Practices and Tools for Servitization

Marko Kohtamäki
Tim Baines • Rodrigo Rabetino
Ali Z. Bigdeli
Editors

Practices and Tools for Servitization

Managing Service Transition

Editors
Marko Kohtamäki
University of Vaasa
Vaasa, Finland

Rodrigo Rabetino
University of Vaasa
Vaasa, Finland

Tim Baines
Aston Business School
Aston University
Birmingham, UK

Ali Z. Bigdeli
Aston Business School
Aston University
Birmingham, UK

ISBN 978-3-319-76516-7   ISBN 978-3-319-76517-4 (eBook)
https://doi.org/10.1007/978-3-319-76517-4

Library of Congress Control Number: 2018942177

© The Editor(s) (if applicable) and The Author(s), under exclusive license to Springer International Publishing AG, part of Springer Nature 2018
This work is subject to copyright. All rights are solely and exclusively licensed by the Publisher, whether the whole or part of the material is concerned, specifically the rights of translation, reprinting, reuse of illustrations, recitation, broadcasting, reproduction on microfilms or in any other physical way, and transmission or information storage and retrieval, electronic adaptation, computer software, or by similar or dissimilar methodology now known or hereafter developed.
The use of general descriptive names, registered names, trademarks, service marks, etc. in this publication does not imply, even in the absence of a specific statement, that such names are exempt from the relevant protective laws and regulations and therefore free for general use.
The publisher, the authors and the editors are safe to assume that the advice and information in this book are believed to be true and accurate at the date of publication. Neither the publisher nor the authors or the editors give a warranty, express or implied, with respect to the material contained herein or for any errors or omissions that may have been made. The publisher remains neutral with regard to jurisdictional claims in published maps and institutional affiliations.

Cover illustration: chinaface/E+/Getty

Printed on acid-free paper

This Palgrave Macmillan imprint is published by the registered company Springer International Publishing AG part of Springer Nature.
The registered company address is: Gewerbestrasse 11, 6330 Cham, Switzerland

Contents

1 **Practices in Servitization** 1
Marko Kohtamäki, Tim Baines, Rodrigo Rabetino, and Ali Z. Bigdeli

Part I Diagnosing Servitization 23

2 **Are You Ready for Servitization? A Tool to Measure Servitization Capacity** 25
Wim Coreynen, Paul Matthyssens, and Heiko Gebauer

3 **Measuring Servitization** 41
S. D. S. R. Maheepala, B. N. F. Warnakulasooriya, and Y. K. Weerakoon Banda

Part II Servitization Strategies and Business Models 59

4 **Business Models in Servitization** 61
Tuomas Huikkola and Marko Kohtamäki

v

Contents

5　Value Constellations in Servitization　　83
　　Saara A. Brax and Filippo Visintin

6　Business Model Innovation: A Process Model and Toolset
　　for Servitizing Industrial Firms　　97
　　Federico Adrodegari, Nicola Saccani, Marco Perona, and Asier Agirregomezkorta

7　Servitization through Product Modularization
　　in Consumer Goods Manufacturing Companies　　121
　　Inmaculada Freije, Alberto de la Calle, and Miguel Ángel Larrinaga

8　Value-Scope-Price: Design and Pricing of Advanced
　　Service Offerings Based on Customer Value　　141
　　Shaun West, Diego Rohner, Dominik Kujawski, and Mario Rapaccini

Part III　Implementing Servitization　　169

9　Overcoming the Challenges of Servitisation: Aligning
　　Responses to Service Strategy　　171
　　Chris Raddats, Jamie Burton, Judy Zolkiewski, and Vicky Story

10　Paradoxes in Servitization　　185
　　Marko Kohtamäki, Rodrigo Rabetino, and Suvi Einola

11　Implementing Servitization Strategies: Trajectories
　　of Capability Development and Offering of Basic
　　and Advanced Services　　201
　　Rui Sousa and Giovani J. C. da Silveira

12	Unboxing the Key Human Competencies for Successful Servitization *Federica Polo*	213
13	BI-in-Practice: A Look at How BI Enacts Framing Contests and Affects the Service Transition Path *Yassine Talaoui*	233
14	Managing Risks for Product-Service Systems Provision: *Introducing a Practical Decision Tool for Risk Management* *Wiebke Reim, Vinit Parida, and David R. Sjödin*	249

Part IV Solution Sales and Co-creation in Servitization 267

15	Selling Solutions by Selling Value *Pekka Töytäri*	269
16	The Virtue of Customising Solutions: A Managerial Framework *Siri Jagstedt, Klas Hedvall, and Magnus Persson*	291
17	Servitization Practices: A Co-Creation Taxonomy *Per Carlborg, Daniel Kindström, and Christian Kowalkowski*	309

Part V Service Ecosystems and Service Supply Chain 323

18	To Servitize Is to (Re)position: Utilizing a Porterian View to Understand Servitization and Value Systems *Rodrigo Rabetino and Marko Kohtamäki*	325

19 Enterprise Imaging: Picturing the Service-Value System 343
Glenn Parry

20 Ecosystems Innovation for Service Development 363
Shaun West, Petra Müller-Csernetzky, and Michael Huonder

21 Service Supply Chain Design by Using Agent-Based Simulation 387
Petri Helo, Javad Rouzafzoon, and Angappa Gunasekaran

22 Servitization in the Public Sector: A Framework for Energy Service Companies 405
María Concepción Peñate-Valentín, Ángeles Pereira, and María del Carmen Sánchez-Carreira

Index 425

Notes on Contributors

Federico Adrodegari is a post-doc fellow at RISE Laboratory (www.rise.it) at the University of Brescia. His research activities concern service and supply chain management, with particular reference to servitization, business model innovation, and digital servitization. He also coordinates the machinery section of ASAP Service Management Forum (www.asapsmf.org), where he carries out research and company transfer projects.

Asier Agirregomezkorta is Product Director in ULMA since 2009. Previously, he was Human Resources and TQM Director for ten years. He holds an MPhil in Production Engineering from the Nottingham Trent University and an MBA in Mondragon Corporation Business School. He is responsible for innovation, production, product support, purchasing, and the control of the forklift trucks rental park of ULMA.

Tim Baines is Professor of Operations Strategy and Executive Director of the Advanced Services Group at the Aston University. He is a leading international authority on servitization and spends much of his time working hands-on with both global and local manufacturing companies to understand servitization in practice and help to transform businesses. His book *Made to Serve* described as an "Essential reading for any companies or executives looking to explore this option for their business" provides a practical guide to servitization, based on in-depth research with leading corporations such as Xerox, Caterpillar, Alstom, and MAN Truck & Bus UK.

Ali Z. Bigdeli is Associate Professor of Industrial Service Innovation at the Advanced Services Group, Aston Business School, Aston University. His interests lie in the organizational change and business model innovation brought about when organizations move toward providing capabilities rather than just selling products on a transactional basis. He is extensively engaged with both multinational and SME manufacturers to understand servitization in practice, and help the acceleration of the adoption of advanced services. His research has been published in leading management journals including *International Journal of Operations & Production Management, Journal of Business Research, Production Planning & Control,* and *International Journal of Production Research.*

Saara A. Brax is a post-doctoral researcher at the Lappeenranta University of Technology. Before joining LUT in 2017, she worked at the Aalto University as a post-doc funded by the Academy of Finland. Her work focuses on industrial and business-to-business services across a broad range of business management and operations management topics.

Jamie Burton is Professor of Marketing and Research Director of the Academic-Practitioner-Customer Management Leadership Group Initiative at Alliance Manchester Business School. His research interests include customer feedback, customer experiences and relationship management, services(s), and servitization.

Giovani J. C. da Silveira is Professor of Operations and Supply Chain Management at the Haskayne School of Business, University of Calgary. He is an expert researcher in operations strategy, mass customization, and supply chain management. He has published widely in scholarly journals. He teaches at undergraduate, MBA, and PhD programs.

Alberto de la Calle is assistant professor and researcher at the Engineering Faculty of the University of Deusto. His research and teaching cover multiple areas of industrial management such as operational research, servitization in manufacturing companies, and supply chain management.

Per Carlborg is Associate Professor of Marketing at the Örebro University, Sweden. Carlborg holds a PhD in Industrial Marketing (2015) from the Linköping University, Sweden. His interest is in service innovation in B2B industry and servitization strategies. Carlborg is involved in several research projects concerning business model transformation in large and small enterprises and new market opportunities in energy sector. He has published in journals such as *Industrial Marketing Management, Service Industries Journal,* and *Service Science* as well as book chapters.

Notes on Contributors xi

Wim Coreynen is researcher at Antwerp Management School in Belgium and the Jheronimus Academy of Data Science (JADS) in the Netherlands. His research revolves around the transformation of industrial companies through servitization, digitization, and business model innovation, and also entrepreneurship.

Suvi Einola is a PhD candidate in the administrative sciences and she works as a project researcher in the Networked Value Systems (NeVS) research group in the School of Management, University of Vaasa (Finland). Her main research interests lie in practices enabling and disabling strategy work in organizations. Her PhD research focuses on paradoxes in strategy work both in public and private organizations. She takes special interest in strategic practices, servitization practices, and business intelligence both in private and public sector contexts. Her empirical projects concentrate on city organizations and industrial companies in Finland, projects funded by Tekes (the Finnish Funding Agency for Technology and Innovation). Besides her research, Einola is leading a management training program in a city organization and acts as a management consultant in the field of participative strategy work.

Inmaculada Freije is Associate Professor of Strategy and a researcher at the Deusto Business School of the University of Deusto and a visiting professor at the Universidad del Salvador, Buenos Aires (Argentina). Her research and teaching is focused on strategic management. She takes special interest in servitization and strategic business and corporate development.

Heiko Gebauer is Visiting Professor of International and Strategic Management at the Linköping University, Sweden. He also leads the Business Innovation group at the Eawag (Aquatic Research Institute of the ETH domain).

Angappa Gunasekaran is the Dean of School of Business and Public Administration at the California State University, Bakersfield, USA. He holds a PhD in Industrial Engineering and Operations Research from the Indian Institute of Technology (Bombay) and has published over 300 articles in peer-reviewed journals. Gunasekaran is interested in researching benchmarking, agile manufacturing, management information systems, e-procurement, competitiveness of SMEs, information technology/systems evaluation, performance measures and metrics in new economy, technology management, logistics, and supply chain management.

Klas Hedvall is an industrial doctoral student at the Department of Technology Management and Economics, Chalmers University of Technology in Gothenburg, Sweden. The research of Klas, who is employed at Volvo Group

Trucks Technology, involves services and solutions in industrial networks, with a specific focus on the transport industry.

Petri Helo is Professor of Industrial Management, Logistics Systems and Head of Networked Value Systems Research Group at Department of Production, University of Vaasa, Finland. His research addresses the management of logistics systems in supply demand networks and use of IT in operations.

Tuomas Huikkola is a post-doctoral researcher in the School of Management at the University of Vaasa. His special interest is in industrial services and the strategy work of growth-seeking companies. His articles have appeared in a number of journals, including *Industrial Marketing Management, Research-Technology Management*, and *Journal of Business and Industrial Marketing*.

Michael Huonder holds a BSc and a BEng (Hons) in Business Engineering and works as an assistant at the Institute of Innovation and Technology Management. He is doing his MSc in Business Engineering and Production. He takes special interest in developing new products, services, and business models with new technologies.

Siri Jagstedt is a doctoral student at the Division of Innovation and R&D Management, Chalmers University of Technology. Her research interests are in the areas of servitization and product-service development, with a focus on efficient development of solutions.

Daniel Kindström is Professor of Industrial Marketing at the Linköping University, Sweden. Kindström's research primarily revolves around market-related innovations and the implementation of proactive market strategies. He is also doing research in the area of the servitization of manufacturing industries and business model innovation. He is involved in research focusing on growth strategies in SMEs and on proactive market shaping and how firms can shape their markets in order to enable new value creation practices. He has published extensively in journals such as *Journal of Service Research, Industrial Marketing Management, Journal of Business Research*, and *Journal of Service Management*, as well as several books and book chapters. He is an editorial board member of *Journal of Business Research and Journal of Service Management*.

Marko Kohtamäki is Professor of Strategy and Director of the "Networked Value Systems" (NeVS) research program at the University of Vaasa. Kohtamäki takes special interest in strategic practices, servitization, co-creation, and business intelligence in technology companies. Kohtamäki has served as a project director in large-scale research and innovation projects, such as "Future Industrial services" and "Solutions for Fleet Management." He has conducted strategy and innovation work with technology companies from large to small (e.g. ABB, Wärtsilä, Prima Power, T-Drill, Cramo), as well as with public sector and non-profit organizations. His articles have appeared in distinguished international journals such as *Strategic Management Journal, International Journal of Operations and Production Management, Industrial Marketing Management, Long Range Planning, Strategic Entrepreneurship Journal, International Journal of Production Economics, Technovation*, and *Journal of Business Research*, among others.

Christian Kowalkowski is Associate Professor of Industrial Marketing at the Linköping University and Assistant Professor of Marketing at Hanken School of Economics. His research focuses on service growth strategies, service innovation, and solutions marketing. Kowalkowski is the Expert Research Panel Chair—Servitization of the *Journal of Service Management*.

Dominik Kujawski is the pricing manager at Regent Lighting and holds an MSc in Engineering from the University of Applied Sciences and Arts, Luzern. He takes a special interest in service pricing, from analysis, strategies and tools to improvement of pricing through a customer-centric approach and Design Thinking methods.

Miguel Angel Larrinaga is an associate professor and researcher at the Deusto Business School of the University of Deusto. His research and teaching cover multiple areas of industrial management such as quantitative analysis, logistics, and supply chain management.

S. D. S. R. Maheepala is a PhD candidate of the University of Sri Jayewardenepura. He takes special interest in sourcing and supply chain and in industrial services. He has more than ten years of middle and senior managerial experience in manufacturing companies. He is also a visiting lecturer at the University of Moratuwa.

Paul Matthyssens is Dean of Antwerp Management School, Professor of Global Strategic Management at the University of Antwerp and Antwerp Management School, and a guest professor at DTU Business in the Lyngby and Fordham University. His research interests include business and industrial marketing, value innovation, global strategy, and purchasing strategy.

Petra Müller-Csernetzky is Professor of Design and Management at the Luzern University of Applied Science and Art and a visiting professor at universities in Germany and Sweden. Her research interest is in service design thinking, design methodology, and visualization as a tool in developing new solutions for product-service systems.

Vinit Parida is Professor of Entrepreneurship and Innovation at the Luleå University of Technology. Parida's research targets the fields of product-service systems, servitization, business modeling, firm capabilities, business opportunity recognition, and early stages of innovation processes. Parida's articles have appeared in leading journals such as Industrial Marketing Management and Strategic Management Journal.

Glenn Parry is Professor of Strategy and Operations Management and Director of the Doctor of Business Administration program at the University of the West of England. His interest is in the meaning of "good business" and value. His research areas include business models, servitization, digital economy, and personal data.

Maria Concepción Peñate-Valentín is an economist and researcher at the Department of Applied Economics of the University of Santiago de Compostela. Her main research focuses on innovation policies and development. In particular, her work studies tools from the demand-side, such as public procurement of innovation.

Ángeles Pereira is an interim part-time lecturer at the Department of Applied Economics, University of Santiago de Compostela and a research associate at ICEDE Research Group. Her main research interests are eco-innovation, servicizing, and circular economy. She has participated in several European and Galician research projects.

Marco Perona is Full Professor of Industrial Logistics at the University of Brescia and Head of the RISE (Research and Innovation for Smart Enterprises) Laboratory. His research activities concern operations management, supply chain management, service management, circular economy, and Enterprise 4.0. Perona is author or co-author of more than 50 publications on international journals or conferences on these topics.

Magnus Persson is an associate professor at the Division of Innovation and R&D Management, Chalmers University of Technology. His research interests are in the areas of platform development, modularization strategies, and innovation through the development of integrated solutions.

Federica Polo is a PhD candidate at the School of Technology and Innovation, University of Vaasa. Her research interest focuses on organizational development; specifically she is studying the impact of training initiatives within organizations and how to use competency management to promote organizational performance and employees' well-being.

Rodrigo Rabetino is Assistant Professor of Strategy in the School of Management and a researcher in the Networked Value Systems research group at the University of Vaasa. His article has appeared in journals such as *International Journal of Operations & Production Management, Industrial Marketing Management, International Journal of Production Economics, Journal of Small Business Management, Research-Technology Management,* and *Journal of Small Business and Enterprise Development*. His research interests include industrial service business, servitization, business intelligence, and small business management.

Chris Raddats is a senior lecturer at the University of Liverpool, having previously had a 20-year marketing career in the telecommunications sector, latterly with an equipment vendor's services division. He now researches how traditionally product-centric businesses can build a chargeable service capability to enhance market differentiation and sales.

Mario Rapaccini is Associate Professor of Innovation Management at the School of Engineering, University of Florence. He is also in the Faculty Staff of University Sant'Anna in Pisa and the School of Business of Milan Polytechnic. His research interests are digital transformation and product-service innovation of manufacturing companies.

Wiebke Reim is a PhD student in Entrepreneurship and Innovation at the Luleå University of Technology. Her research interests include business models, product-service systems, risk management, circular economy, and digitalization. Her articles have appeared in leading journals such as *Journal of Cleaner Production* and *International Journal of Production and Operations Management*.

Diego Rohner is a design assistant at the Institute of Innovation and Technology Management, Lucerne University of Applied Sciences and Arts. He supports teaching and research into design thinking and service design as well as supporting design projects within the university.

Javad Rouzafzoon is a doctoral student and a project researcher in "Networked Value Systems" (NeVS) research program at faculty of technology, Vaasa University. He is interested in supply chain management, logistics, analytical modeling, and software solutions for business decision-making problems.

Nicola Saccani is an associate professor at the University of Brescia, where he is part of the RISE Laboratory. His research activities concern servitization, spare parts demand and inventory management, production and inventory management, digital technologies, and service transformation. He is author of several scientific publications in such fields and national coordinator of the ASAP Service Management Forum.

María del Carmen Sánchez-Carreira is an assistant professor at the Department of Applied Economics, University of Santiago de Compostela, and a member of ICEDE Research Group. Her main research topics are state-owned enterprises, privatization, innovation policies, and public procurement. Apart from academic publications, she has participated in several international and national projects.

David R. Sjödin is Associate Professor of Entrepreneurship and Innovation at the Luleå University of Technology. Sjödin's research targets the fields of servitization, business modeling, open innovation, and inter-organizational collaboration. His articles have appeared in *California Management Review, Industrial Marketing Management, Journal of Engineering Technology Management, Research-Technology Management*, and others.

Rui Sousa is Professor of Operations Management and Director of the Service Management Lab at the Catholic University of Portugal (Porto). He holds a PhD from London Business School and his articles have appeared in leading international journals. His research interests include servitization and operations in technology-enabled services.

Vicky Story is Professor of Marketing and Research Director for the Centre for Service Management at the School of Business and Economics, Loughborough University. Her research interests lie in the fields of innovation and marketing strategy, including entrepreneurial orientation, radical innovation, and servitization

Yassine Talaoui is a PhD candidate and a teaching assistant in the Management Department at the University of Vasa, where he teaches business models and strategic management. His research interests focus on the relationships between business intelligence and strategy research and work.

Pekka Töytäri is a post-doctoral researcher and a research program manager at the Aalto University. His recent research is focused on value-based strategies in industrial markets, including customer value, service-based value creation, value-based selling and sales management, and business model innovation.

Filippo Visintin is Assistant Professor of Service Management at the School of Engineering of Florence University. He is the Scientific Director of the IBIS Lab and co-founder and co-owner of SmartOperations srl. His research interests include servitization of manufacturing and healthcare operations management.

B. N. F. Warnakulasooriya is a professor at the Department of Marketing Management in the University of Sri Jayewardenepura. Warnakulasooriya is also a visiting professor at the University of Colombo, University of Kelaniya, University of Moratuwa, Rajarata University, and University of Peradeniya. He specializes in marketing research.

Y. K. Weerakoon Banda is a professor, PhD coordinator (Mgt), and the founder head of the Finance Department of the University of Sri Jayewardenepura. He is the former dean of the Sir John Kotelawala Defence University. His research interests are corporate finance, valuation, and manufacturing services. He is a visiting professor at the University of Colombo.

Shaun West is Lecturer of Product and Service Innovation at the Institute of Innovation and Technology Management, Lucerne University of Applied Sciences and Arts. He has over 20 years of experience in industrial firms before returning to university where his research interests focus on innovations of digitally enabled product-service systems.

Judy Zolkiewski is Professor of Marketing at Alliance Manchester Business School. Her research interests focus on understanding business markets, relationships, and networks both in the traditional manufacturing and engineering industries and in the evolving business-to-business services sector with specific focus on relationship and network dynamics, servitization, strategy, and technology.

List of Figures

Fig. 1.1	Macro-micro interplay in servitization doings and sayings	12
Fig. 2.1	Template	33
Fig. 2.2	Case results	35
Fig. 3.1	Dimensions of servitization	49
Fig. 4.1	Ideal types of business models	71
Fig. 5.1	Generic value configurations in servitization based on a meta-analysis of the research literature	87
Fig. 6.1	Business model innovation (BMI) process for servitizing industrial firms	106
Fig. 6.2	The brainstorming tool	108
Fig. 6.3	ULMA, STR BM configuration (main elements)	112
Fig. 6.4	ULMA, BM maturity evaluation	113
Fig. 6.5	ULMA, the new data monitoring and data-logger system	117
Fig. 7.1	Integrated business model framework	124
Fig. 7.2	Organizational change (Based on De la Calle Vicente, 2015)	128
Fig. 7.3	Production strategies (regarding OPP) in the proposed model	131
Fig. 8.1	Visual example of traditional and innovative revenue models (based on Bonnemeier, Burianek, & Reichwald, 2010; illustration by Diego Rohner, 2017)	147
Fig. 8.2	Three-step value-scope-price framework (illustration by Diego Rohner, 2017)	150

Fig. 8.3	Value-based pricing framework (based on West & Kujawski, 2016; illustration by Diego Rohner, 2017)	151
Fig. 8.4	The customer and value identification process (illustration by Diego Rohner, 2017)	152
Fig. 8.5	Job-to-be-done to provide insights into the customer's business (illustration by Diego Rohner, 2017)	153
Fig. 8.6	Ecosystem map showing key actors (illustration by Diego Rohner, 2017)	153
Fig. 8.7	Using the value-proposition canvas to describe the business problem (based on Osterwalder et al., 2014; illustration by Diego Rohner, 2017)	154
Fig. 8.8	A process for building and prototyping solutions (illustration by Diego Rohner, 2017)	155
Fig. 8.9	The development of three solutions based on customer problem identification (illustration by Diego Rohner, 2017)	156
Fig. 8.10	Gap analysis for the developed solutions (illustration by Diego Rohner, 2017)	157
Fig. 8.11	Using prototyping to improve the solutions into commercial concepts (illustration by Diego Rohner, 2017)	158
Fig. 8.12	Service value quantification and pricing in detail (illustration by Diego Rohner, 2017)	159
Fig. 8.13	Market benchmark pricing (illustration by Diego Rohner, 2017)	160
Fig. 8.14	Estimating the 'willingness-to-pay' (illustration by Diego Rohner, 2017)	161
Fig. 8.15	Supplier 'fair price' estimation and margins based on cost build-up (illustration by Diego Rohner, 2017)	162
Fig. 8.16	The 'value-scope-price' framework (illustration by Diego Rohner, 2017)	164
Fig. 9.1	Service strategy and challenge road map	177
Fig. 10.1	Organizational paradoxes in servitization: balancing product and solution logics (developed for the context of servitization based on Smith and Lewis, 2011)	189
Fig. 11.1	Desirable trajectory of capability development and service offerings over time	204
Fig. 12.1	Competency framework for servitization (Developed from (Campion et al., 2011))	216

Fig. 12.2	Competency models in servitization: what, why, and how?	218
Fig. 12.3	A systematic approach to competency deployment is servitization process	224
Fig. 13.1	The incongruences causing framing contests as manufacturing and service units shape and gets shaped by BI during servitization. The author's elaboration based on Davidson, 2002; Leonardi, 2013; and Orlikowski & Gash, 1994	236
Fig. 13.2	The types of changes that unfold as collective frames of manufacturing resist the change of servitization. The author's own elaboration based on Oliva & Kallenberg, 2003 and Orlikowski & Gash, 1992	241
Fig. 14.1	PSS risk management decision tree	260
Fig. 15.1	An example of a goal hierarchy, where higher level challenges determine lower level goals	273
Fig 15.2	The goal-driven buying process, adapted from Eades (2004), Rackham and DeVincentis (1999), Töytäri (2015)	274
Fig. 15.3	The framework for value-based solution selling	275
Fig. 15.4	Buying and selling process alignment	278
Fig. 15.5	The connection between goals, challenges, and the solution	283
Fig. 15.6	Price in relation to value created and supplier cost (Adapted from Töytäri and Rajala (2015))	286
Fig. 16.1	Visualisation of the virtual subdivision of a solution	297
Fig. 16.2	A three-layer model representing a solution as three integrated elements: the product(s), the services and the manufacturer–customer interaction	299
Fig. 16.3	Five steps guiding manufacturers when customising solutions	301
Fig. 18.1	Five forces in the propulsion industry. Source: own elaboration based on Porter (1980) and industry reports from 2000 to 2015	330
Fig. 18.2	Service transition map: (re)positioning within the value system. Source: own elaboration based on Davies (2004) and our case company's annual reports from 2000 to 2015. * Each sphere represents one strategic boundary-related move, including new companies, workshops, offices, service facilities, and training/education centers. ** The case company has approximately 20 license agreements worldwide. Only the new license agreements during the period are included in the figure, but not the extensions	334

Fig. 19.1	The background framework for an enterprise image	348
Fig. 19.2	The generic enterprise image	352
Fig. 19.3	The enterprise image of the ATTAC contract	354
Fig. 19.4	Enterprise image of ICU provision	356
Fig. 19.5	Tourism enterprise image	358
Fig. 20.1	Simplified supply chain around a typical product-service system (based on Anderson, Narus, & Narayandas, 2008; illustration by Müller-Csernetzky, 2017)	365
Fig. 20.2	Transformation of the value chain to a value network (based on Anderson et al., 2008; illustration by Müller-Csernetzky, 2017)	366
Fig. 20.3	Transformation of command and control structures to more adaptable team-of-teams (based on McChrystal et al., 2015; illustration by Müller-Csernetzky, 2017)	369
Fig. 20.4	Six-step framework for looking at ecosystem innovation for service business development (based on West, Granata, Künzli, Ouertani, & Ganz, 2017; illustration by Müller-Csernetzky, 2017)	370
Fig. 20.5	The two most used templates (A5 empathy card and A1 ecosystem map) (based on West et al., 2017, adapted from Stickdorn & Schneider, 2012; illustration by Müller-Csernetzky, 2017)	371
Fig. 20.6	Learning about the overall customer value proposition and critical outcomes (Adapted from Osterwalder & Pigneur, 2014; illustration by Müller-Csernetzky, 2017)	372
Fig. 20.7	Identifying the individual actors (based on Künzli, West, Granata, Ouertani, & Ganz, 2016; illustration by Müller-Csernetzky, 2017)	374
Fig. 20.8	Example of a detailed empathy card for the manufacturer (based on West et al., 2017; illustration by Müller-Csernetzky, 2017)	375
Fig. 20.9	Place the actors on the ecosystem map and cluster them when it makes sense to do so (based on Künzli et al., 2016; illustration by Müller-Csernetzky, 2017)	376
Fig. 20.10	An ecosystem map showing the transactions between individual actors (based on West et al., 2017; illustration by Müller-Csernetzky, 2017)	378
Fig. 20.11	Critical points red-flagged on a current state ecosystem map (based on West et al., 2017; illustration by Müller-Csernetzky, 2017)	379

Fig. 20.12	An ecosystem redesigned to provide improve alignment of outcomes (based on Künzli et al., 2016; illustration by Müller-Csernetzky, 2017)	380
Fig. 20.13	The process overview with hints and tips (based on West et al., 2017; illustration by Müller-Csernetzky, 2017)	382
Fig. 21.1	Helsinki service areas from OpenStreetMap data source, © OpenStreetMap contributors (Data is available under the Open Database Licence and cartography is licensed as CC BY-SA: https://www.openstreetmap.org/copyright)	394
Fig. 21.2	Population grid data (1 km × 1 km) in Helsinki city (statistics Finland, 2015) (Licensed as CC BY 4.0: https://creativecommons.org/licenses/by/4.0/deed.en)	395
Fig. 21.3	GIS map with located agents and a service centre—AnyLogic simulation software screenshot	397
Fig. 21.4	Customer processing states and transition within agent	398
Fig. 21.5	Customer flow structure in service delivery	399
Fig. 22.1	Main barriers faced by private companies and public sector. Source: Own elaboration	410
Fig. 22.2	Stages for the public sector to undertake performance procurement. Source: Own elaboration based on European Commission (2015)	417

List of Tables

Table 1.1	Concepts and their meanings	6
Table 2.1	Servitization capacity measurement tool	31
Table 2.2	Case companies	34
Table 3.1	Base, intermediate and advanced services in manufacturing companies	45
Table 3.2	Dimensions and indicators of servitization	50
Table 3.3	Servitization road map example of a manufacturing company	54
Table 4.1	Four service business models for a manufacturer	73
Table 4.2	KONE Corporation's different business models	78
Table 6.1	Contributions to the literature about the development of service-oriented BMs and classification of their steps	100
Table 6.2	Description of the BMI toolkit to support servitizing industrial firms	107
Table 6.3	ULMA, action list	114
Table 7.1	Processes of the demand chain	129
Table 7.2	Processes of the demand fulfilment chain	130
Table 7.3	Process of the strategic alignment chain	132
Table 7.4	Processes and elements of the demand chain	137
Table 7.5	Processes and elements of the demand fulfilment chain	138
Table 7.6	Processes and elements of the strategic alignment chain	138
Table 14.1	Operational PSS risks	255
Table 14.2	PSS risk management	259

Table 15.1	Key differences between value capture and value creation-focused strategies	271
Table 17.1	The 4C framework: relational modes played by servitized firms	314
Table 21.1	Key performance indicators for evaluation, categorized according to agent type (example)	400
Table 22.1	Results of the implementation of ESCOs services	412
Table 22.2	Type of service required from ESCOs depending on the barriers for public procurement	414

1

Practices in Servitization

Marko Kohtamäki, Tim Baines, Rodrigo Rabetino, and Ali Z. Bigdeli

1.1 Introduction

Manufacturers have transitioned from selling products to selling solutions in search of high returns and additional growth opportunities (Matthyssens & Vandenbempt, 2008; Rabetino, Kohtamäki, Lehtonen, & Kostama, 2015). Studies alternatively refer to this expansion as servitization (Vandermerwe & Rada, 1988), service infusion (Brax, 2005; Forkmann, Henneberg, Witell, & Kindström, 2017), service transformation (Martinez, Bastl, Kingston, & Evans, 2010), or service transition (Fang, Palmatier, & Steenkamp, 2008). Servitization is not a simple process, and therefore, positive outcomes cannot be guaranteed

---

M. Kohtamäki (✉) • R. Rabetino
University of Vaasa, Vaasa, Finland
e-mail: marko.kohtamaki@uva.fi; rodrigo.rabetino@uva.fi

T. Baines • A. Z. Bigdeli
Aston Business School, Aston University, Birmingham, UK
e-mail: t.baines@aston.ac.uk; a.bigdeli@aston.ac.uk

© The Editor(s) (if applicable) and The Author(s), under exclusive license to Springer International Publishing AG, part of Springer Nature 2018
M. Kohtamäki et al. (eds.), *Practices and Tools for Servitization*,
https://doi.org/10.1007/978-3-319-76517-4_1

(Gebauer, Fleisch, & Friedli, 2005; Lee, Yoo, & Kim, 2016). This chapter intends to contribute to existing research by framing servitization through a practice lens, in which servitization is regarded as-practice and in-practice. It discusses related approaches and theories, utilizes frameworks and tools, and provides guidelines for advancing servitization in manufacturing companies.

The servitization process can be facilitated by a variety of micro-practices and behavioral foundations. To understand the role of sayings and doings in servitization, practice theory (Bourdieu, 1990) provides a useful framework, which can be utilized to create vocabulary and concepts for doings, tools, and sayings that enable servitization (Luoto, Brax, & Kohtamäki, 2017). Practice theory considers strategy from a micro-perspective, which companies achieve as a compilation of practices (Vaara & Whittington, 2012; Whittington et al., 2003), including not only the practical practice-in-use but also the sayings, discourses, and narratives (Luoto et al., 2017). This inclusion of sayings can be considered to be a central strength in practice theory because sayings frequently become doings in organizations and society (Seidl & Whittington, 2014). When considering practices such as sayings and doings that shape the servitization of manufacturing companies, we refer to a myriad of practices, which practitioners utilize when implementing and facilitating servitization.

This edited book and its articles intend to describe servitization through such lens to demonstrate practices, tools, routines, and frameworks that help practitioners adopt and implement servitization at the micro-level. In addition, this book contributes to our understanding of servitization by facilitating the 'practice turn' through encompassing a large collection of frameworks and tools, which are not restricted to any specific theory. Instead, they are obtained from scholars from different servitization-related streams, such as product-service systems (PSS) and service science, and based on many alternative theoretical approaches, such as services-dominant logic (SDL) and co-creation, resource-based viewpoints, industrial organization, strategy-as-practice, micro-foundations, and institutional theory, which are potential theoretical approaches to gain ideas and frameworks.

The present book could provide a platform to facilitate interdisciplinary collaboration and bridge the different servitization-related communities to enable scholars to answer research questions in a more comprehensive manner. As suggested by Rabetino, Harmsen, Kohtamäki, and Sihvonen (2018), field-level structures serve a fundamental role in the construction of the identity, boundaries, and content of the servitization domain and serve a central role in supporting the acquisition of a high degree of scientific maturity. The evolution of these structures will provide a means to progress and integrate servitization-related research.

1.2 Servitization as a Concept

Servitization research started in the late 1980s, when Vandermerwe and Rada (1988) coined the term. Since then, numerous studies have been published from a variety of different scholars (Lightfoot, Baines, & Smart, 2013), and hence the topic has grown from a trivial topic to a large research domain with multiple sub-fields. In their bibliometric review, which includes more than 1000 articles, Rabetino et al. (2018; see also Lightfoot et al., 2013) identified three main communities in servitization-related research: (1) servitization research, (2) product-service systems, and (3) service science.

In our definition of servitization, we reference Lightfoot et al. (2013, p. 1423) as we consider *servitization as a transition in business model from products to PSS, where product and services are bundled to generate higher use-value, pricing is based on value, and capabilities support customer-dominant orientation*. Although strategy may be surpassing the objects embedded in PSS, strategy materializes via offerings in many cases. When studying the relationship between servitization and performance, studies have often reflected the level of servitization by measuring the scope of service offerings (Partanen, Kohtamäki, Parida, & Wincent, 2017). For many reasons, this perspective is insufficient for addressing the complete scope of servitization; however, it enables separation among servitization strategy, structure (and capabilities), and outcomes (innovation or performance) (Kohtamäki, Hakala, Partanen, Parida, & Wincent, 2015). For long, the strategy literature has delimited environment, strategy, and structure, but in servitization literature, rare studies theorize about their interplay (Kohtamäki & Helo, 2015).

As any major business model transition process, servitization is implemented step-by-step in some cases or through a radical transition process in other cases. The transition from a product-dominant business model to a services-dominant model requires radical changes in strategy, structure, and organizational culture, where the company moves from product emphasis to customer emphasis. Servitization is a highly complex phenomenon, where success is determined by a configuration of multiple dimensions (Baines & Lightfoot, 2013; Rabetino, Kohtamäki, & Gebauer, 2017). Recent studies have begun to utilize configurational analysis or qualitative comparative analysis (e.g. fsQCA) to obtain configurations that explain servitization. In this methodology, studies rely on an equifinality assumption, which suggest that multiple configurations of factors can generate optimal outcomes. In their analysis, Sjödin, Parida, and Kohtamäki (2016) discovered four dimensions that may facilitate servitization in various configurations. The dimensions were service development capability, network management capability, mass service customization capability, and digitalization capability. In a similar fashion, Forkmann, Henneberg, Witell, and Kindström (2017) investigated how service offering, pricing, service capabilities, and their infusion interplay affect servitization. Their study encourages systematic analysis, including supplier, customer, and relationship-oriented factors.

1.3 Product-Service Systems

In this context, the need to distinguish between servitization as a transition process and the concrete offerings from this process is critical. By servitization, we refer to the business model transition (the process) that produces bundles of products and services (the offering) and transforms a product-oriented manufacturing firm toward a service-oriented technology company. Thus, the transition will not make the products obsolete but transform the strategic and operational logic by placing increasing emphasis on customers and services. This transition is a radical shift in the business model and mindset, which changes everything within a company.

Existing studies utilize multiple terms when referring to the offerings from servitization. Derived from the engineering discipline, the term 'product-service systems' (PSS) has gained popularity to describe an offering. Multiple streams of PSS coexist, which have produced an extensive terminology (Table 1.1). Some scholars have focused on designing eco-efficient PSS while examining the impact of these offerings on the environment (Mont, 2002; Tukker & Tischner, 2006). A different group of scholars has focused on functional product (FP) development (Alonso-Rasgado, Thompson, & Elfström, 2004), whereas other scholars have attempted to understand how manufacturers can design technical services to be included in modular life cycle-oriented PSS (Aurich, Fuchs, & DeVries, 2004; Morelli, 2003). Two additional groups have concentrated on the use of engineering methods and computer-aided tools for co-designing life cycle-integrated products and services (Sakao & Shimomura, 2007), and the information and communication technology (ICT)-aided modeling and development of value propositions and service operations processes of PSS (Becker, Beverungen, & Knackstedt, 2010). In addition to the concept of PSS, studies grounded in different disciplines, such as service marketing and service operations management, utilize alternative concepts such as solutions (Paiola, Saccani, Perona, & Gebauer, 2013), customized solutions (Antioco, Moenaert, Lindgreen, & Wetzels, 2008), customer solutions (Biggemann, Kowalkowski, Maley, & Brege, 2013), hybrid offerings (Ulaga & Reinartz, 2011), integrated solutions (Davies, 2004), and fully fledged integrated solutions (Windahl & Lakemond, 2010).

1.4 Servitization and Performance

Manufacturing companies may consider servitization as both a strategy and a process, which de-commoditizes one's offerings and provides a new model of value creation, delivery, and appropriation. This logic seeks to increase firm value, sales, profitability, customer value, and product-service innovation. However, current studies reveal no certainty; in these conditions, these outcomes and logics are realized. This uncertainty is partially attributed to servitization, and the performance is attributed to the complex relationship between these two components. A variety of constructs and issues (components) may interfere with the link between service offering and performance. Studies suggest that the link between

Table 1.1 Concepts and their meanings

Discipline	Concept	Representative description of the integrated offering
Engineering	Product-service system	'A system of products, services, networks of actors and supporting infrastructure that continuously strives to be competitive, satisfy customer needs and have a lower environmental impact than traditional business models' (Mont, 2004, p. 71)
	Functional product	'[A]lso known as "total care products," are products that comprise combinations of "hard" and "soft" elements. Typically, they are described as comprising hardware combined with a service support system' (Alonso-Rasgado, Thompson, & Elfström, 2004, p. 515)
	Industrial product-service systems (IPS2)	'[A] new solution-oriented approach for delivering value in use to the customer during the whole life cycle of a product' (Meier, Völker, & Funke, 2011, p. 1175)
Business (service marketing, service management, service operations management)	Solution	'A solution is a customized, integrated combination of products, services and information that solves a customer's problem' (Sawhney, Wolcott, & Arroniz, 2006, p. 78)
	Product services	'A type of service which is independent from the company's service without consuming its goods' (Mathieu, 2001b, p. 453)
	Full-service	'[A] comprehensive bundle of products and/or services that fully satisfies the needs and wants of a customer related to a specific event or problem' (Stremersch, Wuyts, & Frambach, 2001, p. 2)
	Integrated solutions	'[A] combination of physical products or services, or both, plus knowledge are used to provide a specific outcome fulfilling the customers' needs' (Windahl & Lakemond, 2010, p. 1278)
	Integrated solutions	'[A] bundle of physical products, services and information, seamlessly combined to provide more value than the parts alone, that addresses customer's needs in relation to a specific function or task in their business system; it is long-term oriented, integrates the provider as part of the customer's business system, and aims at optimizing the total cost for the customer' (Brax & Jonsson, 2009, p. 541)
	Installed base service	'[T]he range of product- or process-related services required by an end-user over the useful life of a product in order to run it effectively in the context of its operating process' (Oliva & Kallenberg, 2003, p. 163)
Management/engineering	Complex product systems	'[Integrated solutions] firms design, integrate, and deliver complex products and systems (CoPS) on a project basis in small batches or as one-offs for business users, operators, service providers and/or government agencies' (Brady, Davies, & Gann, 2005, p. 360)

servitization and performance is likely to be moderated and mediated by a variety of other internal and external conditions (Bigdeli et al., 2018). The link between servitization and performance has been determined to be either linear or nonlinear (Fang et al., 2008; Kohtamäki, Partanen, Parida, & Wincent, 2013; Visnjic Kastalli & Van Looy, 2013). Fang et al. (2008) demonstrated a nonlinear effect of servitization on firm value. Kohtamäki et al. (2013) discovered a nonlinear link between the scope of service offerings (servitization) and sales growth. In their configurational study, Ambroise, Prim-Allaz, and Teyssier (2017) conclude that all investigated servitization strategies can cause increased performance but only in the existence of a certain combination of service culture, customer interface, and service delivery system configurations.

1.5 Failures in Servitization

Servitization tends to be 'challenging' (Brady, Davies & Gann, 2005, p. 361), 'painful' (Salonen, 2011, p. 688), where companies 'experience difficulties' (Galbraith, 2002, p. 2) and 'some problems and obstacles' (Turunen & Toivonen, 2011, p. 74) in this process. Servitization 'entails complex implementation challenges that—if not managed properly—may even result in a decline in overall firm performance' (Visnjic Kastalli & Van Looy, 2013, p. 103). Failures have emerged from the incapacity to adopt new service-oriented organizational structures (Galbraith, 2002; Neu & Brown, 2008; Oliva & Kallenberg, 2003), obtain the required capabilities, and allocate resources (Martinez et al., 2010), execute key processes (Fang et al., 2008; Kohtamäki et al., 2013), and change the boundaries of the company (Baines, Lightfoot, Benedettini, & Kay, 2009; Davies, 2004). Cognitive barriers of managers (Allmendinger & Lombreglia, 2005), sales personnel (Neu & Brown, 2005; Rothenberg, 2007), service personnel (Turunen & Toivonen, 2011), and customers (Matthyssens & Vandenbempt, 2010) may also cause failure. These barriers cause risk aversion (Gebauer et al., 2005), failure to recognize productive opportunities (Cohen, Agrawal, & Agrawal, 2006; Spring & Araujo, 2013), or 'a lack of belief in the economic potential of service business' (Gebauer, Fischer & Fleisch, 2010, p. 594).

Servitizing manufacturers must realign their value propositions, processes, organizational structures, mindsets, and resources (Huikkola, Kohtamäki, & Rabetino, 2016; Kindström & Kowalkowski, 2014; Storbacka, Windahl, Nenonen, & Salonen, 2013), which echo tensions or paradoxes that require different coping tools and practices at different organizational levels. Although existing studies have discussed the core challenges, barriers, and many other subjects in the implementation of servitization (Alghisi & Saccani, 2015; Martinez et al., 2010), only a few studies have provided overviews of the key processes and practices needed to successfully execute servitization (Baines & Lightfoot, 2014; Baines & Lightfoot, 2013; Gebauer, 2011; Rabetino et al., 2017; Storbacka, 2011).

1.6 Servitization as a Changing Landscape

Today's notion of servitization is a very different phenomenon than it was ten years ago, which adds new challenges and opportunities regarding strategy implementation and business model innovation. Digitization has enabled novel business models that are based on complex advanced services, which has not only accelerated the implementation of servitization strategies based on smart industrial PSS across industries and ecosystems but also redefined practices, the required capabilities, and operations at different organizational levels. In servitization, the Internet-of-Things and smart connected products serve a significant role and enable a company to collected real-time data, proactively react to service needs, and utilize data to create better PSS. Currently, products are remotely connected from distance—not only a single product but also fleets of products that can be connected, controlled, and operated from control centers. If knowledge has always been the creator of competitive advantage, it will be so more than ever. Data collection, warehousing, analytics, and smart autonomous products will transform business models and create new opportunities for products-as-a-service business models. As suggested by Westerlund, Leminen, and Rajahonka (2014), if expertly exploited, digitization enables a new means of value co-creation. Digitization traverses company strategies, service operations, and connections with many participants in the supply chain. Digitization may enable servitization in the business ecosystems of industrial organizations and may affect inter-organizational service interactions and decision-making practices by amplifying the information intensity and increasing the connectivity of actors.

1.7 Theoretical Approaches Related to Servitization

Servitization has inspired an increasing number of publications (Kowalkowski, Gebauer, & Oliva, 2017) that have accumulated within related but different scholarly communities (Lightfoot et al., 2013) across several academic disciplines that range from the industrial marketing-led and service operations management-led mainstreams to other servitization-related communities that do not explicitly use the term servitization (Rabetino et al., 2018).

Rabetino et al. (2018) have recently identified three main communities. At the core of the servitization mainstream, the solution business community addresses a variety of topics, such as customer solutions, project-based integrated solutions, and operations management in service transition. Research within the community is typically grounded on a resource-based viewpoint and different strategic management and organization theories. The SDL (Vargo & Lusch, 2004) has also gained adherents among marketing scholars. Alternatively, the PSS community focuses on PSS design and development and often emphasizes the environmental aspects of PSS integration and delivery. Articles from the PSS community are typically practical applications that present conceptual discussions without any dominant theory. The service science community, in which the prevailing theory is the SDL, combines organizational, technological, and human understanding to study how service systems should be configured and evolve to foster service innovation and quality and how value is co-created within these dynamic systems (Vargo and Lusch, 2011).

Although the current situation reveals the existence of certain conceptual pluralism, the need for studying the particularities of organizational change processes during servitization is clear (Baines et al., 2017). Most research has been conducted at the firm-level, whereas studies have predominantly misunderstood or neglected the human dimension of servitization. Servitization can provide a valuable context to develop additional studies that add clarity about the micro-perspective of strategic change (Jarzabkowski and Spee, 2009). Strategy-as-practice, for instance, may help researchers study the human dimension of servitization while providing an understanding of how micro-practices develop and how managers' praxis shapes servitization strategies (Rabetino et al., 2017).

1.8 Servitization-as-Practice

Current servitization studies do not utilize practice theory, which provides a useful conceptual landscape to depict routinized micro-level activities. For this purpose, practice theory provides a frame and vocabulary, which can be utilized to describe tools and constructs that enable or disable servitization (Kohtamäki & Rajala, 2016). Practices can be broadly defined as *routinized types of behavior* (Reckwitz, 2002, p. 249). Practice theory considers strategy from a micro-perspective, as a compilation of practices (Vaara & Whittington, 2012; Whittington et al., 2003). From the practice theoretical perspective, the servitization process can be facilitated by a variety of practices that consist of both doings and sayings of practitioners. By talking and acting, managers shape the process of servitization.

In particular, strategy-as-practice provides a literature stream that develops and applies practice theory. Strategy-as-practice is separated into three main concepts: the practice, praxis, and practitioners. Praxis refers to everyday practices conducted by the practitioners (the actual labor or the practical activities conducted); the practice structures the praxis. Thus, practices reference routinized activities, concepts, routines, tools, or processes that provide structure for everyday doings and activities in organizations. Thus, practices carry over time and have been coined as 'background coping skills' (Chia, 2004). In a servitizing company, practices include but are not limited to change management, planning, implementation, planning and follow-up meetings, development tools, templates, discourses, and sayings. These types of routinized practices, which structure the servitization work, can be coined as servitization practices. Thus, practitioners are developers and carriers of practices. Note that practices are not only doings but also sayings when sayings become discourses or narratives.

Sayings also become doings, and therefore, managerial discourses have strong significance for the success of servitization at the company-level (micro-level). Sayings, which include discourses and narratives, have a significant role in practice theory. Despite a few exceptions (Luoto et al., 2017), servitization research has primarily neglected discourses and narratives. Practice theory suggests that frequent sayings become doings, which indicate that the way practitioners talk about the role of services and products in a servitizing company shape the future servitization efforts. Supportive managerial discourses and small stories may facilitate enabling behaviors, whereas talks, which set servitization against the products, may cause stronger organizational inertia instead of regarding servitization as an opportunity it may be considered a threat. Treating servitization as a threat would likely cause resistance, whereas opportunity-discourse would support servitization efforts. One of management's central roles is to influence via discourses and narratives. Managers may be regarded as intentional storytellers who facilitate servitization by acting and talking. Sayings and doings are in constant interplay, when practitioners make sense of activities, and by sayings influence on behaviors.

Servitization is considered to be a firm-level phenomenon that is managed and investigated at the firm-level and primarily focuses on strategic, technological, operational, organizational, and marketing aspects. The macro-environment and micro-level perspectives are lacking with some exceptions. The macro-level indicates the institutional environment, for instance, political technological and social aspects, a value system and a competitive environment. At the broader level, strategy research tends to conceptualize the variety in any business environment by utilizing dimensions, such as dynamism, turbulence, hostility, and resource munificence. In strategy, the competitive landscape is often conceptualized by the concepts that are embedded in strategic groups, value systems, or five-forces. Although contingency theory has contributed to environment-strategy interplay, the micro-level concepts that emerge from practice theory or the micro-foundations movement remain neglected. Figure 1.1 emphasizes the interplay between the macro-level and the micro-level. Because the

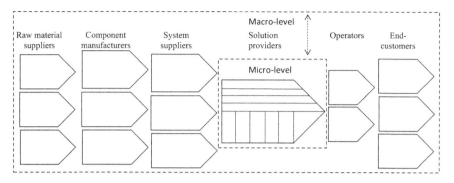

Fig. 1.1 Macro-micro interplay in servitization doings and sayings

activities occur at the micro-level, an in-depth understanding of the macro-micro interplay is important.

1.9 Introduction to the Chapters

The present book includes chapters by authors from different servitization-related scholarly communities and encompasses a variety of topics related to servitization. The chapters in the book intend to offer insight regarding servitization practices from different perspectives, and the topics of different chapters complement each other. The chapters are organized into five different domains: (1) diagnosing servitization, (2) servitization strategies and business models, (3) implementing servitization, (4) solution sales and co-creation in servitization, and (5) service ecosystems and service supply chain. Thus, the topics adequately address the different approaches related to servitization: (a) servitization or service transformation (the core of servitization), (b) product-service systems, and (c) service science and value co-creation (Rabetino et al., 2018).

The first part of the book focuses on a manufacturing firm's readiness for servitization by including a variety of dimensions and components that predicts the firm's capacity to implement service transition. Chapter 2 by Coreynen, Matthyssens, and Gebauer begins by asking an important question: Are you ready for servitization? The chapter provides model and dimensions for companies to obtain appropriate answers to this question. The model presents three dimensions and their measures: (1) a firm's capabilities for service development, (2) a firm's capabilities for service deployment, and (3) service orientation. Chapter 3 by Maheepala, Warnakulasooriya, and Weerakoon Banda provides a measurement method for servitization. This model utilizes the four dimensions: (1) service offering, (2) strategic intent for future service offering, (3) service orientation of the organization, and (4) service revenues of the organization. The chapter also illustrates how to apply the model to analyze and enable servitization.

The five chapters included in the second part of this book address different issues related to servitization and business model innovation. In Chap. 4, Huikkola and Kohtamäki discuss alternative but often coexistent business models of manufacturing companies that have servitized their business operations. As discussed in this chapter, companies must choose a business model that properly addresses customers' concerns and organizes tasks, obtains resources to perform tasks, provides follow-up in the business case, and learns from these cases. In the same manner, Chap. 5 by Brax and Visintin introduces an alternative framework that captures eight generic archetypical configurations of life cycle value constellations along the servitization continuum. The authors discuss how managers can employ the framework for developing and positioning their service-offering portfolios. Complementarily, in Chap. 6, Adrodegari, Saccani, Perona, and Agirregomezkorta focus on business model innovation processes while discussing how capital goods firms should reconfigure the elements of their business models. The chapter describes managerial tools to guide the practical application of the methodology that was specifically developed for supporting business model innovation. Chapter 7 discusses the role of product modularization as a tool for customization in consumer goods servitizing manufacturers. Freije, de la Calle, and Larrinaga analyze how this approach enables the firm to create and nurture customer relationships, and consequently, develop a more sustainable strategy. In the final chapter of this part, West, Rohner, Kujawski, and Rapaccini create a model for companies to fit customer value, service offering, and value-based pricing (value-scope-price). The chapter provides managerial guidelines based on a three-step framework.

The chapters in the third part largely focus on the implementation of servitization strategy and the relevant challenges and facilitators. Raddats, Burton, Zolkiewski, and Story propose a new service strategy and challenge 'roadmap' that includes four primary challenges in implementing servitization within manufacturing (i.e. interpret the market environment, re-orientate from products to services, undertake a structural reorganization, and develop service-related operational processes) and possible responses to each challenge. Chapter 10 is authored by Kohtamäki, Rabetino, and Einola, who develop a paradox approach in servitization, by utilizing the original framework from Smith and Lewis (2011) to create a paradox model for the analysis of servitization process. Model for paradoxes in servitization may assist managers and scholars when trying to understand the challenges in servitization. Kohtamäki et al. suggest that the identified paradox of performing spurs other organizational paradoxes in servitization. The paradox of performing emerges because the manufacturing company intends to customize integrated solutions while trying to preserve efficiency of product manufacturing—both are important, either-or cannot be selected.

Following from this, Sousa and da Silveira employed a value-based perspective and presented a practical framework that guides practitioners in their implementation of servitization. Their framework, particularly, focuses on the relevant capabilities that a manufacturer needs to develop over time while developing different types of service offering (i.e. base and advanced services). Moving from relevant capabilities, Polo's paper explored a set of competencies that can facilitate the implementation of servitization. In this chapter, the author has proposed practical guidelines that enable managers in identifying right service employees, and highlighted the relevant competencies that can translate the strategy and vision into behaviors, skills, and terms that people can easily understand. In the following chapter, Talaoui views servitization as a transformational process conducive to organizational change, and explores the ways in which IT systems can facilitate such change. The author follows the steps proposed by Orlikowski (2000) and adopts the notion of 'technologies-in-practice' to investigate the linkage between organizational units and business intelligence (BI) usage, and demonstrates the ways in which BI influences and gets influenced by the human dynamics in sensemaking. The last chapter of third part is authored by Reim, Parida, and Sjödin. Based on the analysis of the results gathered from a case study of a Swedish manufacturing company and eight of its global dealers, the authors have proposed a practical PSS risk management decision tool that enables manufacturing firms to more proficiently manage risks to offer PSS successfully.

The fourth part of the book includes chapters on solution sales and co-creation in servitization. Töytäri focuses on solution sales with an emphasis on value. He argues the importance of the value-based approach in solution sales, depicts the challenges of value-based selling, and provides a model to guide implementation of the value-based approach when selling solutions. Jagstedt, Hedvall, and Persson provide a managerial framework for customizing solutions. Because manufacturers encounter challenges regarding the customization of solutions (products + services) while attempting to maintain productivity by economies of scale, they encounter difficulties in balancing the two contradictory targets. This chapter provides a managerial framework to customize solutions. Then, Carlborg, Kindström, and Kowalkowski develop a taxonomy for co-creation in servitization. They explore both supplier involvement and customer involvement in the value creation process. The authors delineate and explore the following four roles: caretaker, constructor, cicerone, and consultant.

The fifth part of the book contains four chapters that study service ecosystems and different areas concerning the value system and the service supply chain. In Chap. 18, Rabetino and Kohtamäki apply a Porterian toolkit to highlight the role of industry power as an explanation of vertical re-positioning movement during the implementation of servitization strategies. The chapter illustrates how the power approach complements the prevailing capability viewpoint and contributes to value system analysis in servitization. Chapter 19 by Parry introduces the notion of enterprise image to create a picture of a moment in time of the interaction between a client and a provider in outcome-based agreements. Applied to many different service operations, the approach has proven useful in management decision-making. In the next chapter, West, Müller-Csernetzky, and Huonder focus on ecosystem innovation in service development. In this chapter, the authors provide important and practical steps for ecosystem innovation. In Chap. 21, Helo, Rouzafzoon, and Gunasekaran apply agent-based modeling (ABM) to evaluate operational and structure-related decisions when designing a service delivery system. Chapter 22 examines public procurement as a tool for servitization. Using energy-saving companies (ESCOs) as an illustrative example, Peñate-Valentín, Pereira, and Sánchez-Carreira discuss the role of the public sector, in particular, public procurement of innovation (PPI), as a tool to foster product and service innovation and servitization. The authors provide a framework comprising a set of scenarios for public procurers to take advantage of the potential of PPI to trigger servitization with environmental goals.

References

Alghisi, A., & Saccani, N. (2015). Internal and external alignment in the servitization journey—Overcoming the challenges. *Production Planning & Control, 26*(14–15), 1219–1232.

Allmendinger, G., & Lombreglia, R. (2005). Four strategies for the age of smart services. *Harvard Business Review, 83*(10), 131–145.

Alonso-Rasgado, T., Thompson, G., & Elfström, B.-O. (2004). The design of functional (total care) products. *Journal of Engineering Design, 15*(6), 515–540.

Ambroise, L., Prim-Allaz, I., & Teyssier, C. (2017). Financial performance of servitized manufacturing firms: A configuration issue between servitization strategies and customer-oriented organizational design. *Industrial Marketing Management* (in press).

Antioco, M., Moenaert, R. K., Lindgreen, A., & Wetzels, M. G. M. (2008). Organizational antecedents to and consequences of service business orientations in manufacturing companies. *Journal of the Academy of Marketing Science, 36*(3), 337–358.

Aurich, J. C., Fuchs, C., & DeVries, M. F. (2004). An approach to life cycle oriented technical service design. *CIRP Annals—Manufacturing Technology, 53*(1), 151–154.

Baines, T. S., & Lightfoot, H. W. (2013). *Made to Serve: How manufacturers can compete through servitization and product-service systems*. Chichester: Wiley.

Baines, T. S., & Lightfoot, H. W. (2014). Servitization of the manufacturing firm: Exploring the operations practices and technologies that deliver advanced services. *International Journal of Operations & Production Management, 34*(1), 2–35.

Baines, T. S., Lightfoot, H. W., Benedettini, O., & Kay, J. M. (2009). The servitization of manufacturing: A review of literature and reflection on future challenges. *Journal of Manufacturing Technology Management, 20*(5), 547–567.

Baines, T. S., Ziaee Bigdeli, A., Bustinza, O. F., Shi, V. G., Baldwin, J., & Ridgway, K. (2017). Servitization: Revisiting the state-of-the-art and research priorities. *International Journal of Operations & Production Management, 37*(2), 256–278.

Becker, J., Beverungen, D., & Knackstedt, R. (2010). Service systems: Status-quo and perspectives for reference models and modeling languages. *Information Systems and E-Business Management, 8*, 33–66.

Bigdeli, A. Z., Baines, T., Schroeder, A., Brown, S., Musson, E., Guang Shi, V., & Calabrese, A. (2018). Measuring servitization progress and outcome: The case of "advanced services." *Production Planning & Control, 29*(4), 315–332.

Biggemann, S., Kowalkowski, C., Maley, J., & Brege, S. (2013). Development and implementation of customer solutions: A study of process dynamics and market shaping. *Industrial Marketing Management, 42*(7), 1083–1092.

Bourdieu, P. (1990). *The logic of practice*. Stanford: Stanford University Press.

Brady, T., Davies, A., & Gann, D. M. (2005). Creating value by delivering integrated solutions. *International Journal of Project Management, 23*(5), 360–365.

Brax, S. (2005). A manufacturer becoming service provider—Challenges and a paradox. *Managing Service Quality, 15*(2), 142–155.

Brax, S., & Jonsson, K. (2009). Developing integrated solution offerings for remote diagnostics. *International Journal of Operations & Production Management, 29*(5), 539–560.

Chia, R. (2004). Strategy-as-practice: Reflections on the research agenda. *European Management Review, 1*(1), 29–34.

Cohen, M. A., Agrawal, N., & Agrawal, V. (2006). Winning in the aftermarket. *Harvard Business Review, 84*(5), 129–138.

Davies, A. (2004). Moving base into high-value integrated solutions: A value stream approach. *Industrial and Corporate Change, 13*(5), 727–756.

Fang, E. (Er), Palmatier, R. W., & Steenkamp, J.-B. E. (2008). Effect of service transition strategies on firm value. *Journal of Marketing, 72*(5), 1–14.

Forkmann, S., Henneberg, S. C., Witell, L., & Kindström, D. (2017). Driver configurations for successful service infusion. *Journal of Service Research, 20*(3), 275–291.

Galbraith, J. R. (2002). Organizing to deliver solutions. *Organizational Dynamics, 31*(2), 194–207.

Gebauer, H. (2011). Exploring the contribution of management innovation to the evolution of dynamic capabilities. *Industrial Marketing Management, 40*(8), 1238–1250.

Gebauer, H., Fischer, T., & Fleisch, E. (2010). Exploring the interrelationship among patterns of service strategy changes and organizational design elements. *Journal of Service Management, 21*(1), 103–129.

Gebauer, H., Fleisch, E., & Friedli, T. (2005). Overcoming the service paradox in manufacturing companies. *European Management Journal, 23*(1), 14–26.

Huikkola, T., Kohtamäki, M., & Rabetino, R. (2016). Resource realignment in servitization. *Research-Technology Management, 59*(4), 30–39.

Jarzabkowski, P., & Spee, P. (2009). Strategy-as-practice: A review and future directions for the field. *International Journal of Management Reviews, 11*(1), 69–95.

Kindström, D., & Kowalkowski, C. (2014). Service innovation in product-centric firms: A multidimensional business model perspective. *Journal of Business & Industrial Marketing, 29*(2), 96–111.

Kohtamäki, M., Hakala, H., Partanen, J., Parida, V., & Wincent, J. (2015). The performance impact of industrial services and service orientation on manufacturing companies. *Journal of Service Theory and Practice, 25*(4), 463–485.

Kohtamäki, M., & Helo, P. (2015). Industrial services—The solution provider's stairway to heaven or highway to hell? *Benchmarking: An International Journal, 22*(2), 170–185.

Kohtamäki, M., Partanen, J., Parida, V., & Wincent, J. (2013). Non-linear relationship between industrial service offering and sales growth: The moderating role of network capabilities. *Industrial Marketing Management, 42*(8), 1374–1385.

Kohtamäki, M., & Rajala, R. (2016). Theory and practice of value co-creation in B2B systems. *Industrial Marketing Management, 56*(7), 4–13.

Kowalkowski, C., Gebauer, H., & Oliva, R. (2017). Service growth in product firms: Past, present, and future. *Industrial Marketing Management, 60*(1), 82–88.

Lee, S., Yoo, S., & Kim, D. (2016). When is servitization a profitable competitive strategy? *International Journal of Production Economics, 173*, 43–53.

Lightfoot, H., Baines, T. S., & Smart, P. (2013). The servitization of manufacturing: A systematic literature review of interdependent trends. *International Journal of Operations & Production Management, 33*(11), 1408–1434.

Luoto, S., Brax, S. A., & Kohtamäki, M. (2017). Critical meta-analysis of servitization research: Constructing a model-narrative to reveal paradigmatic assumptions. *Industrial Marketing Management, 60*(1), 89–100.

Martinez, V., Bastl, M., Kingston, J., & Evans, S. (2010). Challenges in transforming manufacturing organisations into product-service providers. *Journal of Manufacturing Technology Management, 21*(4), 449–469.

Mathieu, V. (2001). Service strategies within the manufacturing sector: Benefits, costs and partnership. *International Journal of Service Industry Management, 12*(5), 451–475.

Matthyssens, P., & Vandenbempt, K. (2008). Moving from basic offerings to value-added solutions: Strategies, barriers and alignment. *Industrial Marketing Management, 37*(3), 316–328.

Matthyssens, P., & Vandenbempt, K. (2010). Service addition as business market strategy: Identification of transition trajectories. *Journal of Service Management, 21*(5), 693–714.

Meier, H., Völker, O., & Funke, B. (2011). Industrial Product-Service Systems (IPS2). *The International Journal of Advanced Manufacturing Technology, 52*(9–12), 1175–1191.

Mont, O. (2002). Clarifying the concept of product–service system. *Journal of Cleaner Production, 10*(3), 237–245.

Mont, O. (2004). Reducing life-cycle environmental impacts through systems of joint use. *Greener Management International, 45*, 63–77.

Morelli, N. (2003). Product-service systems, a perspective shift for designers: A case study: The design of a telecentre. *Design Studies, 24*(1), 73–99.

Neu, W. A., & Brown, S. W. (2005). Forming successful business-to-business services in goods-dominant firms. *Journal of Service Research, 8*(1), 3–17.

Neu, W. A., & Brown, S. W. (2008). Manufacturers forming successful complex business services. *International Journal of Service Industry Management, 19*(2), 232–251.

Oliva, R., & Kallenberg, R. (2003). Managing the transition from products to services. *International Journal of Service Industry Management, 14*(2), 160–172.

Orlikowski, W. J. (2000). Using technology and constituting structures: A practice lens for studying technology in organizations. *Organization Science, 11*(4), 404–428.

Paiola, M., Saccani, N., Perona, M., & Gebauer, H. (2013). Moving from products to solutions: Strategic approaches for developing capabilities. *European Management Journal, 31*(4), 390–409.

Partanen, J., Kohtamäki, M., Parida, V., & Wincent, J. (2017). Developing and validating a multi-dimensional scale for operationalizing industrial service offering. *Journal of Business and Industrial Marketing, 32*(2), 295–309.

Rabetino, R., Harmsen, W., Kohtamäki, M., & Sihvonen, J. (2018). Structuring servitization related research. *International Journal of Operations and Production Management*, In press.

Rabetino, R., Kohtamäki, M., & Gebauer, H. (2017, October). Strategy map of servitization. *International Journal of Production Economics, 192*, 144–156.

Rabetino, R., Kohtamäki, M., Lehtonen, H., & Kostama, H. (2015, August). Developing the concept of life-cycle service offering. *Industrial Marketing Management, 49*, 53–66.

Reckwitz, A. (2002). Toward a theory of social practices: A development in culturalist theorizing. *European Journal of Social Theory, 5*(2), 243–263.

Rothenberg, S. (2007). Sustainability through sustainability through servicizing. *MIT Sloan Management Review, 48*(2), 82–91.

Sakao, T., & Shimomura, Y. (2007). Service Engineering: A novel engineering discipline for producers to increase value combining service and product. *Journal of Cleaner Production, 15*(6), 590–604.

Salonen, A. (2011). Service transition strategies of industrial manufacturers. *Industrial Marketing Management, 40*(5), 683–690.

Sawhney, M., Wolcott, R. C., & Arroniz, I. (2006). The 12 different ways for companies to innovate. *MIT Sloan Management Review, 47*(3), 75–81.

Seidl, D., & Whittington, R. (2014). Enlarging the strategy-as-practice research agenda: Towards taller and flatter ontologies. *Organization Studies, 35*(10), 1407–1421.

Sjödin, D. R., Parida, V., & Kohtamäki, M. (2016). Capability configurations for advanced service offerings in manufacturing firms: Using fuzzy set qualitative comparative analysis. *Journal of Business Research, 69*(11), 5330–5335.

Smith, W. K., & Lewis, M. W. (2011). Toward a theory of paradox: A dynamic equilibrium model of organizing. *Academy of Management Review, 36*(2), 381–403.

Spring, M., & Araujo, L. (2013). Beyond the service factory: Service innovation in manufacturing supply networks. *Industrial Marketing Management, 42*(1), 59–70.

Storbacka, K. (2011). A solution business model: Capabilities and management practices for integrated solutions. *Industrial Marketing Management, 40*(5), 699–711.

Storbacka, K., Windahl, C., Nenonen, S., & Salonen, A. (2013). Solution business models: Transformation along four continua. *Industrial Marketing Management, 42*(5), 705–716.

Stremersch, S., Wuyts, S., & Frambach, R. T. (2001). The purchasing of full-service contracts: An exploratory study within the industrial maintenance market. *Industrial Marketing Management, 30*(1), 1–12.

Tukker, A., & Tischner, U. (2006). Product-services as a research field: Past, present and future. Reflections from a decade of research. *Journal of Cleaner Production, 14*(17), 1552–1556.

Turunen, T. T., & Toivonen, M. (2011). Organizing customer-oriented service business in manufacturing. *Operations Management Research, 4*(1–2), 74–84.

Ulaga, W., & Reinartz, W. J. W. J. (2011, November). Hybrid offerings: How manufacturing firms combine goods and services successfully. *Journal of Marketing, 75*, 5–23.

Vaara, E., & Whittington, R. (2012). Strategy-as-practice: Taking social practices seriously. *The Academy of Management Annals, 6*(1), 285–336.

Vandermerwe, S., & Rada, J. (1988). Servitization of business: Adding value by adding services. *European Management Journal, 6*(4), 314–324.

Vargo, S. L., & Lusch, R. F. (2004). Evolving a new dominant logic for marketing. *Journal of Marketing, 68*(1), 1–17.

Vargo, S. L., & Lusch, R. F. (2011). It's all B2B…and beyond: Toward a systems perspective of the market. *Industrial Marketing Management, 40*(2), 181–187.

Visnjic Kastalli, I., & Van Looy, B. (2013). Servitization: Disentangling the impact of service business model innovation on manufacturing firm performance. *Journal of Operations Management, 31*(4), 169–180.

Westerlund, M., Leminen, S., & Rajahonka, M. (2014). Designing business models for the internet of things. *Technology Innovation Management Review, 4*(7), 5–14.

Whittington, R., Jarzabkowski, P., Mayer, M., Mounoud, E., Nahapiet, J., & Rouleau, L. (2003). Taking strategy seriously: Responsibility and reform for an important social practice. *Journal of Management Inquiry, 12*(4), 396–409.

Windahl, C., & Lakemond, N. (2010). Integrated solutions from a service-centered perspective: Applicability and limitations in the capital goods industry. *Industrial Marketing Management, 39*(8), 1278–1290.

Part I

Diagnosing Servitization

2

Are You Ready for Servitization? A Tool to Measure Servitization Capacity

Wim Coreynen, Paul Matthyssens, and Heiko Gebauer

2.1 Introduction

Although the strategic benefits of servitization have often been posited, manufacturers experience much difficulty to move successfully from supplying goods to offering integrated combinations of products and

---

W. Coreynen (✉)
Antwerp Management School (AMS), Antwerp, Belgium

Jheronimus Academy of Data Science (JADS),
's Hertogenbosch, The Netherlands
e-mail: wim.coreynen@ams.ac.be

P. Matthyssens
Antwerp Management School (AMS), Antwerp, Belgium

Department of Management, Faculty of Applied Economics,
University of Antwerp, Antwerp, Belgium
e-mail: paul.matthyssens@ams.ac.be

H. Gebauer
Department of Management and Engineering (IEI), Business Administration (FEK), Linkoping University, Linkoping, Sweden
e-mail: heiko.gebauer@eawag.ch

services, often termed 'hybrid offerings' (Ulaga & Reinartz, 2011), 'product-service systems' (Baines & Lightfoot, 2013) or 'solutions' (Matthyssens & Vandenbempt, 2008). Ample reasons to explain service failure are known, such as the absence of service-oriented values in the firm (Gebauer, Edvardsson, & Bjurko, 2010; Kohtamäki, Hakala, Partanen, Parida, & Wincent, 2015), an ill-suited approach to service innovation (Morelli, 2006) and firms' inability to scale new service activities (Coreynen, Matthyssens, De Rijck, & Dewit, 2017). Yet, servitizing companies generally emphasize the development of new services without considering changes in other aspects of the organization (Kindström & Kowalkowski, 2014).

In this chapter, we address the call for new practice-oriented methodologies that not only focus on improving the hybrid offering itself but also consider the context in which new offerings are created and deployed. A holistic perspective that considers the whole organization (and even beyond) is increasingly used to support manufacturers in servitization. Two such recent examples are 'the Strategy Map of Servitization' (Rabetino, Kohtamäki, & Gebauer, 2016) and 'the Roadmap for Service Strategy in Action' (Kowalkowski & Ulaga, 2017). Following this literature, we introduce a tool that can be used by both practitioners and academics to measure a firm's general capacity for servitization. This instrument complements other tools as a preliminary analytic step before further action. Also, as an internal assessment tool, it complements other methods that focus on the environment in which firms operate, such as assessments of the attractiveness of moving downstream in the value chain (Wise and Baumgartner, 1999).

In the following section, we briefly recap recent work on three organizational factors that contribute to a firm's ability to successfully evolve into a solution provider: (1) capabilities for service development, (2) capabilities for service deployment and (3) the service orientation of corporate culture. Next, we present the tool, explain how to use it and describe two cases where it has been applied. Finally, we conclude by summarizing how the tool can be used to evaluate firms' readiness for servitization and leverage experience among teams, business units and companies.

2.2 Theory

The view on servitization has evolved from a mere complement of product innovation to a multi-dimensional, all-encompassing notion that entails several functions both inside and outside the firm. Servitization is increasingly being considered an organization-wide challenge. Yet, prior studies typically focus on one organizational level, and thereby limit their perspective to function-specific practices. Only a few studies describe the strategic logic of servitization from a company-holistic perspective (Kindström & Kowalkowski, 2014; Rabetino et al., 2016). This perspective though can create benefits for firms as competitors will find it difficult to isolate and copy individual elements of an integrated business model. A holistic approach thus contributes to a better understanding of servitization and strengthens firms' competitive advantage by linking between strategic choices and organizational factors.

According to prior work based on multiple case studies, companies encounter three types of barriers in servitization. From an operational perspective, companies may lack sufficient knowledge or skills to develop a service business, and/or they may not have a go-to-market strategy in place to further deploy services. On top of these two barriers, on an organizational level, companies may not have a culture that is in favor of becoming a solution provider (Coreynen, Matthyssens, De Rijck, et al., 2017). In smaller companies, these operational and organizational levels mostly overlap, but in larger companies, business units or departments can differ heavily in terms of their attitude toward services. In the next three subsections, we discuss these issues in more detail.

2.2.1 Service Development

Many companies feel the importance of extending their offering with (additional) services, yet find it difficult to design solutions and develop a successful business around it. Particularly product-oriented manufacturers, geared toward innovating products, generally lack experience in service innovation. Because such companies are not familiar with integrated product-service design methodologies, they tend to fall back on a traditional product design logic. Consequently, manufacturers that venture into services often remain at the 'service as add-on' stage, providing only basic services.

Manufacturers require specific organizational skills to develop a successful service business. More specifically, they need to be able to (1) sense service opportunities and threats by constantly monitoring the environment, (2) seize opportunities by spreading and applying new knowledge in the organization and (3) reconfigure the company's assets and processes to turn new service activities into a professional business (Fischer, Gebauer, Gregory, Ren, & Fleisch, 2010). These activities are crucial for companies to move toward and maintain an integrated product-service business. They cover, but are not limited to, the capability to gather information on customers' needs and on competitors, make quick and timely decisions and efficiently change internal routines to minimize costs and achieve service profits.

2.2.2 Service Deployment

Besides developing solutions, manufacturers are also often unable to roll out newly added services. The issue of deployment, which focuses on the latter phases of servitization such as production, value selling and delivery, is witnessing more interest in service innovation research. The ability to create attractive business models is a key challenge for manufacturers to make a successful transition toward offering solutions. Companies should be able to monitor costs in service production and delivery, and align incentives to ensure that both revenues and costs remain on target such as not to fall into the service paradox trap (Gebauer, Fleisch, & Friedli, 2005). In addition, companies need to standardize previously customized solutions for repeatability and scalability purposes.

Three important capabilities for deploying product-service combinations relate to the issues of digitization, mass service customization and network management (Rönnberg Sjödin, Parida, & Kohtamäki, 2016). Digitization relates to the ability to leverage digital technologies for improving efficiency and expanding firms' reach into the market (Coreynen, Matthyssens, & Van Bockhaven, 2017). For instance, to what extent does the firm's IT system allow employees to access customer, order, production and/or market-related data (Bharadwaj, Bharadwaj, & Bendoly, 2007)? Mass service customization refers to the ability to offer a large variety of customized offerings without significantly increasing costs or losing quality (Zhang, Zhao, Lyles, & Guo, 2015). Finally, network management relates to the skills necessary for building and coordinating a network of partners by, for example, selecting potential partners and remaining informed about their strategies and goals (Kohtamäki, Partanen, Parida, & Wincent, 2013).

2.2.3 Service Orientation

Due to the inherently different features of products and services, manufacturers often fail to exploit the financial potential of a service extension (Gebauer et al., 2005). There are various explanations why a firm's orientation toward products can block servitization. From a strategic perspective, managers are restrained by several cognitive frames such as a preference toward the tangible features of new products and technologies, a lack of faith in the economic potential of services and fear of taking on risks that were previously carried by the customer. From an operational perspective, employees may resist moving into services as it requires them to develop new skills geared toward solving customer problems; some employees may be reluctant to acquire or apply them.

In order to servitize successfully, manufacturers are advised to move toward a new corporate culture that embraces a service-oriented approach. A service culture, visible in both the values and behavior of managers and employees, is positively associated with companies' performance (Gebauer et al., 2010). Especially management behavior plays a crucial role in initiating a service orientation at the employee level. For example, when companies offer incentives to collaborate, sales channels of different product and service units can more easily clarify common approaches for addressing customer needs.

2.3 A Tool to Measure Servitization Capacity

Based on the theory, we introduce an instrument that can be used as a tool to measure and assess a firm's capacity for servitization. Such a tool can be useful for practitioners to help companies pinpoint their individual strengths and weaknesses for servitization. By bridging the gap between theory and practice, we leverage state-of-the-art knowledge to give companies insight in their readiness for servitization.

2.3.1 The Tool

The tool consists of 48 questions on three service-related organizational factors: (1) capabilities for service development, (2) capabilities for service deployment and (3) the service orientation of corporate culture (see Table 2.1). To capture their complexity and because managers have in-depth knowledge of the organization, the tool comprises only reflective questions that managers need to rate on a 7-point scale (ranging from '0 = entirely disagree' to '7 = entirely agree'). The unit of analysis can be either the whole company, one of the company's business units or teams.

To measure firms' capabilities for service development, we pose 13 items on distinct sensing, seizing and reconfiguring capabilities that are necessary when gradually moving from products to solutions (Fischer et al., 2010). To measure capabilities for deployment, we offer 15 items on digitization, mass service customization (Rönnberg Sjödin et al., 2016) and network management (Kohtamäki et al., 2013). Finally, to measure a firm's service orientation, we pose 20 items that cover the values and behavior of both managers and employees (Gebauer et al., 2010).

To visualize the results, respondents can calculate the average scores for each construct and plot them on a radar chart for their company or business unit (see Fig. 2.1). When respondents from the same team complete the tool, they can either compare their individual charts or calculate total average scores for each construct to create one shared chart. The tool can also be used to compare different business units or companies; this we explain further later.

Table 2.1 Servitization capacity measurement tool

Service development capabilities	
Sensing service opportunities and threats	
We focus on identifying service opportunities to differentiate our total offering	/7
We observe customer needs	/7
We observe competitors' service offerings and behavior	/7
We react quickly to competitors' service activities	/7
Average score	/7
Seizing service opportunities	
We can make quick and timely decisions to create a new dominant design of the total offering	/7
We articulate intended strategies early and clearly to direct information-gathering and filtering mechanisms and focus management attention	/7
We have the capacity to satisfy customers' expressed needs	/7
We can make tactical choices on bundling and charging for goods and services (or charging for them separately)	/7
We have the capacity to commercialize new offerings and communicate changes to the customer	/7
Average score	/7
Reconfiguring assets and processes	
We are able to turn service activities into a professional business	/7
We are able to turn service activities into a profitable business (whereby services are either embedded in product prices or charged separately)	/7
We have procedures and routines to minimize costs related to new service activities	/7
We can overcome internal resistance and conflicts	/7
Average score	/7
Service deployment capabilities	
Digitization	
Our IT system allows us integrated access to the following:	
all customer-related data (e.g. service contracts, feedback)	/7
all order-related data (e.g. order status, handling requirements)	/7
all production-related data (e.g. resource availability, quality)	/7
all market-related data (e.g. promotion details, future forecasts)	/7
Average score	/7
Mass service customization	
We are highly capable of large-scale product-service customization	/7
We can easily add significant product-service variety without increasing costs	/7
We can customize product-services while maintaining high volume	/7
We can add product-service variety without sacrificing quality	/7

(continued)

Table 2.1 (continued)

We can adjust our process design according to customer demand without significantly increasing costs	/7
We can adjust our product-service design according to customer demand without significantly increasing costs	/7
Average score	**/7**
Network management	
We analyze what we would like to achieve with each partner	/7
We remain informed about the goals, potential and strategies of our partners	/7
We determine in advance possible partners with whom to discuss the building of relationships	/7
We appoint coordinators who are responsible for the relationships with our partners	/7
We regularly discuss with our partners how we can support one another in our success	/7
Average score	**/7**
Service orientation	
Service orientation of management values	
Our management …	
recognizes services as a lasting differentiation strategy	/7
considers the combination of products and services as a potential way to improve profitability	/7
uses services to reduce comparability of different suppliers' offerings	/7
aims to exploit the financial potential of services	/7
sees services to compensate fluctuating product sales	/7
considers services as highly profitable	/7
Average score	**/7**
Service orientation of management behavior	
Our management …	
empowers employees to respond to a broad range of customer problems	/7
coaches employees to behave in a service-oriented way	/7
sets rewards for service-oriented employee behavior	/7
supports employees for solving customer problems	/7
Average score	**/7**
Service orientation of employee values	
Our employees …	
recognize the financial potential of services	/7
try to compensate fluctuating product with service sales	/7
consider services as highly profitable	/7
use services to augment the product offering	/7
use services to improve the customer relationship	/7
use services for selling more products	/7

(continued)

Table 2.1 (continued)

Average score	/7
Service orientation of employee behavior	
Our employees …	
serve customers as a reliable troubleshooter	/7
serve customers as a performance enabler	/7
serve customers as a trusted adviser	/7
fulfill the role of problem solvers	/7
Average score	/7

7-point scale: 1, Entirely disagree; 2, Mostly disagree; 3, Somewhat disagree; 4, Neither agree nor disagree; 5, Somewhat agree; 6, Mostly agree; 7, Entirely agree

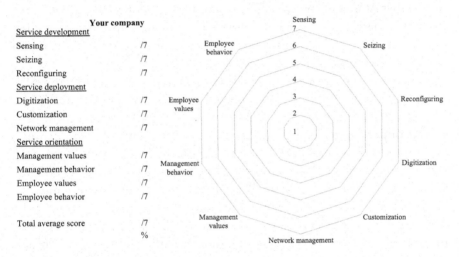

Your company	
Service development	
Sensing	/7
Seizing	/7
Reconfiguring	/7
Service deployment	
Digitization	/7
Customization	/7
Network management	/7
Service orientation	
Management values	/7
Management behavior	/7
Employee values	/7
Employee behavior	/7
Total average score	/7
	%

Fig. 2.1 Template

2.3.2 Case Examples

We invited two manufacturers that have already taken concrete steps toward services to use the tool; they are listed as Alpha and Beta in Table 2.2. Alpha is a relatively young, small company that sells and repairs foot scanners for podiatrists; they also design and manufacture insoles, provide training and advice to podiatrists. Beta is a medium-sized company that supplies sheet metal work, partial and full metal assemblies, and it also provides consulting services on quick response manufacturing

Table 2.2 Case companies

Case	Main products	Company size	Year of incorporation
Alpha	Foot scanners and functional insoles	Micro: 9 employees	2007
Beta	Sheet metal work and assembly	Medium: 63 employees	1998

(QRM) to clients such as original equipment manufacturers (OEM). Both companies promote themselves as being solutions providers.

The results of Alpha and Beta are plotted in Fig. 2.2. At first glance, we can see that Alpha's radar is much larger than Beta's, scoring higher on each construct; therefore, we argue that Alpha has a higher capacity for servitization than Beta. We can also calculate the total score for each case by taking the average of all ten constructs. In this example, Alpha has an average total score of 6.12 out of 7 (87%), and Beta has a score of 4.55 (65%).

Zooming in on the capabilities related to service development, Alpha has consistent high scores for sensing service opportunities and threats, seizing opportunities and reconfiguring the company's assets and processes. Based on several prior interviews with the owners, we affirm the company pays a great deal of attention to observing and satisfying podiatrists' needs. Also, being a small company that fosters close contacts between employees, Alpha can easily overcome internal resistance and conflicts. The company is aware that there is still room for improvement in terms of focusing management attention and minimizing service costs; this is mostly because the owners still manage all customer relations themselves. Beta, on the other hand, scores relatively low on all three service development capabilities, especially in terms of seizing new service opportunities. For instance, the company finds it difficult to satisfy customer needs in their primary activity chain. The CEO explains they are often unable to evolve from being a mere component supplier to offering fully assembled solutions; customers take these decisions on a more strategic level, whereas Beta primarily deals with purchasing managers who oversee only certain components.

On capabilities related to service deployment, Alpha has excellent results on network management and digitization, and a high score for

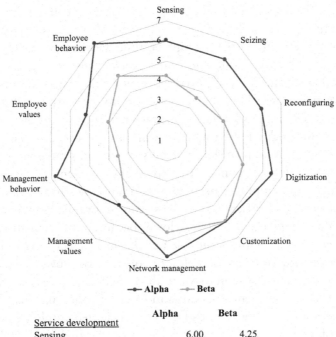

	Alpha	Beta
Service development		
Sensing	6.00	4.25
Seizing	6.00	3.60
Reconfiguring	6.00	4.00
Service deployment		
Digitization	6.50	5.00
Customization	6.00	6.00
Network management	6.80	5.60
Service orientation		
Management values	5.00	4.50
Management behavior	6.75	3.50
Employee values	5.17	4.00
Employee behavior	7.00	5.00
Total average score	6.12	4.55
	87%	65%

Fig. 2.2 Case results

mass service customization. The company invested heavily in its IT system; only for making future forecasts, the company still sees room for improvement. Alpha also works closely together with several strategic partners such as research institutions for testing new types of materials and production methods, business schools for reflecting on new business models and local sports clubs for bundling promotion efforts. In terms of manufacturing insoles, the company is capable of large-scale product customization: they can maintain a high volume without sacrificing quality, yet changes still incur some additional costs. Alternatively, Beta scores highest on customization, followed by network management and digitization. Particularly its IT system can still improve in terms of integrating customer, order and production-related data. The company also admits it does not sufficiently analyze what it wants to achieve through partnerships and does not keep track of partners' goals and strategies.

Finally, on service orientation, Alpha has excellent scores on both management and employee behavior. The company strongly emphasizes its role as a trusted adviser and troubleshooter for podiatrists. In terms of service values, Alpha scores slightly lower because management does not consider services as highly profitable nor do they expect services to compensate for fluctuating product sales. In contrast, Beta overall scores relatively low on service orientation, with a slight increase for employee behavior. Its management does not aim to exploit the financial potential of services nor does it set rewards for service-oriented employee behavior. Also, employees are hesitant to consider services as highly profitable.

2.4 Managerial Conclusions

Using a company-holistic approach, this measurement instrument is a tool that practitioners and researchers can use to assess a firm's capacity for servitization. It supports manufacturers in servitization by pinpointing their strengths and weaknesses regarding organizational factors related to service development, deployment and the corporate culture's service orientation. For instance, the case example Alpha overall receives high scores, yet the company can still benefit from further focusing management attention and minimizing service costs. Beta's scores, on the other hand, are quite low, particularly in the areas of management's orientation toward services and seizing opportunities. Based on such results, companies may start to remedy specific weaknesses for servitization, possibly by involving external parties such as advisers, consultants and training institutions.

A second way to employ the tool is to use it as a means for leveraging experience among different teams, business units and even companies. For instance, respondents in larger organizations can use this method to compare results of different departments, share experiences and learn from each other. For instance, how to observe customer needs, and coach employees to behave in a more service-oriented way? How to further exploit the financial potential of services, and overcome internal resistance and conflicts? A similar exercise can be made during a workshop with several companies to share experiences across different businesses and sectors. For instance, what IT systems allow for integrated access to customer, order and production-related data? How to offer customized products and services without sacrificing quality?

We would like to formulate a few words of caution. Does a high score on all constructs guarantee servitization success? The short answer is 'no'. First, we selected what we consider to be the key capabilities for developing and deploying a successful solution business, but our list is far from limited. There are several additional important factors that we did not include in the tool such as skills related to value selling (Kindström, Kowalkowski, & Alejandro, 2015), methods for personnel recruitment, training and assessment (Kohtamäki et al., 2015) and the proximity of the service organization to the customer (Gebauer, Edvardsson, Gustafsson, & Witell, 2010). Second, we did not include any financial or other performance figures in the tool, so there is no objective way to evaluate the extent to which services have contributed to the company's growth. Third, the results are heavily dependent on the honesty of the respondent as well as the accuracy of his or her perception of the company. For instance, managers might evaluate employees' service values and behavior differently than employees themselves, and vice versa. This issue can be partly overcome by involving an external, objective party such as an adviser or consultant to apply the tool inside your organization.

In sum: high scores do not guarantee servitization success, but they are a strong indicator of the company's readiness for servitization. In the absence of high scores, the tool offers a quick way for companies to assess their capacity for servitization, pinpoint and reflect on potential areas for improvement.

References

Baines, T., & Lightfoot, H. (2013). *Made to serve: How manufacturers can compete through servitization and product service systems* (1st ed.). Chichester, West Sussex: Wiley.

Bharadwaj, S., Bharadwaj, A., & Bendoly, E. (2007). The performance effects of complementarities between information systems, marketing, manufacturing, and supply chain processes. *Information Systems Research, 18*(4), 437–453. https://doi.org/10.1287/isre.1070.0148

Coreynen, W., Matthyssens, P., De Rijck, R., & Dewit, I. (2017). Internal levers for servitization: How product-oriented manufacturers can upscale product-service systems. In *International Journal of Production Research*. Retrieved from http://www.tandfonline.com/doi/abs/10.1080/00207543.2017.1343504

Coreynen, W., Matthyssens, P., & Van Bockhaven, W. (2017). Boosting servitization through digitization: Pathways and dynamic resource configurations for manufacturers. *Industrial Marketing Management, 60*, 42–53. https://doi.org/10.1016/j.indmarman.2016.04.012

Fischer, T., Gebauer, H., Gregory, M., Ren, G., & Fleisch, E. (2010). Exploitation or exploration in service business development?: Insights from a dynamic capabilities perspective. *Journal of Service Management, 21*(5), 591–624. https://doi.org/10.1108/09564231011079066

Gebauer, H., Edvardsson, B., & Bjurko, M. (2010). The impact of service orientation in corporate culture on business performance in manufacturing companies. *Journal of Service Management, 21*(2), 237–259. https://doi.org/10.1108/09564231011039303

Gebauer, H., Edvardsson, B., Gustafsson, A., & Witell, L. (2010). Match or mismatch: Strategy-structure configurations in the service business of manufacturing companies. *Journal of Service Research, 13*(2), 198–215. https://doi.org/10.1177/1094670509353933

Gebauer, H., Fleisch, E., & Friedli, T. (2005). Overcoming the service paradox in manufacturing companies. *European Management Journal, 23*(1), 14–26. https://doi.org/10.1016/j.emj.2004.12.006

Kindström, D., & Kowalkowski, C. (2014). Service innovation in product-centric firms: A multidimensional business model perspective. *Journal of Business & Industrial Marketing, 29*(2), 96–111. https://doi.org/10.1108/JBIM-08-2013-0165

Kindström, D., Kowalkowski, C., & Alejandro, T. B. (2015). Adding services to product-based portfolios: An exploration of the implications for the sales function. *Journal of Service Management, 26*(3), 372–393. https://doi.org/10.1108/JOSM-02-2014-0042

Kohtamäki, M., Hakala, H., Partanen, J., Parida, V., & Wincent, J. (2015). The performance impact of industrial services and service orientation on manufacturing companies. *Journal of Service Theory and Practice, 25*(4), 463–485. https://doi.org/10.1108/JSTP-12-2013-0288

Kohtamäki, M., Partanen, J., Parida, V., & Wincent, J. (2013). Non-linear relationship between industrial service offering and sales growth: The moderating role of network capabilities. *Industrial Marketing Management, 42*(8), 1374–1385. https://doi.org/10.1016/j.indmarman.2013.07.018

Kowalkowski, C., & Ulaga, W. (2017). *Service strategy in action: A practical guide for growing your B2B service and solution business*. Service Strategy Press.

Matthyssens, P., & Vandenbempt, K. (2008). Moving from basic offerings to value-added solutions: Strategies, barriers and alignment. *Industrial Marketing Management, 37*(3), 316–328. https://doi.org/10.1016/j.indmarman.2007.07.008

Morelli, N. (2006). Developing new product service systems (PSS): Methodologies and operational tools. *Journal of Cleaner Production, 14*(17), 1495–1501. https://doi.org/10.1016/j.jclepro.2006.01.023

Rabetino, R., Kohtamäki, M., & Gebauer, H. (2016). Strategy map of servitization. *International Journal of Production Economics*. https://doi.org/10.1016/j.ijpe.2016.11.004

Rönnberg Sjödin, D., Parida, V., & Kohtamäki, M. (2016). Capability configurations for advanced service offerings in manufacturing firms: Using fuzzy set qualitative comparative analysis. *Journal of Business Research, 69*(11), 5330–5335. https://doi.org/10.1016/j.jbusres.2016.04.133

Ulaga, W., & Reinartz, W. J. (2011). Hybrid offerings: How manufacturing firms combine goods and services successfully. *Journal of Marketing, 75*(6), 5–23. https://doi.org/10.1509/jmkg.75.6.5

Wise, R., & Baumgartner, P. (1999, September 1). Go downstream: The new profit imperative in manufacturing. Retrieved July 3, 2017, from https://hbr.org/1999/09/go-downstream-the-new-profit-imperative-in-manufacturing

Zhang, M., Zhao, X., Lyles, M. A., & Guo, H. (2015). Absorptive capacity and mass customization capability. *International Journal of Operations & Production Management, 35*(9), 1275–1294. https://doi.org/10.1108/IJOPM-03-2015-0120

3

Measuring Servitization

S. D. S. R. Maheepala, B. N. F. Warnakulasooriya, and Y. K. Weerakoon Banda

3.1 Introduction

No business strategy, no matter how relevant, can be brought to a success unless the tactical support for its execution is in place. One of the primary decisions that the senior management of an organization must make is regarding how the progress of the strategy is to be measured. As such, this chapter introduces a matrix to measure servitization, so that progress towards strategic goals can be monitored. Strategies that are measured are more likely to be successful than those that are not. Specially, the strategies of an organization need to be properly measured using key performance indicators (KPIs) to accommodate business responsiveness. By understanding the elements of the strategy that can be measured, an organization can allocate resources to successfully execute it and periodically assess its progress. It is also easy to obtain the consent from the relevant stakeholders, if the measurements of the strategy's success are clear.

S. D. S. R. Maheepala (✉) • B. N. F. Warnakulasooriya • Y. K. Weerakoon Banda
University of Sri Jayewardenepura, Nugegoda, Sri Lanka
e-mail: neville@sjp.ac.lk; weerakon@sjp.ac.lk

Over the past decade, there has been a growing interest in servitization as a strategy of manufacturing companies to enhance business performance. Moreover, over the current decade servitization has been identified as a major strategy to remain competitive for manufacturing organizations (Brennan et al., 2015). It is important to understand how organizations measure the intensity of servitization and compare it with other organizations. Unless a concept is measured, it is not possible to maintain or improve beyond the current level. Although more objective variables such as net profit, sales growth, return on capital employed can be measured directly, abstract concepts applicable to the organizational context need to use carefully developed measurement scales. Therefore, this chapter explains how servitization can be measured and compared across the organizations, industries and countries. It is also important that the scale accurately measures what it intends to measure (validity) and consistently measures it (reliability). In other words, this chapter proposes a scale that meets measurement properties such as reliability and validity to measuring servitization so that practicing managers can use it to improve the different aspects of servitization in their organizations.

Manufacturing/Technology firms that also offer services to their clients are usually called as servitized organizations. In other words, the manufacturing/technology companies that offer at least one service to their clients can be considered as servitized manufacturers, while the manufacturers that do not offer any service can be categorized as pure manufacturers. The number of services delivered by manufacturing companies have often been used as a measure of industrial service offerings. Some studies measured servitization using the share of service revenues in manufacturing companies. Further, the percentage of service turnover has been used to measure the servitization intensity. Direct and indirect service revenues have also been used to measure servitization, while the service orientation of a manufacturing firm is often used to represent the extent of the industrial service strategy of a firm. Homburg, Hoyer, and Fassnacht (2002) measured the service orientation of a business strategy using the number of services offered, broadness of each service and emphasis on services. Moreover, Gebauer (2009) measured the service business orientation of manufacturing firms using indicators such as services offered, on how many customers these services are offered and how strongly these services are emphasized on a 5-point scale. Recently, Kohtamaki, Hakala, Partanen, Parida, and Wincent (2015) measured the service orientation of a firm using service orientation of corporate values of the firm, service orientation of employee's behaviour of the firm and service orientation of personnel recruitment of the firm.

Rabetino, Kohtamäki, Lehtonen, and Kostama (2015) explained the concept of life-cycle service offering where they identified and mapped ranges of services as services supporting customers' processes, services supporting products, transactional-based services and relational-based services. More recently, Partanen, Kohtamäki, Parida, and Wincent (2017) explained the dimensions of industrial services pre-sales services, product support services, product life-cycle services, R&D services and operational services.

From these past studies, it is obvious that servitization is a multi-dimensional construct and therefore, it is sine qua non to use a suitable scale for measuring the extent of the servitization in a firm. As previously mentioned, this chapter proposes a comprehensive scale, including the dimensions and indicators of the servitization.

3.2 Theory

This section focuses on the relevant theories and the extant literature on the measurement scale. Servitization is deemed as the strategy of an organization and can be defined as follows:

> Servitization is the strategy of service integration into the core business in manufacturing organizations in order to enhance the competitive position and performance of the organization. (Maheepala, Warnakulasooriya, & Weerakoon Banda, 2016, p. 202)

When discussing a strategy that integrates services into the core business, it is important to understand the four dimensions to measure such a strategy. First, the current service offering of the organization needs to be understood. Second, it is important to understand the strategic intent for future service offering, to clarify whether the organization is offering services as a strategic approach or as a tactical approach. Third, the service orientation of the company is an important aspect of the servitization strategy, since the execution of service strategy is strongly connected to the service orientation of the firm. Finally, service revenue will show the financial implications of the servitization strategy and would be the fourth important aspect to monitor when measuring servitization. The measurements of the above four aspects are discussed in details in the subsequent sections.

3.2.1 Measures of Current Service Offering

The current service offering of the organization explains the strength of the existing service portfolio of the manufacturing firm. This includes the number of services the organization offers to the customers and the organizations personalized admiration expressing the intensity to their customers in the course of service delivery. As per Homburg, Fassnacht, and Guenther (2003), the number of services offered to their customers clearly reflects the scope of the service strategy of an organization, where the number of services itself is an important facet of a service-oriented strategy. This is because the more the services that an industrial company offers, the greater is the ability of the organization to augment the product offering. Further, they explained that the number of services is similar to the breadth of product range which is considered to be a key strategic decision in the field of product management. When the company is combining the products and services, it is important to look at the breath of the service portfolio through the number of services. For a given number of services offered, companies have the option of offering them actively to customers or offering them only when customers explicitly ask for them. Therefore, in addition to the number of services offered, it is important to examine the emphasis placed on these services (Homburg et al., 2003). The number of services the company offers and the depth and the intensity of how the organization offers those services to their customers are important factors in order to accurately reflect the current scope of service strategy in the organization. The nature of the services offered means whether they are narrow activities centred on the production capability of the organization (e.g. spare part provision) or are offered to ensure the state and the condition of the product. For example, technical support and maintenance services or whether the company offered services which are usually internal to the customer are important when assessing the level of servitization (Baines & Lightfoot, 2013). The base services typically focus on product provision and the company uses its production competence to deliver these types of services. Installation service, spare parts provision and technical support are examples of base services. Intermediate services are broader activities than base services and are mainly focused on ensuring the state and condition of the product/equipment. Product research for customers, design and development services, and customer trainings are some examples of intermediate services. As per Baines, Lightfoot, Smart, and Fletcher (2013) apropos of advanced services stretching out the manufacturing enterprise over a wider area, to take on activities that are usually internal to the customer. Furthermore, they explained that advanced services focus on outcome assurance and

Table 3.1 Base, intermediate and advanced services in manufacturing companies

Base services (narrow activities centred around organizations production competences)	Intermediate services (stretched services based on existing production competences/customer maintenance services)	Advanced services (stretched activities that are usually internal to the customer)
Installation service	Product research for customers	Service for operating customer's process
Spare part provision	Customer training	Distribution, wholesaling, retailing, branding for customer
Technical support	Sourcing services	Consulting services
Analyses on product's manufacturability	Recycling service	Financing services for customers
Procurement services	Product design and development service	Start-up assistance for customers
Warranty	Repair and maintenance	Customer support agreements
Product demonstrations	Product upgrade service	Outcome-based performance services

usually involve themselves in higher risk than base and the intermediary services. Some examples for advanced services are customer support agreements, retailing and branding support for customers, and start-up assistance for customers. Table 3.1 explains some of the base, intermediate and advanced services identified in manufacturing companies.

It is important to understand that the current service offering of an organization can be measured using the three indicators, namely (1) number of services offered, (2) the depth of service offered and (3) whether they are base, intermediate or advanced services.

3.2.2 Measures of Strategic Intent for Future Service Offering

In addition to current service offering, it is important to understand the companies' strategic intent to develop further services in the future. Servitization is a conscious and explicit strategy, with services becoming one of the main differentiating determinants in a totally integrated products and service offering of manufacturing companies (Baines, Lightfoot, Benedettini, & Kay, 2009). The strategic intent of service offering explains whether the organization is offering services as a strategic weapon or whether organization offers services as a tactical solution for customer demand. If the company does not have a plan for future service offerings, it will not be able to invest and develop its current service offering of the organization. As such, while understanding the current service offering, it is equally important to grasp the focus of for the future service offerings. In a servitized organization, it is imperative for a future service portfolio to pay the same attention to the future product portfolio. Lay, Copani, Jäger, and Biege (2010) explained that the strategic intent for future service offering needs to be identified in terms of service breadth and service depth. The organizational intent to increase the number of services in the future explains the company's expectation to broaden its current service activities. The strategic intent to improve the current services and the company's anticipation to increasing the depth of service offerings need to be clearly reflected in its servitization strategy. While traditional manufacturing companies may deliver some services due to customer pull, servitized companies use services to differentiate themselves and co-create value with the customers. Consequently, it is essential to understand the strategic intent of future services when measuring and comparing the extent of servitization of an organization.

3.2.3 Measures of Company Service Orientation

Servitization describes the manufacturer's transformation towards a service-oriented business strategy (Baines et al., 2009). As per Lytle and Timmerman (2006), service orientation is best understood as an organizational predisposition—a strategic organizational affinity or preference for service excellence. Service-oriented organizations plan, pro-actively engage in and reward service giving practices, processes and procedures that reflect well the belief to the effect that service excellence is a strategic priority and that services significantly affect the creation of superior value. Service orientation of a company is a great reflection on the success or failure of the servitization strategy, which then can be used to measure and compare servitization. Lytle and Timmerman (2006) further explained that the service orientation of the employee behaviour and management behaviour is a clear and significant reflection of the company's service orientation, and it can be measured by considering how individual employees and managers are service oriented. The service orientation of human resource activities when recruiting, training and providing compensation is also important when evaluating the service orientation of the entire organization. Specifically, the service orientation of recruitment refers to the extent to which the selection of the workforces focuses on service-related aspects, service orientation of the employee training captures the degree to which the employees are trained for interactions with customers and service orientation of compensation refers to the extent to which service-related performance is evaluated and rewarded within the organization (Homburg et al., 2003). In addition to the activities related to the employee and management, it is also important to understand the service orientation of corporate values of the organization when determining the service orientation of the manufacturing companies (Homburg et al., 2003). Ideas, opinions and attitudes or the mindset regarding the importance of services need to be embedded into the corporate culture in order to succeed in servitization. This organizational belief reflects the customer views of how much the value of services is subsisted in the organization. It is important to understand the service orientation dimension of servitization can be measured using the six indicators such as (1) service orientation of employee's behaviour, (2) service orientation of management behaviour, (3) service orientation of employee recruitment, (4) service orientation of employee training, (5) service orientation of employee compensation and (6) service orientation of corporate values. In other words, these six areas are important in order to improve the servitization within the manufacturing firm.

3.2.4 Measures of Service Revenue

Service revenue is another important dimension in measuring servitization. Servitized companies have the opportunity to increase their revenues through product-service combinations, by strategically infusing services with products and technologies. The extent of servitization thus can be understood from the revenue generated through services in such companies. However, it is important to note that service revenue may not be separable from the product sales in manufacturing companies. For example, the research and development service of manufacturing companies may not be charged separately to the customer, meaning it will be added into the product price when the company offers new products to the clients. In such situations, Lay et al. (2010) deemed that the revenue is generated by the company directly and indirectly through the service offerings to their customers. The premium charged for the product due to the service component would then be considered as the indirect revenue from the service offerings. As such, it is appropriate to consider both the directly and the indirectly invoiced service shares of the manufacturing firms when measuring the service revenue.

3.3 Framework

It is sine qua non for companies embarking on a servitization strategy to focus on the following four areas: (1) current service offering, (2) strategic intent for future service offering, (3) service orientation of the company and (4) services revenue. When comparing and measuring the servitization all four areas are equally important as they reflect a unique aspect of the servitization strategy of the organization. Therefore, it is important to improve all the four areas to enhance the servitization level within the organization (Fig. 3.1).

The current service offering is clearly get reflected in the number of services offered, depth of company offering and the nature of service offering whether they are basic, intermediary or advanced. These three indicators measure the current service portfolio of a manufacturer. Further, the strategic intent of services measures the company's strategic intent to improve the breadth and depth of its services offering in future. Any strategy needs to have a future state. Hence, the strategic intent of the manufacturer to offer services in the future plays a pivotal role in the servitization strategy of an organization. The third component of servitization is the service orientation of the company which can be measured using the service orientation of the company's corporate values, management behaviour, employee behaviour and employee recruitment, training and compensation. The service orientation of the organization elucidates the overall readiness of the manufacturer to offer services. The fourth component to measure the level of servitization is service revenue, and it measures direct and indirect service revenue of the company. The summary of this model is depicted in Table 3.2

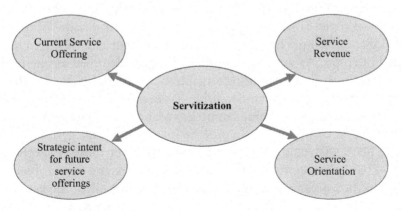

Fig. 3.1 Dimensions of servitization

Table 3.2 Dimensions and indicators of servitization

Dimensions	Indicators
Current service offering	Number of services currently offered
	Base, intermediate, advanced service offering
	Depth of services delivered
Strategic intent for future service offering	Strategic intent to develop a service breadth
	Strategic intent to develop a service depth
Service orientation of the company	Service orientation of corporate values
	Service orientation of management behaviour
	Service orientation of employees behaviour
	Service orientation of employee recruitment
	Service orientation of employee compensation
	Service orientation of employee training
Service revenue	Direct revenue from service offerings
	Indirect revenue from service offerings

3.4 Managerial Conclusions

Due to overstated competition and advancements in the marketplace over the current decade, organizational offerings to their customers have become more complex. Therefore, manufacturers operate more close to the customer needs than ever before in the current decade. Moreover, traditional capabilities have been widened by manufacturers through servitized offerings. As such, servitization has been identified as one of the key strategies in manufacturing organizations (Brennan et al., 2015). Further, servitization of manufacturing has become the trend in both the developed and the developing countries (Maheepala, Warnakulasooriya, & Weerakoon Banda, 2017). In order to manage any strategy, it is important to first understand how it can be measured. The measures explained in this chapter are appropriate for managers to assess the extent of servitization in their organizations and benchmark it to those of the key competitors. The set of measures proposed here provides mangers a quick and comprehensive view of the service-oriented business strategy of the organization. For example, managers can review their current product/service portfolio and the strategic intent for future offering with their key competitors. When assessing and comparing current service offering, it is important to consider the number of services the company offers, depth of the service delivery and whether the portfolio includes basic, intermediate and advanced services.

The senior management of an organization that is embarking upon a servitization strategy needs to have a meticulous understanding about the service offerings in that particular industry, market leaders and their competitors. They can then assess whether the number of services the company offers and their depth are adequate or there are opportunities to improve these aspects. Furthermore, the company can compare the types of services in its current portfolio whether they are basic, intermediate or advanced. Because the risk and return of those that are different from basic, intermediate and advanced services. For example, HeiQ Materials AG—a global textile chemical company that provides advanced technologies to its clients—has integrated several services to co-create value together with the clients. As a result, they tailor service offerings to customer's specific needs and extend the depth of each service to meet customer expectation. The company service portfolio features a combination of base (technical support, trouble shooting, legal compliance services), intermediary (customer training, mill recommendations, environmental health safety and sustainability support) and advanced services (usually internal to customer, e.g. testing customers product, marketing support, ingredient branding). The company had a strong technology/product portfolio inclusive of service offering to their customers and uniquely combined the offering to the existing and new customers. With the unique approach, HeiQ co-creates value together with its customers through its business offerings. As a result, this company has achieved a 30% compound annual growth rate in sales over the last five years.

In addition to the current service offering, the company needs to consider the strategic intent to widen and intensify the future service offerings. Measuring the strategic intent to develop the service breadth and depth helps managers to understand the magnitude and direction of the organizational maturation and proliferation, apropos of the service-oriented business strategy. As such senior managers need to craft the servitization road map and develop either long- or medium-term plan and then pass those to the middle-level management for the execution. If the strategy is long term, the managers must measure the progress over the analysed period with sensible milestones. Middle-level management needs to develop clear KPIs and delegate to junior management. It helps to agree to the proposal of using the relevant KPIs with each layer and plan resource requirements to achieve those KPI's. For example, if the organization needs to set up a separate division or department to successfully extend the current service offering, it also needs to budget the resources and develop a proper action plan at all levels.

The service orientation of the organization clearly echoes preference for service excellence within the organization and often reflects on the belief that service excellence is a strategic priority of the organization. Service orientation is often measured and compared in service organizations such as banking, airlines and hotels. However, service orientation is equally important for servitized manufacturing/technology companies, which they aim to compete by means of outstanding product-service combinations. In such situations, organization-wide commitment to relatively enduring organizational practices, procedures and policies which support and reward service-oriented behaviours is essential in determining what demands to be measured, monitored and cultivated. The six indicators in Table 3.2 can be used in a subjective manner to compare the service orientation of a manufacturing/technology company internally, longitudinally and externally. IBM is a good example on the shift from a product-dominant culture to service-oriented culture. The company created a new service vision and anchored its service culture to become the leading servitized organization in the industry. Service revenue generated directly and indirectly due to service infusion provided a good indication to the management to understand the financial implications of the servitization strategy. Organizations expect to improve their revenues, as well as profits, via transition to the stage of servitized organizations. A higher servitization level should thus reflect a higher percentage of service revenue compared to product revenue. For example, highly servitized companies such as IBM, Rolls-Royce Aerospace, BP, Shell, Boeing and Xerox have a higher percentage of service sales than those of the less servitized competitors. Thus, it is important to measure and place controls to monitor such trends and take appropriate remedial actions.

Different dimensions of servitization would be helpful when shaping and executing a service-based business strategy because the previously discussed four dimensions reflect different aspects of servitization. When managers measure the servitization using these four dimensions, it is possible to identify flank areas. The framework in Table 3.2 would thus be helpful to draw an action plan and build KPIs to measure servitization. Table 3.3 exemplifies how a manufacturer can develop a road map to increase servitization over three years based on the framework in Table 3.2. This example considers all elements on the servitization scale to improve the current position and develop a plan to enhance servitization. The company is planning to extend the current service offering of its two basic services to seven, including intermediary and advanced services. Furthermore, they have planned to extend the intensity of each service to their customers to increase the service revenue from the current 5% to 25% over three years. The related organizational change in culture, management behaviour, employee behaviour and human resources practices has been planned accordingly. Similarly, they can measure the outcome based on the developed KPIs for each action. Firms wishing to compete by using a servitization strategy have to constantly monitor the current offering and design future offering. To this end, the proposed scale can be used as a diagnostic tool to identify and improve specific areas. The organization can use an external benchmark at the industry level to compare itself to major competitors. As previously illustrated, top management can use this framework to develop an overall strategy for the product/service offerings of the organization. Middle-level managers can use the framework to set clear policies for the success of servitization. Changing the management and employee behaviour, training and development, and reward systems are also considered in the framework.

The servitization scale can also be used by academics to conduct empirical studies to measure servitization and develop relationships. Researchers can thus compare the extent of servitization among different companies, industries or countries using this scale.

In summary, practicing managers can use this framework to estimate the current position and use it as a standard measure to benchmark

Table 3.3 Servitization road map example of a manufacturing company

Indicators	Current position (2017)	Y1 (2018)	Y2 (2019)	Y3 (2020)
Number of services offered	Currently offers two services known as procurement of raw material and technical support when required	Add sourcing services and product design and development services	Add product research service and product innovation service to our customers	Add distribution and wholesaling services
Base services, intermediate services, advanced service offering	Currently offers only base services	Add one intermediary services into service portfolio	Add one more intermediary services	Add one advanced services
Depth of services delivered	Offer for selected customers when required and do not align with customer expectation	Offer for all customers and align with customer expectation	Offer for all customers and align with customer expectation	Offer for all customers and exceed customer expectation
Strategic intent to develop a service breadth	Add services selectively. At least one service each year in next three years	Supplement two new services in 2017	Supplement two new services in 2018	Add one new service in 2019
Strategic intent to develop a service depth	Plan to increase the intensity of each service company is offering. strengthen and resource the procurement and technical support department	Introduce sourcing as a parallel function in procurement department and strengthen the resources.	Product research would become a key offering to all customers and establish a separate R&D department	Exceed customer expectation in product research, sourcing and other services offered. Set up a strategic alliance/joint venture with the customer for a distribution centre in Asia

(continued)

Table 3.3 (continued)

Indicators	Current position (2017)	Y1 (2018)	Y2 (2019)	Y3 (2020)
Service orientation of corporate values	Customer service is not currently a core value in our corporate culture	Revise the company mission by incorporating the service business	Establish high-quality customer service as a key priority of the organization	Establish the company internally and externally as comprehensive solution provider in the footwear industry
Service orientation of employees behaviour	Currently, there is no mechanism to measure the service orientation of the employees	Create awareness among employees about the importance of a comprehensive customer service	Establish service mentality of the employees	Engage employees strongly as solution providers to the customers' specific need
Service orientation of employee recruitment	Currently, company does not have a mechanism to recruit high-quality service staff	Consider the ability for customer service as a key criterion in new recruitments when recruiting employees for service function	Consider readiness for customer service as a major factor in new recruitments for all employees of the organization	Company recruits best solution providing staff to their customers in the industry
Service orientation of employee compensation	Currently, company does not have a mechanism to differentiate service staff	Introduce customer service as a component in annual performance review	Evaluate customer service as a component in annual performance review and link to annual performance	Recognize the best solution providing staff quarterly and appreciate their effort and embed those practices into the culture

(continued)

Table 3.3 (continued)

Indicators	Current position (2017)	Y1 (2018)	Y2 (2019)	Y3 (2020)
Service orientation of employee training	Current trainings are more focused on manufacturing related	Include the social competence into the company training matrix	Identify the training gaps of service-related activities and train the key staff members	Identify the training gaps of service-related activities and train all the staff members
Service orientation of management behaviour	Senior management currently understands and supports the shift from product dominant to solution (product/service) dominant approach	Management development programme for middle-level management to implant solution provision culture from traditional manufacturing orientation	Management needs to coach employees to become solution providers	Reflect best management behaviour for solution-oriented foot wear manufacturing company
Direct revenue from service offerings	Less than 2.5%	Directly invoiced services need to generate 5% of total sales	Directly invoiced services need to generate 10% of total sales	Directly invoiced Services need to generate 15% of total sales
Indirect revenue from service offerings	Less than 2.5%	Service needs to generate additional 5% of sales included in the product price	Service needs to generate additional 7.5% of sales included in the product price	Service needs to generate additional 10% of sales included in the product price

against others, whereby specific actions can be implemented in the organization. The above example of how to use the framework to enhance the servitization level of the organization will help managers to improve their position. In addition to the practicing managers, the scale is also deemed appropriate for academics to measure and reflect upon the extent and the level of servitization according to their research settings.

References

Baines, T., & Lightfoot, H. W. (2013). Servitization of the manufacturing firm. *International Journal of Operations & Production Management, 34*(1), 2–35.

Baines, T., Lightfoot, H. W., Benedettini, O., & Kay, J. (2009). The servitization of manufacturing. *Journal of Manufacturing Technology Management, 20*(5), 547–567.

Baines, T., Lightfoot, H. W., Smart, P., & Fletcher, S. (2013). Servitization of manufacture. *Journal of Manufacturing Technology Management, 24*(4), 637–646.

Brennan, L., Ferdows, K., Godsell, J., Golini, R., Keegan, R., Kinkel, S., … Taylor, M. (2015). Manufacturing in the world: Where next? *International Journal of Operations & Production Management, 35*(9), 1253–1274.

Gebauer, H. (2009). An attention-based view on service orientation in the business strategy of manufacturing companies. *Journal of Managerial Psychology, 24*(1), 79–98.

Homburg, C., Fassnacht, M., & Guenther, C. (2003). The role of soft factors in implementing a service-oriented strategy in industrial marketing companies. *Journal of Business-To-Business Marketing, 10*(2), 23–51.

Homburg, C., Hoyer, W., & Fassnacht, M. (2002). Service orientation of a retailer's business strategy: Dimensions, antecedents, and performance outcomes. *Journal of Marketing, 66*(4), 86–101.

Kohtamaki, M., Hakala, H., Partanen, J., Parida, V., & Wincent, J. (2015). The performance impact of industrial services and service orientation on manufacturing companies. *Journal of Service Theory and Practice, 25*(4), 463–485.

Lay, G., Copani, G., Jäger, A., & Biege, S. (2010). The relevance of service in European manufacturing industries. *Journal of Service Management, 21*(5), 715–726.

Lytle, R., & Timmerman, J. (2006). Service orientation and performance: An organizational perspective. *Journal of Services Marketing, 20*(2), 136–147.

Maheepala, S., Warnakulasooriya, B., & Weerakoon Banda, Y. (2016). Servitization in manufacturing firms and business performance: A systematic literature review. *International Journal of Business and Social Science, 7*(5), 200–210.

Maheepala, S., Warnakulasooriya, B., & Weerakoon Banda, Y. (2017). Servitisation and business performance in developing countries: An evidence from Sri Lanka. *International Journal of Services Sciences, 6*(2), 132.

Partanen, J., Kohtamäki, M., Parida, V., & Wincent, J. (2017). Developing and validating a multi-dimensional scale for operationalizing industrial service offering. *Journal of Business & Industrial Marketing, 32*(2), 295–309.

Rabetino, R., Kohtamäki, M., Lehtonen, H., & Kostama, H. (2015). Developing the concept of life-cycle service offering. *Industrial Marketing Management, 49*, 53–66.

Part II

Servitization Strategies and Business Models

4

Business Models in Servitization

Tuomas Huikkola and Marko Kohtamäki

4.1 Introduction

To escape the commoditization trap, globalization and price erosion and take advantage of the new emerging and digitized technologies, manufacturers have to reinvent their business models to sustain their advantages. Hence, manufacturers have implemented services, service contracts, operational services, and performance services to increase their customer value, customer engagement, downstream movements, financial value, revenue stability, and profits. Despite the seemingly evident motivation to generate the service business model and move from pure products to customer solutions, manufacturers have struggled to adopt the right business model for dedicated customers and service products.

For researchers and practitioners, the question of the appropriate service business model is far from simple since the potential business model of a manufacturer can consist of various configurations that can each lead

---

T. Huikkola (✉) • M. Kohtamäki
University of Vaasa, Vaasa, Finland
e-mail: Tuomas.huikkola@uva.fi; marko.kohtamaki@uva.fi

© The Editor(s) (if applicable) and The Author(s), under exclusive license to
Springer International Publishing AG, part of Springer Nature 2018
M. Kohtamäki et al. (eds.), *Practices and Tools for Servitization*,
https://doi.org/10.1007/978-3-319-76517-4_4

to optimal outcomes. In strategy research, this phenomenon is called "equifinality" (Sjödin, Parida, & Kohtamäki, 2016). Thus, understanding the possible service-oriented business models for a manufacturer is complex and context-dependent. Context influences on the success potential of any business model and the relationship between a service business model and success is far from linear. In fact, the relationship between the business model configuration and success may be non-linear, with many variables intervening, mediating, or moderating the relationship. The current servitization literature falls short with respect to the discussion of business models, and it leaves options to study many viable configurations. This chapter intends to address the gap and understand the key elements of the alternative business models in servitization.

This chapter suggests that servitized manufacturers can successfully and simultaneously apply multiple business logics, since it is rare that any empirical configurations are pure. Instead, in theory, we can define ideal types that then take different forms when companies apply them. Even more importantly, companies may apply different business models for different customers or customer segments. Hence, in many cases, companies are not utilizing just one business model but are using multiple simultaneous business models or configurations. In this chapter, following the similar logic of organizational ambidexterity, we propose that the suggested business models are complementary rather than contradictory, and they help manufacturers address different customer needs and business concerns.

4.2 Theory

The servitization literature has acknowledged that manufacturers should configure service strategies to meet business objectives (Gebauer, Gustafsson, & Witell, 2011), realign resources and capabilities (Huikkola, Kohtamäki, & Rabetino, 2016), align product-service offerings (Kowalkowski & Ulaga, 2017), and decide on a pricing model. This allows them to establish their business model for creating, delivering, and capturing value (Storbacka, Windahl, Nenonen, & Salonen, 2013). The extant literature has used many dimensions to represent different service offerings (e.g., Mathieu, 2001) and strategies (Oliva & Kallenberg, 2003). For instance, Ulaga and Reinartz (2011) have categorized four service offerings based on their value propositions and service orientation. The nature of the value proposition in each of these services is whether they are input-based or output-based, and the service orientation is linked whether we are addressing the supplier's good or the customer's process. They have categorized these offerings into (1) product life-cycle services, (2) asset efficiency services, (3) process support services, and (4) process delegation services. However, much of the discussion in the servitization literature has conceptualized service product strategies or overall service business strategies, neglecting the importance of business models. Therefore, this chapter sheds light on how a firm can create, deliver, and capture value through alternative service business models.

The business model approach well fits the intention to understand appropriate configurations of building blocks to reach high performance. Osterwalder and Pigneur (2010) have established *the business model canvas*, which has been widely adopted by practitioners and academics to understand, define, and select a firm's key partners, activities, resources, value propositions, customer relationships and segments, channels, cost structures, and revenue streams. Furthermore, Johnson, Christensen, and Kagermann (2008) identified four intertwined elements that help firms to create and deliver value. These elements are (1) superior value propositions to their clients (the most important element), (2) the profit formula (includes revenue model, cost structure, margin model, and resource velocity), (3) key resources (includes tangible and intangible resources), and (4) key processes (includes rules, metrics, and norms) required when designing a business model.

While it has been stated that the business model is something between the firm's detailed business plan and overall strategy, it has been acknowledged that a single firm or business unit may adopt multiple simultaneous business models (Bertini & Tavassoni, 2015), and they can be dynamic and systemic by nature (Storbacka et al., 2013). By utilizing the concept of equifinality, typological research suggests that multiple logics may lead to optimal outcomes and that firm should find the configuration of building blocks that fits their purposes when operating with different customers. In theoretical models, researchers can specify pure models (called Weberian ideal types), but empirical configurations are rarely if ever pure. Instead, in an empirical world, companies mix elements from different business model configurations, especially when operating with different customers or customer segments. Because of strong customer-orientations in services, firms can utilize different business models with different customer segments, which may even lead to a customized business model for each key customer. For a firm, it is a challenge to define and understand the models it utilizes and on what grounds. The application of multiple logics makes the organization more difficult to manage.

4.3 Framework

Based on hundreds of executive interviews, company consultancy work, studying the action research method applied in companies, company observations, and numerous servitization workshops during the last eight years, we have compiled a comprehensive understanding of manufacturers that have servitized their businesses. We have identified and classified four distinct business models for manufacturers: (1) the product business model, (2) the service-agreement business model, (3) the process-oriented business model, and (4) the performance-oriented business model. The first two business models focus on products, while the two latter models focus on the customer's process development. In the product and service-agreement business models, the customer owns the process or product, while in the process-oriented and performance-oriented business models the supplier owns the process or product on the customer's behalf.

4.3.1 Product Business Model

The product business model builds on the manufacturing, selling, and delivering a product and the add-on services. Selling and delivering a tire is an example of the product business model. For instance, the Finnish tire manufacturing company Nokian Tires Plc sells highly innovative and differentiated tires with premium prices to dedicated customers (car drivers, SUV drivers, truck and van drivers) in dedicated market areas (Nordic countries, Russia, Middle-Europe, and North America). The corporation's separate service unit (and directly owned sales channel) Vianor supports the company in selling more tires and tire-related services directly to the customers, and helps the company to better understand its end-users' needs through its direct contact with consumers.

The product business model serves B2B customers or purchasers who are mainly technologists and require services that typically support product development, procurement, usage, delivery, functioning, or disposal. The key service products provided in this business model include various research and development (R&D) services, documentation services, maintenance services, instructions, repairs and spare parts for certain supplier's products, warranties, financial services, or technical backup services.

The product business model is transaction-based and mostly focused on the product itself, its development, sales, delivery, repair, or disposal. This is also its strength because it is less complex than others are. It is suitable for customers or purchasers whose earnings logic is based on exceeding their fixed costs. Once they have covered their fixed costs, they are able to generate high profit margins from every additional transaction made. Particularly, traditional customers in traditional industries appreciate the simplicity related to this business model. The disadvantage for manufacturers is related to the customer's potential use of an arm's length mechanism, price erosion, and the lack of true differentiation. Key sales arguments and value propositions are related to emphasizing product features, delivery times, and product superiority. The profit formula is based on low product margins but relatively big yet infrequent deals. Key performance indicators (KPIs) are the fill rate and repayment period for the customer. A firm's overall profits are based on the traditional manufacturing logic and exceeding fixed costs. Inventory turnover is high in this business model.

The key resources are the firm's distribution channels (such as dealers) and production facilities (e.g., factories and production lines). The key processes are related to R&D, and its strategic orientation is technology-oriented rather than customer-focused. Thus, the approach in development activities is inside-out. This business model initially attempts to profit from new breakthrough products (black-box types of development) or scale advantages (low costs). The services provided in this business model are initially meant to support product sales, development, delivery, use, and (to a lesser extent) functionality. This business model is probably the most popular among current manufacturers.

4.3.2 Service-Agreement Business Model

The second alternative model focuses on service agreements. For instance, the Finnish forest machine manufacturer Ponsse Plc sells two-level service agreements (Ponsse Active Care/Ponsse Active Care+) to contractors. These service agreements enable Ponsse's customers to improve harvesters' reliability and resale value.

The service-agreement business model is meant to serve B2B customers or purchasers who are "fleet managers". "Fleet managers" source services that improve equipment's total productivity, decrease products' total-cost of ownership (TCO), and help them to more efficiently manage their fleets. The services provided in this business model mainly support the use of equipment, product availability, and reliability/functionality. Examples of services provided are fixed-price service contracts, predictive maintenance, extended warranties, customer/user training, modernization services, remote services, and product upgrades.

The service-agreement business model's strengths are related to the predictability and stability of income for the manufacturer. The demand for services among customers is constant since services are typically needed with respect to the usage of equipment. The service-agreement business model is suitable for customers and purchasers who appreciate the product's availability and reliability. The business model's disadvantage is the potential commoditization of spare parts or threats of new substitutes or emerging technologies, such as 3D-printing. For instance, traditional car manufacturers' established after-sales business markets may decay as the number of electric cars increases. For instance, the Chevrolet Bolt, an electric car manufactured by General Motors, has only 24 moving parts while the traditional Volkswagen Golf has 149 moving parts. Tesla's maintenance interval for batteries, the engine, and the gearbox are 1.6 million kilometers compared to 15,000–30,000 kilometers for traditional cars. The key sales arguments and value propositions in the service-agreement business model are related to the product's availability (e.g., short response time/time-to-fix rate) and reliability for the customer. The profit formula is based on high service margins. Instead of highlighting the customer's repayment period, the supplier often emphasizes increased return on investment (ROI) to the customer in order to justify possible higher prices. Manufacturer's overall profits in this model are based on exceeding the variable costs (typically every transaction requires increased labor or materials) or premium pricing. Higher product prices can be achieved through the identification, communication, and verification of product's life-cycle costs and increased returns for the customer's tied equity. The inventory turn in this service business model is low.

The key resources are the firm's installed base of products and existing service contracts, service-aware salespeople, field personnel (such as technicians), service depots, and spare part centers. The key processes are related to fleet management developmental activities. The approach in the developmental activities is both inside-out and outside-in. On the other hand, manufacturers should be able to calculate its customers' overall costs and productivity, lock-in the customers, and improve its internal productivity (gray-box type of development). Services are typically organized under profit-and-loss responsibilities and separate service units that have their own management team, workforce, and business targets. This business model is typically well adopted in manufacturing companies who have reported large profits from service businesses.

4.3.3 Process-Oriented Business Model

Sales outsourcing, operations management, equipment upkeep, remote diagnostics, project management, and equipment rental services are a few examples of service products provided in the process-oriented business model. For instance, Konecranes Plc, a Finnish crane manufacturer, offers broad-scope maintenance outsourcing services to its industrial customers (e.g., commitment maintenance program). The key idea behind outsourcing services is to decrease the customer's overall costs or increase customer's overall productivity through new ways of organizing the work. Hence, the customers' top managers are typically responsible for sourcing such services, and suppliers' representatives should be more interested in the customer's business-oriented issues (e.g., profit formula, revenue model, or balance sheet benefits) than technical details.

The strength of the process-oriented business model is the movement toward more value-added operations in the industry's value system. However, this business model requires the ability to discuss operational services' monetary value with customers' top managers. This is typically difficult for the old product sales and after-sales sales forces since the needed capabilities in these businesses remarkably differ from each other. The process-oriented business model is suitable for customers who are planning to outsource part of their production or business processes. Customers typically outsource part of the operations to generate cost savings, transfer fixed costs to variable costs, increase its productivity and flexibility, achieve better KPIs, or reallocate resources to new business areas. Suppliers can benefit through scale advantages, learning benefits, or an improved production utilization rate. The manufacturer's disadvantage in this business model is the potential threat of becoming a subcontractor and not a partner. Then, customers can use the price-based governance mechanism every time the contract is renewed. The customers' disadvantages are related to realized cost savings (that may be lower than thought), lack of control and trust, or difficult-to-measure transaction costs. Therefore, customers should always evaluate the opportunity costs regarding the outsourcing decision and its alternatives. The key sales arguments and value propositions in this business model are fact-based numbers such as increased productivity/sales or decreased costs. This typically requires open-book principles and trust from both parties.

The key resources are manufacturer's existing customer relationships, customer references for such projects, project teams, and a dedicated and direct sales force to sell more comprehensive operational services. The key processes are related to risk and project management issues. Typically, the sales teams responsible for selling services under the process-oriented business model are separated from traditional product and service sales, and consists of senior-level managers and experienced salespeople. The sales cycles for such services are high since the decision-making process is relatively lengthy as customer's top managers are typically involved in the sourcing process. This business model is currently adopted by manufacturers who, for example, offer maintenance outsourcing services to their current customers.

4.3.4 Performance-Oriented Business Model

Sales operations and maintenance services (O&M), consulting services, turnkey solutions, integrated solutions, and data analytics services are examples of solutions sold under the performance-oriented business model. For instance, Outotec Plc, a Finnish technology company that provides processing machinery and process engineering solutions to customers operating in the metal and minerals processing sector, offers comprehensive O&M solutions to its customers operating in the mining sector. In these offerings, Outotec is responsible for running the customer's mining operations by guaranteeing and selling *costs per ton* instead of selling pure equipment or traditional projects. In these O&M solutions, customers source comprehensive solutions to run dedicated business operations. Customers buy such solutions to (1) *buy or loan* competencies from external firms or (2) *release* resources for the reallocation of capital or other resources. Typically, companies in developing countries lack the technological capabilities to run businesses, even though they may possess superior financial competencies. Therefore, they want help from external firms to obtain the technical capabilities to run the business or process. On the other hand, established companies in developed countries typically outsource these business operations to external firms to release resources for other purposes. Customers may move to another strategic direction, which requires new resources. This business model involves top executives from both sides since these contracts are the most demanding to sell and buy. For a manufacturer, adopting this business model requires careful consideration as it enters customers' businesses. Therefore, manufacturers need to acquire competencies to run the customer's business. This may mean that some of its existing customers consider manufacturers as their direct rivals.

This business model's strength is that it is the most difficult to replicate by competitors. Moreover, it is also the most demanding business model to accomplish since it requires active involvement in the development of the firm's strategic and operational activities. The performance-oriented business model is suitable for firms whose leading strategic customers are attempting to move ahead in the value system. This requires careful consideration from the manufacturer's strategists as firm's competitive landscape will be dramatically changed. (Will it start to compete with its other customers? How many customers are scared of this movement?) For an O&M provider, this usually includes the acquisition of blue-collar workers since running the dedicated business operations requires workers such as builders, cleaners, or technicians. The customer's business logic in this business model is based on the confirmation of the variable costs. Hence, when a customer knows the exact variable costs to produce a certain end-result (good or service), it is able to better price the sold outcome and thus evaluate its own margins. The manufacturer's profit formula is based on the traditional partnership model where profits and losses are mutual and, in this sense, companies are somewhat inter-dependent. In these types of cases, relationships are often built on mutual trust and the existence of a win-win scenario where both parties have to gain from the created benefits.

The key resources include the capabilities and competencies required in the other three business models since the performance-oriented business model is the most systemic and integrative of all the servitized manufacturer's business models. Even though this business model is built on the resources required in the three other business models, manufacturers should focus on developing the capabilities related to contract management and IT infrastructure development. Since the sales processes are the most demanding and firms must rely mainly on external firms' capabilities, it must perform good contracts. Therefore, a firm typically needs to hire lawyers or establish a legal unit in order to facilitate contract management competencies. Additionally, manufacturer typically starts to internalize its IT activities as it needs to know how the end-result is produced and how much producing the outcome has cost. A manufacturer typically wants control over the produced end-result. From the salespeople, this requires consultative sales competencies. Salespeople must identify, quantify, communicate, and verify the customer value during the business relationship. Business agreements in the performance-oriented business model are relatively long. For instance, the Finnish marine solution provider Wärtsilä announced a 12-year strategic performance-based partnership with its strategic customer the Carnival Corporation (a leisure travel company) in a deal worth almost 1 billion euros. In this agreement, Wärtsilä Plc handles, maintains, and monitors Carnival's 79 vessels. The main target for Wärtsilä and Carnival is to decrease the vessels' overall fuel consumption, increase productivity, and optimize the ships' routes.

Figure 4.1 visualizes the link between a customer's key needs and a manufacturer's capacity and readiness to run the customer's business process. In the product business model, the customer wants and has the capacity to run the business process himself. In the service-agreement business model, the customer wants to own the business process but is ready to outsource some of the non-core activities (e.g., maintenance and personnel/user training) to a specialized company. The customer also has the capacity to operate the business process but may lack or want to buy some specific competencies from external firms. Therefore, the customer should evaluate its opportunity costs regarding the distribution of work. In the process-oriented business model, the customer lacks the readiness to run the business process and is ready to outsource part of its sub-

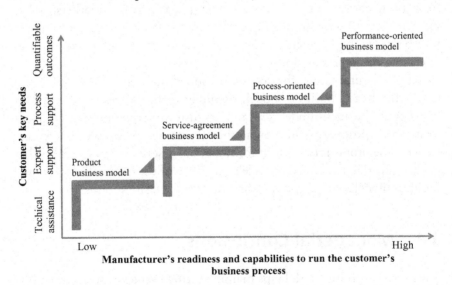

Fig. 4.1 Ideal types of business models

processes to external firms. It may be that the customer has recognized the lack of capabilities to effectively operate the business process, or that the customer wants to release resources for other purposes. In other words, the customer may possess the capability to run the business but wants to redirect its resources to other purposes for other reasons (e.g., to acquire other, more urgent, or strategic competencies). In the performance-oriented business model, the customer's willingness to run the business process is low. A customer may also lack the capabilities to independently operate the business process, even though it would like to autonomously operate the business process. This is the typical situation in developing countries where the customer wants the manufacturer to teach them how to run the business. For example, it may take five years for the customer to build the critical competencies necessary to run the business. The opposite situation occurs with established customers or customers in developed countries where the customers possess the capabilities to run the business process, but they want to outsource the operations to an external company for other reasons. In this case, the customer typically wants to release resources to focus on other more important business areas. Therefore, the demand for performance-oriented services comes from both competent and incompetent players in the markets. Thus, Fig. 4.1 is not an all-embracing model but rather an illustration of the link between the business models and customers' key characteristics in operating the business process.

Table 4.1 summarizes the above-mentioned business models, the rationale behind each business model, examples of the service products provided by the business model, key targeted customer segments, the supplier's focus areas, process/product ownership (customer *vs.* supplier), key customer value propositions, profit formulas, key resources and processes that are developed in the business models, examples of the materialization of the business models, and suggestive time frames for business deals.

4.4 Managerial Conclusions

The presented framework helps manufacturing managers to consider different configurations of service business models. Initially, no business model is better than another, but rather they are just different by their

Table 4.1 Four service business models for a manufacturer

	Simple ----------			---------- Complex
	Product business model	Service-agreement business model	Process-oriented business model	Performance-oriented business model
Process ownership Product vs. Process	Customer owns the process		Supplier owns the process	
	Supplier's focus is on the product		Supplier's focus is on the customer's process	
Customer segments	Technologist	Fleet manager	Outsourcer	Business partner
Examples of services provided to the clients	– R&D services – Documentation – Product training – Instruction services – Product maintenance – Repair services and spare parts for own products – Warranty – Technical support/ backup – Financial services	– Maintenance and spare parts for competitors' equipment or third-party products – Predictive maintenance – Service contracts – Extended warranties – Customer training – Modernization services – Remote services – Product upgrades	– Outsourcing services – Operations services – Comprehensive upkeep of the equipment – Remote diagnostics – Customer projects – Equipment rental/ leasing	– Operations and maintenance services (O&M) – Consulting services – Turnkey solutions – Integrated solutions – Data analytics services

(continued)

Table 4.1 (continued)

	Simple ←――――――――――――――――――――――――――――――――→ Complex			
	Product business model	Service-agreement business model	Process-oriented business model	Performance-oriented business model
Customer value proposition	– Technical features – Product superiority – Fill rates – Short repayment periods	– Shorter response times – Better availability – Increased returns on investment (ROIs)	– Increased utilization rate of production – Increased productivity of the process – Decreased transaction costs – Decreased and verified cost savings	– Risk outsourcing (risk evaluation is transferred to the supplier) – Increased overall business performance – Making outcome-related costs planned and predictable
Profit formula	– Low margins (few units sold) – Overall profits are based on exceeding fixed costs – High inventory turnover – Infrequent payments	– High service margins (services are sold frequently) – Overall profits are based on exceeding the variable costs – Low inventory turnover – Frequent payments (e.g., monthly or biannually)	– Profits are based on project success – Usage-based pricing	– Profits are based on customer's business performance – Value-based pricing – Pay-per-outcome

(continued)

Table 4.1 (continued)

	Simple————————————————————————————————Complex			
	Product business model	Service-agreement business model	Process-oriented business model	Performance-oriented business model
Key resources and processes	– Distribution channel (dealers) – Production plants – R&D – Installed base of products	– Installed base of products and service contracts – Service-aware salespeople – Field personnel (technicians) – Service depots and spare part centers – Fleet management development	– Existing customer relationships – References (reputation) – Project teams – Direct sales force (senior managers) – Risk management – Project management	– Solution sales workforce (includes also executives) – System suppliers – Contract management – IT infrastructure and IoT development – Customer value identification, quantification, communication, and verification processes – Risk management – Network management
Rationale behind the business model	– Easy for everyone to understand – Relatively big deals	– Predictability – Income stability – Customer lock-in	– Customer lock-in – Project-based business logic	– Win/win situation – Partnership – The most difficult BM to copy

(continued)

Table 4.1 (continued)

	Simple ———————————————————————————— Complex			
	Product business model	Service-agreement business model	Process-oriented business model	Performance-oriented business model
Examples of associated products, services, and solutions	– Truck tire and add-on services (remolding services) – Elevators and escalators – Engines and spare parts – Services to support product purchase and delivery	– Tire and wheel contracts – Service agreements for elevator, escalator, and automatic doors (service level depends on contract type) – Engine maintenance contracts – Product life-cycle services	– More extensive tire and wheel contracts – People flow solutions (large projects) and people flow analyses – Engine leasing – Operating services	– Michelin's fleet solutions (kilometers charged) – People flow optimization solutions – Power-by-the-hour solutions – Total solutions
Typical time frame for deals	<1 year	0–4 years	2–5 years	5–30 years

natures. Additionally, hybrid forms are available for a single company or a business unit. Alternative business models are even recommended since different customers have various business pains and gains. For instance, the Finnish elevator manufacturer KONE Plc may adopt several simultaneous business models. First, KONE may sell only elevators and escalators to a hotel chain. Second, KONE may make a service agreement to cover spare parts and maintenance for the elevators, escalators, and automatic doors in a dedicated business area, country, continent, or hotel branch. Third, the same customer can consult KONE about the optimal number of products and the most effective movement of customers inside the building. Fourth, KONE can optimize its hotel chain's customers' movements inside the buildings. For example, KONE may guarantee and verify how smoothly or conveniently hotel chain's customers move. KONE may have to pay penalties to the customer if there is an error in the elevator and the elevator users have bad customer experiences due to the broken elevator.

Table 4.2 exemplifies KONE Corporation's four distinct business models and the elements related to its value proposition (target customers, jobs that need to be done, and products/services/solutions), profit formula (revenue model, cost structure, margin model, and resource velocity), and resources/processes (tangible and intangible resources, processes, rules & metrics, and norms).

To conclude, a manufacturer can successfully adopt multiple concurrent service business models, and it is even desirable. Therefore, we ask how a manufacturer can know the appropriate business model(s) in each case. It depends on the initially defined customer's problems, needs, gains, and pains that the manufacturer has already identified and the value propositions that have been proactively designed to meet those requirements. After this, the company must choose the right business model that best addresses the customer's concerns. Finally, the firm must organize the work, obtain the resources to perform the job, follow up on the business case, and learn from the cases. Eventually, the firm may need to change its business model when customer needs and capabilities evolve.

Table 4.2 KONE Corporation's different business models

		Product business model	Service-agreement business model	Process-based business model	Performance-oriented business model
Value proposition	Key customer needs	Technical assistance	Expert support	Process support	Guaranteed and quantified outcomes
	Target customer(s)	Traditional builders (e.g., NCC, YIT, Skanska), architects, consultants	Condominiums, hotel chains, airports (e.g., Heathrow), construction companies, shopping centers (e.g., Stockmann), process industry, hospitals, users, property maintenance companies	Commercial real-estate companies, construction companies	Real-estate investment company, airport operators (e.g., Finavia), global hotel chains (e.g., Hilton)
	Job to be done	Ensuring the delivery, installation, and usage of elevators, escalators, and automatic doors	Ensuring the product's functionality and availability	Ensuring the project's delivery on time and cost-effectively	Ensuring end-user's experience and B2B customer's business performance
	Products/ services/ solutions	Escalators, elevators, and automatic doors, access systems, their delivery and installation, spare parts and maintenance services	Service contracts (different levels)	KONE major projects, marine solutions, solutions for process industry and hospitals, turnkey solutions	People flow analysis, 24/7 connections, performance services, integrated solutions

(continued)

Table 4.2 (continued)

		Product business model	Service-agreement business model	Process-based business model	Performance-oriented business model
Profit formula	Revenue model	High scale advantages, (high) price x (moderate) volume, negative working capital because of advanced payments	(Low) Price x (high) volume, negative working capital because of advanced payments	(High) price x (low) volume	Dependent on the usage of the equipment, in line with customer's business development
	Cost structure	Relatively high fixed costs, high share of outsourcing to component suppliers	Little investments, relatively high fixed costs because of the high number of service personnel	Variable costs	Variable costs
	Margin model	Product margins ~10%	Service margins 25–35%	Project margins	Margins depend on both supplier's and customer's success
	Resource velocity	High inventory turnover, moderate lead times	Low inventory turnover, short lead times	Moderate lead times	Long lead times

(continued)

Table 4.2 (continued)

		Product business model	Service-agreement business model	Process-based business model	Performance-oriented business model
Key resources and processes	Tangible resources	Production plants, agents, dealers, distributors, technology, component suppliers	Service depots, spare part centers, installed base of products	Equipment delivered, local project network	Equipment included in the contract
	Intangible resources	Patents, product personnel know-how, brand	Field personnel's (technicians') know-how, brands, data acquired from the products (IBM Watson)	Project managers and personnel, project handbooks	Top managers' competencies, strategic partners, such as IBM's (Watson) know-how, contract management, existing customer relationships, ICT competencies
	Processes	Product development, manufacturing, sourcing, after-sales development	Service process development, fleet management, operational productivity, service factory	Project management development and optimization, project data collected, project reviews, project auditing	Customer process development and optimization, understanding end-users' preferences and behaviors
	Rules and metrics	Delivery times, production efficiency	Customer retention rates (90–95%), response times, time-to-fix rates, product availability, tracking service	Project-related metrics, tracking the project's costs and development regularly	Customer value verification, tracking the output (possible root cause analysis of end-result production)
	Norms	No product tailoring, products in different price categories (typically premium pricing)	Service level determines the response times, standardized service levels and agreements, in-house service personnel	Standardized project protocols	Penalties possible if KONE cannot deliver good customer experience (minute-based charging for every time the elevator is broken/not in use)

References

Bertini, M., & Tavassoni, N. (2015). Case study: Can one business unit have 2 revenue models? *Harvard Business Review, 93*(3), 121–123.

Gebauer, H., Gustafsson, A., & Witell, L. (2011). Competitive advantage through service differentiation by manufacturing companies. *Journal of Business Research, 64*(12), 1270–1280.

Huikkola, T., Kohtamäki, M., & Rabetino, R. (2016). Resource realignment in servitization. *Research-Technology Management, 59*(4), 30–39.

Johnson, M. W., Christensen, C. M., & Kagermann, H. (2008). Reinventing your business model. *Harvard Business Review, 86*(12), 50–59.

Kowalkowski, C., & Ulaga, W. (2017). *Service strategy in action: A practical guide for growing your B2B service and solution business*. Scottsdale, AZ: Service Strategy Press.

Mathieu, V. (2001). Product services: From a service supporting the product to a service supporting the client. *Journal of Business & Industrial Marketing, 16*(1), 39–61.

Oliva, R., & Kallenberg, R. (2003). Managing the transition from products to services. *International Journal of Service Industry Management, 14*(2), 160–172.

Osterwalder, A., & Pigneur, Y. (2010). *Business model generation: A handbook for visionaries, game changers, and challengers*. Hoboken, NJ: Wiley.

Sjödin, D. R., Parida, V., & Kohtamäki, M. (2016). Capability configurations for advanced service offerings in manufacturing firms: Using fuzzy set qualitative comparative analysis. *Journal of Business Research, 69*(11), 5330–5335.

Storbacka, K., Windahl, C., Nenonen, S., & Salonen, A. (2013). Solution business models: Transformation along four continua. *Industrial Marketing Management, 42*(5), 705–716.

Ulaga, W., & Reinartz, W. J. (2011). Hybrid offerings: How manufacturing firms combine goods and services successfully. *Journal of Marketing, 75*(6), 5–23.

5

Value Constellations in Servitization

Saara A. Brax and Filippo Visintin

5.1 Introduction

The literature abounds in studies proposing typologies and examples to describe the offerings that servitizing firms provide to their customers. A recent literature review identified over 90 different conceptualizations of such offerings (Brax & Visintin, 2017). How can managers grasp the range of options in providing industrial product service system (PSS) offerings and select the best value constellations to pursue from such set of options? To help managers to identify and understand the options available to provide extended value propositions for their customers, this chapter presents a framework (Brax & Visintin, 2017) that captures the

---

S. A. Brax (✉)
School of Business and Management, Lappeenranta University of Technology, Lappeenranta, Finland
e-mail: saara.brax@lut.fi

F. Visintin
Department of Industrial Engineering, University of Florence, Florence, Italy
e-mail: filippo.visintin@unifi.it

different generic configurations that have been presented in the servitization literature. The framework arranges the generic value configurations into a pattern that reflects the companies' level of servitization in terms of the types of offering they provide.

5.2 Meta-Modeling Servitization

5.2.1 Servitization and Evolving Value Constellations

Established product businesses, especially original equipment manufacturing companies (OEMs), are extending their business to deliver their customers services and 'integrated solution offerings' that combine both physical products and services (Brax & Jonsson, 2009), following the value chain in their industry 'downstream'(cf., Davies, 2004). The various forms of this phenomenon are referred to as 'servitization' of the manufacturing industries (Baines et al., 2007). In particular, manufacturers of capital goods are organizing themselves to support their installed base of manufactured goods. The extended life cycle of such products typically requires maintenance and support activities that can become those that are offered as services (cf. Rabetino, Kohtamäki, Lehtonen, & Kostama, 2015).

For manufacturers, in fact, services provide continuity and a more stable income from a broadening customer base, protecting them against economic turmoil. The physical products become an 'installed base' for the OEM; a technology layer that needs services to run. An extreme example is the Xerox Corporation that accounted over 77% of its total revenues as annuity-based, coming from service contracts, maintenance of equipment, consumables, and financing services in 2016 (Xerox Annual Report 2016). More broadly and beyond the customer base associated with the installed base, needs and buying practices in companies are changing and organizations are increasingly looking for full-service solutions for specialized activities (Baines, Lightfoot, Smart, & Fletcher, 2013; Visnjic, Jovanovic, Neely, & Engwall, 2017).

Downstream extensions involve building services to support the core, that is, the capital good, as well as the customer's business function associated with this installed base. Some offerings extend upstream as companies often provide expert services that help customers to diagnose their needs more precisely. The range and maturity of the service solutions available can vary broadly within an industry. Within a single firm, value propositions with different scope and target can be provided. Changes in the total offering of the companies have been conceptualized as shifts of strategic focus or as extensions of the range of the offerings.

Researchers and consultants in the field have proposed numerous concepts and frameworks to capture the different options that companies have in designing their service-based value propositions. Recently, we conducted a systematic literature review in the servitization literature and identified around 90 different concepts or models of value constellations—all with distinctive names but many of them shared similar concepts (Brax & Visintin, 2017). Since it is not efficient to study all of them, we need a meta-model that reduces the number of concepts and focuses on the key aspects. Working on a structured analysis approach, we identified eight structurally different configurations, forming a framework of generic value constellations associated with servitization. This chapter explores the eight generic configurations that provide the backbone for variation when firms innovate value propositions of differing scopes and targets. The generic framework provides a map for managers to identify and analyze different solution offering strategies, no matter how these are branded and labeled.

5.2.2 A Framework of Generic Value Constellations

The identified generic value configurations are explained against the analytical framework that was used in the study to recognize them. The underlying rationale of the framework takes the life cycle of the PSS as its starting point and allows to connect the various value propositions to the bigger picture of servitization. It compares three main elements we observed in the value constellations presented in studies: PSS life-cycle stages, revenue model elements, and actors.

Servitization was defined here as the transition of manufacturing companies toward more service-dominant offerings. Hence, this change is associated with the delivery of tangible goods and systems to the customer to support the customers in their operations. These tangible assets are often called the OEM's *installed base* as they create a platform for services across its entire life cycle; increases in complexity, life-cycle duration, and cost of the systems typically require more advanced services as customers must rely further on their provider's expertise and support. For example, Visintin, Porcelli, and Ghini (2014) report the case of a global supplier of human to machine electronic controls operating in the aerospace industry that signed a major contract with an aircraft manufacturer for the provision of several critical systems and related services. These systems needed to be installed on a new type of aircraft for which the manufacturer had already been ordered 600 units. These aircrafts were supposed to enter in service in the following seven years, and to require support for the following 20 years at least.

In sourcing a business function, customer companies can choose from various alternatives, including the options to own their equipment and perform all activities in-house or to fully outsource—and many variations in between the two extremes. The basic, non-servitized model is the traditional 'arms-length' approach: the manufacturer sells the equipment, and its services focus on the sales phase. On the other extreme, the customer can purchase performance as full service through long-term contracts without taking owner's responsibility for the PSS. Companies implementing a servitization approach can sell various combinations of goods, services, and information to match the customers sourcing and operations strategies. We call the archetypical combinations that we identified in the meta-analysis as generic value configurations of servitization.

To develop the framework, we first compared the literature and business practices to identify the major steps in the PSS life cycle: (1) production, (2) business analysis, (3) solution design, (4) supply network design, (5) implementation, (6) operation, (7) support, and (8) disposal. During the analysis, we discovered that case studies very rarely separate the stages of the business analysis and supply network design. Often these activities were included in the design of the solution, which in the illustration covers both technical integration and business design activities (see Fig. 5.1).

Value Constellations in Servitization 87

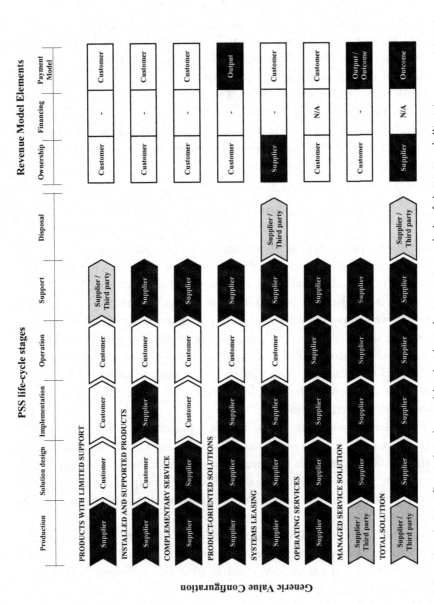

Fig. 5.1 Generic value configurations in servitization based on a meta-analysis of the research literature

Second, in addition to the life cycle stages, three revenue model elements were identified: (a) ownership of the system, (b) payment model, and (c) financing for the capital good. The key difference between the revenue models is how payments are determined; based on inputs, direct outputs, or more broadly defined outcomes.

Third, three parties were identified in the analysis; either the PSS supplier (S), the customer (C), or a third party (T) can take operational responsibility of each life cycle stage or revenue model element. All stages are characterized by interaction between the supplier's and customer's resources (Tuli, Kohli, & Bharadwaj, 2007).

5.2.3 The Pattern of Servitization

While most studies represent servitization as a rather straightforward, although challenging, process, there has been some discussion about whether the view of servitization as a uni-directional transition or shift is the whole truth (Kowalkowski, Gebauer, Kamp, & Parry, 2017). Davies (2004) noted that systems integrators are evolving upstream or downstream the industry value chain depending on their original role. Finne, Brax, and Holmström (2013) looked at two cases, one of them being Xerox, and reported the cases that showed a pattern of *reverse servitization*, as the case companies withdrew from their servitized business back to the product-focused model.

What the meta-analysis shows is that a pattern of value propositions with increasing emphasis on service-based elements exists, and according to the empirical research reviewed, these generic value configurations seem to be progressing sequentially. However, companies may provide several types of configurations side by side, meaning their strategy is an extension rather than a full shift to services.

Next, we will take a closer look at the eight different value configurations and explain what the offering strategy for them looks like. In the broader literature, the term value constellation (cf. Normann & Ramirez, 1993) is often used for such configurations.

5.3 The Value Constellations

5.3.1 Products with Limited Support

This is the most basic type of value constellation. In this case, the supplier manufactures a system and sells it to customers along with some basic services, typically break-fix, maintenance and customer support services. The system is not tailored to customer-specific needs. Customers assess their needs, select the system best matching these needs, implement the system in their environment, and operate it. The payment model is input-based. This is the case of many consumer electronic products, small household devices, but also of more complex product. For example, Wikhamn, Ljungberg, and Styhre (2013), describing the servitization journey of Volvo, point out how, back in the early 2000s, this constellation was the prevailing one in the automobile industry. At that time, suppliers' focus was just on providing basic after sales services such as maintenance service and spare parts. Nowadays, top players in the automobile industry (as well as in many other) have definitely switched toward more sophisticated constellations.

5.3.2 Installed and Supported Products

With this configuration, the supplier takes on the responsibility of installing the (new) system at the customer site and of maintaining it over time. The scope of the services being offered may vary, but the distinguishing feature of these value constellations is the product implementation. The system design activities, in general, are not based on customer-specific input and the system delivered can include components manufactured by third parties. Implementation activities imply some customization. The customers' socio-technical environment, in fact, can vary and the supplier has the responsibility to make the system work in different environments. The dominant payment model is still input-based even though services in this category can have a relational basis. Visintin (2012), referring to the case of Océ (a former Dutch manufacturer of printing devices now part of the Canon Group), describes how this configuration became very popular, in the nineties, in the professional printing industry. In those days, former analogue and disconnected products became digital and connected. Suppliers, thus, were expected to be able not only to deliver a product (e.g. a plotter) at the customer site but also to make it work in the customer environment. Rapidly evolving networks, operating systems, and applications characterized such an environment. Different customers had different environments and being good at performing smooth implementations (as well as the capability to deal with continues update in the environment) turned out to be a key differentiation factor.

5.3.3 Complementary Services

With this configuration, an OEM provides consultancy and R&D-oriented services (also) disjointedly from their main systems. The services provided may include design services, diagnostic services, consultation, logistics, managed inventories, and training. In addition, in this case, the payment model is based on the input being provided. Parida, Sjödin, Wincent, and Kohtamäki (2014) provide a nice example of this constellation. The authors report the case of LKAB, a Swedish mining company, which offers its customers an R&D service that consists in the possibility to use an experimental blast furnace to test blast furnace equipment and the blast furnace process. This service, which is offered either as part of a wider solution or as a separate service, allows customers to collect early test results without investing in an expensive and highly specialized piece of equipment.

5.3.4 Product-Oriented Solutions

In this case, the supplier delivers a comprehensive package including solution design, implementation, and support. With respect to the previous constellations, support services are relational in nature (often contract-based), and the prevailing payment model is the output-based one. As in the previous cases, the asset ownership remains on the customer side, and customer operates the system.

This constellation is spreading very quickly in the office equipment market (Visintin, 2014). Here former photocopier OEMs such as Xerox, Canon, Ricoh—to mention a few—are offering a wide set of solutions aiming at optimizing and managing the customers' document output environment. Such an environment includes (Visintin, 2014) photocopiers, scanners, printers, and fax machines, the relevant consumables, the processes that these devices enable (mailing, scanning, copying, faxing, archiving, distributing, sharing), and the people operating them. These solutions are usually regulated by multiyear contracts, where the provider is asked to supply the hardware equipment (which may replace or add up to the equipment customer already owns) as well as the software and services required to operate them efficiently. Customers are usually charged a pay-per-page fee that covers the supplies, the service, and the cost of the equipment. Depending on the contract, the hardware can be owned by the customer but also rented or leased. Some contracts also include guarantees of certain outcomes (e.g. in terms of reduction of overall print volumes, CO_2 emissions).

5.3.5 Systems Leasing

As in product-oriented solutions, also in this case, the supplier provides a solution including design, implementation, and support services, and the customer has the responsibility to operate the system provided. However, the asset ownership is not transferred to the customer, and the payments are input-based. Van Ostaeyen, Van Horenbeek, Pintelon, and Duflou (2013) provide an example of this configuration in the space heating and cooling market. They hypothesize the case of a supplier of space heating radiator that sells packages including the design, implementation, and maintenance (including cleaning and spare parts) of heat radiators, and charges them per day when the system is available for the customer, regardless of how much equipment is being used in that period.

5.3.6 Operating Services

Here, in addition to designing, implementing, and maintaining the provided system, the supplier takes on the responsibility of operating it on the customer's behalf under an input-based payment model. Contrary to the previous case, though, the customers own the system that is operated by the supplier. With respect to this constellation, Windahl and Lakemond (2010) discuss the case of a manufacturer of steam and gas turbines that back in 2000 signed its first operations and maintenance contract. Such a contract implied that over a six-year period, the supplier was responsible for running the plant and delivering power to the national grid, and steam and power to a paper mill. The customer was asked to pay a fixed monthly fee, plus a variable fee based on operational uptime.

5.3.7 Managed Service Solutions

As for the operating services, also in this case, suppliers design, implement, support, and operate a system that is owned by the customer (whose hardware or software components can also be sourced from third parties). The distinguishing feature of this configuration, though, is that the payment model is either output- or outcome-based. In their popular studies, Davies and coauthors provide detailed examples of how companies such as Ericsson moved toward this type of configuration in the early 2000s (Davies, 2003; Davies, Brady, & Hobday, 2006, 2007). Specifically, they show how Ericsson switched from selling mobile handsets, mobile system, and subsystem products (e.g. radio base stations, base station controllers, mobile switches, operating systems) to designing, building, and operating mobile phone networks, and supporting (through their own consultancy organizations, Ericsson Global Services) customers in developing their strategies for mobile communications.

5.3.8 Total Solutions

This value constellation is the most complex one. Here again, the supplier is responsible for all the activities from design to support and operation, and the payment model is based on the outcome. Contrary to managed service solutions, however, the provider owns the systems and the contract period is typically very long. Windahl and Lakemond (2010) present the case of a Swedish manufacturer of (a wide range of) air compressors that has developed a new technology to optimize their customers' use of compressed air. Instead of just selling air compressors, it offers to produce compressed air for its customers for (typically a) five-year period, and asks them to pay a fixed monthly fee based on their consumption. To do so, such a company buys the customers' old equipment (that are usually used as backup) and installs new equipment and systems that are used to run the customer plant efficiently.

5.4 Managerial Conclusions

As the Fig. 5.1 shows, a gradually increasing pattern toward more complex, service-based offerings emerges from the mapping of the value configurations reported in the servitization literature. This visualization explicates how operational responsibilities across the PSS life cycle are transferred from the customers to the OEM-suppliers or third-party service providers during servitization moves. Yet, the results indicate an emphasis on the OEM over third parties as the dominant player in this game. Vertically, the framework illustrates expansion from product-focused business to service-based business. Horizontally, it also illustrates how manufacturers expand by following their products 'downstream' the industry value chain.

The analysis revealed how terminology in the research field of servitization has proliferated during the past 15 years of research, making it challenging for both researchers and managers to make comparisons between the various offerings. The framework presented provides a robust conceptual tool for comparing the different business models in servitization beyond their different names and labels. The identified eight configurations are based on structural analysis of the offerings, ignoring the original names of the value constellations. The model also crosses industry boundaries, allowing companies to identify useful approaches beyond those that are provided in their industry.

The framework also suggests a clear direction for managers to describe their range of offerings to their clients and actors in the supply network. Most importantly, for strategic planning, the framework suggests a roadmap of different servitization strategies to be considered as managers develop the firm's portfolio of offerings. What are the configuration options the company wants to provide to its customers, and what options are not preferred?

References

Baines, T., Lightfoot, H. W., Evans, S., Neely, A., Greenough, R., Peppard, J., ... Wilson, H. (2007). State-of-the-art in product-service systems. *Proceedings of the Institution of Mechanical Engineers, Part B: Journal of Engineering Manufacture, 221*(10), 1543–1552. https://doi.org/10.1243/09544054 JEM858

Baines, T., Lightfoot, H. W., Smart, P., & Fletcher, S. (2013). Servitization of manufacture: Exploring the deployment and skills of people critical to the delivery of advanced services. *Journal of Manufacturing Technology Management, 24*(4), 637–646. https://doi.org/10.1108/17410381311327431

Brax, S. A., & Jonsson, K. (2009). Developing integrated solution offerings for remote diagnostics: A comparative case study of two manufacturers. *International Journal of Operations & Production Management, 29*(5), 539–560. https://doi.org/10.1108/01443570910953621

Brax, S. A., & Visintin, F. (2017). Meta-model of servitization: The integrative profiling approach. *Industrial Marketing Management, 60*(1), 17–32. https://doi.org/10.1016/j.indmarman.2016.04.014

Davies, A. (2003). Integrated solutions. The changing business of systems integration. In A. Prencipe, A. Davies, & M. Hobday (Eds.), *The business of systems integration* (pp. 333–368). New York: Oxford University Press.

Davies, A. (2004). Moving base into high-value integrated solutions: A value stream approach. *Industrial and Corporate Change, 13*(5), 727–756. https://doi.org/10.1093/icc/dth029

Davies, A., Brady, T., & Hobday, M. (2006). Charting a path toward integrated solutions. *MIT Sloan Management Review, 47*(3), 39–48.

Davies, A., Brady, T., & Hobday, M. (2007). Organizing for solutions: Systems seller vs. systems integrator. *Industrial Marketing Management, 36*(2), 183–193. https://doi.org/10.1016/j.indmarman.2006.04.009

Finne, M., Brax, S., & Holmström, J. (2013). Reversed servitization paths: A case analysis of two manufacturers. *Service Business, 7*(4), 513–537. https://doi.org/10.1007/s11628-013-0182-1

Kowalkowski, C., Gebauer, H., Kamp, B., & Parry, G. (2017). Servitization and deservitization: Overview, concepts, and definitions. *Industrial Marketing Management, 60,* 4–10. https://doi.org/10.1016/j.indmarman.2016.12.007

Normann, R., & Ramirez, R. (1993). From value chain to value constellation: Designing interactive strategy. *Harvard Business Review, 71*(4), 65–77.

Parida, V., Sjödin, D. R., Wincent, J., & Kohtamäki, M. (2014). Mastering the transition to product-service provision. *Research Technology Management, 57*(3), 44–52. https://doi.org/10.5437/08956308X5703227

Rabetino, R., Kohtamäki, M., Lehtonen, H., & Kostama, H. (2015). Developing the concept of life-cycle service offering. *Industrial Marketing Management, 49*(Suppl C), 53–66. https://doi.org/10.1016/j.indmarman.2015.05.033

Tuli, K. R., Kohli, A. K., & Bharadwaj, S. G. (2007). Rethinking customer solutions: From product bundles to relational processes. *Journal of Marketing, 71*(3), 1–17. https://doi.org/10.1509/jmkg.71.3.1

Van Ostaeyen, J., Van Horenbeek, A., Pintelon, L., & Duflou, J. R. (2013). A refined typology of product–service systems based on functional hierarchy modeling. *Journal of Cleaner Production, 51,* 261–276. https://doi.org/10.1016/j.jclepro.2013.01.036

Wikhamn, B. R., Ljungberg, J., & Styhre, A. (2013). Enacting hard and soft product offerings in mature industries: Moving towards servitization in Volvo. *International Journal of Innovation Management, 17*(4), 1–23. https://doi.org/10.1142/S136391961350014X

Windahl, C., & Lakemond, N. (2010). Integrated solutions from a service-centered perspective: Applicability and limitations in the capital goods industry. *Industrial Marketing Management, 39*(8), 1278–1290. https://doi.org/10.1016/j.indmarman.2010.03.001

Visintin, F. (2012). Providing integrated solutions in the professional printing industry: The case of Océ. *Computers in Industry, 63*(4), 379–388. https://doi.org/10.1016/j.compind.2012.02.010

Visintin, F. (2014). Photocopier industry: At the forefront of servitization. In G. Lay (Ed.), *Servitization in industry* (pp. 23–43). Springer International Publishing.

Visintin, F., Porcelli, I., & Ghini, A. (2014). Applying discrete event simulation to the design of a service delivery system in the aerospace industry: A case study. *Journal of Intelligent Manufacturing, 25*(5), 1135–1152.

Visnjic, I., Jovanovic, M., Neely, A., & Engwall, M. (2017). What brings the value to outcome-based contract providers? Value drivers in outcome business models. *International Journal of Production Economics, 192*(Suppl C), 169–181. https://doi.org/10.1016/j.ijpe.2016.12.008

6

Business Model Innovation: A Process Model and Toolset for Servitizing Industrial Firms

Federico Adrodegari, Nicola Saccani, Marco Perona, and Asier Agirregomezkorta

6.1 Introduction

The transition from a traditional business model (BM), based on product sales, to a service-oriented BM constitutes an opportunity for increasing revenues and achieving competitive advantages in industrial firms. In particular, faced with the commoditization of goods, declining profitability and customers with complex needs, an increasing number of companies are reorienting their offering from selling products to providing solutions. However, to be successful in this transformation,

---

F. Adrodegari (✉) • N. Saccani • M. Perona
RISE Laboratory, Department of Mechanical and Industrial Engineering, University of Brescia, Brescia, Italy
e-mail: federico.adrodegari@unibs.it; nicola.saccani@unibs.it; marco.perona@unibs.it

A. Agirregomezkorta
ULMA Servicios de manutencion, Onati, Spain
e-mail: asagirre@manutencion.ulma.es

manufacturers should not only shift their value proposition but also need to redesign their BM (Baines, Lightfoot, Benedettini, & Kay, 2009). But service-oriented BMs, particularly in capital goods companies, have received limited attention to date, and both the practitioners and the academia have limited knowledge on how to implement them (Adrodegari & Saccani, 2017). In fact, this transition implies several challenges, including a cultural shift from an engineering- and product-centred core culture to a more relational and customer-oriented one; a new strategy matching customers and business needs, providing them a clear value proposition; the redesign of products and processes. The company has to adapt its supply chain to set up a delivery network capable of distributing the service components of its offering. Thus, it is not surprising that, despite their potential benefits, a limited application of service-oriented BMs has been observed in the capital goods sector, particularly by the Small and medium-sized enterprises (SMEs) that find it extremely difficult to embrace the transformation and face the above-mentioned challenges. To date, few managerial guidelines have been developed to support this decision-making regarding such BM transformation (Reim, Parida, & Örtqvist, 2015). To provide a first step into closing this gap, this chapter presents a new business model innovation (BMI) process, a holistic and integrated multi-step methodology to support firms' transition towards service-oriented BMs. Different from other works, this methodology provides a formalized service-oriented BM framework that helps companies in structuring and managing, in an integrated way, the relevant elements that have to be taken into account in this transition. Moreover, a toolkit has been developed in order to enable the application of the BMI process in the real world.

6.2 Theory

BM innovation is generally seen as a vehicle through which companies transform themselves and achieve superior performance. Scientific research in this field has increased significantly in recent years (Wirtz,

Pistoia, Ullrich, & Göttel, 2016), but it has generally adopted a rather static perspective and there is a need to better explore tools and methods for achieving BM innovation (Cavalcante, Kesting, & Ulhøi, 2011). In fact, although several studies have addressed service innovation from a BM perspective (e.g. Barnett, Parry, Saad, Newnes, & Goh, 2013; Parida, Sjödin, Wincent, & Kohtamäki, 2014; Visnjic, Wiengarten, & Neely, 2016), only a few of them have developed a structured approach to this transition. In particular, research has still not paid sufficient attention to the applicability and availability of practical tools to support the ideation and implementation of service-oriented BMs (Baines et al., 2009; Adrodegari & Saccani, 2017). In Table 6.1, the main contributions found in literature in this regard have been collected and briefly described.

As shown in Table 6.1, although BMI's core elements (i.e. steps) of the analysed papers are somehow different, they could be grouped into five main phases that can be tracked back to the general BMI literature. These steps are (i) idea generation, (ii) selection of the (most promising) idea, (iii) requirements analysis, (iv) implementation and (v) evaluation (assessment of economic feasibility and environmental impact of the new BM).

With the only exception of the fifth step, these phases are considered in the majority of the papers analysed, but with little detail. Moreover, few of these works provide and describe tools to support the adoption of the proposed methodology. As an example, several works indicate creativity techniques such as brainstorming for the Idea Generation phase. Methods for business analysis (e.g. market, industry, stakeholder analysis, opportunity and risk analysis, visual thinking) are used in the second step. Methods for quali-quantitative market research (e.g. survey, interviews, group discussions) and for corporate analysis (e.g. SWOT, customer analysis, gap analysis, customer feedback) are often presented in the third step. Evaluation scenario techniques, life-cycle assessment tools and business plan are then used in the last steps.

However, there is a lack of integrative frameworks that comprise all stages and specific tools to generate and develop innovative BMs, helping managers to design and implement them.

Table 6.1 Contributions to the literature about the development of service-oriented BMs and classification of their steps

Paper	Contribution	Idea generation	Idea selection	Requirements analysis	Implementation	Evaluation
Van Halen et al., (2005)	Propose a complex decision methodology with a step-by-step approach of phases and decision nodes associated with tools that can be used in the Product-Service-System (PSS) development process.	Strategic analysis Idea development	Exploring opportunities	Concept design	Development and implementation	
Maxwell et al., (2006)	Propose a step approach for the implementation of Sustainable Product and/or Service Development (SPSD) that focus on the concept design phase when PSS ideas can be integrated into design		Planning Offering development	Detailed design Testing	Production	Offering launch and marketing

(continued)

Table 6.1 (continued)

Paper	Contribution	Idea generation	Idea selection	Requirements analysis	Implementation	Evaluation
Copani et al., (2008)	Propose a new framework consisting of a multi-step methodology for the selection and design of the most appropriate business models in machine tools companies. The methodology represents an operative instrument guiding machine builders towards the offer of value added services.		Identification	Definition of value proposition		
Muller & Stark (2008)	Propose an activity-based method to sustain the development of a PSS business model. The paper also proposes a PSS meta-model, which can be used to document and compare PSS ideas.	Analysis	Derive requirements	Formalize requirements		

(continued)

Table 6.1 (continued)

Paper	Contribution	Idea generation	Idea selection	Requirements analysis	Implementation	Evaluation
Pawar et al., (2009)	Propose three stages of developing Product-Service-Organisation. The framework provides the foundations for a process to develop PSS: it highlights the organisational challenges and suggests that a systematic yet iterative process can be devised to create and deliver value	Define value	Design value	Design value	Deliver value	
Shih et al., (2009)	Propose an integrated two-phase approach for PSS design and evaluation, with six major methods.	Potential idea for new BM	Supporting operation	Market responses and customers' preferences		General evaluation and life-cycle assessment
Ho et al., (2011)	Propose a process approach of service BM innovation to assist service business executives and policy makers in managing and promoting service innovations for sustained competitive advantage	Service paradigms	Concept development	Prototyping	Execution	Assessment and evaluation

(continued)

Table 6.1 (continued)

Paper	Contribution	Idea generation	Idea selection	Requirements analysis	Implementation	Evaluation
Lee et al., (2011)	Propose a reference model that can be used in the ideation process of the business design. The reference model, referred to as a business model design template, consists of predefined building blocks, each of which represents specific features or ideas that could be applied to create the new PSS business model.	Identify product or service element	Business model theming	Value creation mechanism	BM implementation	
Van Ostaeyen et al., (2011)	Propose a roadmap that includes a series of analyses that need to be carried out to define the value proposition that suits better the customers' value-in-use business model.	Strategic analysis	Options generation	Option filtering	Simulation and design Implementation plan	

(continued)

Table 6.1 (continued)

Paper	Contribution	Idea generation	Idea selection	Requirements analysis	Implementation	Evaluation
Martinez & Turner (2011)	Propose the first two phases of a generic method to design a PSS business model for a manufacturer of investment goods.	Analysis	Value proposition	Gap analysis	New BM Plan Strategy alignment	
Ehrenhöfer and Kreuze (2012)	Adapt the toolbox of the BM Canvas complemented by specific methods and tools from the service engineering approach, to show how complex service systems can be developed in a systematic and holistic manner.	Understand	Design		Implement - Manage	
Barquet et al., (2013)	Propose a framework that aims to analyse companies in terms of PSS requirements and to define actions to implement the BM concept to support the adoption of PSS.	Business context	Selection of types	PSS characteristics	PSS characteristics	

(continued)

Table 6.1 (continued)

Paper	Contribution	Idea generation	Idea selection	Requirements analysis	Implementation	Evaluation
Dimache and Roche (2013)	Propose a comprehensive systematic decision support methodology (TraPSS) and toolkit that supports decision-making regarding the transition from one position to another along the PSS BM continuum.	Establish goals	Identify criteria for decision making	Assess impact of the transition	Evaluate and make decision	
Wiesner et al., (2014)	Propose a methodology to provide a clear roadmap for the development of a new strategy for Extended-Product BMs.	Analysis	Find and create		Development	

6.3 The Business Model Innovation Process

To support managers in undertaking servitization, a new methodology has been designed, consisting of (i) a multi-step BMI process for the selection and design of the most appropriate service-oriented BM and (ii) tools to support managers in deploying the different steps of the methodology. Figure 6.1 illustrates the process, described in the remainder of this section. Table 6.2, instead, briefly describes the toolkit developed.

6.3.1 BM Idea Generation

The aim of the first step is to establish a shared language within the company, framing different expectations and defining the rationale, scope and main objectives of the new BM. Specific tools have been designed to support this step, helping companies to structure and present preliminary ideas more effectively. This step is divided in three main tasks:

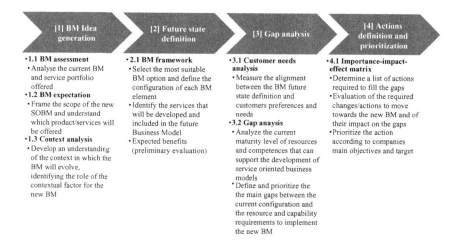

Fig. 6.1 Business model innovation (BMI) process for servitizing industrial firms

Table 6.2 Description of the BMI toolkit to support servitizing industrial firms

Step	BMI tool	Purpose of the tool	Method/Format
1. BM Idea generation	1.1 BM assessment	Assess the current BM configuration; Identify the services that are already offered	Interviews; Excel sheet with list and classification of services; competitive positioning
	1.2 BM expectation	Define the main elements of the new idea and the boundaries (products/service/customer) of the new business model; Identify the services that will be developed and included in the new BM	Brainstorming; Excel sheet with list and classification of services
	1.2 Context analysis	Identify the role of contextual factors for the new BM (market and environment): inhibitors, obstacles, facilitators and opportunities	Excel tool with a set of factors to be analysed concerning the market and external environment
2. Future state definition	2.1 BM framework	Define and formalize the new BM, according to a structured framework encompassing the relevant elements and variables	Excel sheet to be filled based on detailed analysis and BM design
3. Gap analysis	3.1 Customer needs analysis	Measure the alignment of customers preferences and needs with the new BM	Guidelines to support customer interviews and survey design
	3.2 Gap analysis	Define the maturity level and gaps of a set of aspects related to the new BM (resources, capabilities, tools and procedures)	Excel sheet to support internal or external audit about resources and capabilities for the new BM
4. Actions definition and prioritization	4.1 Importance-Impact-effect matrix	Based on the Gap Analysis (3.2) a list of actions is defined to implement the new BM. Actions are prioritized according to an evaluation of their implementation efforts and expected benefits/relevance	Excel sheet to support a qualitative and/or quantitative evaluation

1. "BM Assessment". It consists of depicting the company with the aid of a BM analysis framework (a simplified version of what is presented in Sect. 6.3.2) and carrying out an analysis of the current service portfolio. A specific tool provides guidelines for collecting information to achieve a good understanding of a company's current BM configuration.
2. "BM Expectations". It aims to define the project boundaries and generate business ideas. This phase still remains a creative stage where new service-based concepts are generated and/or new opportunities are identified. A brainstorming tool has been developed that allows companies to frame the scope and objectives of their new BM. It consists of 10 key questions that are connected to each other in a "circular" process. As exemplified in Fig. 6.2, reviewing the answers allows for achieving a greater consistency.
3. "Context analysis". It aims to develop an understanding of the context in which the BM will evolve, assessing the industry context, the market trends and the role of the company in the supply chain. This task

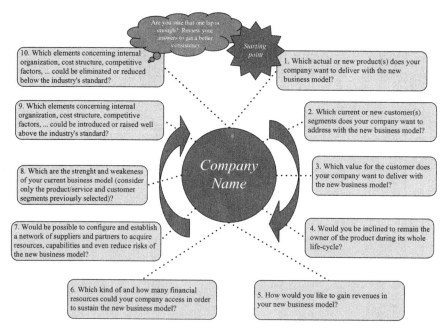

Fig. 6.2 The brainstorming tool

allows for pointing out the role of specific contextual factors for the new BM: inhibitors, obstacles, facilitators or opportunities. Again, a specific tool was developed to support the implementation in practice of this task. In particular, this tool can help companies in achieving a concrete perception of the role of three different categories of "contextual factors", namely industry context, internal environment, and market and customers.

6.3.2 Future State Definition

The concepts generated in the Idea Generation step are then translated into specific BM characteristics. The idea is formalized according to a specific BM framework based on the well-known BM Canvas (Osterwalder & Pigneur, 2010), in order to facilitate a common understanding of the phenomenon for both researchers and practitioners. Differently from the Canvas, this is a two-level hierarchical framework that encompasses a broad set of elements—derived from literature—to be evaluated and characterized when designing the servitization transformation. In order to simplify the practical application, the framework includes a set of questions to guide managers in identifying the characteristics of each element of the new BM (for a detailed description of the framework, see Adrodegari, Saccani, Kowalkowski, & Vilo, 2017). At the end of this step, the business idea selected is formalized as a structured and coherent BM.

6.3.3 Gap Analysis

In the third step, the company identifies the gaps with respect to relevant processes/procedures, capabilities and resources of the firm that are needed to deploy the new BM. This allows for identifying the actions needed to successfully implement the new BM. This step consists of two tasks: "Customer need analysis" and "Maturity evaluation".

First, the customer need analysis collects information among (current or potential) customers to assess the importance they assign to different potential value sources embedded in the new company offering, and their interest towards the (new) revenue model and services the company wishes to offer. This activity also allows for fine-tuning the BM configuration based on the feedback collected from customers.

Second, the "Maturity Evaluation" task has been designed in order to assess the service orientation of the company's key resources, capabilities and procedures. To support this task, a *Maturity Evaluation Tool* has been developed. The tool is based on existing maturity models in literature, but is specifically designed in order to evaluate the service orientation of each variable of the BM framework defined in the second step of the BMI process (see Sect. 6.3.2) through a five-level scale. This allows for pointing out gaps in resources, capabilities, tools and procedures needed to properly support the new BM, by comparing the actual configuration with the theoretical maturity required by the specific service-oriented BM chosen by the company (see Fig. 6.4 in the case example).

6.3.4 Actions Definition

The fourth step supports the company in the definition of a list of actions needed to fill the gaps and/or to implement the new BM. They are prioritized according to the expected impact and feasibility. A specific tool ("Importance-Effect-Matrix") was developed and aims to help the company to evaluate and select the most relevant actions to build the required resources, capabilities, tools and procedures to support the new BM. The tool provides a list of predefined actions that can be enriched and adapted by the company, and supports the company in assessing (qualitatively) the expected impact of each action in the specific case.

Then, it computes, thanks to an automatic calculation, an overall score for each action that represents an indicator of the effectiveness of the action. Moreover, through this tool, a preliminary cost evaluation of each action may be carried out.

6.4 BMI Process and Toolkit Application: ULMA Forklift Trucks

The BMI process and toolkit have been applied in the company ULMA within T-REX, a project funded by the European Commission. ULMA is a Spanish forklift truck distributor and after-sales service provider that successfully developed a new service-oriented BM based on short-term rental (STR), also thanks to the methodology described in this chapter. At the beginning of this decade, in order to face competition and the economic crisis, ULMA has radically changed its organization: from being a traditional forklift truck reseller it progressively became a forklift rental company. As a result, to date the company has more than 2000 forklift trucks on long-term rental (LTR) and has a solid business supported by financial and after-sales services. In order to take further advantage of the company's fleet mobility, ULMA has decided to develop a new service-oriented BM aiming to expand its customer base and better exploit its installed base: the STR of forklift trucks. In order to develop a clear understanding of the STR concept and to identify the transformations needed to implement the new BM, ULMA has applied the BMI Process described in this chapter. As a first step, the preliminary idea was shared within the company and refined (*Step 1* of the BMI process). In particular, the main guidelines for the development of STR were defined as follows:

- To reduce the internal costs of the new business, relying as much as possible on the structure, processes and information systems of the LTR business;
- To define an accurate and complete BM design and action plan to develop the new STR business.

Then, using the tool provided in *Step 2*, the preliminary idea of STR was translated into specific BM characteristics, structuring and mapping the idea according to the BM framework tool. The main characteristics of the new STR BM are summarized in Fig. 6.3, through the BM Canvas representation (Osterwalder & Pigneur, 2010).

Key Partners	Key Activities	Value Proposition	Customer Relationships	Customer Segments
The development of the STR is based on the existance of the current LTR partnerships. Specific partners for STR are a reliable logistic service provider and other forklift rental companies. These are critical in order to answer immediately to customers requests	1) During the product design phase a set of design techniques should be used: design for reliability, design for maintainability/serviceability, design for reuse/recoverability and life cycle. 2) Product modularization and reliability assessment techniques are critical. 3) Other key activities in the STR are: Marketing and e-commerce tools, logistics (stock -type and number-, proximity and travel companies), quick and efficient Service, product retrofit and efficient internal management and control (revision, scarp or sale decision, bad use invoicing, call center to attend demands.) supported by accurate and quick fleet operation and maintenance information.	Access and use of the product from 1 day to 6 months, with competitive prices, quick response (proximity), wide number of forklifts in perfect technical and apperance state to attend peaks of demand, full service, product usage monitoring and civil responsibility insurance	Relationships in STR are shorter than in LTR. On the other side, specific marketing activities are in place to collect information that are critical to identify the right customers for STR. Collect information about truck usage and service activities carried out to STR customers	In STR customers can be classified (a) according to the sector (LTR customers that have to attend peaks of demand -70%- and seasonal customers -30%(~) and (b) period of time the truck is rented (f.e. less / more than 3 months). Focus on seasonal demand customers (agiculture, Fair and Events, food industry...)
	Key Resources		**Channels**	
	ICT: 1) ERP; 2) Integrated fleet management system; FINANCIAL: high Finance capabilities required; exploitation of LTR fleet; HR: same skills to LTR; new specific, dedicated and efficient "call center" are developed.		Use of LTR channels, with focus on sales and marketing actions. Development of a new e-commerce tool (i.e. check availability and reserve forklift trucks)	
Cost Structure				**Revenue Streams**
Personnel costs, Service costs, Transport costs and Product depreciation (finance). Risks: low utilization rate, unpayment, product damages.				STR expected income for the first year is 250.000€ (Basque Country Area): 84,8% rental contracts, 8,2% transport, 3,9% insurance, 3,1% others

Fig. 6.3 ULMA, STR BM configuration (main elements)

In particular, using the information collected in the initial step through the brainstorming tool and further discussing the new value proposition configuration in internal company workshops, the distinctive sources of value for the customer were clearly identified. They are:

- Total flexibility on the usage of the product. Although there is a daily hours limit, this can be negotiated at any time (changing the daily rental fee);
- A full service contract that includes field service support in no more than eight hours and the replacement of the forklift if the problem cannot be solved in two days;
- Wide number of forklifts ready to be used for many different applications;
- Civil responsibility insurance that covers all damages caused to third parties;
- Condition monitoring that provides key information to the customer.

Following *Step 3* of the BMI process, a "Maturity evaluation" was carried out to map the current configuration of the LTR BM elements in ULMA (red line) against the future expected configuration needed to support the new STR BM (green line).

Figure 6.4 shows that the current configuration is generally close to the future needs, and it is not a radical innovation for the company. In fact,

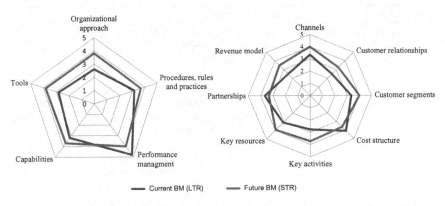

Fig. 6.4 ULMA, BM maturity evaluation

in the new STR BM, most of the needed resources (e.g. trucks, service personnel, spare parts) would come from the existing LTR business. Moreover, because of the recent shift from a reseller to a rental demand, the company has modified some key parts of the organization and the main processes to answer to this new scenario, and this will suit also the STR BM needs. As expected, a relevant gap identified was related to ICT and monitoring technologies that are critical to sustaining the STR BM.

Then, following *Step 4* of the BMI process, ULMA used the "Importance-Effect-Matrix" tool in order to select the actions needed to overcome the identified gaps and achieve the new BM configuration. In particular, this tool supported the company in the choice of the most appropriate actions, by prioritizing them according to their feasibility and expected impact on the highlighted gaps.

ULMA has defined over 30 actions to be implemented. Table 6.3 reports the top-priority actions.

As emerges from Table 6.3, in order to develop the new STR value proposition, ULMA needed a more accurate fleet management system—compared to the LTR business—in order to:

- Monitor the main signals of the forklift: for example, working hours, battery situation, temperature of engine, impacts, operator identification;

Table 6.3 ULMA, action list

Selected actions	Detailed description
Implementation of a health and fleet management system (and KPIs)	New STR business: it is intended to have a Fleet Management system for: – Product usage monitoring and utilization rate information – Monitoring of the main signal of the forklift (working hours, battery situation, temperature of engine, impacts, operator identification) – Recording the history of maintenance activities performed (day, technician, problem solved, number of hours per type of maintenance, costs, etc.) – Monitoring the status and activity of the fleet (total number of forklifts per area, number of hours per day working, etc.)

(continued)

Table 6.3 (continued)

Selected actions	Detailed description
Implementation of monitoring technologies on product/systems	Condition monitoring devices, sensors and tools: condition monitoring for batteries and key components will enable preventive/predictive maintenance and life-cycle ext. – Data acquisition for operation conditions – Event logs (impacts, operator identification, etc.) – Status reports for diagnostics (actual and predictive)
Development of CRM portal	Web-based applications for customer (STR): ticketing and renting; configuration of the forklift
GPS localization	Geolocalization of Service Engineers and Sales Personnel using a Mobile APP (e.g. localization of the closest Serviceman to attend an urgent repair at a customer's site)
Documentation and formalization of data analysis processes (procedures and workflows)	Formalization of workflows (to be shared within the company). Define procedures that formalize and standardize the data collection, interpretation and processing, on data that refers to both product and process and service (i.e. how to collect and interpret usage/performance/health state and customer process data from an installed base and formalize/report this information or feedback from service engineers).
Improvement of the Battery life cycle and data collection	Adaptive electronic battery regeneration by pulses: (a) with the pulses, the sulphatation of the battery it is delayed, maintaining the capacity of the "heart" of the trucks and (b) communicate the battery state with the truck operations and condition monitoring system.
Additional device for the connectivity of the forklift (data logger)	Development of an external device able to acquire data from the sensors installed on the forklift with the possibility to connect it to the monitoring system in order to collect and analyse data without the on-site intervention of a technician. The communication can be activated remotely (with Wi-Fi or GPRS) or locally (with a USB or serial output) whenever needed.
Monitoring of energy consumption	Monitoring the electric energy consumption will help to understand the real usage of the battery and when it needs to be regenerated.
Development of dedicated marketing activities	Marketing initiatives for STR (advertisement and communication). Marketing and commercial approach to target specifically seasonal demand customers

- Configure the forklift: for example, mast type, attachments, section of the company where it is working;
- Record all maintenance activities performed, collecting data such as *date, technician, problem solved, number of hours per type of maintenance, costs*;
- Monitor the status and overall activity of ULMA's forklift truck fleet: for example, total number of forklifts per area, number of hours per day working;
- Increase the timeliness and efficiency of maintenance operations and start exploring the adoption of predictive maintenance practices.

In order to collect all the data and signals required from the new fleet management system, several sensors were added to the forklift (to measure temperature, impacts, working hours, etc.). In particular, within the T-REX project, a specific data-logger system was developed to collect those signals from the forklift as well as to monitor the usage and efficiency of the battery that represents the critical part of electric forklifts. Figure 6.5 shows the system and the main signals collected.

6.5 Managerial Conclusions

This chapter provides an integrative framework that links service strategy and operational practices, supporting managers of industrial companies in the development of servitized BMs, through a BMI process and the related toolkit. As the ULMA case shows, the methodology and tools can be used by companies to formalize and guide the transformations needed towards servitization. Moving through the different steps of the BMI process, companies can better understand where their current BM stands, identify where they want to go, and point out and address the relevant gaps needed to successfully deploy the new BM. As shown by the empirical application, this methodology can be of particular help to SMEs that, due to limited internal resources and limited ability to arrange service strategy, may need a rigorous yet practical methodological support to undertake such an important change, thus reducing the risk of failure. Therefore, the proposed model and tools contribute to filling a gap and favouring a broader diffusion of service-oriented BM within capital goods

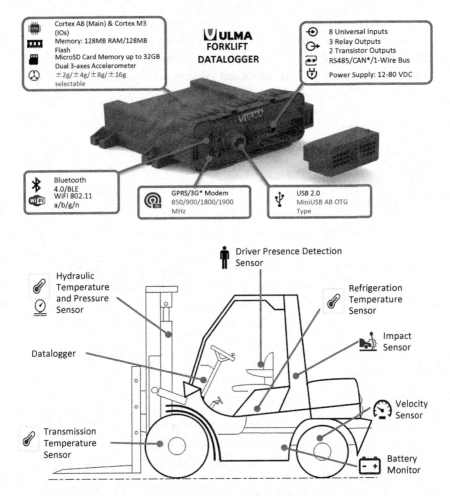

Fig. 6.5 ULMA, the new data monitoring and data-logger system

companies. Moreover, from the ULMA case, it is apparent that companies often need managing different BMs simultaneously (e.g. the LTR and STR in the analysed company). The BMI methodology helps companies formalize the configuration of their different BMs, highlighting and orchestrating synergies, and pointing out the relevant differences. In such cases, the success of service business development initiatives becomes also a matter of balancing the co-existing BM elements and strategically deciding where to place more emphasis.

Finally, it has to be noted that this research is mainly based on the analysis of industrial firms belonging to capital goods sectors. An extension of the empirical research to different sectors is required to achieve a greater generalization of the proposed BMI process and a fine-tuning of the tools.

Acknowledgements

The work described in this chapter has been conducted as part of the project T-REX (Lifecycle Extension Through Product Redesign And Repair, Renovation, Reuse, Recycle Strategies For Usage and service-oriented business model), a research project funded by the European Union Seventh Framework Programme (FP7/2007-2013) under grant agreement no 609005 (http://t-rex-fp7.eu).

References

Adrodegari, F., & Saccani, N. (2017). Business models for the service transformation of industrial firms. *The Service Industries Journal, 37*(1), 57–83.

Adrodegari, F., Saccani, N., Kowalkowski, C., & Vilo, J. (2017). PSS business model conceptualization and application. *Production Planning & Control, 28*(15), 1251–1263.

Baines, T. S., Lightfoot, H. W., Benedettini, O., & Kay, J. M. (2009). The servitization of manufacturing: A review of literature and reflection on future challenges. *Journal of Manufacturing Technology Management, 20*(5), 547–567.

Barnett, N. J., Parry, G., Saad, M., Newnes, L. B., & Goh, Y. M. (2013). Servitization: Is a paradigm shift in the business model and service enterprise required? *Strategic Change, 22*, 145–156.

Barquet, A. P. B., de Oliveira, M. G., Amigo, C. R., Cunha, V. P., & Rozenfeld, H. (2013). Employing the business model concept to support the adoption of product-service systems (PSS). *Industrial Marketing Management, 42*(5), 693–704.

Cavalcante, S. A., Kesting, P., & Ulhøi, J. P. (2011). Business model dynamics and innovation: (Re)establishing the missing linkages. *Management Decision, 49*(8), 1327–1342.

Copani, G., Marvulli, S., & Tosatti, L. M. (2008). An innovative pattern to design new business models in the machine tool industry. In *Innovation in manufacturing networks* (pp. 317–324). Springer US.

Dimache, A., & Roche, T. (2013). A decision methodology to support servitisation of manufacturing. *International Journal of Operations & Production Management, 33*(11/12), 1435–1457.

Ehrenhöfer, C., & Kreuzer, E. (2012). The role of business model design in the service engineering process: A comparative case study in the field of cloud computing to join service engineering with business model design. In *SRII Global Conference, IEEE* (pp. 283–292). San Jose, CA: IEEE.

Ho, J. C., Tseng, F. M., & Lee, C. S. (2011). Service business model innovation: A Conceptual Model and a Framework for Management Consulting. In *Service Sciences International Joint Conference IEEE* (pp. 247–251). Taipei, Taiwan: IEEE.

Lee, J. H., Shin, D. I., Hong, Y. S., & Kim, Y. S. (2011). Business model design methodology for innovative product-service systems: A strategic and structured approach. *SRII Global Conference, IEEE* (pp. 663–673). San Jose, CA: IEEE.

Martinez, V., & Turner, T. (2011). Designing competitive service models. In *service design and delivery* (pp. 61–81). Springer US.

Maxwell, D., Sheate, W., & van der Vorst, R. (2006). Functional and systems aspects of the sustainable product and service development approach for industry. *Journal of Cleaner Production, 14*(17), 1466–1479.

Osterwalder, A., & Pigneur, Y. (2010). *Business model generation: A handbook for visionaries, game changers, and challengers.* Hoboken, NJ: John Wiley & Sons, Inc.

Parida, V., Sjödin, D. R., Wincent, J., & Kohtamäki, M. (2014). Mastering the transition to product-service provision: Insights into business models, learning activities, and capabilities. *Research Technology Management, 57*(3), 44–52.

Pawar, K. S., Beltagui, A., & Riedel, J. C. (2009). The PSO triangle: Designing product, service and organisation to create value. *International Journal of Operations and Production Management., 29*(5), 468–493.

Reim, W., Parida, V., & Örtqvist, D. (2015). Product–Service systems business models and tactics—a systematic literature review. *Journal of Cleaner Production, 97*, 61–75.

Shih, L. H., Chen, J. L., Tu, J. C., Kuo, T. C., Hu, A. H., & Lin, S. L. (2009). An integrated approach for product service system development (I): Design phase. *Journal of Environmental Engineering and Management, 19*(6), 327–342.

Van Halen, C., Vezzoli, C., & Wimmer, R. (2005). *Methodology for product service system innovation: How to develop clean, clever and competitive strategies in companies*. Uitgeverij Van Gorcum.

Van Ostaeyen, J., Neels, B., & Duflou, J. R. (2011). Design of a product-service systems business model: Strategic analysis and option generation. In *Functional thinking for value creation* (pp. 147–152). Springer Berlin Heidelberg.

Visnjic, I., Wiengarten, F., & Neely, A. (2016). Only the brave: Product innovation, service business model innovation, and their impact on performance. *Journal of Product Innovation Management, 33*(1), 36–52.

Wiesner, S., Padrock, P., & Thoben, K. D. (2014). Extended product business model in four manufacturing case studies. *Procedia CIRP, 16*, 110–115.

Wirtz, B. W., Pistoia, A., Ullrich, S., & Göttel, V. (2016). Business models: Origin, development and future research perspectives. *Long Range Planning, 49*(1), 36–54.

7

Servitization through Product Modularization in Consumer Goods Manufacturing Companies

Inmaculada Freije, Alberto de la Calle, and Miguel Ángel Larrinaga

7.1 Introduction

This chapter focuses on servitization through product modularization in consumer goods manufacturing companies. While servitization has been developed and explored considerably in other markets, it has received little attention to date in industrial markets. Servitization is particularly interesting for companies in mature, traditional and highly competitive arenas facing aggressive competition and an erosion of profits due to competitors from low-cost countries.

Modularization is a useful way to customize products and increase the level of servitization, paving the way to a more sustainable competitive strategy. Not only is it more difficult to imitate by low-cost competitors but it also allows the firm to create and nurture customer relationships. Customization changes the traditional way of product development, as the weight of the relationship with the customer moves from pure transactional to relational.

I. Freije (✉) • A. de la Calle • M. Á. Larrinaga
Universidad de Deusto, Bilbao, Spain
e-mail: ifreije@deusto.es; acalle@deusto.es; miguel.larrinaga@deusto.es

However, such a change is very challenging for companies. In the following sections, both a framework to develop that strategic change and a business case are presented. These can be useful for consumer goods manufacturing companies considering new business opportunities, as there is a lack of servitization models in the literature, mainly in B2C.

7.2 Theory: Servitization and Modularization

Servitization can take very different forms, from just adding some peripheral services to total solutions, which also implies different levels of change (named servitization level). High level of servitization broadens the interaction with customers from transaction to relationship, giving a customized solution to its problems or desires. Customization modifies the scope of change both internally and externally, and the number of agents involved in the change (Martinez, Bastl, Kingston, & Evans, 2010). Although customization in servitization is usually more focused on B2B markets, we are referring here to B2C markets, which are traditionally mass-production sectors. When considering consumer goods, usually the number of customers grows sharply and, consequently, customization multiplies costs. In this context, customization through modularization offers interesting possibilities to personalize the offer while also making it possible to contain the costs by taking advantage of certain scale economies in the modules. Modules have to be designed to be combinable to create final products and services that fit better with the particular customers' tastes, choices and needs, which increase the value offered by the company. Through modularization, companies can also achieve cost reductions along with product range broadening, dealing with the difficult trade-off between standardization and customization. At the same time, as value is defined by and co-created with the customer, it allows the company to avoid intense rivalry, frequent in standardized consumer products.

This approach has many implications in the company as it supposes a profound impact on the current business model of the company along with other cultural and managerial changes. There are important challenges surrounding the transition from a product-centric to a servitized organizational structure. These not only involve developing and manufacturing the new customized products or marketing and delivering them but also human resources, and cultural issues. Ultimately everything should be considered under the new strategy. Rabetino, Kohtamäki, and Gebauer (2017) propose a strategy map of servitization to guide company managers in this process for companies that are shifting their focus to project-based customer solutions.

When a manufacturing company competing in mass production wishes to implement a servitization strategy through modularization, it also needs to conduct a solid analysis to define a new business model and thereby generate a sustainable competitive advantage.

The business model refers to the benefit that the company will deliver to its customers, how it will be organized in order to achieve it and how it will capture a part of that value being delivered (Teece, 2010). The following section proposes a conceptual framework for defining such a strategy based on this approach.

7.3 Framework

We shall therefore structure a framework to facilitate the definition of a servitization strategy through modularization in three interrelated parts (Fig. 7.1). This integrated framework can be used for supporting companies facing this strategic change as it covers: (Part 1) the definition of the value proposition to be delivered to the customers; (Part 2) the delineation of the changes to the current organization of the company considering the business resources, capabilities and processes and (Part 3) the design of the mechanisms for value capture.

7.3.1 Definition of the Value Proposition

The definition of the value proposition constitutes the core element of the competitive strategy. It is also the starting point for the configuration of the value chain that is required to develop and deliver the offering and, therefore, determine its costs and revenues that might be obtained in the

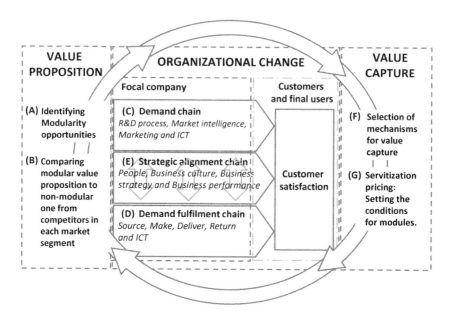

Fig. 7.1 Integrated business model framework

process. The value proposition that the company makes to the market includes all the benefits that it offers (from physical or technical aspects, to other aesthetic, brand or prestige, term, personal attention, information, etc.) along with the trade-offs that the customer will have to assume. The most common trade-off is the payment of a price, but there are many others, such as participation in the service at any time: in the design, development or delivery of the product or service. This term is highly related to the concept of 'value co-creation' (Prahalad & Ramaswamy, 2004).

In the definition of its value proposition, the company therefore determines what services or benefits it will cover for the customer and which, on the other hand, will be left for the customer itself to cover in some other way.

Servitization is often understood to be a process that completes the features covered by products along with others that are delivered with the services, sometimes by adding services and, at other times, by offering products or solutions. However, broader service coverage is not the only method. Due to the evolution of technologies and customer capabilities, as well as their changing expectations and habits, increasing opportunities are also observed to be derived from greater participation of customers in the final coverage of their needs. The definition of new value propositions based on customer participation in their service has enabled some companies to develop business models with highly sustainable advantages, such as the paradigmatic case of Ikea in the furniture industry.

Consequently, the definition of value proposition involves the need to analyse what combination of benefits that will be included and benefits that will not be offered to the customer (for the customer to cover itself) will be most highly appreciated by potential customers. Appreciation will logically be different depending on the tastes, wishes, capabilities, jobs to be done and needs of different customers, that is, market segments. If we can modularize that offer, we can multiply the possibilities for adapting to customer particularities, considerably broadening the possible combinations offered.

We therefore distinguish between two fundamental steps for the definition of value proposition: (A) the identification of opportunities for modularization and (B) the comparison of these modular value propositions with other non-modular ones in the different market segments.

– (A) Identifying modularity opportunities

The aim of this definition is to look for the more attractive combination of benefits to the customers. It implies determining what benefits will not be offered to the customer (for the customer to cover itself). The company and the customer should do what each is best positioned to do, as long as there are no difficulties combining their respective contributions. Otherwise, it would be more appropriate to offer total solutions (Freije & Freije, 2009). Based on the said approach, we propose answering three questions:

- Is the consumer in a better position than the provider company to make this contribution?
  The customer may be in a better condition than the supplier to cover some aspects for different reasons, such as knowledge or mastery of the

technology, better access to resources or being better positioned in the cost-productivity ratio. Commonly suppliers have an advantage in these areas because of their professional position and their potential for specialization due to catering for a larger customer base, especially in consumer markets. However, some research has highlighted the better position of users in relation to their specific needs and the context of use, while suppliers tend to have a greater capability to improve products by applying their technical knowledge to aspects that are already known to be of interest (Von Hippel, 2010). Consequently, the inclusion of customer participation in the final configuration of the product-service can open up interesting possibilities for differentiation, including those derived from customization.

- Do consumers appreciate their participation in the service or the potential individualized outcome?

  Sometimes, the participation of customers in the service is not justified by them being better placed than the supplier with regard to knowledge, resources or costs but rather because it is participation itself that generates value, or because it is the particular result that the customer especially appreciates.

  In the former case, customer participation generates enjoyment, learning or other benefits, such as personal or professional prestige.

  In the latter case, participation enables results in terms of personalization that would not be achieved any other way. This justifies how, in many cases, customers are willing to pay a clearly higher price for personalized products in which they have played a part in the process.

- Is there any barrier to modularity?

  The response arising from the services as a whole requires a connection between the benefits covered by the company and those which the customer fulfils itself. Links are sometimes very simple, which opens opportunities for the modularization of these aspects. To do so, and in many sectors, it is common to offer the possibility of access to financing, transport or different types of delivery. On the other hand, when fits are difficult, the opportunities for customer participation in the service can be limited, opening more opportunities for broader offerings.

- (B) Comparing modular value proposition to non-modular value proposition of competitors in each market segment.

The definition of the value proposition requires identification of the market segments in which the modular proposition could offer possible competitive advantages. On the one hand, potential customers have different capabilities, needs and conditions of use and context, which gives rise to different assessments of these combinations. They might not only obtain different results, but might also evaluate participation in the service in different ways.

Moreover, competitors do not always target all market segments, so the value propositions of current and potential, and direct or indirect, competitors that are presented as alternatives to our own will differ between segments.

The decision in this phase will depend on our estimation of the possibilities for the new modularized value proposition to compete in the market. The company should target customers that appreciate the customized proposition opened through modularization. These kinds of customers are usually against standard products.

7.3.2 Delineation of Changes to the Current Company Organization

The modularization process requires major changes to the company to fit with the new value proposition in terms of customer relationships and offerings. The firm must have a proper understanding of customer needs in order to adapt, or otherwise completely renew, the way that things are done, for example, how it interacts with the customer to capture and process useful information for the design of products and services or how it organizes production processes to meet or surpass expectations.

The complexity of the change with regard to the modularization strategy will fundamentally depend on the point where the customers start making decisions on processes pertaining to the company. This point is called the Order Penetration Point (OPP) or Customer Order Decoupling Point (CODP) (Wikner, 2014).

The required changes involve not only processes and resources (activities), but also demand a change in business mind-set, thus affecting people and the business culture itself. The challenge also resides in how all the elements that make up the essence of the company need to be aligned. Given this view, the changes can be read from the perspective of the relation with the customer, from that of the factory or production line, or from that of the management of people and resources. Consequently, we propose a model that differentiates between the elements of the organization that would be affected by servitization: on the one hand, processes and resources and, on the other, people and the business culture. Furthermore, among the former, a differentiation is made between those that involve a relation with the customer and those concerning the physical flow of materials.

Therefore, the model features three chains (Fig. 7.2): (C) Demand Chain, (D) Demand Fulfilment Chain and (E) Strategic Alignment Chain.

- The Demand Chain is focused on capturing and processing information related with customers and markets, as well as stimulating demand. This is used to try to understand the customers' needs and

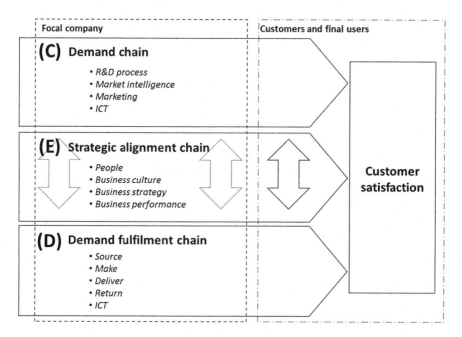

Fig. 7.2 Organizational change (Based on De la Calle Vicente, 2015)

expectations, with this information useful to design an attractive product-service approach. Thus, the Demand Chain would seek to respond to the questions arising in the modularization strategy from the perspective of the customer. The processes associated to this chain are described in Table 7.1.

- The Demand Fulfilment Chain analyses the situation from the perspective of physical and information flow associated with materials and products from the suppliers, to delivery to and returns by the customer. The processes associated to this chain are described in Table 7.2. Again, ICTs are the enablers of these processes.

The Demand Fulfilment Chain responds to the changes brought about by the implementation of the modularization strategy on a production process level. Production strategy is clearly affected by the position of

Table 7.1 Processes of the demand chain

Processes	Description
Research and Development (R&D)	During the R&D process, it must be determined what parts of the product can be modularized and which cannot. Through the creation of modules, the company can create a basic platform and seek synergies among the possible combinations that could be offered to the customer.
Market Intelligence	The surveillance system must be defined through this process to gain more in-depth knowledge about the customer such as tastes and purchase pattern.
Marketing	In this process should be defined the marketing strategy. This makes it possible to provide customers with the best value proposition in keeping up with their needs and to respond with the what, where and how that they seek.
Information and Communication Technologies (ICTs)	Increasing customer participation in activities that were formerly conducted by the company means implementing technologies to facilitate customer-company interaction. Furthermore, the use of ICTs allows the company to gather key information about the customer—what customers say, how they say it and how they interact with the system. Some examples of the use of ICTs are website, social networks or customer relationship management (CRM).

Table 7.2 Processes of the demand fulfilment chain

Process	Description
Source	Supply policy is clearly affected by the position of the OPP. Taking customer opinion into consideration in the early stages of manufacture implies that the supply of raw materials occurs as late as possible in order to avoid high storage costs, use of space, low rotation, risk of obsolescence, and so on. This in turn involves asking whether the supplier will be able to respond to an increase in the number of orders and a smaller batch per order. Likewise, working with parts rather than a product raises the need to pay special attention to the coordination of availabilities.
Make	This process needs consideration of the flexibility required for the resources used, and the type of process by which production is organized. If the OPP is located in the early stages of manufacture, the level of customization will be greater and so the level of resource flexibility will be more critical.
Deliver	Modularization therefore offers the possibility of increasing the level of customization, which complicates distribution as it is more difficult to group products for a single dispatch. In this case, criteria need to be set to control the dispatch of orders: delivery time and cost.
Return	The strategy for managing returns for different reasons or for recovering the product at the end of its life cycle must also be analysed in consideration of the modularization strategy. Among others, the key aspects for the definition might be decisions regarding guarantees, policy for maintaining spare parts and making use of product modules.
ICT	Information systems are instruments that support decision-making processes in this chain. They can be used to plan, execute, track and develop improvements to optimize the different processes involved in this chain. Barcode or radio frequency for identifying products and Manufacturing Execution Systems (MES) are some examples of ICT use.

the OPP, which determines how far the interaction with the customer goes (Fig. 7.3).

A production strategy that is associated as far as the OPP tends to be a push strategy, where the supply or manufacture of material is conducted based on demand forecasts, uncertainty level and/or service levels fixed by the focal company. In a Make to Stock (MTS) strategy,

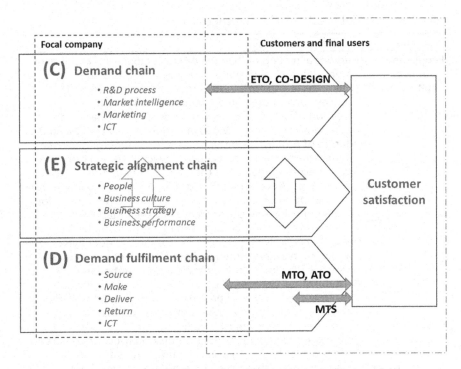

Fig. 7.3 Production strategies (regarding OPP) in the proposed model

the customer may choose the point of sale from a range of ready-made products. On the other hand, in intermediate strategies with regard to the position of the OPP, such as Assemble to Order (ATO) or Make to Order (MTO), there is a higher level of customer interaction/participation. An Engineering to Order (ETO) strategy would imply co-design of the ordered product with the customer, and it therefore appears in the Demand Chain in Fig. 7.3.

- The Strategic Alignment Chain concerns the strategic fit of the Demand and Demand Fulfilment Chains. The Strategic Alignment Chain covers the essential aspects of business management: people, culture, business strategy and business performance (Table 7.3). The Strategic Alignment Chain pools together the sometimes-contradictory targets of differentiation and operational excellence. The former is

Table 7.3 Process of the strategic alignment chain

Processes	Description
People and business culture	Traditional models of manufacturing companies bring to mind more clearly departmentalized organizations with hierarchical structures and bureaucratized processes. The concept of a strategy like modularization requires the creation of spaces and opportunities for coordination and collaborative learning. Modularization implies rethinking the design of products and therefore seeking synergies between them, which makes interaction between R&D and production more necessary than ever. The Demand Chain exerts pressure on the production model in that it determines the interest in customization of products. Another example is the need for communication and transparency between Market Intelligence and Source, between Marketing and Deliver. In summary, the issue here is to determine the right values on which the business should be based in order to encourage effective development between the different areas of the organization. In order to do so, it is essential to eliminate past mental models and prejudices, confronting the challenge based on values such as collaboration and transparency.
Business strategy and business performance	The business strategy must be defined, evaluated and monitored to help make decision-making processes quicker and provide them with as much information as possible. The modularization strategy must consider whether the company's response is really aligned with the customers' needs and expectations. In order to properly monitor performance, indicators can be defined and measurement systems articulated. In the Demand Chain, measurements can be made of brand value, customers' level of satisfaction with the modular offer, and so on. Demand Fulfilment can monitor the level and cost of storage, the level of resource use, assembly quality, delivery times, and so on. A balance scorecard can be used for monitoring the strategy implementation. The use of ICT supports the management of the strategy implementation. In this sense, companies usually implement Enterprise Resource Planning (ERP) systems.

most commonly sought by the Demand Chain opposed to the focus on operational effectiveness of the Demand Fulfilment Chain. However, the aim is to strike a balance to foster the coherence and sustainability of the business model.

7.3.3 Design of Mechanisms for Value Capture

Historically, most companies captured part of the value delivered to customers by setting a price for the acquisition of ownership of the product or enjoyment of the service. The pricing could take many forms, from a single payment to a periodical quota or payment for the time of use, as well as combinations of all these. In recent years, technological developments and access to ICTs by a large part of the population have drastically changed consumer culture, expectations and behaviour. Consequently, many companies now have to deal with the easiness of making immediate comparisons between product prices and the custom of receiving many services free. The determination of the way in which the company will recover the value that it delivers to the customer has therefore become, in some cases, one of the most complex elements of developing a sustainable model, especially in new business models associated with the internet and digital transformation. Two questions need to be dealt with here: (F) the selection of mechanisms for value capture and (G) the setting of conditions for modules.

– (F) Selection of value capture mechanisms

There are different ways of capturing value other than the traditional method of charging a price for the acquisition of physical units of products or the right to use services (McGrath, 2010). Some of these are more traditional, such as maintenance after warranty is over (a source of income that has historically been used by durable and capital goods) or cross-subsidization. This latter case, commonly used in complementary strategies such as 'razor and blades', involves totally or partially relinquishing the profit margin on some products or services, normally those that give access to others that replace them or are more commonly needed, and which is therefore where the profit margins lie. Examples can be found both in industrial markets, for example, to promote maintenance services or continuous supplies of energy, spare parts, and in consumer markets such as mobile telephones, printers and cartridges, coffee machines and capsules. A similar approach is that of promotions in general, where there is no strict complementarity between the products/services offered, and it is enough for the customer to be the same.

The Freemium option stems from a combination of free and premium and involves offering a free product to obtain profit margins via greater value-added (premium) services or products and offering upgraded versions to the current customer base that, unlike the former, are not free. For instance, in the automotive sector, some Original Equipment Manufacturers (OEMs) begin to charge for advance services when a new and improved vehicle is launched. Another is what is known as barter, whereby the customer must offer something in return for receiving a free service, such as filling in screens with personal data or information. Finally, in the 'free' or 'gift model', customers offer their time or contribution in exchange for the product, or upgrades or adaptations of the same, for example, in the case of medical surgery equipment (Von Hippel, 2010). This mechanism offers cost savings rather than a source of revenue, so it will need to be complemented by one of the previously mentioned methods. It is the same in other cases.

However, when manufacturing companies give some services for free, frequently, customers are reluctant to start paying for them. Consequently, it is important that the customer understands the value of the provided service, even if it is free. Otherwise, in the future, it could be difficult to profit from the whole business.

– (G) Fixing the conditions for modules

In the case of customization via modularity, an important aspect in terms of the mechanism for value capture is the method used for billing and setting module prices. The company must define which modules require payment and which are included in the minimum or base price. Sometimes, methods can be found to reduce the base price of modules, although this does not tend to be common. In the definition of what constitutes the base product and its price, as well as that of modules, aspects other than the cost are involved, such as the estimation of customer appreciation and comparison with the competition.

7.3.4 Case Study

To provide a better understanding of the challenge of servitization and guidance on how best to proceed in developing new business models to address it, the main aspects of this model are going to be viewed through the analysis of a Spanish bicycle manufacturing company, Orbea (www.orbea.com). The company designed a customization strategy to cope with the important competitive difficulties that it was facing in the standard bicycle global market. Consequently, it is immersed in strategic change as it evolves from the production of a standardized product to a customized one through modularity. Orbea has defined a new value proposition where customers can participate in the design of their own bicycle. Consequently, profound changes in the processes and managerial systems have been implemented. Fortunately, the results are generating greater revenues as well as being received very favourably by the customers.

1. Value proposition

Regarding the features that Orbea leaves in the hands of the customer, we identify:

- The design of the bicycle is done in conjunction between Orbea (which defines the possible modules) and the customer, who chooses from among the alternatives and uses the combination to define their particular bicycle. From the different criteria, we are able to observe that the customer knows his/her specific tastes and needs better regarding aspects of aesthetic (colours, logos and inscriptions, frame shape, etc.) and functional design (sizes, crank-set and cassette, fork, etc.), and is therefore better positioned to configure the best result from his/her point of view. On the other hand, should the company make inquiries in order to offer a particular proposal to the customer, it would be impossible to make this process profitable.
- The customer therefore positively evaluates being able to participate in the design of the bicycle, as there is enjoyment to be gained from configuring the characteristics, and logically, he/she expects the result to be more in keeping with his/her tastes and needs. The name adopted for the strategy looks to cover all these aspects: MyOrbea 'MyO'. It is also a play on words as the Spanish word 'mío' means 'mine'.

The new offer is consequently expected to be more highly valued by market segments with greater knowledge of their needs and greater definition in terms of tastes, for which standard offers are not deemed sufficient.

2. Changes to the organization

The impacts of modularization on the processes in the different chains are shown in the following tables (Tables 7.4, 7.5 and 7.6).

3. Value capture

The mass customization in the case of Orbea does not imply any special difficulty in terms of the design of value capture mechanisms as the different components that the customer adds to his/her customized bicycle admit different prices depending on their effect on the cost, and some choices are even free. The greatest difficulty is getting the price levels right with respect to the segments.

At MyO, and depending on the model, the basic price can vary from less than €3000 to more than €8000. Then there are elements of both the design (gloss or matte, frame colours, etc.) and components that suppose no additional cost and can even reduce the cost by incorporating simpler components, which is a valid option for different models. Meanwhile, there are others, such as certain frames, wheels, tyres or chain wheels, which increase the price.

When adding new modules, they can see the effect in the final price. This process is naturally accepted as customer was previously accustomed to pay for extra parts after buying standard bicycles. However, perhaps it could be interesting to add price to every single choice (even if is not going to be charged, showing the discount or gift) so as to avoid that customer does not value these modules.

Finally, Orbea has chosen a cooperative strategy through which the same commission is generated for the stores even if the customer makes all the process by their own. That way it avoids conflicts and assures distribution and after-sales involvement.

Table 7.4 Processes and elements of the demand chain

Process/Element	Impacts
Market intelligence	The MyO strategy is centred on determining the interests and experience that the customer expects to get from the product (the bicycle). It is a case of not just collecting but also understanding the customer's needs and expectations. So, data processing systems are activated to classify and analyse them, and turn them into useful information for decision making.
Marketing	The maximum number of channels for communication with the customer has been opened (omni-channel marketing): from the most famous social networks to more traditional in-store services. The relationship with the channel (fundamentally specialized stores) on opening direct sales via internet demands adaptation of the policy. Rather than cutting it out, it is integrated as a key element. Therefore, the agreement with distribution centres involves user guidance, setting up the bicycle (transport is in individual boxes but with certain components unassembled) and encouragement to share the user experience on social networks. The company has also sought to boost the brand experience through initiatives like races in emblematic locations and user gatherings.
ICT	The company has made a major effort in this area by completely redesigning the website, making it a place to exchange experiences and where the customer interacts with the company in order to satisfy his/her needs. Communication systems are tools for gathering data regardless of the source and treating that data to gain valuable information.
R&D	MyO's strategy means that when new models are developed or new models are integrated in this strategy, the criteria of modularity and standardization of components are taken into consideration. It also has customers that are professionally involved with cycling that try out new designs and technologies.

Table 7.5 Processes and elements of the demand fulfilment chain

Process/Element	Impacts
Source	This has involved renegotiating agreements with suppliers to increase the frequency of deliveries and reduce the number of pieces per order. This has involved expanding the materials storage zone.
Make	There has been a shift from MTS type production to MTO. Modularization has also supposed process postponement.
Deliver	Delivery to the customer is maintained via a network of external stores.
Return	This is the only process that has not changed, catering for and resolving any claims generated as quickly as possible.
ICT	The goal here has been traceability of each product. The technology applied is barcodes and QR codes. This also means that not only each unit can be located but that stock times, operation times and delivery times can be measured. Orbea can also share the information with the user so that he/she is aware on real-time of the location of his/her order.

Table 7.6 Processes and elements of the strategic alignment chain

Process/Element	Impacts
Business culture	Orbea is very aware of the values that facilitate the implementation of a strategy of these characteristics. As it is a cooperative company, such values as cooperation, collaboration and transparency form part of its DNA. But it must battle against the inertias of the previous strategy.
People	Orbea has made a major effort to provide people with the tools and knowledge required to carry out their work. It has highly flexible training protocols depending on the people and jobs that require it.
Business strategy	The manager of each process understands the strategy on his/her strategic, tactical and operative level while also being aware of the interdependencies between their responsibilities and those of their colleagues.
Business performance	The strategy is monitored using a continuous assessment system of the same: control panels and indicators by area and for the company as a whole that enable corrective actions to be deployed almost immediately.

7.4 Managerial Conclusions

Like Orbea, other consumer goods manufacturing companies competing in mass-production markets, which are increasingly commoditized and feature high pressure on costs, could find modularization to be a way of personalizing the product to gain more sustainable competitive advantages, as they require a change to the business model in order to be replicated. At the same time, modularization allows companies to adapt the products without assuming increasing costs, as they can achieve scale economies in the modules. However, this strategy implies sound changes in the business model. These changes pose some very important challenges that the company needs to face if it wants to improve its competitiveness.

This chapter proposes a framework for an analysis and definition of the changes required for such a servitization strategy, which contemplates the key elements of the three components of the business model: value proposition, adaptation of processes and the people, and mechanisms of value capture. In addition, the implications in the case of Orbea can help to better understand how the model works.

It might be a valuable practical tool for companies considering servitization strategies through modularization.

References

De la Calle Vicente, A. (2015). *La integración de la cadena de suministro como herramienta competitiva: el caso de la industria manufacturera del País Vasco* (Doctoral dissertation). Universidad de Deusto, Bilbao, Spain.

Freije, A., & Freije, I. (2009). *Estrategia empresarial con método*. Bilbao: Ed. Desclée de Brouwer.

Martinez, V., Bastl, M., Kingston, J., & Evans, S. (2010). Challenges in transforming manufacturing organisations into product-service providers. *Journal of Manufacturing Technology Management, 21*(4), 449–469.

McGrath, R. (2010). Business models: A discovery driven approach. *Long Range Planning, 43*, 247–261.

Prahalad, C. K., & Ramaswamy, V. (2004). *The future of competition: Co-creating unique value with customers*. Boston: Harvard Business School Press.

Rabetino, R., Kohtamäki, M., & Gebauer, H. (2017). Strategy map of servitization. *International Journal of Production Economics, 192*, 144–156.

Teece, D. J. (2010). Business models, business strategy and innovation. *Long Range Planning, 43*, 172–194.

Von Hippel, E. (2010). Innovación impulsada por los usuarios. *Innovación. Perspectivas para el siglo XXI*. BBVA.

Wikner, J. (2014). On decoupling points and decoupling zones. *Production & Manufacturing Research, 2*(1), 167–215.

8

Value-Scope-Price: Design and Pricing of Advanced Service Offerings Based on Customer Value

Shaun West, Diego Rohner, Dominik Kujawski, and Mario Rapaccini

This chapter gives the reader a structured 'how-to' guide to design and price a product-service system. We integrate service design thinking, service science, and the customer value proposition canvas to develop a step-by-step framework. This helps the reader to focus on the customer problem and value expectations and define the scope of a product-service system with different options. From this, a price can be set that, starting from the market benchmark, considers the pains and gains achieved by each different option in the product-service system.

S. West (✉) • D. Rohner
Lucerne University of Applied Sciences and Arts, Lucerne, Switzerland
e-mail: shaun.west@hslu.ch; shaun.west@mailhec.com; diego.rohner@hslu.ch

D. Kujawski
Regent Beleuchtungskörper AG, Basel, Switzerland
e-mail: d.kujawski@regent.ch

M. Rapaccini
University of Florence, Florence, Italy
e-mail: mario.rapaccini@unifi.it

© The Editor(s) (if applicable) and The Author(s), under exclusive license to Springer International Publishing AG, part of Springer Nature 2018
M. Kohtamäki et al. (eds.), *Practices and Tools for Servitization*,
https://doi.org/10.1007/978-3-319-76517-4_8

We start by discussing the relevance of integrating pricing and scoping strategies for product-service systems. This leads to considering why the pricing approaches of product-centric companies should be revisited to make the service business grow. Then, we introduce and explain the value-scope-price framework: the value baseline that is used to graphically determine the customer's 'willingness-to-pay' a given product-service system. Finally, we compare different pricing schemas and revenue models.

This approach has the advantage of helping to define the goal and scope of the product-service system in a way that is consistent with the customer's problems. It is then natural to construct a solution with different options/features that address the job-to-be-done by the customer and his pains and gains. Using this how-to framework enables the reader to see the value of the solution to the customer and price accordingly.

The value of this approach to a company is demonstrated in a 2011 study (Hogen, 2011), which showed that companies using value-based pricing principles are 36% more profitable than those that lean toward cost- or market-share-driven pricing. These results were confirmed by Hinterhuber and Snelgrove (2016), who reported that industrial companies that had a structured methodology for measuring and buying based on value were 35% more profitable than similar companies that lacked this kind of value-based procedure.

8.1 Why It is Difficult to Price and Scope in Product-Service Systems

Marketing literature has been debating the best pricing strategies for products and services for many years. Traditionally, the price of industrial goods is determined by adding a target margin to the production cost, taking as a reference the prices of rival products as imposed by market (price) leaders (Dorward, 1987). Value-based pricing (e.g., setting prices based on value created in the customer's context) is not often used, although for advanced services, it is widely recognized to be superior (Hinterhuber, 2004; Rapaccini, 2015). The current 'status quo' is being challenged with the shift to service businesses that are forcing industrial firms to rethink their managerial practices. This is very much the case where digital services are bundled with more traditional services or where new pricing (or revenue) models are offered that focus on performance and outcomes.

How much value should be captured by service sales is a key question (Auguste, Harmon, & Pandit, 2006). However, before we answer this, we must understand value, scope, and price and how they impact paying customers and users (Anderson, Narus, & Narayandas, 2009).

8.1.1 Tying Together Value, Scope, and Price

Changing the scope of what a manufacturing firm offers to its customers can also be a force to change traditional pricing strategies and consider new revenue models (e.g., pay-per-use). These new revenue models can be designed to align with the customer's value-creation process. This is useful in situations—such as performance-based contracting—in which the manufacturer shifts from 'moving boxes' to selling 'outcomes'. In some service contracts, the manufacturer continues to own the equipment and is paid by monthly subscription fees, as in a rental business. Revenues can also come from product access and/or use (i.e., pay-as-you-go, pay-per-click, pay-per-page, and pay-per-use), and adjusted according to the performance delivered.

The pricing of product-service systems can be cumbersome. Osterwalder, Pigneur, Bernarda, and Smith (2014) suggest prices should be coherent to the value proposition, that is, the value the solution promises to the customer, as it solves some of the problems, versus the next best alternative. It is indisputable that the customer only wants the options that contribute to value in that customer's context. Instead of filling a solution with features of limited usefulness, the value of the solution's scope should be calculated. No one is willing to pay for features they do not need, so the rule-of-thumb is easy: 'don't under-scope or over-scope'.

As a guideline, this chapter provides a three-step framework that builds on service science foundations, as well as on our personal experiences with multinational companies and SMEs. It is based on the following assumptions:

- The framework can be applied to both product-service systems (that are sold as integrated bundles or solutions) and to hybrid offerings in which services are delivered as add-ons;
- There is genuine knowledge about the customer's needs (i.e., pains and gains, what is 'valuable' for the customer, what is the 'job-to-be-done');
- There is knowledge about the roles that the manufacturer and customer want to play in the value-creation process, and how these are linked to the company's value propositions and to the solution's options.

In service design, at least three options should be considered to generate value (Campbell, Maglio, & Davis, 2011). The customer can create value independent of the manufacturer (i.e., 'do-it-yourself'); it can be created interactively, with the manufacturer and the customer collaborating to co-create the value (i.e., 'do-it-with-me'); or the manufacturer can create the value on behalf of the customer (i.e., 'do-it-for-me'). In this last case, the customer only sees (and takes advantage of) the outcome produced because the task is done entirely by the solution provider.

8.2 Gaining Insights Into Value, Customers, and Revenue Models

This section offers academic theory to help support the value, scope, and pricing model described in Sect. 8.3. It starts with a short introduction to 'value', which has many more dimensions than simply monetary cost. The section on understanding how customers perceive value helps to create a detailed understanding of customers and users. This makes it possible to build a picture of their 'willingness-to-pay' and their individual roles within both the buying process and service delivery. Finally, we consider different service classifications and revenue models to establish which are useful.

8.2.1 The Perception of Value

According to many authors (Grönroos & Helle, 2010; Malleret, 2006), customers expect benefits from product-related services such as economic utility, a sense of security, or a gain in emotional or social status.

In a business setting, Campbell et al. (2011) argue that services are focused on increasing the efficiency of a production process, reducing cost and resource consumption, and decreasing process timing. In this context, a customer could also be willing to pay to provide a better experience to the end user: for example, a faster response time, or ensuring greater accessibility and availability of products.

Other studies from the organizational buying behavior literature (Selviaridis, Spring, & Araujo, 2013) investigate the buying decisions of business organizations, and introduce the idea that when a customer purchases a product, they take the risks associated with the product's performance (e.g., malfunctioning, unavailability, or misuse). In many cases, these risks have higher cost implications than the price of the original equipment. Service solutions can be focused to reduce these risks, or the corresponding costs. Consequently, the customer perceives that an integrated product-service offer delivers far more benefits than costs if the services associated with the product can reduce these risks. This can make the product-service solution much more attractive to the customer, who shows greater 'willingness-to-pay'.

8.2.2 Paying Customers and Users Who Drive Value

First, we define 'customer' in this chapter, with no discrimination between paying customers and solution users. 'Customer' is also used to indicate the recipient of the value delivered by the product-service system. By thinking in this way, we can relate the 'willingness-to-pay' for the solution to its full potential. Everyone who is involved with the equipment—its operation, planned and unplanned maintenance, routine maintenance, and asset management—should be considered, whether they are involved in the buying process or not, even if in a conventional description, they are neither customers nor users.

The price at which a product-service system should be sold depends on the value it creates in the customer's context. This is because the customer's 'willingness-to-pay' is related to their expectation of value. However, 'willingness-to-pay' is influenced by subjective factors such as personal traits, beliefs, attitudes, skills, and mood, as well as by individual and collective goals (e.g., company targets, department objectives). For instance, if a company wants to reduce its capital expenditure (CAPEX), a solution that is based on renting or leasing could be preferable for financial—if not technical—reasons. It is important to remember that solutions are often situation-specific and that renting can be viable in cases where decisions are based on short-term needs.

It follows that the price charged for a product-service system should be in line with the customer's 'willingness-to-pay', which in turn depends on their value expectations (Hinterhuber & Snelgrove, 2016). Higher prices are likely to be difficult to accept for the buyer—whereas lower prices bring losses for the supplier. We assume that the customer is always aware—somehow—of their value expectations. This can be expressed in terms of net benefits, that is, benefits that the customer expects ('what you get') minus the costs that may accrue ('what you sacrifice'), to procure and run the solution (Anderson et al., 2009). Unfortunately, these constructs are often difficult to determine, as they are dependent on the situation and context (Khalifa, 2004).

8.2.3 Service Classifications and Revenue Models

Services and product-service solutions can be classified in many ways. Three categories used to distinguish the value proposition of a product-service system offering (Smith, Ng, & Maull, 2012) are product-related, use-related, or outcome-related services. Each of these can have similar or different associated revenue models, as shown visually in Fig. 8.1. It is worth considering that even outcome-based services may have a product component in their revenue model and that fixed fees may be hidden in an agreement as 'operational assumptions'.

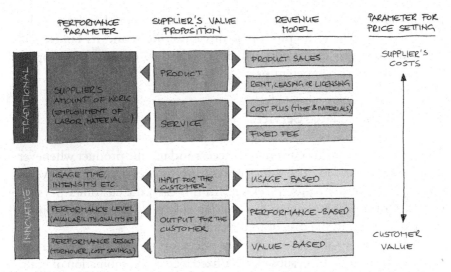

Fig. 8.1 Visual example of traditional and innovative revenue models (based on Bonnemeier, Burianek, & Reichwald, 2010; illustration by Diego Rohner, 2017)

8.2.3.1 Product-Related Services

These typically includes product-support services that focus on increasing the availability of the products after sale, often in support of the warranty. Here the value proposition is 'to reduce the risk of having unsatisfied customers due to poor performance or early failure'. Examples of these services are planned maintenance, spare parts provision, field inspection, and repair interventions. Usually, they are billed on the basis of the inputs consumed (e.g., the time spent performing the intervention and the type and amount of spare parts used). Price lists that show the unit price of the different inputs (e.g., EUR/hour, EUR/unit) are agreed between the customer and the provider. In case of particular requirements, the provider starts a quotation process (that takes time and effort).

Traditional input-based pricing poorly communicates the value that can be created in the customer context, as services are sold 'as-a-product' and priced on the basis of cost plus (or mark-up). It may, in fact, provide poor value to the customer. For the customer, the risk of incurring large consequential losses is increased when they lack the skills required to support planned or unplanned maintenance. Consequential losses are also more relevant where the product is mission critical, and its failure will affect the business continuity, which may lead to outsourcing support services to a more competent party.

8.2.3.2 Use-Related Services

These services allow the customer to access and use the product whenever and wherever needed. The value proposition focuses on 'anytime/everywhere access to easy-to-use products'. In this case, the customer pays on the basis of product usage and has to be able to undertake some tasks themselves (e.g., in the case of tool rental).

These kinds of solutions are usually priced on the basis of pay-per-use agreements (variable fees), subscription/fixed fees, or a combination of both. Fixed fees are normally used to cover the fixed costs, with variable fees covering the variable costs (e.g., consumables, spares, maintenance, and field support). Again, with this strategy, the price is not always in line with the value the product-service system actually creates in the customer's context.

8.2.3.3 Outcome-Related Services

These services are the most knowledge-intensive and focus on delivering outcomes that are of interest to the customer. In fact, even if a product is working correctly and can be accessed and used, there could be factors preventing the anticipated outcomes being achieved. In this case, the value proposition aims at ensuring that these desired outcomes can be continually attained. This can be done if the provider either directly runs the process on behalf of the customer or supports the customer in running it.

Revenues are generated because the customer pays a fee (i.e., a fixed-fee, per barrel of oil lifted, or use-related fees) for delivering the services with satisfactory performance (e.g., a minimum volume of units produced, packages shipped, and prints managed). Outcomes are often aligned with a risk share system (e.g., liquated damage/bonus) related to performance—failing to meet target performance means reduced revenues for the supplier, while over-achievement means a bonus payment. In this case, the customer shows the highest 'willingness-to-pay', as there are new ways to create more value.

8.2.3.4 Revenue Models for Services

The way in which prices are set and revenues or fees are generated can be structured in many ways, and with more advanced services, they are often a mix of several different forms. The structure of the fees becomes a core part of the value proposition as different customers have different preferences. Some prefer fixed fees, others variable; some prefer levelized fees, others prefer lumpy fees; some wish to pay in 30 days, other will not pay for 90 days; some wish to pay for inputs (or cost drivers), others for outputs (revenue drivers); some are concerned with the overall price, others the net present value; some prefer a low headline price with add-ons, others an all-inclusive price. A model that is often used is separating the new equipment sale from the service sales—even in the case of advanced services. It is worth remembering that the separation of products from services was a result of the Xerox photocopier anti-trust case in the 1970s.

In use-based and outcome-based service contracts, the customer and the supplier should agree on what is and is not within the scope of the contract. Out-of-scope service activities could be charged for in many ways, such as requesting specific quotations, using a price list, or traditional time and material agreements. Customers need to be careful in these arrangements, as sometimes suppliers use a low entry point to start an agreement knowing that scope creep will make up for any initial loss of profitability.

8.3 A Three-Step Framework for Value Discovery, Scope Identification, and Price Setting

The value-scope-price framework supports teams to design (or re-design) customer value propositions to better fit the customer's problem. It also provides different ways to deliver the services, based on customer preferences. The use of prototyping further improves the process of value discovery for customers. Finally, the use of modules helps to increase the flexibility of the services while also improving the reliability of delivery. The three-step model is shown graphically in Fig. 8.2 and builds upon the theory in Sect. 8.2.

It is important not to over-focus on the current solution being offered. Rather, it is useful to develop three 'standard' solutions that are built up from modules, as this allows for rapid customization for individual customers, with the addition of 'wild card' solutions created for specific customers. The situational aspects are considered in step 3; for many industrial B2B solutions, it is worth considering installation, maintenance or conversions, modifications, and upgrades.

Involving the customer means that the solutions will be closer to their needs. Firms are often concerned about customer involvement early in the process. With a structured process, there is little to fear, as service is a relationship business and by definition is concerned with co-creation of value and design of new service offerings, requiring input from many different sources, including the customer.

The approach to pricing is based on the value-based pricing framework (West & Kujawski, 2016), which is shown in Fig. 8.3. This model assumes that value is best defined by the 'value in use' model. Thus the value can only be defined by the customer who is using the equipment and requires the services. This means that two different customers with the same

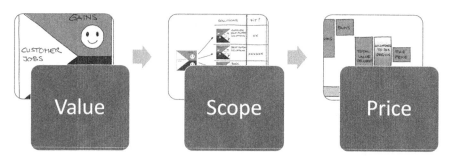

Fig. 8.2 Three-step value-scope-price framework (illustration by Diego Rohner, 2017)

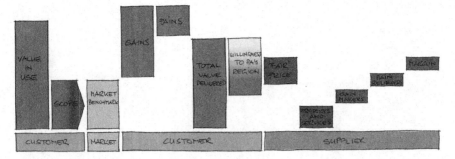

Fig. 8.3 Value-based pricing framework (based on West & Kujawski, 2016; illustration by Diego Rohner, 2017)

equipment, requiring the same service, may have a different value. The value is always related back to the context, and this can be complicated to define. This is the reason why so many firms fail to move to (customer) value-based pricing.

8.3.1 Step 1 Value—Identifying Customers and Value

The objective of this step is to identify every customer and every stakeholder and discover what they value. Each of the stakeholders will have a different view on what value is—remember that different situations can create different amounts of value. This is why for a value-discovery process, a careful analysis is required to better understand the customer's problems. The process is shown graphically in Fig. 8.4.

It is worth considering the context that the customer is in, as well as the situation. Input is required from a number of sources—not just sales or purchasing, but anyone who can provide insight into the customer, their business, and their thinking. This also helps to share the results around the firm. Other useful sources of information are customers' websites, Wikipedia, and trade associations. With the internet, much of this material is freely available.

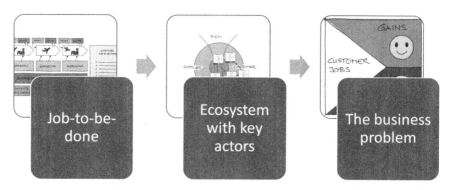

Fig. 8.4 The customer and value identification process (illustration by Diego Rohner, 2017)

8.3.1.1 Understanding the Customers' Value-Creation Process and Job-to-be-Done

This step provides a detailed understanding of the customer's value-creation process and the ultimate job-to-be-done of the business. Figure 8.5 provides a template that allows the value-creation processes to be clearly described. It is based on the job-to-be-done model and has been extended to capture other insights. Once it has been completed, there should be a clearer understanding of the customer's core and supporting jobs. How the 'customer job-to-be-done' fits into the whole business needs to be seen clearly: core tasks, inputs/outputs, supporting tasks, business KPIs and activity metrics are important. Often these are overlooked, with only the technical aspects considered. This is short-sighted and can lead to misunderstandings and to an inability to price (or scope) correctly.

8.3.1.2 Ecosystem Mapping to Understand the Key Actors and Stakeholders

The process of customer identification starts with ecosystem mapping and is shown in Fig. 8.6. The different actors and their roles need to be clearly named, described, and placed on the ecosystem map. Analyzing empathy maps helps to understand what could be seen as 'irrational' behavior and identifies motivations for each of the actors in the ecosystem.

Value-Scope-Price: Design and Pricing of Advanced Service... 153

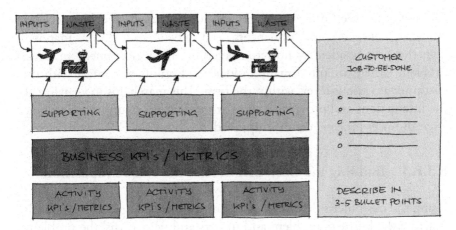

Fig. 8.5 Job-to-be-done to provide insights into the customer's business (illustration by Diego Rohner, 2017)

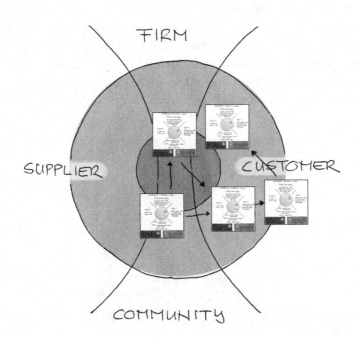

Fig. 8.6 Ecosystem map showing key actors (illustration by Diego Rohner, 2017)

Exchanges between different actors should be shown, and key decision makers, gatekeepers, and influencers need to be identified. This map will help the firm to identify how to overcome the 'procurement manager problem'. There are often many unidentified points of contact with the customer at various levels within the firm. This map helps to visualize all the interactions and provides a focus around which solution design (and later, the sales process) can be improved.

8.3.1.3 Building the Customer Side of the Value Proposition

Using the customer side of the value proposition, it is possible to clearly describe the business problem and understand who 'owns' the problem. It also gives a clear understanding of the business' value-creation process. Each 'customer job' and how it fits into that value-creation process can quickly be transferred to the 'customer job' definition. The three to five key actors can explain the main pains and gains that are associated with the service that they require. Keeping the language simple and jargon-free means that the information can be shared more easily. Where there are questions about the language, it may be easier to use simple sketches, as they can often provide more insight into the customer's business problem. The customer side (business problem description) of the customer

Fig. 8.7 Using the value-proposition canvas to describe the business problem (based on Osterwalder et al., 2014; illustration by Diego Rohner, 2017)

value proposition is shown in Fig. 8.7. This can be used internally to share lessons learnt as it provides a simple overview of the problems your customers have.

8.3.2 Step 2 Scope—Building and Prototyping Solutions

The objective of this step is to build and prototype solutions based on the customer problem that was defined in Step 1. Each solution that is proposed should address the business problem. The framework develops three to five different solutions: the 'complete' solution, a 'basic' solution, and the 'best match', plus one or two 'wild card' solutions (see Fig. 8.8). For each solution, three to five additional options or features should be created that can be linked to the customer's pains (pain-relieving options) and gains (gain-creating options). It is important to evaluate the customer's willingness to pay for the different options, in relation to the customer's budget, operating expenses, (OPEX) and CAPEX.

To help with this process, it is useful to consider the two extremes of 'do-it-yourself' and 'do-it-for-me', as well as a more normal 'do-it-with-me' delivery model. There is always more than one 'right' solution and customer situations change over the equipment's lifetime. There are many different models that can be drawn from. However, it is important to

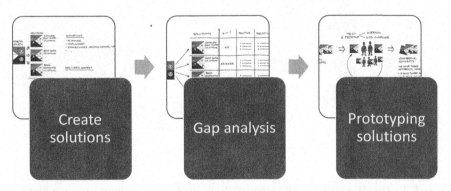

Fig. 8.8 A process for building and prototyping solutions (illustration by Diego Rohner, 2017)

remember that all customers face different situations, so we need to learn about and address their outcomes and not assume what is best for them.

8.3.2.1 Creating Solutions

The model used for the initial design of solutions is given in Fig. 8.9. As explained above, it is good practice to develop many solutions and to create options around each solution.

Challenge the mixed team to consider a 'basic/economy' solution, a 'gold-plated' complete solution, and one that it considers the 'best match', as well as a 'wild card' option. This should be done considering different situations (at least planned and unplanned initially) and for different delivery contexts ('do-it-for-me', 'do-it-with-me', 'do-it-yourself'). Do not allow current company policies (or legal considerations) to stop dif-

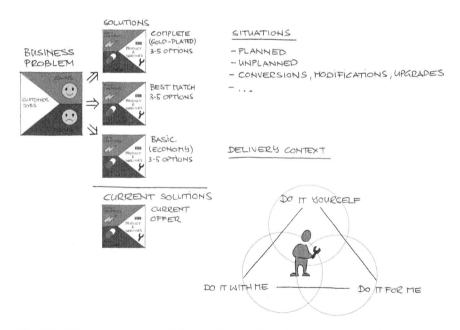

Fig. 8.9 The development of three solutions based on customer problem identification (illustration by Diego Rohner, 2017)

ferent solutions being created: it is important to create new solutions and to measure them against the customer's business problem. Here the different fee structures should also be considered—input-based, outcome-based, performance commitments, and for out-of-scope services.

8.3.2.2 Gap Analysis—What Is the 'Best' Fit? Don't Assume

The gap analysis, in Fig. 8.10, provides a deeper measure of the problem-solution fit. The results of the analysis can be transferred to the design or re-design of the customer value proposition and help to target the solution to the right 'job'. The aim of gap analysis is to identify and close the gaps between the customer's expectation and the actual services provided at different stages of service delivery. Measure every solution for a simple fit and then give both positive and negative commentary to each. Here is where the weaker solutions are weeded out, which is why it is better to

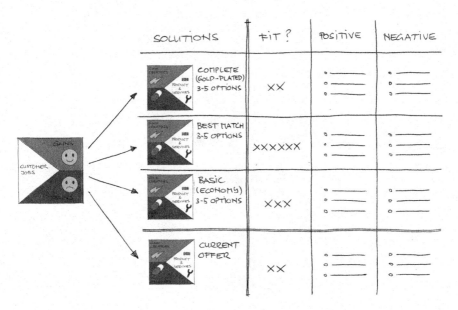

Fig. 8.10 Gap analysis for the developed solutions (illustration by Diego Rohner, 2017)

have more solutions to consider. By the end of the gap analysis, there should be a 'winner' in each of the three groups and a detailed understanding of the weaknesses and strengths of the current solution. This process means that new hybrid solutions may also be created during the team review. The final task here is to confirm the findings with customers in a clear and understandable way to avoid any possible confusion.

8.3.2.3 Prototyping Solutions

While completing the three solutions for the customer's problem, it is time to create three draft brochures. These should be based on the customer value propositions that have been designed. The brochures are tangible materials that can be used to test the solutions both internally and externally with customers (at least five of them). The feedback on these prototyped solutions allows improvements to be made before testing again, a process shown in Fig. 8.11. It should become possible to move quickly from the initial concepts to basic commercial concepts.

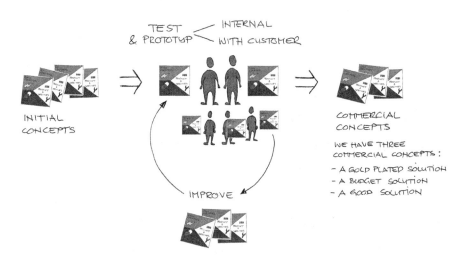

Fig. 8.11 Using prototyping to improve the solutions into commercial concepts (illustration by Diego Rohner, 2017)

Value-Scope-Price: Design and Pricing of Advanced Service... 159

8.3.3 Step 3 Price—Quantifying Service Value and Pricing

This step offers guidance toward pricing value-based services, considering the most important aspects of pricing, as the model in Fig. 8.12 shows. It helps to identify the value-based price that the customer is willing to pay. It is possible that this step will show the customer has been overcharged, and it may be necessary to reduce the pricing in the medium term to improve customer relationships. Conversely, it is likely that with more advanced services, the current pricing is too low and does not reflect the value created for the customer. Where this is the case, value capture should be approached carefully, as it can be dangerous to suddenly increase prices. This is where having three solutions can give the flexibility needed to allow adjustments to the pricing, helping to increase the margins, while at the same time improving customer satisfaction.

8.3.3.1 Market Benchmark

The customer will often have a price in mind for the service. This will be from experience of some form or other, and is shown in Fig. 8.13. Often in services, labor rates are an emotive topic, and can become a problem area, even where the rate chosen by the customer is inappropriate. It is

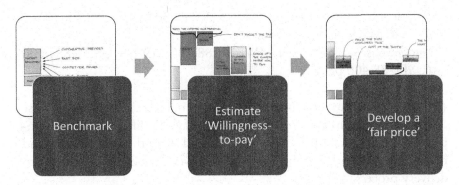

Fig. 8.12 Service value quantification and pricing in detail (illustration by Diego Rohner, 2017)

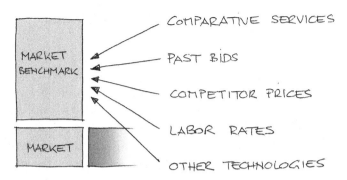

Fig. 8.13 Market benchmark pricing (illustration by Diego Rohner, 2017)

important to understand the benchmarks the customer will be using and why they are using them. Other elements that are valuable to consider in benchmarking are past bids, comparative services, and competitor prices, as well as alternative technologies (particularly useful for conversions, modifications, and upgrades).

From the benchmarks, it is simple to provide a budget for the service—this can be very helpful in the early stages to understand the 'normal' price. For example, there is published data for wind turbine maintenance costs of USD0.01 per kWh. From this number, it is relatively simple to provide a budget cost for the ten-year maintenance agreement with 30% availability and 30 MW of capacity:

- Production = 8760 hours × 10 years × 30% × 30 MW = 788,400 MWh (78,840 MWh per year);
- Budget cost = USD10 per MWh × 788,400 MWh = USD7,884,000 (USD788,400 per year).

It is important to remember that different markets and regions will use different benchmarks and that customers may use different (or inappropriate) benchmarks. In all cases keep, use and share the benchmarks (and resulting budget prices) with everyone involved in the service design and delivery process.

8.3.3.2 Customer Value Delivered and 'Willingness-to-Pay'

Getting to understand the range of customer 'willingness to pay' (Fig. 8.14) is important both internally and externally, that is, with the customer. Start by assuming that the market benchmark for the generic service is 'about right'. Now, by quantifying the gains and the pains, it is possible to get to the total value delivered to the customer. This means that all (or as many as possible) of the gains need to be quantified in monetary terms; the same process must be done for the pains. Once this has been completed, the total value delivered can be estimated. This process increases customer understanding within the service firm. However, the quantification of value is not easy; it requires input from many stakeholders, including customers. It is often best done using simple calculations that can be easily understood, rather than using large complex models.

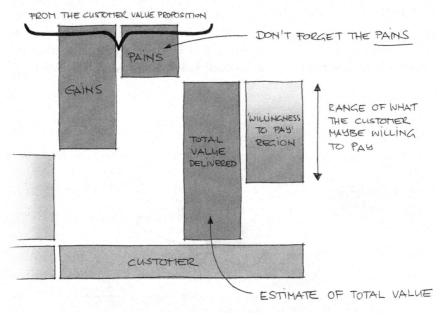

Fig. 8.14 Estimating the 'willingness-to-pay' (illustration by Diego Rohner, 2017)

Once the total value has been calculated, the emotional aspect of estimating the range of the customer's 'willingness-to-pay' needs to be considered. This stage must capture input from many people within the firm; it is partly experience, partly hard work, and partly luck. Also, embedded in this range are the different fee structures—a monthly fee based on performance may encourage the customer to pay a higher sum than they would for a one-time up-front fee for the same service.

8.3.3.3 Supplier 'Fair Price' Estimation and Margins

With an understanding of the customer's 'willingness-to-pay', it is time to estimate the 'fair price' for the service (Fig. 8.15). In essence, what is the 'correct amount' of value to capture from the customer? Too much and the price cannot be justified, too little and it may be 'too good to be true'. The price here must be 'about right' and be justifiable, and it must lie within the customer's 'willingness-to-pay' range. The whole service design team must come to a consensus on the 'fair price'—it cannot be left to the sales team alone. Once agreed, it can be further refined so that the base price is based on the benchmark being reflected in the customer

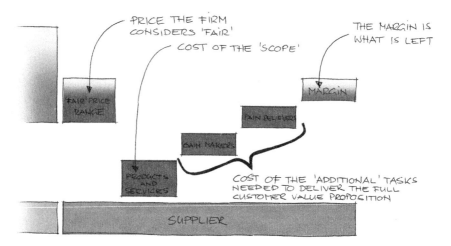

Fig. 8.15 Supplier 'fair price' estimation and margins based on cost build-up (illustration by Diego Rohner, 2017)

gains and pains, so that the customer value propositions can be fully reflected in the fee structures.

The final stage is the cost build-up for the full solution—this means bringing together the costs for the products and services, the gain makers and the pain relievers. Finally, the difference between the fair price and the costs is the margin. It may be higher or lower than previously offered, and it may be that the more basic service creates more margin than the gold-plated solutions.

8.3.4 Prototype the Modular Offerings

The value discovery, scope identification, and pricing process are complete. The result is the first set of modular service offerings that are scoped and priced according to value. Lessons need to be learned from the first commercial offers made using them, and those lessons can then be incorporated into the design process. Competitors will react, and the firm needs to be ready to counter.

8.4 Managerial Conclusions

This chapter has worked through a thorough process that has developed pricing of services for specific customers based on customer value. In doing so, the process has focused on customer value creation, helping to develop the scope based on the customer value proposition, and culminates in pricing the services. It has used service design/design thinking approaches as well as more classical Kellogg approaches, also integrating some approaches from operations management, to help with value quantification. The overview of the 'value-scope-price' framework is shown in Fig. 8.16.

The approach starts with the customer and value identification. Every customer and stakeholder within the buying process has a different view on value, and different situations create different amounts of value, so careful analysis is needed for the key actors during the value-discovery process. 'Value in use' is the main approach used to understand customer value creation (or destruction), as this approach helps quantify value.

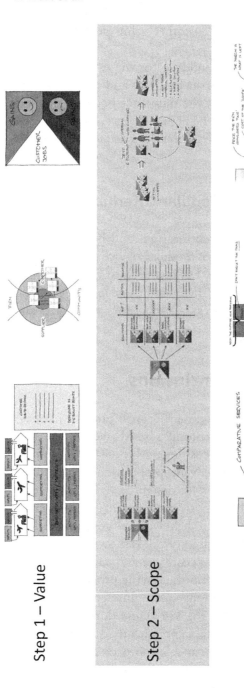

Fig. 8.16 The 'value-scope-price' framework (illustration by Diego Rohner, 2017)

Using a 'job-to-be-done' approach and empathy maps of the key actors and the firm, it is possible to define the customer problem in the customer value proposition. Finding the right level of detail is tough, but grouping helps here. Once the customer problem is described, it is natural to start to construct the solution. Here the objective is to create three to five solutions as this helps with creativity: a 'basic' version, a 'gold-plated solution', a 'normal' solution, and two other wild-card solutions. These can be clarified with the customer to help identify the scope that best suits their needs. Considering three additional extremes here also helps—'do-it-for-me', 'do-it-with-me', and 'do-it-yourself'.

Services built from these basic building blocks (or modules) help to provide a flexible yet standardized service offering. Different pricing structures or revenue modules should be identified at this point; all customers will have a preference, as will all suppliers. For instance, it would be unrealistic to ask for 100% of a ten-year advanced service contract in advance; monthly or 'per hour' pricing might be more appropriate. Cash flow can be an important and often forgotten part of the customer value proposition, particularly with outcome-based agreements where risk is transferred and liquidated damages and bonuses are used to incentivize the service provider.

Pricing is the next stage to consider: what should the price be and how should it be charged or structured? The value delivered to the customer has already been quantified; the appropriate (or inappropriate) benchmarks have been found; the supplier scope described. Each of these will provide a different price range and help to describe the range of 'willingness-to-pay'. The art is now to identify the 'fair-price' range and this is a team game that requires each team member to give their own views.

Finally, structuring of the price in the offer for the service needs to be agreed—even with a simple offer, there may be negotiations of basic payment terms. With more advanced services, a fixed monthly fee may be agreed with 'per-the-hour' billing or a contract term that provides a floor on the number of operational hours per year that create the per-the-hour billing. Other customers may wish to be 'in charge' and use rate sheets; and in many cases basic rate sheets will, in fact, be required for activities that are out of scope.

Now please go and try to create services and discover customer value, and find out how to capture a fair share of the value that is created from services using our value-scope-price model. Learn and share the learning, so that the business becomes more effective at pricing and scoping services. The expectation is that by being better in pricing, a firm providing a service will improve customer relationships and increase average margins.

References

Anderson, J. C., Narus, J. A., & Narayandas, D. (2009). *Business market management: Understanding, creating, and delivering value*. Pearson Prentice Hall.

Auguste, B. G., Harmon, E. P., & Pandit, V. (2006). The right service strategies for product companies. *The McKinsey Quarterly, 1*, 41–51.

Bonnemeier, S., Burianek, F., & Reichwald, R. (2010). Revenue models for integrated customer solutions: Concept and organizational implementation. *Journal of Revenue & Pricing Management, 9*(3), 228–238.

Campbell, C. S., Maglio, P. P., & Davis, M. M. (2011). From self-service to super-service: A resource mapping framework for co-creating value by shifting the boundary between provider and customer. *Information Systems and E-Business Management, 9*(2), 173–191.

Dorward, N. (1987). *The pricing decision: Economic theory and business practice*. London: Harper & Row.

Grönroos, C., & Helle, P. (2010). Adopting a service logic in manufacturing. Conceptual foundation and metrics for mutual value creation. *Journal of Service Management, 21*(5), 564–590.

Hinterhuber, A. (2004). Towards value-based pricing—An integrative framework for decision making. *Industrial Marketing Management, 33*(8), 765–778.

Hinterhuber, A., & Snelgrove, T. (2016). *Value first then price: Quantifying value in business to business markets from the perspective of both buyers and sellers*. Abingdon, Oxfordshire, UK: Routledge.

Hogen, J. (2011). Building a leading pricing capability: Where does your company stack up? Retrieved from https://www2.deloitte.com/content/dam/Deloitte/us/Documents/strategy/us-consulting-building-a-leading-pricing-capability.pdf

Khalifa, A. S. (2004). Customer value: A review of recent literature and an integrative configuration. *Management Decision, 42*(5), 645–666.

Malleret, V. (2006). Value creation through service offers. *European Management Journal, 24*, 106–116.

Osterwalder, A., Pigneur, Y., Bernarda, G., & Smith, A. (2014). *Value proposition design: How to create products and services customers want.* John Wiley & Sons.

Rapaccini, M. (2015). Pricing strategies of service offerings in manufacturing companies: A literature review and empirical investigation. *Production Planning & Control, 26*(14–15), 1247–1263.

Selviaridis, K., Spring, M., & Araujo, L. (2013). Provider involvement in business service definition: A typology. *Industrial Marketing Management, 42*(8), 1398–1410.

Smith, L., Ng, I., & Maull, R. (2012). The three value proposition cycles of equipment-based service. *Production Planning & Control, 23*(7), 553–570.

West, S., & Kujawski, D. (2016). Service pricing strategies in maintenance services. *Proceedings of the 23rd EurOMA conference*, Trondheim, Norway.

Part III

Implementing Servitization

9

Overcoming the Challenges of Servitisation: Aligning Responses to Service Strategy

Chris Raddats, Jamie Burton, Judy Zolkiewski, and Vicky Story

9.1 Introduction

Manufacturers that have traditionally been product-focused face challenges in their transition to become more servitised businesses. These challenges include interpreting the market environment to understand whether servitisation is appropriate, reorienting the business from products to services, determining the correct organisational structure to deliver a new service strategy, and developing the necessary

---

C. Raddats (✉)
University of Liverpool, Liverpool, UK
e-mail: Chrisr@liv.ac.uk

J. Burton • J. Zolkiewski
University of Manchester, Manchester, UK
e-mail: jamie.burton@manchester.ac.uk; judy.zolkiewski@manchester.ac.uk

V. Story
Loughborough University, Loughborough, UK
e-mail: v.m.story@lboro.ac.uk

service-focused processes. While the benefits of servitisation are often espoused, the complexity and difficulty of overcoming these challenges is sometimes underestimated, leading to poorer outcomes from servitisation than might have been expected (this is sometimes termed the 'servitisation paradox').

Most research to date has treated servitisation challenges as isolated issues and has not explicitly recognised the interconnections between them. From a practical perspective, this is unhelpful since managers seeking to develop more servitised businesses must consider all the possible challenges they will face and, if they are interconnected, their approach to dealing with them should, likewise, be integrated. Equally, the number and specifics of these challenges also depend on the service strategy a manufacturer adopts, with approaches to overcoming challenges that facilitate the most servitised outcomes not necessarily being appropriate for all companies. Thus, for manufacturers aiming for less servitised outcomes, there are, potentially, fewer challenges to overcome and different approaches that can be adopted.

This chapter discusses the interlinked challenges of servitisation, aligned to the various service strategies manufacturers may adopt, and articulates potential responses to these challenges. It builds on work that brings together previously fragmented research on servitisation challenges (Alghisi & Saccani, 2015; Zhang & Banerji, 2017). However, unlike previous work, this chapter provides a 'road map' of servitisation challenges and responses, helping manufacturers to better understand how the service strategy they adopt requires them to sequentially address specific challenges to achieve their goals.

9.2 Service Strategies, Servitisation Challenges and Responses

This section considers (1) different service strategies that manufacturers might adopt and (2) the main servitisation challenges faced and possible responses to these challenges.

9.2.1 Manufacturers' Service Strategies

Manufacturers' service strategies have been variously categorised in the literature, with most researchers extolling the value of having more services in the mix of customer offerings (Ostrom et al., 2010). This may not, however, be the unidirectional process often envisaged in the literature (e.g., Oliva & Kallenberg, 2003), with manufacturers needing to balance service expansion and standardisation activities and manage the co-existence of products and services (Kowalkowski, Windahl, Kindström, & Gebauer, 2015). Indeed, there is evidence that manufacturers offer customers different types of services, from base services (e.g., installation, repair) through to advanced services (i.e., that involve payment based on performance or outcome), in order to cater for diverse customer needs (Baines & Lightfoot, 2014).

To deal with the plurality of manufacturers' service strategies, academics have developed two main typologies, which cater for a large range of manufacturers, not just those which are highly servitised. Gebauer (2008) developed a four-type service strategy typology aligned to manufacturers' business environments, with each strategy reflecting different degrees of servitisation. After-sales Service Providers (ASPs) concentrate on ensuring that their products function correctly. Customer Support Providers develop services to enable service differentiation. Outsourcing Partners take over activities that might have previously been performed in-house by customers, while Development Partners provide research and development services to customers. This typology addresses some of the heterogeneity in manufacturers' service strategies but aligns a 'strategy' to a type of service offering; for example, ASPs are assumed to offer after-sales services such as maintenance. Thus, the typology neglects service strategies where multiple service offerings are made.

To overcome this weakness in the Gebauer (2008) typology, Raddats and Kowalkowski (2014) developed a three-type service strategy typology based on manufacturers' 'enthusiasm' for services. Service Doubters (hereinafter termed Doubters) view services as offering limited differentiation and, therefore, offer few services; Service Pragmatists (hereinafter termed Pragmatists) view services as a means to create product differentiation for their own products; Service Enthusiasts (hereinafter termed Enthusiasts) view services as a primary means of growth and offer advanced services on their own and other vendors' products. Subsequent work has, however, questioned whether three types are sufficient, suggesting that Enthusiasts represent too large a group, with the possibility of an additional type, Restrained Enthusiasts, who primarily offer advanced services for their own, rather than multi-vendor, products (Burton, Story, Raddats, & Zolkiewski, 2017). This work also questions the use of the term Doubters, suggesting a negative view about services that might be too strong, and that Conservatives more accurately reflects a cautious proponent of services.

9.2.2 Servitisation Challenges and Responses

The first challenge manufacturers face concerns the need to interpret the market environment and whether servitisation is an appropriate response. For example, a multinational manufacturer may encounter varying regulatory environments for services in different international markets, meaning that the extent of servitisation may vary, with local service companies protected from international competitors in some countries (Neto, Pereira, & Borchardt, 2015). Manufacturers also need to consider the evolution of customers' needs and customers' likelihood of accepting the procurement of services from product suppliers rather than in-house service operations or dedicated service providers. This is highlighted in several industries, often those with complex product offerings (e.g., aerospace), with these customers more likely to seek assistance from their product suppliers in terms of financing capital equipment, improving service processes and risk mitigation (Ng, Parry, Smith, Maull, & Briscoe, 2012).

If the market environment is suitable for services, then manufacturers must deal with the second challenge, reorientation from products to services. This challenge is multi-faceted and concerns how a traditionally product-dominant firm can embrace services, overcoming the inherent cultural inertia of this transformation (Ostrom et al., 2010). To successfully reorientate to services, manufacturers need service leaders capable of overseeing the transformation (Raddats, Burton, & Ashman, 2015), with this service focus not just within a service strategic business unit (SBU) but also at the top of the company. This transformation might entail the development of new outcome-based business models—that is, payment for achieved performance outcomes rather than payment for products and services per se (Visnjic, Wiengarten, & Neely, 2016). Manufacturers also need new service-related capabilities to enable these business models (Huikkola, Kohtamäki, & Rabetino, 2016), such as new (or retrained) staff to sell and deliver these offerings (Baines & Lightfoot, 2014).

Even if a manufacturer is transforming its business from products to services, without overcoming the third challenge, that of structural reorganisation to deliver a new service strategy, its efforts may not be that effective (Alghisi & Saccani, 2015). There are two main options to consider. If services are primarily designed to 'defend' existing product businesses, then combined product/service SBUs may be appropriate (Auguste, Harmon, & Pandit, 2006). If, however, services are primarily there to 'grow' the business, a separate service SBU may be appropriate, which allows services to be developed independently from products, offering greater accountability for performance and enabling a services culture to develop (Auguste et al., 2006). However, a separate service SBU may not be the optimal organisational design; for example, in highly servitised businesses, customer-facing SBUs could be the optimal structure, integrating products and services into customer offerings. In this situation, the disadvantages of separate product and service business SBUs (e.g., potentially not working together on a customer offering) may outweigh the benefits.

The fourth challenge concerns the need to develop service-related operational processes. This challenge is applicable to all manufacturers, although each process is not applicable to every manufacturer. Even if services are not an important differentiator for manufacturers, there is still a need for some limited processes to deal with base services (Lay, Schroeter, & Biege, 2009). As services become more central to a manufacturer's customer offerings, the interlinkages and alignment between new service development (NSD) and new product development (NPD) become important (Spring & Araujo, 2013). However, NSD and NPD may compete for scarce resources, so firms need to balance these competing interests carefully to enable both to flourish (Eggert, Thiesbrummel, & Deutscher, 2015). As manufacturers develop advanced services, NSD must take greater account of customer needs, particularly during the early stages of the process (Santamaría, Nieto, & Miles, 2012). The sales process also needs to reflect this change and embrace 'value-based selling' (Sheth & Sharma, 2008), while the delivery process may include new technologies as part of remote monitoring and management of equipment (Opresnik & Taisch, 2015). As services start to address customers' business problems, it becomes less likely that these problems can be solved just with the manufacturer's products. Thus, service processes may need to encompass other vendors' products, with critical issues relating to knowledge sharing and organisational interfaces (Raddats & Easingwood, 2010).

9.3 Service Challenge and Strategy Road Map

The four service strategies and challenges are set out in the following road map (Fig. 9.1). The road map is based on interviews with 24 managers and documentary evidence from four large manufacturers: SecurCo, from the security sector; ChemCo, from the chemical sector; TelCo, from the telecommunications sector; and AeroCo, from the aerospace sector. Each manufacturer followed a different service strategy and the study investigated the servitisation challenges they faced and their responses to them.

The road map provides an original perspective on how manufacturers adopting different service strategies respond to servitisation challenges. It highlights the sequential nature of servitisation challenges. The four service strategies are adapted from previous research and highlight the differing roles that services can play within manufacturers, thus supporting the plurality of approaches identified in the literature. In summary, these strategies are:

- Conservative (SecurCo)—cautious adopter of services;
- Pragmatist (ChemCo)—understands the benefits of services linked to its own products;

Overcoming the Challenges of Servitisation: Aligning... 177

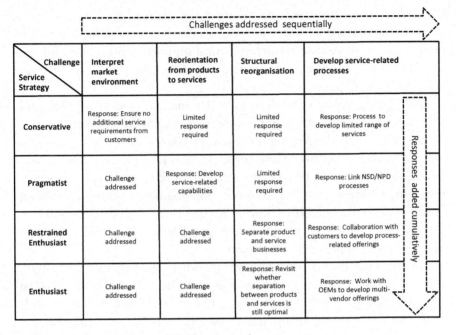

Fig. 9.1 Service strategy and challenge road map

- Restrained Enthusiast (TelCo)—clear on the benefits of services and focused on developing advanced services aligned to its own products that take over operational processes previously performed by customers (e.g., availability contracting);
- Enthusiast (AeroCo)—strongly focused on developing advanced serviced, which include offerings developed from multi-vendor products.

The road map can help facilitate servitisation since it enables manufacturers to identify the type of service strategy they are adopting (or considering) and then relate this to the challenges they will face and how they might respond to them (in the order they need to be addressed). The road map shows that overcoming servitisation challenges is a four-stage sequential process. Those that choose to take an enthusiast strategic approach will need to progress through all four stages; the others will need to move through fewer stages, depending upon their particular strategy.

So, a Conservative needs to interpret the demand for services in its markets and develop a limited range of service processes to facilitate such offerings (e.g., spares and repairs, technical support), while maintaining a watching brief on whether customers might require more services from their product suppliers.

A Pragmatist already understands the market, and recognises and responds to a need to reorientate to services, mainly focused on its own products, typically developing more complex service offerings than those offered by firms adopting a Conservative strategy. To do this, new service-related capabilities will be required in addition to those identified as necessary for Conservatives, for example, skill engineers who can maintain products. Equally, the NPD process needs to be adapted to account for differences in the development of services, although these will largely be offerings that support existing products.

A Restrained Enthusiast will have to address the first two challenges, and then, in choosing to enable greater value from services, will need to consider setting up a separate service SBU to help nurture a service culture, and delineate reporting and reward systems for products and services. Given that manufacturers adopting this strategy will start to offer advanced services, such as availability contracting on their own products, it is imperative to further develop their service processes in addition to those already developed by Pragmatists. For example, account managers need to focus on understanding how products are used in the operational environment and their customers' pain points, in order to design offerings that deliver better performance than customers can achieve through in-house provision.

Finally, an Enthusiast will already have responded to the challenges of interpreting the market environment and reorientating from products to services. However, it will need to revisit whether a separate service SBU is the optimal organisational design, with customer-facing SBUs providing product/service offerings sometimes more appropriate. Equally, in addition to the service processes developed by Restrained Enthusiasts, Enthusiasts will need to commit to developing effective practices for working with other manufacturers (e.g., exchanging technical data on products) to develop customer offerings that include multi-vendor products.

9.4 Conclusion

Given that manufacturers are at different stages of their servitisation 'journeys' and have different destinations, this road map should assist managers to understand better where they are currently positioned (in terms of their service strategy) and the challenges that need to be overcome to reach their servitisation goals. The road map provides an original perspective, and by linking to existing academic literature, managers can seek more detailed guidance from individual papers on specific service strategies, challenges and responses as befits their needs. Servitisation has become a key opportunity and challenge for many manufacturers, as they seek to develop service offerings that help to differentiate their products, grow revenue and address evolving customer needs. However, it must be borne in mind that manufacturers need to have service strategies that best reflect their capabilities and the opportunities that their markets present, which in some cases may not be based on services at all.

For some manufacturers, for example, Conservatives, services may not be perceived as valued by customers, their products might not be amenable to complex service additions or they may lack some key capabilities, resources or knowledge to develop more advanced services. It is, however, important that these manufacturers continue to research the market to ensure that emerging trends, such as new customer requirements and/or competitor offerings, are assessed to ensure that service opportunities are not overlooked. Even these manufacturers will offer some services to improve the reliability of their products, for example, spares and repair and technical support. These services are unlikely to require service-specific processes, as these offerings will be catered for as part of the NPD process. There are unlikely to be many challenges to providing these services, given they are intrinsically linked to product offerings. For these manufacturers, differentiation could be sought through product innovation, customer centricity or cost leadership, rather than services.

For other manufacturers, for example, Pragmatists, services can play an important role in creating product differentiation. These services might include installation, maintenance and upgrades. They might also encompass other manufacturers' products on a case-by-case basis, if customer demand dictates, and the products in question do not directly compete against a manufacturer's own. To make this move into services, it is assumed that the manufacturer will have identified a market requirement and, therefore, needs to focus on developing suitable service-related capabilities. These are likely to include service engineers capable of delivering more complex service offerings, IT systems that enable service provision and sales people who can articulate the value of these service offerings. Given that services are now a distinguishable (and probably chargeable) element of a manufacturer's offerings, it is important that NPD/NSD processes are adapted to support the development of services. While services will generally be closely linked to products in terms of organisational structure (i.e., products and services in the same SBUs), it is important that they are managed as separate offerings, to avoid them being 'given away' (i.e., the cost absorbed into the product price). For many manufacturers, being a Pragmatist is the extent of their servitisation efforts, with more developed approaches either not being required by customers or requiring a fundamental realignment of strategy, organisational structure and capabilities that might negatively impact their existing product-focused business models.

For Restrained Enthusiasts, services are an approach to product differentiation and also an opportunity to grow revenue and address changing customer needs, for example, a desire to outsource formerly in-house operational processes, where the risk and responsibility is assumed by the manufacturer or shared between the manufacturer and customer. These offerings may guarantee the availability of the supplied products, with the customer paying for this availability, rather than the products themselves and other discrete services. To make this change, it is almost inevitable that the firm will have assessed the market environment, considering both customer needs and competitor responses to these needs. Equally, they will already have established services as a separate offering from products. To develop and deliver service offerings may require a major structural reorganisation within the business, for example, setting up a separate service SBU. Such an organisational separation between services and products may be required to enable a sufficiently strong services culture or mindset to develop and service-specific targets to be set and measured. Service-focused senior managers are also likely to be needed to lead this change. Beyond this structural challenge, manufacturers need to develop very close operational linkages with customers to fully understand their existing product-related processes. This challenge should not be underestimated as manufacturers' traditional expertise is in product design and possibly manufacturing, not the operational use of these products. This can also be a concern from the perspective of customers who may need convincing that manufacturers possess the expertise to take over what were formerly in-house processes. Equally, customers may perceive risks in sharing intimate details of their operations with suppliers as well as losing the knowledge to perform these activities in-house should the strategy to outsource them be reversed. Only by building strong, trusting relationships with customers are manufacturers likely to develop a deep understanding of these processes, their costs and risks, to enable suitable performance-based offerings and prices to be developed. It should be noted that these performance-based offerings are not likely to replace the existing portfolio of product-attached services but rather complement them, especially when a manufacturer's customers do not have homogeneous service requirements. Indeed, one customer may have heterogeneous service requirements for different products.

The final group of manufacturers, termed Enthusiasts, has the most developed approach to services, taking on performance-based contracts for their own products and being able to extend these two products from other manufacturers and third parties. These manufacturers will already possess a sophisticated understanding of the market environment and have established services as a separate line of business within the firm. The main organisational challenge that Enthusiasts face is whether the separation of services from products starts to be counterproductive, with unhelpful competition for resources (e.g., financing new offerings) and over prioritising services or products in pursuit of SBU-specific financial targets. Thus, organisational separation may no longer be necessary. Instead, customer-facing teams can use components from product and service SBUs (and indeed from other manufacturers) to create multi-vendor offerings for customers. Manufacturers will have less knowledge of other manufacturers' in-service product performance, so this heightens the risk of providing these complex, multi-vendor advanced services. Delivering these types of services requires Enthusiasts to develop strong relationships with other manufacturers to gain access to technical knowledge about their products, and this may need to be reciprocated. Even with strong supplier partnerships, Enthusiasts require high levels of technical expertise and strong risk management procedures. Customers may also perceive heightened risks from a manufacturer supplying products for which it is not the Original Equipment Manufacturer (OEM). As with Restrained Enthusiasts, these offerings are likely to sit alongside more traditional service offerings, so manufacturers need to be able to provide a suite of offerings that befits the needs of their customers. Managers should be aware that becoming an Enthusiast is generally an incremental, non-linear process spanning several years or even decades, requiring significant commitment from senior management to instigate the required degree of cultural change. Thus, being an Enthusiast is likely to be the exception rather than the rule.

References

Alghisi, A., & Saccani, N. (2015). Internal and external alignment in the servitization journey—Overcoming the challenges. *Production Planning and Control, 26*(14/15), 1219–1232.

Auguste, B. G., Harmon, E. P., & Pandit, V. (2006). The right service strategies for product companies. *McKinsey Quarterly, 1*(1), 40–51.

Baines, T. S., & Lightfoot, H. (2014). Servitization of the manufacturing firm: Exploring the operations practices and technologies that deliver advanced services. *International Journal of Operations and Production Management, 34*(1), 2–35.

Burton, J., Story, V. M., Raddats, C., & Zolkiewski, J. (2017). Overcoming the challenges that hinder new service development by manufacturers with diverse services strategies. *International Journal of Production Economics, 192*, 29–49.

Eggert, A., Thiesbrummel, C., & Deutscher, C. (2015). Heading for new shores: Do service and hybrid innovations outperform product innovations in industrial companies? *Industrial Marketing Management, 45*, 173–183.

Gebauer, H. (2008). Identifying service strategies in product manufacturing companies by exploring environment—Strategy configurations. *Industrial Marketing Management, 37*(3), 278–291.

Huikkola, T., Kohtamäki, M., & Rabetino, R. (2016). Resource realignment in servitization: A study of successful service providers explores how manufacturers modify their resource bases in transitioning to service-oriented offerings. *Research-Technology Management, 59*(4), 30–39.

Kowalkowski, C., Windahl, C., Kindström, D., & Gebauer, H. (2015). What service transition? Rethinking established assumptions about manufacturers' service-led growth strategies. *Industrial Marketing Management, 45*, 59–69.

Lay, G., Schroeter, M., & Biege, S. (2009). Service-based business concepts: A typology for business-to-business markets. *European Management Journal, 27*(6), 442–455.

Neto, G. Z., Pereira, G. M., & Borchardt, M. (2015). What problems manufacturing companies can face when providing services around the world? *Journal of Business and Industrial Marketing, 30*(5), 461–471.

Ng, I., Parry, G., Smith, L., Maull, R., & Briscoe, G. (2012). Transitioning from a goods-dominant to a service-dominant logic: Visualising the value proposition of Rolls-Royce. *Journal of Service Management, 23*(3), 416–439.

Oliva, R., & Kallenberg, R. (2003). Managing the transition from products to services. *International Journal of Service Industry Management, 14*(2), 160–172.

Opresnik, D., & Taisch, M. (2015). The value of big data in servitization. *International Journal of Production Economics, 165*, 174–184.

Ostrom, A., Bitner, M., Brown, S., Burkhard, K., Goul, M., Smith-Daniels, V., … Rabinovich, E. (2010). Moving forward and making a difference: Research priorities for the science of service. *Journal of Service Research, 13*(1), 4–36.

Raddats, C., Burton, J., & Ashman, R. (2015). Resource configurations for services success in manufacturing companies. *Journal of Service Management, 26*(1), 97–116.

Raddats, C., & Easingwood, C. (2010). Services growth options for B2B product-centric businesses. *Industrial Marketing Management, 39*(8), 1331–1342.

Raddats, C., & Kowalkowski, C. (2014). A reconceptualization of manufacturers' service strategies. *Journal of Business-to-Business Marketing, 21*(1), 19–34.

Santamaría, L., Nieto, M. J., & Miles, I. (2012). Service innovation in manufacturing firms: Evidence from Spain. *Technovation, 32*(2), 144–155.

Sheth, J. N., & Sharma, A. (2008). The impact of the product to service shift in industrial markets and the evolution of the sales organization. *Industrial Marketing Management, 37*(3), 260–269.

Spring, M., & Araujo, L. (2013). Beyond the service factory: Service innovation in manufacturing supply networks. *Industrial Marketing Management, 42*(1), 59–70.

Visnjic, I., Wiengarten, F., & Neely, A. (2016). Only the brave: Product innovation, service business model innovation, and their impact on performance. *Journal of Product Innovation Management, 33*(1), 36–52.

Zhang, W., & Banerji, S. (2017). Challenges of servitization: A systematic literature review. *Industrial Marketing Management, 65*, 217–227.

10

Paradoxes in Servitization

Marko Kohtamäki, Rodrigo Rabetino, and Suvi Einola

10.1 Introduction

Alternatively referred to as servitization (Vandermerwe & Rada, 1988), service infusion (Brax, 2005; Forkmann, Henneberg, Witell, & Kindström, 2017), service transformation (Martinez, Bastl, Kingston, & Evans, 2010), or service transition (Fang, Palmatier, & Steenkamp, 2008), the transformation from selling standardized products (+ add-on services) to offering customized solutions (+ advanced services) is far from easy (Baines, Ziaee Bigdeli, Bustinza, Shi, Baldwin, & Ridgway, 2017; Forkmann et al., 2017). Therefore, also the outcomes of servitization may be uncertain (Gebauer, Fleisch, & Friedli, 2005; Lee, Yoo, & Kim, 2016). Servitizing manufacturers typically face a variety of significant challenges in the transition process that lead to difficulties in capturing the financial value from servitization, so called service paradox (Gebauer et al., 2005). As such, servitization studies

M. Kohtamäki (✉) • R. Rabetino • S. Einola
University of Vaasa, Vaasa, Finland
e-mail: marko.kohtamaki@uva.fi; rodrigo.rabetino@uva.fi; suvi.einola@uva.fi

have found that servitization may have a non-linear effect on company performance, such as on sales growth (Kohtamäki, Partanen, Parida, & Wincent, 2013), profitability (Visnjic Kastalli & Van Looy, 2013), and firm value (Fang et al., 2008). Our work suggests that the challenges manufacturing companies face in servitization result from the paradoxical tensions related to the co-existence of two strategic logics, which create the paradox of performing: 1) offering customized solutions (+ advanced services) while 2) trying to maintain efficiency of product manufacturing. Mere co-existence of these two strategic logics in a servitizing manufacturing company is the reason for other organizational paradoxes to emerge. Hence, the paradox theory is utmost relevant when trying to understand the bottlenecks in service transition.

Whereas the service transition is by no means limited to offerings, it often begins from offerings expanding to all dimensions of the manufacturing firm's business model. Hence, we concur with Fischer, Gebauer, Gregory, Ren, and Fleisch (2010), who argue that manufacturing companies should free themselves from the "straightjacket" of seeing servitization mostly through spare parts, repair, or maintenance, and consider the opportunities created by more advanced life-cycle services (Rabetino, Kohtamäki, Lehtonen, & Kostama, 2015). However, poor outcomes with servitization typically lead companies to stop the service transition or eventually trigger a de-servitization process (Kowalkowski, Gebauer, & Oliva, 2017). This is often unnecessary, and results from wrong interpretations of causes and effects when servitizing the company. Instead of deciding between efficient product manufacturing and customized integrated solutions, the company management should find ways to accept and balance with these paradoxical tensions. This is not to say that companies should not develop modularity of integrated solutions, but instead that despite developing modularity of solutions, tensions between efficiency of manufacturing and delivery and customization of integrated solutions will persist, and these tensions cannot be solved by simple either-or choices.

The tensions that manufacturers face when transitioning from manufacturing products toward the provision of customized integrated solutions are often paradoxical in nature (Einola, Kohtamäki, & Rabetino, 2017). Paradoxical tensions refer to *contradictory yet interrelated elements that exist simultaneously and persist over time* (Smith & Lewis, 2011, p. 386). Reflecting the tensions that emerge in organizational change processes such as service transition, the paradox approach provides an alternative to the contingency theory suggesting that instead of trying to solve the organizational tensions, an organization should accept, embrace, and cope with them (Jay, 2013). While the paradox theory has gained increasing attention in organization studies, some have suggested it becoming almost the "new normal" in organizations (Gaim, 2017), and perhaps in organization science.

The paradox approach has been utilized to a limited extent in servitization. According to prior research a service paradox results from the coexistence of different strategic logics, such as services versus products that vary substantially (Gebauer et al., 2005) creating a *tension between a service and a product/manufacturing culture* that *is likely to be a constant challenge* (Kindström & Kowalkowski, 2009, p. 157). Previous studies highlight the importance of the underlying tensions between product-oriented and services-oriented (or customized integrated solutions) business models. These tensions stretch from financial factors to organizational structure and culture, all the way to people working between different divisions (Visnjic Kastalli & Van Looy, 2013; Visnjic Kastalli, Van Looy, & Neely, 2013). Despite servitizing, firms need to maintain efficiency of product manufacturing, and hence after servitization, a servitized firm has both maintained the old organizational culture of efficient product/technology organization and created a new more effective customer-oriented culture of integrated solutions and advanced services. In many cases, servitized organizations find it difficult to provide customized integrated solutions while maintaining efficiency of product manufacturing—these organizations face the paradox of performing emerging when maintaining efficiency of product manufacturing while offering customized solutions and advanced services. This paradox of performing spurs other organizational paradoxes that cannot be resolved, but should be accepted, embraced, and coped with. By accepting the organizational paradoxes and their persistency, managers can bring order in to the chaos, tone down the messiness of the organization, and move toward workable certainty (Lüscher & Lewis, 2008).

This chapter extends the above discussion by considering servitization through the paradox lens. Based on an empirical work with professionals from leading Finnish manufacturing companies that have been involved in servitization processes, we discuss about the paradox theory, create a model to analyze the paradoxical tensions in servitization, and provide some managerial guidelines on how to cope with these paradoxes in order to alleviate their negative impact and facilitate servitization (Vaara &

Whittington, 2012; Whittington et al., 2003). We build upon the model on organizational paradoxes developed by Smith and Lewis (2011). The developed framework provides assistance for managers responsible for manufacturing firms' servitization efforts.

10.2 Paradox Theory

Strategy and organization theories suggest a variety of either-or choices, such as differentiation versus the low cost (Porter, 1980), market versus hierarchy (Williamson, 1975), or exploration versus exploitation (March, 1991). Creating an alternative for the classic contingency theory, the paradox theory challenges the environment-strategy-structure fit (Chandler, 1962), and suggest that, a firm should alternatively accept tensions between the competing strategies and implement them in parallel. Therefore, instead of choosing either-or, firms should accept both-and, and try to cope with competing demands, by selecting a hybrid strategy, hybrid governance mechanisms, or ambidexterity, to name a few examples of concepts used in different research fields. Hence, studies suggest that these paradoxical tensions cannot be resolved, but they persist, and firms should thus learn how to cope with them (Calton & Payne, 2003; Jay, 2013; Poole & van de Ven, 1989).

In their original model, Smith and Lewis (2011) scrutinize four organizational paradoxes: (a) *learning*, (b) *organizing*, (c) *performing*, and (d) *belonging*. The paradox of learning underlines the tension between single- and double-loop learning (Argyris, 1991; e.g. exploitative and explorative learning)—different types of learning strategies that are both central for short- and long-term performance (March, 1991; Raisch & Birkinshaw, 2008). The paradox of organizing may emerge in between routines and change, flexibility and adaptation, direction and empowerment. The paradox of performance arises between the short- and long-term goals, company-level and divisional targets, or between organizational and individual optimization—all important tensions stretching to different directions. Finally, the paradox of belonging refers to organizational identity, the paradoxical tensions between product and service identity, or between standardized and customized. While these do not capture all the potential paradoxes, they provide important examples of persistent organizational paradoxes, which may not be solved but have to be accepted and coped with.

10.3 Paradoxes in Servitization

Our main argument is that the organizational paradoxes in servitization are actually caused by the tensions triggered by a manufacturer moving from standardized products (+ add-on services) toward customized solutions (+ advanced services). While the servitized manufacturer offers customized solutions and advanced services, it also has to maintain efficiency of product manufacturing. This logic is aligned with the paradox of performing. Hence, we suggest that the paradox of performing spurs other paradoxes in servitization. Our suggestion also highlights the dynamic nature of the paradox theory—Paradoxes tend to spur other paradoxical tensions within the organization. Figure 10.1 draws from Smith and Lewis (2011), and develops their original model to servitization context, depicting organizational paradoxes in servitization. In particular, we build on the existing research on servitization, and the service paradox coined by Gebauer et al.

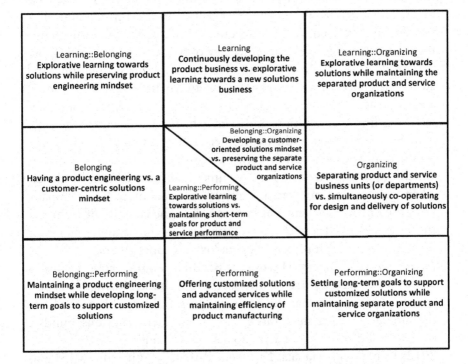

Fig. 10.1 Organizational paradoxes in servitization: balancing product and solution logics (developed for the context of servitization based on Smith and Lewis, 2011)

(2005). In their study, Gebauer et al. (2005) present the service paradox as a situation where a company invests in services, but is incapable of capturing the value of investments as higher returns due to increased costs. The current chapter extends the paradox approach in servitization by developing concept and theory on the paradoxes in servitization.

Based on a previous research conducted in the fields of servitization and organizational paradoxes, and the significant empirical work we have conducted in the last seven years in four manufacturing companies, we developed the model of organizational paradoxes in servitization.

According to our findings, the main paradoxes in servitization could be coined as:

1. *Paradox of Performing*: **Offering customized solutions and advanced services while maintaining efficiency of product manufacturing**. We define the paradox of performing emerging in between the customization of solutions and advanced services while maintaining the efficiency of product manufacturing. As we explained in the Introduction, this paradox may be such that it spurs other paradoxes, as the manufacturing company has to maintain efficiency of product manufacturing and service delivery, while trying to develop customized solutions and advanced services. Thus, the paradox emerges in between customization and efficiency. The paradox of performing is highly persistent for manufacturing firms, or solution providers, which have to customize integrated solutions to meet their customer needs. Customization increases production and transaction costs, in contrast to standard products which can be produced in larger volumes and more efficiently. Hence, when customizing integrated solutions, the manufacturing company faces the difficult challenge of how to utilize the capacity of manufacturing efficiently. These challenges generate an important paradox for the manufacturing company—a paradox that spurs others.
2. *Paradox of Belonging*: **Having a product engineering versus a customer-centric solutions mindset**. From the servitizing firm's perspective, this means that the organization should be able to facilitate the emergence of a new, more customer-centric solutions mindset (Gebauer, Edvardsson, & Bjurklo, 2010; Gebauer & Kowalkowski, 2012; Kohtamäki, Hakala, Partanen, Parida, & Wincent, 2015) and

organizational culture, while trying to preserve and cherish the product-engineering mindset. Both are important, so the manufacturing company cannot choose either-or.

3. *Paradox of Learning*: **Continuously developing the product business versus explorative learning toward a new solutions business.** From the servitizing firm's perspective, this paradox suggests that while exploratively learning toward integrated solutions, the organization should also continue developing the product business. This paradox emphasizes the radical innovation needed when moving toward customized integrated solutions—in many ways questioning the traditional product-oriented processes, while still maintaining the incremental development of product manufacturing and delivery processes. Understandably, it is a very challenging balancing act to perform. Studies suggest that firms need dynamic capabilities to succeed in servitization efforts (Fischer et al., 2010; Huikkola, Kohtamäki, & Rabetino, 2016; Kindström, Kowalkowski, & Sandberg, 2013).

4. *Paradox of Organizing*: **Separating product and service business units (or departments) versus simultaneously co-operating for design and delivery of solutions.** For practitioners in servitization and servitizing firms, this paradox suggests a need for setting different practices to support product-service bundling to facilitate solutions integration, while the product and service units remain separated. While separate units for products and services are important for the facilitation of their performance, they tend to cause sub-optimization, and difficulties regarding integration of products and services into customized solutions. Studies suggest the importance of capabilities related to product-service bundling especially in multi-divisional organizations, where product and service units have been separated (Huikkola & Kohtamäki, 2017; Rabetino, Kohtamäki, & Gebauer, 2017; Ulaga & Reinartz, 2011).

Then again, according to our findings, the emerging paradoxes could be coined as:

5. *Emerging Paradox of Learning::Belonging*: **Explorative learning toward solutions while preserving a product-engineering mindset.** This emerging paradox refers to a situation where a servitizing

firm struggles when trying to develop a radically new business in integrated solutions, while the mindset and culture of the organization still cherishes the product, technology, or manufacturing. Hence, it is the engineering mindset that clashes with explorative learning toward solutions.

6. *Emerging Paradox of Learning::Organizing:* **Explorative learning toward solutions while maintaining the separated product and service organizations.** This paradox implies the difficulties of learning to integrate products and services into integrated solutions when products and services are delivered by separate units. Thus, the sub-optimizing organizational structure may provide significant obstacles to servitization—yet, the separated product and service organizations are important for effective order-delivery of products and services. Easily, the sub-optimizing, separated, and exploitative organizational units turn into core rigidities (Leonard-Barton, 1992), exploitation (Sirén, Kohtamäki, & Kuckertz, 2012), or competence (Fischer et al., 2010) traps in servitization (Huikkola et al., 2016).

7. *Emerging Paradox of Performing::Organizing:* **Setting long-term goals to support customized solutions while maintaining separate product and service organizations.** This paradox references to a situation where the servitizing firm needs to set long-term targets to facilitate the sales of integrated solutions while having sub-optimizing product and service organizations. In many ways, setting and receiving long-term targets may feel frustrating in the product and service organizations, while they would rather focus on product and service sales that may provide quicker returns. In these occasions product-centric cultures may thwart development of integrated solutions (Oliva & Kallenberg, 2003).

8. *Emerging Paradox of Belonging::Performing:* **Maintaining a product-engineering mindset while developing long-term goals to support customized solutions.** Setting long-term goals clashes with the product-engineering mindset and culture—the organizational discourse at the micro-level continues to emphasize technology and products, while the top management intends to influence the organizational orientation by setting long-term targets that emphasize customized integrated solutions. Thus, the organization cannot choose either-or (engineering mindset vs. customized integrated

solutions), but has to preserve also the engineering mindset, although it generates a paradox with the management system being developed to support the strategic transition towards customized, customer-centric, integrated solutions. Organizational identity clashes with the performance management system.

9. *Emerging Paradox of Belonging::Organizing*: **Developing a customer-oriented solutions mindset while preserving the separate product and service organizations.** In this paradox, it is the separated product and service organization that clashes with the customer-oriented solution mindset. In prior research, for instance, Gebauer et al. (2010, p. 238) suggest that *value, meanings, beliefs and goals related to services may create conflicts with product-oriented organizational units leading an internal resistance*. While the manufacturing company maintains separate product and service organizations, it has to develop also customer-centric solutions mindset to succeed in customizing solutions and advanced services. Hence, the organizational structure with separate and often sub-optimizing product and service organizations clash with the development of customer-centric mindset, customer orientation. For instance, how to develop customer-centric mindset in a product division, which should collaborate across the divisional boundaries to facilitate integration of customized solutions and advanced services.

10. *Emerging Paradox of Learning::Performing*: **Explorative learning toward solutions while maintaining short-term goals to support also product and service performance.** Short-term goals in separate product and service organizations maintain an exploitative product and add-on service focus, while simultaneously the organization intends to develop toward integrated solutions. Thus, short-term performance interests in product and service organizations clash with explorative learning toward customized integrated solutions.

10.4 Conclusions

When moving toward a servitized business model, toward customization of solutions and advanced services, manufacturing companies face major challenges—these challenges are significant as they may be creating the straightjacket to see servitization through spare parts and basic maintenance activities (Fischer et al., 2010). The present chapter argued that these challenges are paradoxical and emerge as a result of the paradox of performing that arises between efficient manufacturing of products and delivery of add-on services, and the new business models required for configuring and delivering customized integrated solutions including advanced services. As the companies cannot stop from manufacturing products when servitizing the company, they face tensions between the juxtapose demands to manufacture and deliver products highly efficiently while simultaneously developing more advanced and customized product-service systems. We interpret this as the paradox of performing and argue that this paradox spurs other organizational paradoxes depicted in Fig. 10.1.

We utilized and developed the model from Smith and Lewis (2011) for the analysis of paradoxes in servitization. While the paradox theory seems to almost emerge as the new normal science in the organization theory, very limited number of works have so far utilized the concept in servitization research (Brax, 2005; Gebauer et al., 2005; Johnstone, Wilkinson, & Dainty, 2014; Visnjic Kastalli & Van Looy, 2013). This chapter developed the model to address the unique challenges manufacturing companies face when servitizing their business models.

As the paradoxes are in definition tensions that persist, manufacturing companies need to learn how to live with them. Organizations should learn how to accept, appreciate, make sense of, and cope with paradoxes (Beech, Burns, Caestecker, MacIntosh, & MacLean, 2004; Lewis, 2000). In servitizing manufacturers, acceptance begins from the paradox between efficient manufacturing of products and customization of integrated solutions. As this tension persists, it continues spurring other organizational tensions and paradoxes.

For managers in charge of managing the transition process toward a servitized business model, we provided a contextualized version of the Smith and Lewis (2011) framework to understand the paradoxes in servitization. The created model intends to support managers in developing understanding on how to cope with the paradox between products and customized integrated solutions. Accepting the tensions is central for managers to bring order into chaos. While the role of senior leaders and top managers is of importance, the role of middle managers should be emphasized in servitization, as they are often the ones that actually face the tensions and experience the dilemmas, where any either-or decision would feel irrational. Hence, the paradox model may help the middle managers to make sense of the paradoxes encountered in servitization. In search of alignment between different divisions and units, the management system plays a central role. The management system should support both-and, and hence, instead of enforcing one way over another, balance dynamically when needed, as both the products and integrated solutions are important for the company success.

A servitizing firm may try to cope with the paradoxes by using different coping practices, such as accepting, accommodating, differentiating, and integrating (Smith, 2014). In servitization, accepting and embracing implies that both strategies are embraced, products and customized integrated solutions. Accommodation would mean that the organization juxtaposes the contradictory elements and accommodates them—for example, mass customizes hardware, software, and advanced services to integrate and deliver as efficiently as possible. Differentiating and integrating would provide other options too. Differentiation suggests separating and appreciating both products and customized, integrated solutions. Integrating suggests finding and arguing synergies between products and customized integrated solutions. The paradox approach encourages managers to ask how we can develop servitization and a value-based business model without sacrificing efficient product manufacturing—how to implement both-and (Smith, Binns, & Tushman, 2010).

Overall, to cope with the paradoxical tensions of servitization, manufacturers need tools and practices. While some of our previous studies (Huikkola et al., 2016; Kohtamäki & Rajala, 2016; Rabetino et al., 2017) and, in particular, other chapters in this book provide good illustrations of tools and practices, here we will only mention a few concrete examples; for instance, the paradox of organizing call for appropriate service-oriented structures to support the delivery of solutions while keeping up the effective operations in product and service units. Manufacturers can set a separate unit for solutions (either formal or an ad-hoc project team), which can develop its own organizational capabilities, processes, and resources, and be run separately. In addition, the solutions unit could facilitate coping with the paradox of performing—develop modular solutions to minimize production and delivery costs without sacrificing the customization.

The paradox of belonging highlighted a tension between the product-engineering mindset and the customer-oriented culture related to provision of customized integrated solutions. Thus, the organization would need a capacity to balance between these different types of identities. Again, accepting the paradox, and separating the solutions activities into a separate unit might provide an answer—however, it is important to acknowledge that having a separate unit for solutions will not remove the paradoxical tension, but it persists and should be accepted by the practitioners. This is important also for the tension between exploitative and explorative learning (Paradox of learning). Finally, we believe that the paradox theory provides a valuable lens to consider the challenges manufacturing companies face when moving toward customized integrated solutions. Servitization literature needs alternative narratives (Luoto, Brax, & Kohtamäki, 2017) in addition to valuable contingency theoretic perspectives (Rabetino, Harmsen, Kohtamäki, & Sihvonen, 2018) when developing theory to support decision making in servitizing manufacturing companies.

References

Argyris, C. (1991). Teaching smart people how to learn. *Harvard Business Review, 69*(May–June), 99–109.

Baines, T., Ziaee Bigdeli, A., Bustinza, O. F., Shi, V. G., Baldwin, J., & Ridgway, K. (2017). Servitization: Revisiting the state-of-the-art and research priorities. *International Journal of Operations & Production Management, 37*(2), 256–278.

Beech, N., Burns, H., De Caestecker, L., MacIntosh, R., & MacLean, D. (2004). Paradox as invitation to act in problematic change situations. *Human Relations, 57*(10), 1313–1332.

Brax, S. (2005). A manufacturer becoming service provider—Challenges and a paradox. *Managing Service Quality, 15*(2), 142–155.

Calton, J., & Payne, S. (2003). Coping with paradox: Multistakeholder learning dialogue as a pluralist sensemaking process for addressing messy problems. *Business Society, 42*(7), 7–42.

Chandler, A. D. (1962). *Strategy and structure: Chapters in the history of the American industrial enterprise.* Cambridge, MA: Massachusetts Institute of Technology Press.

Einola, S., Kohtamäki, M., & Rabetino, R. (2017). Paradoxes in servitization. In *Servitization spring conference 2017*.

Fang, E.. (Er), Palmatier, R. W., & Steenkamp, J.-B. E. (2008). Effect of service transition strategies on firm value. *Journal of Marketing, 72*(5), 1–14.

Fischer, T., Gebauer, H., Gregory, M., Ren, G., & Fleisch, E. (2010). Exploitation or exploration in service business development?: Insights from a dynamic capabilities perspective. *Journal of Service Management, 21*(5), 591–624.

Forkmann, S., Henneberg, S. C., Witell, L., & Kindström, D. (2017). Driver configurations for successful service infusion. *Journal of Service Research, 20*(3), 275–291.

Gaim, M. (2017). *Paradox as the new normal: Essays on framing, managing and sustaining organizational tensions.* Umeå: Umeå School of Business.

Gebauer, H., Edvardsson, B., & Bjurklo, M. (2010). The impact of service orientation in corporate culture on business performance in manufacturing companies. *Journal of Service Management, 21*(2), 237–259.

Gebauer, H., Fleisch, E., & Friedli, T. (2005). Overcoming the service paradox in manufacturing companies. *European Management Journal, 23*(1), 14–26.

Gebauer, H., & Kowalkowski, C. (2012). Customer focused and service focused orientation in organizational structures. *Journal of Business & Industrial Marketing, 27*(7), 527–537.

Huikkola, T., & Kohtamäki, M. (2017). Solution providers' strategic capabilities. *Journal of Business & Industrial Marketing, 32*(5), 752–770.

Huikkola, T., Kohtamäki, M., & Rabetino, R. (2016). Resource realignment in servitization. *Research-Technology Management, 59*(4), 30–39.

Jay, J. (2013). Navigating paradox as a mechanism of change and innovation in hybrid organizations. *Academy of Management Journal, 56*(1), 137–159.

Johnstone, S., Wilkinson, A., & Dainty, A. (2014). Reconceptualizing the service paradox in engineering companies: Is HR a missing link? *IEEE Transactions on Engineering Management, 61*(2), 275–284.

Kindström, D., & Kowalkowski, C. (2009). Development of industrial service offerings: A process framework. *Journal of Service Management, 20*(2), 156–172.

Kindström, D., Kowalkowski, C., & Sandberg, E. (2013). Enabling service innovation: A dynamic capabilities approach. *Journal of Business Research, 66*(8), 1063–1073.

Kohtamäki, M., & Rajala, R. (2016). Theory and practice of value co-creation in B2B systems. *Industrial Marketing Management, 56*(7), 4–13.

Kohtamäki, M., Hakala, H., Partanen, J., Parida, V., & Wincent, J. (2015). The performance impact of industrial services and service orientation on manufacturing companies. *Journal of Service Theory and Practice, 25*(4), 463–485.

Kohtamäki, M., Partanen, J., Parida, V., & Wincent, J. (2013). Non-linear relationship between industrial service offering and sales growth: The moderating role of network capabilities. *Industrial Marketing Management, 42*(8), 1374–1385.

Kowalkowski, C., Gebauer, H., & Oliva, R. (2017). Service growth in product firms: Past, present, and future. *Industrial Marketing Management, 60*(1), 82–88.

Lee, S., Yoo, S., & Kim, D. (2016). When is servitization a profitable competitive strategy? *International Journal of Production Economics, 173*, 43–53.

Leonard-Barton, D. (1992). Core capabilities and core rigidities: A paradox in managing new product development. *Strategic Management Journal, 13*(1), 111–125.

Lewis, M. W. (2000). Exploring paradox: Toward a more comprehensive guide. *The Academy of Management Review, 25*(4), 760–776.

Luoto, S., Brax, S. A., & Kohtamäki, M. (2017). Critical meta-analysis of servitization research: Constructing a model-narrative to reveal paradigmatic assumptions. *Industrial Marketing Management, 60*(1), 89–100.

Lüscher, L. S., & Lewis, M. W. (2008). Organizational change and managerial sensemaking: Working through paradox. *Academy of Management Journal, 51*(2), 221–240.

March, J. G. (1991). Exploration and exploitation in organizational learning. *Organization Science, 2*(1), 71–87.

Martinez, V., Bastl, M., Kingston, J., & Evans, S. (2010). Challenges in transforming manufacturing organisations into product-service providers. *Journal of Manufacturing Technology Management, 21*(4), 449–469.

Oliva, R., & Kallenberg, R. (2003). Managing the transition from products to services. *International Journal of Service Industry Management, 14*(2), 160–172.

Poole, M. S., & van de Ven, A. H. (1989). Using paradox to build management and organization theories. *The Academy of Management Review, 14*(4), 562–578.

Porter, M. (1980). *Competitive strategy.* New York: Free Press.

Rabetino, R., Kohtamäki, M., & Gebauer, H. (2017). Strategy map of servitization. *International Journal of Production Economics, 192*(October), 144–156.

Rabetino, R., Harmsen, W., Kohtamäki, M., & Sihvonen, J. (2018). Structuring servitization related research. *International Journal of Operations and Production Management*, In press.

Rabetino, R., Kohtamäki, M., Lehtonen, H., & Kostama, H. (2015). Developing the concept of life-cycle service offering. *Industrial Marketing Management, 49*(August), 53–66.

Raisch, S., & Birkinshaw, J. (2008). Organizational ambidexterity: Antecedents, outcomes, and moderators. *Journal of Management, 34*(3), 375–409.

Sirén, C., Kohtamäki, M., & Kuckertz, A. (2012). Exploration and exploitation strategies, profit performance and the mediating role of strategic learning: Escaping the exploitation trap. *Strategic Entrepreneurship Journal, 6*(1), 18–41.

Smith, W. K. (2014). Dynamic decision making: A model of senior leaders managing strategic paradoxes. *Academy of Management Journal, 57*(6), 1592–1623.

Smith, W. K., Binns, A., & Tushman, M. L. (2010). Complex business models: Managing strategic paradoxes simultaneously. *Long Range Planning, 43*(2–3), 448–461.

Smith, W. K., & Lewis, M. W. (2011). Toward a theory of paradox: A dynamic equilibrium model of organizing. *Academy of Management Review, 36*(2), 381–403.

Ulaga, W., & Reinartz, W. J. W. J. (2011). Hybrid offerings: How manufacturing firms combine goods and services successfully. *Journal of Marketing, 75*(November), 5–23.

Vaara, E., & Whittington, R. (2012). Strategy-as-practice: Taking social practices seriously. *The Academy of Management Annals, 6*(1), 285–336.

Vandermerwe, S., & Rada, J. (1988). Servitization of business: Adding value by adding services. *European Management Journal, 6*(4), 314–324.

Visnjic Kastalli, I., & Van Looy, B. (2013). Servitization: Disentangling the impact of service business model innovation on manufacturing firm performance. *Journal of Operations Management, 31*(4), 169–180.

Visnjic Kastalli, I., Van Looy, B., & Neely, A. (2013). Steering manufacturing firms towards service business model innovation. *California Management Review, 56*(1), 100–123.

Whittington, R., Jarzabkowski, P., Mayer, M., Mounoud, E., Nahapiet, J., & Rouleau, L. (2003). Taking strategy seriously: Responsibility and reform for an important social practice. *Journal of Management Inquiry, 12*(4), 396–409.

Williamson, O. E. (1975). *Markets and hierarchies*. New York: Free Press.

11

Implementing Servitization Strategies: Trajectories of Capability Development and Offering of Basic and Advanced Services

Rui Sousa and Giovani J. C. da Silveira

11.1 Introduction

Research on the impact of servitization on firm performance remains inconclusive, with several studies suggesting this is more complex and fine-grained than originally envisaged (Eggert, Hogreve, Ulaga, & Muenkhoff, 2014; Kastalli & van Looy, 2013; Kohtamaki, Partanen, Parida, & Wincent, 2013; Visnjic, Wiengarten, & Neely, 2016). Our understanding of how to implement servitization strategies over time to attain increased financial performance is in many ways incomplete.

First, although investments in capabilities may explain declines in performance after servitization (e.g., Martinez, Bastl, Kingston, & Evans,

---

R. Sousa (✉)
Católica Porto Business School, Universidade Católica Portuguesa,
Porto, Portugal
e-mail: rsousa@porto.ucp.pt

G. J. C. da Silveira
Haskayne School of Business, University of Calgary, Calgary, AB, Canada
e-mail: giovani.dasilveira@haskayne.ucalgary.ca

2010), few studies addressed the capability antecedents and performance outcomes of servitization in an integrated manner. Second, empirical research has often not distinguished between different types of servitization strategies, for example, based on basic services (BAS) or advanced service (ADS) offerings (Gebauer, Fleisch, & Friedli, 2005). Third, although different servitization trajectories have been proposed (e.g., from BAS to ADS; Martinez et al., 2010; Kowalkowski, Windahl, Kindström, & Gebauer, 2015), their occurrence and impact on performance have not received sufficient examination in large-scale empirical studies.

To address these knowledge gaps, we present a framework for the effective implementation of servitization strategies over time, namely, in terms of a sequence of offering different types of services and developing supporting capabilities in parallel to that process. The framework distinguishes between BAS and ADS, which require different capabilities and have different impacts on financial performance. The core contribution is the proposal of a desirable servitization trajectory consisting of (i) a balanced growth of BAS and ADS over time, using BAS as a platform for selling ADS and (ii) building appropriate capabilities over time, recognizing that BAS and ADS require different types of capabilities. The framework was validated with data from a large-scale survey of 931 manufacturers from different countries and sectors. The research that developed the framework is reported in detail in Sousa and da Silveira (2017).

11.2 Theory

The servitized manufacturer co-creates value with the customer through interactions associated with service provision. In order to understand the performance impact of servitization strategies over time, we look at the value creation and appropriation processes associated with service offerings (Kastalli & van Looy, 2013). Service offerings affect financial performance through supply-side effects (capabilities) and demand-side effects (customer perceived value and product substitution). On the supply side, servitization may increase costs by demanding investment in new capabilities to provide services (service capabilities). On the demand side, servitization may increase revenue by leading to price premiums associated with product-service bundles, which are perceived by customers to have higher value than standalone products and services (Eisenmann, Parker, & Van Alstyne, 2011). However, servitization may also reduce revenue through decreasing product sales, due to longer product life cycles resulting from better maintenance services.

Value creation and appropriation processes strongly depend on the types of services offered by the manufacturer (Eggert et al., 2014; Smith, Maull, & Ng, 2014). Specifically, we distinguish between BAS and ADS (Sousa & da Silveira, 2017). BAS aim to install and maintain basic product functionality. Examples include product installation, provision of spare parts, maintenance, and repair. BAS involve limited customer interaction and customer value co-creation. ADS involve the adaptation of the product use to the customer's unique needs and usage situation, aiming to co-create value that goes beyond basic product functionality and entailing more intense interactions with customers (Smith et al., 2014). Examples are training in using the product, product upgrades, consulting, and product rental. ADS are a key component of high-value integrated solutions that address a specific customer's need.

Drawing on these theoretical concepts, we next present a framework to guide managers in the development of servitization strategies, namely, in what concerns capability development and the offering of different types of services (basic and advanced) over time.

11.3 Trajectories of Capability Development and Offering of Basic and Advanced Services

The framework for implementing servitization strategies is depicted in Fig. 11.1. Our central argument is that BAS and ADS require different capabilities and have different associations with performance, resulting in naturally occurring servitization trajectories. This is because they involve

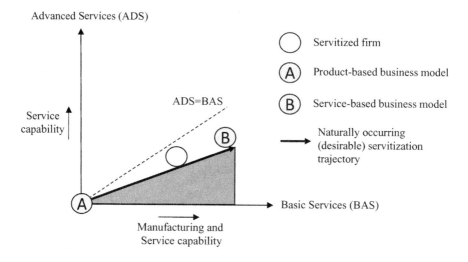

Fig. 11.1 Desirable trajectory of capability development and service offerings over time

distinct value co-creation and appropriation processes by the servitized manufacturer and the customer (Kastalli & van Looy, 2013; Sousa & da Silveira, 2017). We propose that BAS require manufacturing-based capabilities, while both BAS and ADS require service-specific capabilities. We also argue that offering BAS is a necessary condition for offering ADS. Moreover, we argue that BAS have a neutral or negative impact on financial performance, while ADS have a positive impact. Based on these arguments, we propose a natural trajectory to implement servitization over time, based on a balanced growth of BAS and ADS provision in tandem (i.e., BAS increase first, followed by ADS). That is, ADS build on BAS, with BAS acting as a platform to sell ADS. We next elaborate on the different components of the framework.

11.3.1 Capabilities

BAS require manufacturing-based capabilities, including expertise in product design and product/process engineering (Ulaga & Reinartz,

2011). For example, maintenance services require knowledge about parts' failures and durability over the product life cycle. Consistent with this, customers tend to value technical expertise when they buy product-based services. Because ADS are not product-centric, they do not directly require the development of manufacturing capabilities.

However, service-specific capabilities are required for the offering of both BAS and ADS. Offering services requires the ability to design services and products jointly (e.g., product design for serviceability; Ulaga & Reinartz, 2011). In addition, it demands expertise in designing and delivering service processes, which entail more frequent and complex interactions with customers than manufacturing processes. It may also involve setting up a separate organization to manage service provision, hiring and developing service-centred employees (e.g., with strong values of customer orientation, customization, flexibility, and quick response), and changing the incentive systems in order to foster integrated product-service performance (Baines & Lightfoot, 2014).

11.3.2 BAS as a Necessary Condition to ADS

We argue that a manufacturer's entry point into a service relationship with a customer requires offering BAS first. As the customer benefits from the initial product-BAS bundle, which increases confidence in the manufacturer's ability to provide quality services, it becomes more willing to contract higher-risk, higher-priced ADS (Gebauer et al., 2005). In addition, the offering of BAS enables the manufacturer to map the installed product base and learn about how customers use the products in their specific use environment. It is this customer-specific knowledge that paves the way for customized, high-value-added ADS offerings. For example, by obtaining historical product failure data through BAS, manufacturers can estimate risk and develop better pricing policies for product rental services; or, by observing how customers use products, they may co-design solutions that are more tailored to customer needs (Porter & Heppelmann, 2014). Hence, ADS build on BAS, with BAS acting as a platform to sell ADS.

11.3.3 Performance Impacts of BAS and ADS

BAS offerings are typically not differentiated and must compete against independent service providers, as well as customers' in-house maintenance departments. Thus, BAS sales margins are often low or even negative (frequently, customers expect these services to be provided free of charge). Moreover, because BAS lead to longer product lives due to better maintenance, product sales may decrease (product substitution effects). Therefore, BAS are not expected to lead to increased aggregate sales revenues (product and service sales). Because BAS still require investments in manufacturing and service capabilities, they are expected to have a negative impact on profitability. Overall, although the customer receives an enhanced value proposition, the manufacturer is not able to appropriate that value.

ADS offerings (or solutions) co-create value in use with customers beyond that which is embedded in basic product operation. Thus, they provide significant differentiation, creating strong customer lock-in effects (Ulaga & Reinartz, 2011) and commanding premium prices. Because ADS are not aimed specifically at improving product functionality, they do not lead to product substitution effects, resulting in higher overall sales. Although ADS require significant investments in service-specific capabilities, because they are highly differentiated, the manufacturer is able to charge premium prices and recoup the investment. As a result, ADS are expected to lead to increased sales and profitability.

11.3.4 Desirable Servitization Trajectories

Based on the previous arguments, we propose a naturally occurring (desirable) servitization trajectory, from a baseline manufacturing (product-based) business model towards increased levels of servitization maturity (see Fig. 11.1). Servitization maturity represents the extent to which the business model is based on service offerings versus products (Kowalkowski et al., 2015). In this trajectory, the manufacturer gradually introduces BAS to learn about how customers create value through product usage in the customer's specific context, and follows with ADS afterwards. BAS and ADS work closely together: the manufacturer initiates the service relationship with a customer with BAS and consolidates its market position by providing ADS. Over time, this pattern (BAS, followed by ADS) is extended to a larger number of customers, leading to increased levels of servitization maturity. BAS are employed to penetrate the service market (i.e., developing market breadth by offering services to additional customers), followed by ADS for developing market depth (offering higher levels of service [ADS] per customer) in coordination.

This trajectory is justified by the previous discussion. Service provision starts with BAS because these services make use of existing manufacturing capabilities (Sect. 11.3.1). BAS facilitate the development of a service culture (Gebauer et al., 2005) and allow time to develop service capabilities for higher-level service offerings. ADS are offered later because they require BAS not only for market entry but also to learn how individual customers create value through product usage (Sect. 11.3.2). The manufacturer's goal in progressing through this trajectory is to offer as high a level of ADS as possible (using BAS as a platform), because it is ADS and not BAS that lead to improved financial performance (Sect. 11.3.3).

11.3.5 Empirical Testing

The framework was empirically validated with data from a survey of 931 manufacturers from different countries and sectors, carried out in 2013–14. The data was collected as part of the International Manufacturing Strategy Survey (IMSS), a periodic study of the operations strategies, practices, and performance of manufacturing companies. The companies belong to ISIC sectors 25–30, which include manufacturers of fabricated metal products, machinery, instruments, and equipment. Their plants were located in 22 countries in Europe, America, and Asia. Questionnaires were responded by directors of manufacturing, operations, or equivalent, and the response rate was 13%. The unit of analysis was the business unit. IMSS data have been used for decades in several operations management studies in areas such as operations strategy, technology, and supply chain management, among others.

We tested the framework using indicators available from the survey. BAS and ADS were measured by the extent that manufacturing units offered services to accompany their product sales. BAS included typical product services such as maintenance, installation, and provision of spare parts. ADS included value "co-creation" services such as product leasing, upgrading, helpdesk, training, and consulting. Capabilities were measured by the ability of labour and equipment in the unit to deal with complex products and processes (manufacturing capability [MANCAP]) and to design and deliver services to customers (service capability [SERVCAP]). Financial performance was measured by the unit profitability (return on sales [ROS]) and annual revenue (SALES).

With those variables, we expected to find support to specific hypotheses. Units with stronger SERVCAP should offer more BAS and ADS. MANCAP should also be associated with BAS, but not necessarily with ADS. As illustrated in Fig. 11.1, BAS should be a "necessary condition" for ADS, that is, ADS could only be found in units that also offered BAS. Finally, we expected BAS to have no specific effect on SALES, and an even negative effect on ROS, whereas ADS should associate positively with both performance indicators. All those relationships should be found even by controlling the effects of unit size (number of employees), industry sector (ISIC), and country endowments (GDP per capita).

Results from our analyses supported those hypotheses, and therefore the framework. SERVCAP related positively with both BAS and ADS, but MANCAP related only with BAS. There were many cases of manufacturing units with low BAS and low ADS, and with high BAS and high ADS. We also found (albeit comparatively fewer) cases with high BAS and low ADS, but no cases with low BAS and high ADS. Finally, only ADS related positively with ROS and SALES. As further evidence to the servitization trajectory posited in Fig. 11.1, we found that units that offered more BAS and ADS also had more intensive investment in "sustainability, globalization, and servitization" initiatives (7.7% against 4.4% of sales turnover on average), obtained more revenue from service sales (13.0% against 5.9% of total sales turnover on average), and gave higher strategic importance to customer services (4.0 against 3.4 points on average on a five-point scale). This suggests that indeed as firms progress along the trajectory depicted in Fig. 11.1, they show increased levels of servitization maturity and financial performance.

Further analyses presented by da Silveira and Sousa (2017) indicated that ADS might be consistent with the implementation and success of a competitive differentiation strategy. Offering ADS may be a means for manufacturers in competitive markets to set their sales portfolios apart from competitors and offer superior value to customers. This can be an important advantage particularly if customers have difficulties distinguishing between alternative offerings based only on information about product features and performance.

11.4 Managerial Implications

The framework's key takeaway is that manufacturers wishing to servitize should distinguish between BAS and ADS. BAS and ADS require different capabilities: BAS require manufacturing-based capabilities, while both BAS and ADS require service-specific capabilities. Moreover, only ADS lead to increased sales and profitability. These differences result in a naturally occurring (desirable) servitization trajectory, consisting of (i) a balanced growth of BAS and ADS over time, using BAS as a platform for selling ADS and (ii) building appropriate capabilities over time, recognizing that BAS and ADS require different types of capabilities.

It is important to note that servitization strategies based on the offering of BAS in isolation (product-centric business model) do not seem to provide performance advantages and may be less sustainable in the long term. The offering of ADS to a significant level, however, seems to represent a substantially different business model, leading to increased servitization maturity and performance advantages (Baines, Lightfoot, Benedettini, Whitney, & Kay, 2010). Accordingly, our proposed trajectory differs from prior recommendations, namely, those involving the provision of BAS first to a high extent across customers, and only then follow with ADS. While we recognize that BAS are necessary for ADS at the level of individual customers, our findings suggest that a trajectory in which a provider offers BAS significantly across customers but not ADS (i.e., market breadth without market depth) is less sustainable. This is because BAS do not provide sufficient returns to support the required investments in manufacturing and service capabilities. Therefore, we propose a trajectory in which BAS and ADS developed in parallel (combining market breadth and depth), rather than strictly sequentially (BAS first with high breadth followed by ADS). It is feasible to follow with ADS shortly after BAS have been introduced to a specific customer (market depth), without building scale in the offering of BAS across different customers (market breadth). This is because economies of scale are less important for ADS due to its customized nature.

Nevertheless, manufacturers should be prepared to withstand a decline in profits at the initial stages of the servitization trajectory—characterized by low or medium levels of BAS and low levels of ADS—because the rise in costs associated with capability development is not made up by sufficient returns. This is because BAS do not lead to higher profits and the level of ADS offering is low. It is only when manufacturers offer significant levels of ADS that they achieve increased performance.

Although BAS do not directly lead to performance, they play two roles in servitization strategies. First, they can increase the value offered to customers, even though the manufacturer is not able to appropriate this value significantly. In some cases, BAS are offered due to coercive pressures from customers (Martinez et al., 2010). Thus, BAS can play a defensive role for the product business, acting as market qualifier (Eggert et al., 2014). The second role of BAS is to penetrate the service market and support profitable business models, based on the offering of ADS and synergies between BAS and ADS. As discussed earlier, the offering of BAS in isolation may be less sustainable in the long term. Thus, BAS also play an offensive role in the service market, acting as platform for ADS and service-based business models (Baines et al., 2010).

Besides those strategic and financial effects, implementing the trajectory might have benefits to marketing and customers' perception about the company service capabilities. Companies attempting to offer ADS without a BAS foundation might find it harder to be trusted on their ability to offer consulting or training services focused on exploiting their products utilization in the field. If manufacturers still rely on external contractors to perform seemingly standard services such as product installation and maintenance, how should they be able to inform about advanced practices to extend product utilization and life cycle? Thus, implementing the servitization trajectory might help not only to improve the company's *ability* to perform advanced services in the user's operating environment but also to boost customers' *perception* and trust on that ability.

Looking at the future, developments such as the Internet of things and smart, connected products (Porter & Heppelmann, 2014) will likely affect servitization strategies and trajectories. These technologies are expected to increase the efficiency in the provision of BAS by embedding them in products (e.g., remote monitoring and maintenance via sensors) (Wünderlich et al., 2015). In this context, BAS will result in faster learning about how customers use products. In addition, such technologies may allow for some types of ADS to be provided in a more efficient way, through the products themselves (e.g., products may autonomously learn and adapt to user preferences) (Porter & Heppelmann, 2014). As a consequence, in the future, BAS and ADS may become more closely interconnected than at present, leading to the ability to achieve higher levels of service per customer (market depth) at a faster pace.

References

Baines, T., & Lightfoot, H. (2014). Servitization of the manufacturing firm: Exploring the operations practices and technologies that deliver advanced services. *International Journal of Operations & Production Management, 34*(1), 2–35.

Baines, T., Lightfoot, H., Benedettini, O., Whitney, D., & Kay, J. (2010). The adoption of servitization strategies by UK-based manufacturers. *Journal of Engineering Manufacture, 224*(5), 815–829.

da Silveira, G. J. C., & Sousa, R. (2017). Does servitization influence manufacturing strategy and performance? In *15th International Research Symposium on Service Excellence in Management (QUIS15)*, Porto, Portugal, June 12–15 (abstract).

Eggert, A., Hogreve, J., Ulaga, W., & Muenkhoff, E. (2014). Revenue and profit implications of industrial service strategies. *Journal of Service Research, 17*(1), 23–39.

Eisenmann, T., Parker, G., & Van Alstyne, M. (2011). Platform envelopment. *Strategic Management Journal, 32*(12), 1270–1285.

Gebauer, H., Fleisch, E., & Friedli, T. (2005). Overcoming the service paradox in manufacturing companies. *European Management Journal, 23*(1), 14–26.

Kastalli, I., & van Looy, B. (2013). Servitization: Disentangling the impact of service business model innovation on manufacturing firm performance. *Journal of Operations Management, 31*(4), 169–180.

Kohtamaki, M., Partanen, J., Parida, V., & Wincent, J. (2013). Non-linear relationship between industrial service offering and sales growth: The moderating role of network capabilities. *Industrial Marketing Management, 42*(1), 1374–1385.

Kowalkowski, C., Windahl, C., Kindström, D., & Gebauer, H. (2015). What service transition? Rethinking established assumptions about manufacturers' service-led growth strategies. *Industrial Marketing Management, 45*(2), 59–69.

Martinez, V., Bastl, M., Kingston, J., & Evans, S. (2010). Challenges in transforming manufacturing organisations into product-service providers. *Journal of Manufacturing Technology Management, 21*(4), 449–469.

Porter, M., & Heppelmann, J. (2014). How smart, connected products are transforming competition. *Harvard Business Review, 92*(11), 64–88.

Smith, L., Maull, R., & Ng, I. (2014). Servitization and operations management: A service dominant-logic approach. *International Journal of Operations & Production Management, 34*(2), 242–269.

Sousa, R., & da Silveira, G. J. C. (2017). Capability antecedents and performance outcomes of servitization: Differences between basic and advanced services. *International Journal of Operations & Production Management, 37*(4), 1–52.

Ulaga, W., & Reinartz, W. (2011). Hybrid offerings: How manufacturing firms combine goods and services successfully. *Journal of Marketing, 75*(6), 5–23.

Visnjic, I., Wiengarten, F., & Neely, A. (2016). Only the brave: Product innovation, service business model innovation, and their impact on performance. *Journal of Product Innovation Management, 33*(1), 36–52.

Wünderlich, N., Heinonen, K., Ostrom, A., Patrício, L., Sousa, R., Voss, C., & Lemmink, J. (2015). "Futurizing" smart service: Implications for service researchers and managers. *Journal of Services Marketing, 29*(6/7), 442–447.

12

Unboxing the Key Human Competencies for Successful Servitization

Federica Polo

12.1 Introduction

Servitization is the process that changes the business models of firms from selling products and rudimentary services to delivering customized solutions (Baines et al., 2007). This process, however, brings serious challenges to organizations regarding organizational strategy, transformation, and the acquisition of service capabilities (Oliva & Kallenberg, 2003; Wise & Baumgartner, 1999). Traditionally, manufacturers nurture specific competencies related to either technology or products' offerings, which, in turn, develops myopia toward other competencies particularly the services-related (Neu & Brown, 2005). To overcome this trap and facilitate servitization, manufacturers ought to invest in the development of capabilities proprietary to the design of services and their integration into customer-specific solutions, selling, and delivery (Paiola, Saccani, Perona, & Gebauer, 2013). Therefore, the successful implementation of

F. Polo (✉)
School of Technology and Innovation, University of Vaasa, Vaasa, Finland
e-mail: fpolo@uwasa.fi

servitization requires a substantial change in existing characteristics of traditional industrial organizations and necessitates employees with new qualification profiles composed of complementary and necessary competencies (Gotsch, Hipp, Erceg, & Weidner, 2014).

In this context, organizations undergoing servitization need to ensure the sustainability of competitive advantage in the long run by investing in their processes and human capital (Gratton, Hope-Hailey, Stiles, & Truss, 1999). Nevertheless, before such a decision takes place, organizations should be able to uncover the competencies salient to servitization. In this regard, firms must seek to answer the following question: for a successful servitization, what competencies should employees possess and how can these competencies be defined in the long run?

In response, the present chapter contributes to the servitization community (managers and scholars) by exploring the set of competencies that can undergird servitization. By so doing, this chapter seeks to provide valuable guidelines to corporations for the implementation of a competency-based model that helps the top management identify the competencies that service employees should possess and highlights competencies that could translate the strategy and vision of the organization into behaviors, skills, and terms that people can easily understand and implement (Sanchez & Levine, 2009).

12.2 Competencies Deployment in Servitization Process: State of the Art

12.2.1 Definition of Competency

In the literature, there is a conceptual ambiguity and lack of consensus on the definition of competencies (Robinson, Sparrow, Clegg, & Birdi, 2007; Shippmann et al., 2000). For some, the concept refers mostly to behavioral aspects, while for others the term connects to abilities and personal characteristics, other researchers also subsume the outcomes of actions in the definition of competency (Iles, 2001). Given this multifaceted nature of competency that behooves a comprehensive view, it should be considered as a construct (Lahti, 1999) that is not directly observable and measurable but based on measurable and observable data. In light of this, competency is defined in this chapter as a set of observable dimensions comprising knowledge, skills, abilities, behaviors, and values that are necessary for effective performance in the job in question (Shippmann et al., 2000). These dimensions are tailored to the specific nature and needs of the organization and customized for the business objectives and strategy (Rodriguez, Patel, Bright, Gregory, & Gowing, 2002). Although most interpretations explicitly narrow the concept of competency to the individual level, many conceptualizations extend the focus to the team and organizational level (Robinson et al., 2007). However, this chapter pictures the three levels as strictly interrelated and forms joint organizational competencies that are embedded in the strategy formulation process (Fleury & Tereza Fleury, 2003). Therefore, the set of organizational competencies required within the organization should be determined and operationalized to support and improve the competitive strategy of the firm (Fleury & Tereza Fleury, 2003).

12.2.2 Competency Modeling in Servitization

The transition from product-based firm to service-based firm implies the realignment of employees to the new strategy and goals, which carries an impact on both individual competencies and organizational capabilities. Naturally, with the emerging new business needs related to servitization, it seems necessary for companies to implement new methods to face the change in competencies identification (Athey & Orth, 1999). In this regard, competency models act as a guide for the organization in the identification and deployment of new competencies tailored for servitization. The implementation of competency-based methods in servitization requires a shift in perspective from the individual level of analysis—in the definition of specific skills and behaviors—to the organizational level. Indeed, organizational and process competencies need to be jointly identified within the organization to combine and leverage individual knowledge, skills, and attitudes (KSAs) to increase organizational advantage (Athey & Orth, 1999). As Fig. 12.1 illustrates, the competencies' definition process is a continuous loop between individual and organizational level. Indeed, organizational competencies are created when individual

Fig. 12.1 Competency framework for servitization (Developed from (Campion et al., 2011))

KSAs are broadly shared across the organization (Dai & Liang, 2012). In turn, it becomes fundamental for the organization to define and manage the individual KSAs to support specific organizational competencies and strategic directions (Lawler, 1994). Therefore, competencies, defined as KSAs, need to be directly linked to business objectives and strategy (Campion et al., 2011). The attempt of aligning competencies to organizational goals during servitization can generate particularly complex or multidimensional patterns. In this regard, an appropriate use of competency models facilitates and simplifies the identification and definition of the required competencies. Furthermore, when competencies are identified in light of the strategy, it becomes important to deploy them in terms of observable job behaviors to help employees understand them and ensure a successful implementation of the strategy (Vakola, Eric Soderquist, & Prastacos, 2007).

In light of these considerations, the following paragraph, based on the extant literature and practical insights from real-case companies, outlines the main characteristics that competency models should have for a successful implementation of servitization strategy.

12.2.3 Characteristics of Competency Models in Servitization

As previously mentioned, competency models have a crucial role in linking together individual KSAs with the organizational strategy. Moreover, they are implemented to facilitate the identification of competencies required to better perform in a specific job, organization, or industry (Shippmann et al., 2000), as well as the evolution and definition of the needs related to changes in the business environment due to servitization (Athey & Orth, 1999). However, changes in business needs and the nature of work (e.g., the necessity of real-time knowledge work in the case of servitization) have created several challenges to consider in the implementation of competency methods, which in turn suggests the adaptation and amendment of these methods to face changes (Athey & Orth, 1999). Figure 12.2 exhibits the four main pillars for the implementation of competency models in servitization, described below.

1. *Facilitate servitization by linking competency models to organizational strategy and goals:*

The effectual implementation of servitization is strictly related to the understanding of the company's strategic logic (Rabetino, Kohtamäki, & Gebauer, 2017). Therefore, the focus should be oriented to the logic behind the strategy implementation, rather than the strategy itself (Kaplan & Norton, 2006). The connection between strategic logic and soft organizational factors is a very crucial and critical point in service-oriented organizations (Homburg, Fassnacht, & Guenther, 2003). Understanding the logic behind the strategy allows the deduction of specific business objectives and organizational targets, based on which the KSAs needed to achieve them are defined. Deploying the competencies needed for organizational strategy and goals and translating them

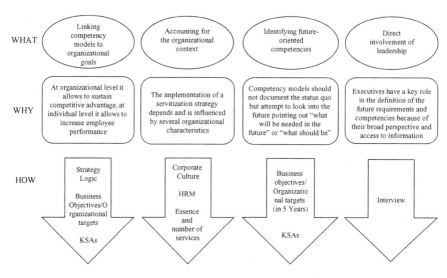

Fig. 12.2 Competency models in servitization: what, why, and how?

into observable KSAs support their understandability and applicability and that of the strategy itself (Vakola et al., 2007). Moreover, the integration of employees' competencies and business strategy plays a very important role both at the organizational level (in sustaining competitive advantage) (Barney, 1991) and at the individual level (in performing better the job aligning their competencies to the business strategy).

2. *Facilitate servitization by accounting for the organizational context:*

Competency models should be developed and tailored to the specific organizational context. The implementation of a servitization strategy depends on and is influenced by several organizational characteristics. For instance, corporate culture and human resource management need to be taken into consideration in the strategy implementation (Davis, 1983), as well as in the competencies' deployment for its effective strategy implementation. Further elements characterizing the organization in the servitization process are the typology and number of services offered by the organization (Homburg et al., 2003). All these elements characterize the organization and need to be included in the competencies' definition.

3. *Facilitate servitization by identifying future-oriented competencies:*

Competencies are usually defined by comparing past behaviors, rather than anticipating future performance requirements. After reviewing the extant literature, we can affirm that competencies deployment is mostly the result of the comparison between people considered as high performers and people considered average performers within an organization (Athey & Orth, 1999). To support servitization, it is therefore important to change this perspective. Consequently, competency models should not document the *status quo*, but attempt to look into the future (Campion et al., 2011) pointing out "what will be needed in the future" or "what should be done" for a successful implementation of servitization.

4. *Facilitate servitization through the direct involvement of leadership in implementing competency models:*

Even though it is not possible to predict the future with certainty, organizations have some insights about future business directions in terms of products, services, markets, resources, challenges, and competitive issues. As mentioned by Campion et al. (2011), executives and top managers have a key role in the definition of the future requirements and competencies because of their broad perspective and overall view, access to information on new developments, business changes and needs, and role in shaping the future of the company. Therefore, involving them in the competencies' definition allows their support for the project, which becomes one of the most important advantages of competency modeling (Campion et al., 2011).

12.3 Competencies Deployment in Servitization: A Systematic Approach

12.3.1 Methodological Approach

Identifying the most appropriate and effective methodology in organizational analysis always represents a complex issue. Indeed if, on the one hand, the aim is to implement the most accurate modality of observation; it is, on the other hand, necessary to consider the lack of time and resources to dedicate to these activities especially in larger organizations (Athey & Orth, 1999). Moreover, the complex procedures proposed in traditional approaches to competency modeling are worthless for organizations involved in servitization, where the structure, processes, and requirements are rapidly changing (Vakola et al., 2007). To face this problem, it becomes important to identify an agile processual methodology that ensures the effective implementation of a competency-based model in the organization. In the case of competency models, the literature (e.g., Campion et al., 2011) suggests a focus on the core idea; not every detail needs to be included to facilitate the implementation and maximize the results. Therefore, the proposed methodology permits to identify a set of competencies needed during the servitization journey to implement the business strategy and work effectively at both individual and team levels. The goal is to propose a *vademecum* for the applicability of competency models. This guide will help companies to identify the competencies required to implement the servitization strategy in the long run successfully. The following section describes in detail each step based on the literature.

Identification of the main objectives a company seeks to achieve through servitization: (This step answers two questions: How to identify the underlying objectives? And who are the main actors to include in the identification process?)

Research shows that the most controversial aspect managers need to face is the translation of the strategy into individual competencies required to implement and operationalize the business strategy effectively (Kaplan & Norton, 2005). Frequently, organizations adopt a prescriptive approach to competencies providing job descriptions aligned with the strategic objectives (Sparrow, 1997). This approach implies a static view of competencies focused on what the organization already does (Vakola et al. 2007). Therefore, to dynamically adapt to the strategy evolution, it becomes important to start the competencies' definition based on the organizational objectives the company is going to achieve in a future-oriented perspective. This approach is based on the initial identification of the organizational targets, interviewing the most relevant actors within the organization (Campion et al., 2011) to draw an overall picture of what is the foundation of core business areas and what is the strategic direction the company is going to undertake. Indeed, through interviews or focus groups with executives and top managers, it is possible to depict the future directions, markets, resources, challenges, and competitive issues the company is going to undertake.

Definition of the organizational targets within a time frame: (This step seeks to answer two questions: What is the most appropriate time frame to consider and why? And why is it important to define competencies in a future-oriented perspective?)

One of the most important elements in the determination of future competency requirements is to establish how far we want to seek into the future (Robinson et al., 2007). The definition of the time frame is a crucial passage because looking at the immediate future we risk identifying competencies that are slightly different from the current ones. On the other hand, looking too far we risk to speculate rather than provide an accurate prediction (Robinson et al., 2007). Gow and McDonald (2000) suggest that the future time horizon should be a minimum of five years.

As mentioned before, competencies are commonly defined through the comparison of the top with the average performers. At best, this approach tends to focus on the present; at worst, it dwells on the past (Iles, 2001). Adopting such a perspective in a transition period constitutes a risk for the organization that might become stuck in the past (Robinson et al., 2007) rather than look ahead through the competencies' definition. Therefore, the ability to forecast future requirements represents a strategic leverage for the organization depicting hypothetical future scenarios and predicting future business changes. The interviewer or researcher should support executives and managers by delving beyond vague images of the future to identify specific features that describe how the business should operate successfully in the future (Athey & Orth, 1999).

Translation of organizational targets and organizational-level competencies into individual competencies via KSAs: (This step seeks to answer two questions: What kind of approach to adopt? And how to identify individual competencies?)

The choice of the right approach to defining competency requirements has been debated extensively in the literature. The two main streams can be classified as top-down and bottom-up approaches (Robinson et al., 2007). In the top-down approaches, the competencies' definition is carried out by a previously defined set of competencies to which we re-conduct the competencies needed for the specific job analyzed. On the contrary, the bottom-up approaches aim to explore data without any pre-existing competency frames. In this research, a bottom-up approach was adopted. Although bottom-up approaches are more demanding and time-consuming, they ensure major adherence between the identified competencies and the role analyzed as opposed to competencies defined through top-down approaches (Robinson et al., 2007).

The investment in the deployment of individual competencies may vary following the needs and resources available in the organization. Lahti (1999) suggests six main steps for defining individual competencies: the first step is represented by (1) the review of the available documentation: company policies, strategic view, mission, and vision; whereby (2) the targets to achieve are defined. Once the main goals are identified, it is important to (3) identify the process and criteria for collecting information (e.g., methodology, actors to involve, and information to seek). Consequently (4) information is collected and (5) elaborated following the criteria of accuracy, importance, and representativeness. Through this process, we (6) define the competencies at the individual level.

Adoption of granularity in the definition of competencies: (This step seeks to answer one question: How many details should be included in the definition of competencies?)

The number of details to include in the competencies' definition is one of the main challenges to face in the implementation of competency models. This problem emanates from an obsession with detail on the one hand, and the need for simplification and usability on the other (Shippmann et al., 2000). Therefore, the suggestion that comes from the literature is not only to limit the number of competencies identified but also to reduce the amount of detail in the description of each competency (Campion et al., 2011).

Emphasis on the distinction between different competencies' layers: cross-jobs, job-specific and managerial competencies: (This step seeks to answer one question: How to categorize the identified KSAs?)

In order to create a detailed but efficient competency framework, it is necessary to identify the individual-level competencies following the organizational-level competencies and to categorize them according to generic/transversal competencies (common to different jobs and required in several circumstances to better perform), job-specific competencies (required to perform a specific job), and managerial or leadership competencies (specific of managerial roles).

Definition of a methodology for the collection and elaboration of data: (This step seeks to answer one question: How to collect data, how to corroborate evidence, and how to counterproof evidence?)

Data can be collected using different methods such as interviews, observations, and focus groups to identify potential competency information (Campion et al., 2011). The sample of people to interview should be broad enough to represent a range of business units and offer diverse and complementary perspectives on the future orientations and needs of the organization (Robinson et al., 2007).

The transcripts of the interviews/focus groups/observations are subject of a content analysis to identify the most recurrent themes and the indicators behind them (Kandola & Pearn, 1992). Approaching the content analysis, without preconceptions and with the support of an external observer, ensures that the indicators emerge in a bottom-up manner (Robinson et al., 2007). As described in Fig. 12.3, the emerged indicators need to be organized in a matrix that will summarize the future of the business along with several key organizational criteria or characteristics (Athey & Orth, 1999). Subsequently, these business priorities need to be deployed in terms of specific requirements and KSAs. Once identified, the KSAs are classified into generic/transversal, job-specific, and managerial competencies. Finally, it is necessary to examine and redefine the competency framework with a panel of experts from the organization to ensure comprehensiveness and understandability of the framework.

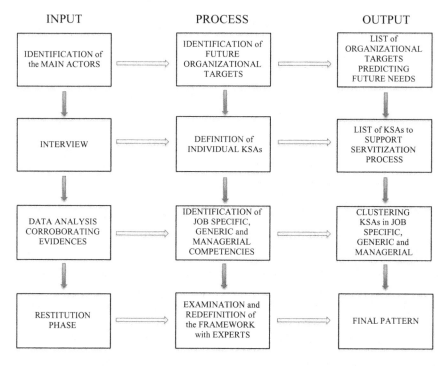

Fig. 12.3 A systematic approach to competency deployment is servitization process

12.3.2 An Illustrative Case Example

The case company where the methodology was developed and tested is a large company operating in the sector of advanced technologies and life-cycle solutions for the marine and energy sector. During the case study, the company has undergone the transition from products to services and integrated solutions.

The competency model implementation started with the identification of the main actors, from each unit, to involve in the project. The criteria adopted in the selection of key figures to interview were the role and access to relevant information of the candidates. The competency model implementation witnessed the involvement of 1 chief, 6 vice-presidents, 15 directors, 7 general managers, 2 managers, 2 project managers, and 1 senior proposal engineer.

Data were collected through interviews (face to face or via teleconference). The duration of each interview was 30 minutes on average. Four open questions were used to stimulate the discussion. The time frame adopted for the definition of the main targets, the company is going to achieve and the consequential competencies needed, is five to ten years, as suggested in the literature and confirmed through a follow-up with the managerial team. Once data were elaborated, the results have been discussed with a panel of experts within the organization to verify their robustness.

From the analysis of the interviews, we identified four main areas of focus for the company in the next years, summarized as follows: digitization; energy sector; production and services; and business and technology. Subsequently, these business priorities were deployed in terms of specific requirements and KSAs and were clustered into generic/transversal, job-specific, and managerial competencies. In this chapter, the results are presented in a summarized and narrative version to give the reader an overview of the outcomes the company obtained through the implementation of a systematic competency-based methodology.

Data revealed that, in the long run, the company would go through an increasing need for services related to products updating and upgrading during their life cycle. As a consequence, it is necessary to develop a good product and system understanding. Moreover, the company is moving from selling products to selling solutions, integrating different systems. To implement this change of perspective effectively, an increase of technical capabilities of all professionals is required, and particularly for salespeople to have a better technical understanding of the solutions sold. Furthermore, the focus on solutions also requires competencies in process understanding and process design.

One element emerged as a crucial factor in sustaining servitization is the need for professionals that have both the business understanding and technical capabilities, can combine different disciplines, and have a strong ability to think at the system level. There is the need to combine the business and engineering acumens to ensure that the technical experts have also a business mindset and can think strategically, while the business experts possess technical capabilities and can understand the products and solutions of the company. The strategic mindset is a crucial characteristic; employees will need it for all business functions, especially to understand how to enter new businesses and conduct market analysis. Also, the ability to use and adapt technology to create new businesses and improve operational effectiveness is strongly required.

The central element will be the customer value and centricity. The company is selling full solutions that need to bring value to the customer. The key competence to meet this requirement is the ability to understand how to create value for the customers. This is possible combining a very deep technical understanding, that allows implementing a value-based selling, and a positive attitude toward clients, understanding their interests and points of view.

Furthermore, it is important to develop competencies in big data analysis in order to provide the company crucial information to customize solutions and products on the basis of customers' needs. For instance, understanding customers' needs allows the firm to operate cost-effectively. Moreover, digitizing the delivery chain, sharing information with the customer, and planning the delivery time would add value to the customer. Therefore, the ability to maintain the relationship with the customer is a key element in the value creation process.

In order to meet these requirements, generic/transversal competencies are considered crucial within the organization to work effectively. In particular, communication among people and team members is considered a key element to maintain a good working climate. The communication includes the ability to build relationships and to understand people. Another important element is the ability to select and extrapolate the information needed out of a discussion, avoiding misinterpretations and stereotypes. Moreover, it is important to develop employees' presentation skills regarding the ability to summarize and prioritize information and transmitting the message clearly to impact the audience.

Today, the work dimension is the team. Therefore, employees need to be able to work in groups, collaborating and cooperating with colleagues, developing effective reporting skills and the capacity to share information and responsibility. The core of teamwork is the ability to combine different expertizes and competencies profitably.

The case company operates in a global environment; employees need to be prepared to work in global networks as well as in a virtual environment. Therefore, employees need to develop social skills in a virtual environment, as well as the awareness and understanding of the multicultural context in which the communication occurs. Indeed, the knowledge and skills regarding *cultural intelligence* are much recommended to work efficiently in global networks. Furthermore, the ability to speak different languages is very well recommended to facilitate the relationship with the customer and to tear down the barriers between the seller and the customer.

Regarding the promotion and maintenance of a good organizational and group climate, employees need to have a good approach toward learning and the right attitude toward change, developing a mindset that enables the change. Being open, questioning and challenging the findings and facts is crucial to working efficiently in the organization as well as the stress management and agility in programming and managing the work in critical situations, when people need to find solutions and revise their plan fast.

The basics of negotiations and the ability to sell ideas internally and externally are well recommended as well as a good attitude toward problem-solving. In the next years, firms will need professionals with different characteristics in different areas. There will be the need for professionals with a strong technical background and solid knowledge in their field "experts," as well as the need for more adaptable and flexible professionals with extrovert and communicational personality, who are able to create new business occasions, to lead teams, and to bring innovations into the organization.

The work in the company is becoming more and more project-oriented. Therefore, the service employee should have a flexible way of working, changing fast and working with uncertainty. Moreover, working on projects requires the capability of bringing and adapting the individual way of working to the project, sharing it with all the project members.

The results of the interviews show that the manager in service-based organizations will still need a deep technical understanding but will not be the best expert on the team anymore. Indeed, he or she will need to have the ability to lead and guide the group, uncover their potential, and foster the creation of a good work environment. Moreover, the manager will be a team member. Indeed, the managerial model will not be hierarchic and centralized anymore, but it will be based on autonomy and shared responsibilities among the group members.

The manager will coach people, challenge them and give them the opportunity to develop and implement their competencies. He/she will have a support function enabling others to work efficiently. He/she should be capable of motivating and empowering people. For this reason, good communication skills, adopting new ways of sharing information, and the ability to listen to people and understand their needs are important. Moreover, the manager of service-based organizations is approachable by people and able to transmit trustworthiness even when absent.

An interesting aspect arisen is related to problem-solving. Indeed, the manager will not provide answers to problems but will create the circumstances and support problem-solving within the group, as well as he/she will involve people in decision-making.

Social skills will be crucial for managers in leading the team, for instance, empathy in understanding people's needs and in respecting diversity has been stressed as a fundamental aspect. Indeed, respondents highlighted that promoting the success of an organization is not only about completing tasks but also about the individuals behind the tasks. Therefore, the manager should be able to adapt his/her style to people's characteristics. In fact, there can be team members who might need more micromanagement and guidance, and other members who like to work with grater authonomy.

Last but not least, the manager in service-based organizations should have a good business acumen, with a global vision about business, and the ability to combine different factors. Strategic thinking and planning will be the key elements in order not only to run the business today but also to develop it for tomorrow.

12.4 Conclusion

Despite the considerable amount of research on servitization, the implementation of competency methods as tools for the realignment of organizational and individual competencies to the new business needs remains little explored. Throughout the years, scholars stressed the importance of the integration of competency methods and business planning processes as leverage to emphasizing future emerging competencies to facilitate and accelerate the change (Athey & Orth, 1999). Nevertheless, this topic still finds little room for application in the everyday business life, where companies usually invest a huge amount of resources in the initial phase of competencies analysis neglecting the importance of sustaining the implementation of the competency models in the long run (Campion et al., 2011). Therefore, this chapter offers to companies undertaking the servitization journey an integrated and flexible approach to help managers in the translation of the business strategy in future competencies requirements, ensuring the development of capabilities proper of services and solutions. Furthermore, the practical case presented in this chapter can guide companies through a more efficient use of competencies in the servitization process, as well as points out a pattern of competencies arisen in the case company analysis that can be adaptable to other organizational contexts.

References

Athey, T. R., & Orth, M. S. (1999). Emerging competency methods for the future. *Human Resource Management, 38*(3), 215–225.

Baines, T. S., Lightfoot, H. W., Evans, S., Neely, A., Greenough, R., Peppard, J., … Alcock, J. R. (2007). State-of-the-art in product-service systems. *Proceedings of the Institution of Mechanical Engineers, Part B: Journal of Engineering Manufacture, 221*(10), 1543–1552.

Barney, J. (1991). Firm resources and sustained competitive advantage. *Journal of Management, 17*(1), 99–120.

Campion, M. A., Fink, A. A., Ruggeberg, B. J., Carr, L., Phillips, G. M., & Odman, R. B. (2011). Doing competencies well: Best practices in competency modeling. *Personnel Psychology, 64*(1), 225–262.

Dai, G., & Liang, K. (2012). Competency modeling research and practice in China: A literature review. *Journal of Chinese Human Resources Management, 3*(1), 49–66.

Davis, S. M. (1983). Corporate culture and human resource management: Two keys to implementing strategy. *Human Resource Planning, 6*(3), 159–167.

Fleury, A., & Tereza Fleury, M. (2003). Competitive strategies and core competencies: Perspectives for the internationalisation of industry in Brazil. *Integrated Manufacturing Systems, 14*(1), 16–25.

Gotsch, M., Hipp, C., Erceg, P. J., & Weidner, N. (2014). The impact of servitization on key competences and qualification profiles in the machine building industry. In *Servitization in Industry* (pp. 315–330). Springer International Publishing.

Gow, K., & McDonald, P. (2000). Attributes required of graduates for the future workplace. *Journal of Vocational Education and Training, 52*(3), 373–396.

Gratton, L., Hope-Hailey, V., Stiles, P., & Truss, C. (1999). Linking individual performance to business strategy: The people process model. *Human Resource Management, 38*(1), 17–31.

Homburg, C., Fassnacht, M., & Guenther, C. (2003). The role of soft factors in implementing a service-oriented strategy in industrial marketing companies. *Journal of Business to Business Marketing, 10*(2), 23–51.

Iles, P. (2001). Employee resourcing. In J. Storey (Ed.), *Human resource management: A critical text* (pp. 133–164). London: Routledge.

Kandola, R., & Pearn, M. (1992). Identifying competencies. In R. Boam & P. Sparrow (Eds.), *Designing and achieving competency* (pp. 31–50). London: McGraw-Hill.

Kaplan, R. S., & Norton, D. P. (2005). The office of strategy management. *Strategic Finance, 87*(4), 8.

Kaplan, R. S., & Norton, D. P. (2006). How to implement a new strategy without disrupting your organization. *Harvard Business Review, 84*(3), 100.

Lahti, R. K. (1999). Identifying and integrating individual level and organizational level core competencies. *Journal of Business and Psychology, 14*(1), 59–75.

Lawler, E. E. (1994). From job-based to competency-based organizations. *Journal of Organizational Behavior, 15*(1), 3–15.

Neu, W. A., & Brown, S. W. (2005). Forming successful business-to-business services in goods-dominant firms. *Journal of Service Research, 8*(1), 3–17.

Oliva, R., & Kallenberg, R. (2003). Managing the transition from products to services. *International Journal of Service Industry Management, 14*(2), 160–172.

Paiola, M., Saccani, N., Perona, M., & Gebauer, H. (2013). Moving from products to solutions: Strategic approaches for developing capabilities. *European Management Journal, 31*(4), 390–409.

Rabetino, R., Kohtamäki, M., & Gebauer, H. (2017). Strategy map of servitization. *International Journal of Production Economics, 192*, 144–156.

Robinson, M. A., Sparrow, P. R., Clegg, C., & Birdi, K. (2007). Forecasting future competency requirements: A three-phase methodology. *Personnel Review, 36*(1), 65–90.

Rodriguez, D., Patel, R., Bright, A., Gregory, D., & Gowing, M. K. (2002). Developing competency models to promote integrated human resource practices. *Human Resource Management, 41*(3), 309–324.

Sanchez, J. I., & Levine, E. L. (2009). What is (or should be) the difference between competency modeling and traditional job analysis? *Human Resource Management Review, 19*(2), 53–63.

Shippmann, J. S., Ash, R. A., Batjtsta, M., Carr, L., Eyde, L. D., Hesketh, B., … Sanchez, J. I. (2000). The practice of competency modeling. *Personnel Psychology, 53*(3), 703–740.

Sparrow, P. R. (1997). Organizational competencies: Creating a strategic behavioral framework for selection and assessment. In N. Anderson & P. Herriot (Eds.), *International handbook of selection and assessment* (pp. 343–368). Chichester: John Wiley.

Vakola, M., Eric Soderquist, K., & Prastacos, G. P. (2007). Competency management in support of organizational change. *International Journal of Manpower, 28*(3/4), 260–275.

Wise, R., & Baumgartner, P. (1999). Go downstream: The new profit imperative in manufacturing. *Harvard Business Review, 7*, 133–141.

13

BI-in-Practice: A Look at How BI Enacts Framing Contests and Affects the Service Transition Path

Yassine Talaoui

13.1 Introduction

Today, the convergence of cloud computing, Web 3.0, social media, video content, Internet of things, industry 4.0, and big data promises a surge in the frequency of change facing the business environment (Heisterber & Verma, 2014). In response to such a shaky context, industrials convert their old manufacturing business models into ones that offer customized solutions to end-users, in an attempt to sustain growth or secure higher margins (Matthyssens & Vandenbempt, 2008; Sawhney, 2006). This transition, dubbed servitization (Vandermerwe & Rada, 1988), is writ large a transformational process conducive to organizational change (Benedettini, Neely, & Swink, 2015; Kowalkowski, Brehmer, & Kindström, 2009). It requires various technological drivers (Gephart, 2004); of which, business intelligence (BI) tops most IT budgets (Gartner Press, 2014). Unfortunately, when the dominant culture

---

Y. Talaoui (✉)
University of Vaasa, Vaasa, Finland
e-mail: Yassine.talaoui@uva.fi

(manufacturing) and counter-culture (service) engage in making sense of BI, inertia or implementation failure takes over signaling the clash of two cultures (Gebauer, Fleisch, & Friedli, 2005). Notwithstanding this, the servitization research seems more focused on exploring the role of IT as a catalyst or booster of servitization (e.g., Kowalkowski & Brehmer, 2008; Kowalkowski, Kindström, & Gebauer, 2013), rather than understanding what causes the clash when the two cultures make sense of BI.

As any process of change, servitization adheres to an interpretative process (Barr, 1998; Davidson, 2006) in which the manufacturing and service cultures rely on their schemata of interpretations to make sense of BI as they socially construct a new reality, that is, the service transition (Berger & Luckmann, 1967). Besides, BI is the sum of technologies that comprise multiple features that can be utilized independently from one another as one sees fit, which in turn can generate different outcomes (Burton-Jones & Straub, 2006; Leonardi, 2013). Therefore, neither culture will use BI in the same manner. Instead, both the manufacturing and service cultures will view BI differently based on the choices they make about using its features (Leonardi, 2013; Markus & Silver, 2008). In a nutshell, each of the cultures has its assumptions, attributes, and needs that shape the way it uses BI, whereas BI offers features that shape the way the manufacturing and service mindsets think about and make use of it (Leonardi, 2013; Markus & Silver, 2008). In light of the preceding elements, this chapter pictures servitization as an interpretive process during which BI shapes and gets shaped by the manufacturing and service units' interpretations of reality as both mindsets think about and use BI to fulfill the service transition. This chapter brings to fore the notion of BI-in-practice to shed light on the bundle of human and technology that interact to support servitization. This motivation emanates from the evidence suggesting that technologies-in-practice encourage social interactions among actors with different interpretations of reality (Orlikowski, 2000), which in turn yields contestations over meaning and generate unintended outcomes (Orlikowski & Gash, 1992). Therefore, this chapter presents a conceptual discussion that addresses two questions: (1) how BI enacts contests when the manufacturing and service cultures interact with BI to support servitization? And (2) what happens to the service transition path when BI enacts the framing contests?

13.2 BI and the Enactment of Framing Contests

When firms transition to services, the manufacturing and service cultures often clash (Gebauer et al., 2005). A culture, nevertheless, is an enacted reality that was socially constructed by people drawing on their schemata of interpretations or frames of reference to interpret, experience, and plan action (Orlikowski & Gash, 1994; Brummans et al., 2008). Therefore, an analysis of frames of reference of both cultures uncovers how meaning forms as people of both cultures make sense of BI (Orlikowski & Gash, 1994). These schemata are termed technological frames of reference (TFR) and refer to *the subset of actors' frames that concern the assumptions, expectations, and knowledge they use to comprehend technology...and includes not only the nature and role of the technology itself, but the specific conditions, applications, and consequences of that technology...* (Orlikowski & Gash, 1994, p. 178). In this vein, Fig. 13.1 draws on Galbraith's (2002) study of product-centric (manufacturing) versus customer-centric (service) cultures to illustrate the TFR that guide the way the manufacturing and service units make sense of BI and act upon it (Orlikowski & Gash, 1994). In light of these differences in the respective TFR of manufacturing and service cultures, what follows is a discussion of the conflicts in expectations and actions about BI as the two cultures make sense of BI during servitization.

The TFR of manufacturing and service mindsets regarding the way they think about and use BI fall into three domains. First, the *nature of BI*, which answers the question of what images of BI and understanding of its features and utility people hold. Second, the BI *strategy*, which answers the question of what do people think motivated the adoption of BI and its relative value. Third, the *BI in use*, which answers the question of how people view the daily use of BI and its associated outputs

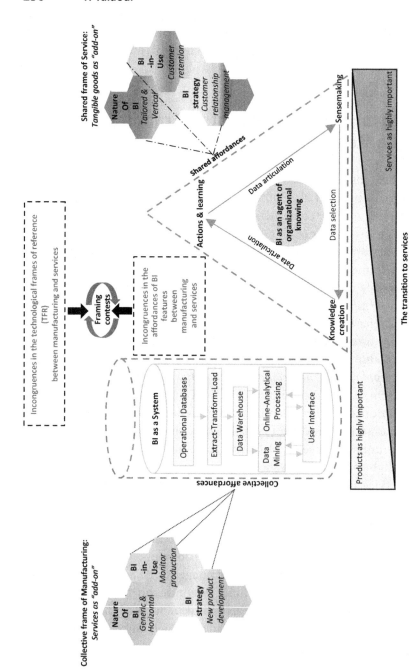

Fig. 13.1 The incongruences causing framing contests as manufacturing and service units shape and gets shaped by BI during servitization. The author's elaboration based on Davidson, 2002; Leonardi, 2013; and Orlikowski & Gash, 1994

(Orlikowski & Gash, 1994). The domains of TFR indicate that BI in manufacturing is generic and horizontal across the organization, as opposed to service culture where BI is synonymous with a vertical solution that is tailored to facilitate the service function (Galbraith, 2002). In manufacturing, BI is adopted to develop new products and improve existing ones.

In services, though, BI is implemented to improve customer relationship management and seek new business opportunities (Galbraith, 2002). BI in use also reveals incongruences between manufacturing and service cultures. In the former, BI is used daily to monitor indicators of production efficiency (e.g., number of new products, % of revenue from products, and market share). In service culture, BI usage aims customer retention through a daily search for expressed and latent customer needs, and customization of the best combination of products to meet customers' needs (Galbraith, 2002). The above-mentioned incongruences—that ensue from thinking about BI and interacting with it (Pinch & Bijker, 1987)—represent the first cause of contests between the manufacturing and service cultures as their assumptions, attributes, and needs shape the way they use BI in servitization (Orlikowski & Gash, 1994).

Furthermore, while people can perceive the technology features, the utility of that technology hinges upon the goals, needs, and behavior of the person considering it (Gibson, 1986). Therefore, the utility of the technology does not depend solely on the technology or the human but the relational interaction between both as technologies offer features and humans choose to appropriate the ones they believe propel action (Leonardi, 2013; Markus & Silver, 2008). This idea is termed "affordances" and represents the way people choose to appropriate certain features of technology (IT use) if they feel such technology offers them affordances (utility) to act upon (Leonardi, 2013; Markus & Silver, 2008). In this case, BI as a technology used by a group of people can offer various affordances to each one of them and thereby each one will enact a different affordance or a combination of affordances as they utilize it (Davern, Shaft, & Te'eni, 2012; Kaptelinin & Nardi, 2006). In this regard, for the manufacturing and service environments, the number of features of BI will generate two different group-level affordances described in Fig. 13.1 as collective and shared affordances (Leonardi, 2013).

A collective affordance is collectively enacted by a group to accomplish something they could not do otherwise (Leonardi, 2013). This type of affordance is often created in environments such as manufacturing where interdependence is limited, and tasks are performed at the individual level then combined to generate the outcome (Leonardi, 2013; Thompson, 1967). The manufacturing environment is characterized by a configurational structure of technology use, that is, group members use BI at maybe the same frequency but in different ways as different BI features offer multiple affordances that might benefit the various tasks they are involved in (Leonardi, 2013). In such a context, a traditional application of BI dominates a system that supports decision-making (Shollo & Galliers, 2016). Accordingly, BI offers manufacturers a formal rational mechanism that integrates internal and external data, analyzes and conceives intelligence out of it, then communicates it through the user interface that offers the option to manipulate it as the business user sees fit (Chaudhuri, Dayal, & Narasayya, 2011). While the BI system relies on an intertwined bundle of technologies, each user will enact affordances they believe are conducive to their task. For instance, planners might use the data mining engine to run predictive analyses of different scenarios, while product designers may see more affordances in the online analytic processing (OLAP) to slice and dice the data for a benchmark of their existing product line with that of competitors. Operational users, on the other hand, will likely utilize the relational database management system (RDBMS) to rapidly execute queries across internal data to quickly eliminate bottlenecks and maintain a lean production.

In contrast, *a shared affordance* occurs in environments like service business where group members use technology in the same way because their work environment involves high reciprocal interdependence and thus necessitates a high degree of interaction, dependability, and coordination to accomplish the project (Guzzo & Shea, 1992; Leonardi, 2013). In the service business, the structure of use is shared as group members use BI at the same frequency and share the same affordances about it, which in turn help them enact the same capabilities and coordinate efficiently to achieve group goals (Leonardi, 2013). Accordingly, BI arises as an agent, which thanks to its practices of data selection and articulation orchestrates an ad infinitum process of organizational knowing that ranges from sensemaking to knowledge creation and learning (Choo, 2002; Shollo & Galliers, 2016). Following this rationale, BI offers a high capability of data scrutiny that when combined with the interpretations of users can articulate new distinctions across variables that call for comparison, which in turn crystallize common patterns across the different interpretations of users and help them formulate factual hypotheses (Shollo & Galliers, 2016). As a result, BI helps users articulate their gut feelings into acceptable claims by offering them a legitimate format that promotes dialogues and contestations while drilling down into low-level data and rolling up for the high-level ones (Schultze, 2000; Shollo & Galliers, 2016). During this interaction, individuals add meaning to data via the cyclical practices of data selection and articulation where the former produces knowledge, whereas the latter adds meaning to it by uncovering patterns across multiple interpretations, which in turn yields knowledge sharing (Shollo & Galliers, 2016). Only then, organizational learning can commence, and actions can ensue (Shollo & Galliers, 2016). In sum, the incongruences between the types of affordances manufacturing and services enact from BI features represent the second cause of contests between manufacturing and services as BI features shape the way the two mindsets make use of it during servitization (Orlikowski & Gash, 1994).

13.3 BI and the Unintended Outcomes of Servitization

As a change process, servitization (intentionally or unintentionally) shapes or is shaped by the collective frames of groups involved in it (Bartunek & Moch, 1987). This happens because existing collective frames are difficult to alter and influence the way people perceive, interpret, act, and commit to the change (Tichy, 1974). In this vein, old manufacturing collective frames that might turn obsolete and inadequate when servitization occurs will most likely continue to guide the sensemaking of change agents, which in turn will generate conflictual situations and constrain the transformation process and generate unintended outcomes (Orlikowski & Gash, 1992). What follows is an attempt to delineate how such deviation unfolds and at what stage of servitization.

The foregoing literature indicates that organizational change occurs through two hierarchical forms: first-order change and second-order change (e.g., Bartunek & Moch, 1987; Orlikowski & Gash, 1992). The first type of change is an incremental modification of existing collective assumptions and frames that happens within and seeks to reinforce an established modus operandi; the second order of change is a radical modification of collective frames that seeks to reverse the status quo (Bartunek & Moch, 1987; Orlikowski & Gash, 1992). It is worth mentioning though that these orders are non-sequential and vary according to the context of the focal organization, that is, environment, organization, structure, or organizational agents (Orlikowski & Gash, 1992). Therefore, this chapter views servitization as a first-order change based on ample evidence suggesting that service infusion follows an incremental migratory path (Kowalkowski, Kindström, Alejandro, Brege, & Biggemann, 2012; Matthyssens & Vandenbempt, 2008). Afterward, I juxtapose the typology of change outcomes (Orlikowski & Gash, 1992) against the service transition stages (Oliva & Kallenberg, 2003) to examine the nature of change that unfolds during the three stages of servitization (consolidating product-related services, entering the installed base service market, and expanding to relationship-based services). Based on evidence from Oliva and Kallenberg's (2003) study of 11 German capital equipment manufacturers transitioning to services, Fig. 13.2 presents an index of change outcomes (aligned intended, partial intended, and unintended). This index assesses the nature of outcomes ensuing from the manufacturing and service framing contests that BI enacts (Orlikowski & Gash, 1992).

13.3.1 Stage 1: Consolidating Product-Related Services

The idea here is that since most manufacturers offer services to undergird their products, they only need to consolidate their existing service base under a separate unit as a starting point for servitization (Oliva & Kallenberg, 2003). This step is often motivated by a willingness to integrate fragmented services to boost product sales and enhance customer

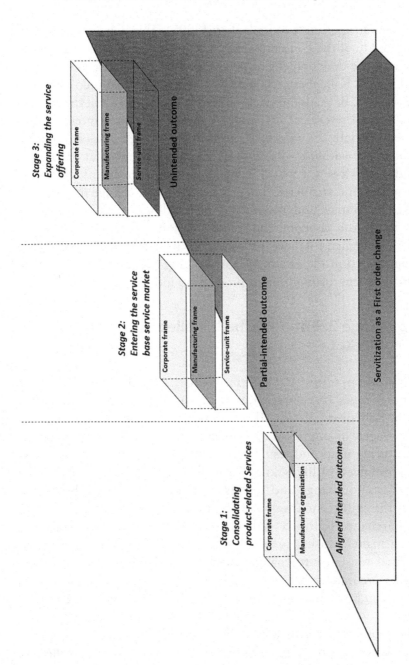

Fig. 13.2 The types of changes that unfold as collective frames of manufacturing resist the change of servitization. The author's own elaboration based on Oliva & Kallenberg, 2003 and Orlikowski & Gash, 1992

satisfaction ratings (Oliva & Kallenberg, 2003). This step emanates from a strong desire of the corporate unit to improve the delivery of services offered and the development of new ones to diversify the services provided (Oliva & Kallenberg, 2003). During the consolidation of product-related services, BI is adopted to monitor service delivery and the share of services in total revenues. This stage generates an aligned intended outcome because both the corporate and manufacturing frames are congruent. This stage witnesses a dominant corporate frame that intends to consolidate services, for which it enjoys support, agreement, and commitment from the manufacturing unit since the new change rhymes with its collective frames and necessitates no modification in the existing frames to fit the concomitant transformation (Oliva & Kallenberg, 2003). This aligned intended outcome also reflects a traditional understanding, rooted in the existing manufacturing frames, of BI usage as a horizontal system for monitoring production indicators.

13.3.2 Stage 2: Entering the Installed Base Service Market

When a new opportunity for profit emerges, organizations experience different changes (processes or structures) to fit the service market (Oliva & Kallenberg, 2003). This new reality, however, jeopardizes the previous degree of alignment and agreement between the corporate and manufacturing units and results in a partial-intended outcome following two instances (Orlikowski & Gash, 1992). First, the manufacturing group resists to change and retains its pre-change frames because it involves the shift from a frame of equipment design to a one of repair and maintenance (Oliva & Kallenberg, 2003). Further, the collective frames of manufacturing centered on the notion of services as add-ons fuel further resistance to change when it senses the need for a shift to new collective frames that view goods as add-ons (Oliva & Kallenberg, 2003). Second, the new service unit exhibits collective frames that fit the change intended by the corporate and sees its BI system run as a separate profit center (Oliva & Kallenberg, 2003). Further alignment emerges as the corporate guards the service unit against the collective frames of manufacturing to develop an efficient service organization and expand its installed base service market.

13.3.3 Stage 3: Expanding to Relationship-Based Services

Once a fully operational service unit is put in place, expanding to relation-based services then follows via two transitions: from transaction to relationship contracts and from product efficacy to process-oriented services (Oliva & Kallenberg, 2003). The transition toward relationship contracts is rooted in a wish to capitalize on the separate service unit and augment its capacity utilization (Oliva & Kallenberg, 2003). This scenario engenders an unintended outcome as the service unit accepts the change but perceives it as incongruent with its collective frames for the new transition requires the outsourcing of its maintenance function and a lengthy process of establishing enduring relationships with the end-user. This incongruence also dictates a shift in BI usage from one that offers affordances to track inventory and repairs to another that monitors customer relationship management. Likewise, the transition toward process-oriented services shifts the focus from the product at the heart of the value proposition to the product as part of the end-user's process (Oliva & Kallenberg, 2003). This scenario also generates an unintended outcome as the new collective frames centered on solutions attempt to supplant the existing collective frames of manufacturing (Oliva & Kallenberg, 2003). Both instances suggest a high likelihood for the existing collective frames of manufacturing and services to engage in a different vision from the one initially intended by the corporate.

13.4 Conclusion

Servitization is a complex and iterative process that implies a shift in mindsets toward a service-enthusiastic culture (Gebauer et al., 2005; Homburg, Fassnacht, & Guenther, 2003). There exists, nonetheless, a chasm among scholars regarding the best form of initiating a service-oriented culture with minimum internal challenges (Storbacka, Windahl, Nenonen, & Salonen, 2013). While some suggest that a separate service unit would infuse service orientation without disrupting the manufacturing culture (Oliva & Kallenberg, 2003), others recommend cross-functional integration between units to dodge organizational conflicts between the product and service units (Kindström, Kowalkowski, & Nordin, 2012; Storbacka et al., 2013). Notwithstanding this, both scenarios eventually witness more interactions between the service and manufacturing units, which in turn might translate into a clash between a dominant culture (manufacturing) and counter-culture (service) and veer the organization from the service transition path toward "the service paradox" (Gebauer et al., 2005). In response, this chapter follows the steps of Orlikowski (2000) and presents the notion of BI-in-practice to shed light on BI as a material artifact that could trigger sensemaking of people and stimulate action (Garreau, Mouricou, & Grimand, 2015; Jarzabkowski & Kaplan, 2015). The key word here is "stimulate action" which hints that the importance of artifacts lays in the outcomes they produce through their usage (Jarzabkowski & Kaplan, 2015). Accordingly, this chapter demonstrates that when two divergent mindsets (manufacturing and service) make sense of BI and act upon it the result is meaning contests and unintended outcomes (Orlikowski & Gash, 1992). In this vein, this chapter examines the usage of BI in the context of servitization. Particularly, the way BI influences and gets influenced by the manufacturing and service mindsets in the dynamics of sensemaking. In this regard, this chapter uncovers two sources of framing contests that arise as the manufacturing and service mindsets interact with BI. First, the incongruences across the three domains of TFR ensue when the manufacturing and service units think about BI and interact with it. Second, the incongruences between the types of affordances manufacturing and services enact as they use BI. Accordingly, the service transition process involving the manufacturing and service cultures is unlikely to occur unless both groups converge on a shared appropriation of BI features (Leonardi, 2013). Put differently, each time the two cultures fail to realize the affordances BI provides jointly, the service transition will witness unintended outcomes at the installed base service market (Oliva & Kallenberg, 2003).

References

Barr, P. (1998). Adapting to unfamiliar environmental events: A look at the evolution of interpretation and its role in strategic change. *Organization Science, 9*, 644–669.

Bartunek, J. M., & Moch, M. K. (1987). First-order, second-order, and third-order change and organization development interventions: A cognitive approach. *The Journal of Applied Behavioral Science, 23*(4), 483–500.

Benedettini, O., Neely, A., & Swink, M. (2015). Why do servitized firms fail? A risk-based explanation. *International Journal of Operations & Production Management, 35*(6), 946–979.

Berger, P., & Luckmann, T. (1967). *The social construction of reality*. New York: Anchor Books.

Brummans, B., Putnam, L., Gray, B., Hanke, R., Lewicki, R. J., & Wiethoff, C. (2008). Making sense of intractable multiparty conflict: A study of framing in four environmental disputes. *Communication Monographs, 75*(1), 25–51.

Burton-Jones, A., & Straub, D. W. (2006). Re-conceptualizing system usage: An approach and empirical tests. *Information Systems Research, 17*(3), 228–246.

Chaudhuri, S., Dayal, U., & Narasayya, V. (2011). An overview of business intelligence technology. *Communications of the ACM, 54*(8), 88.

Choo, W. C. (2002). Sensemaking, knowledge creation, and decision making: Organizational knowing as emergent strategy. In C. W. Choo & N. Bontis (Eds.), *Strategic management of intellectual capital and organizational knowledge* (pp. 79–89). Oxford: Oxford University Press.

Davern, M., Shaft, M., & Te'eni, D. (2012). Cognition matters: Enduring questions in cognitive IS research. *Journal of the Association for Information Systems, 13*, 273–314.

Davidson, A. (2002). Technology frames and framing: A socio-cognitive investigation of requirements determination. *MIS Quarterly, 26*(4), 329–358.

Davidson, E. (2006). A technological frames perspective on information technology and organizational change. *The Journal of Applied Behavioral Science, 42*(1), 23–39.

Galbraith, J. R. (2002). Organizing to deliver solutions. *Organizational Dynamics, 31*(2), 194–207.

Garreau, L., Mouricou, P., & Grimand, A. (2015). Drawing on the map: An exploration of strategic sensemaking/giving practices using visual representations. *British Journal of Management, 26*(4), 689–712.

Gartner Press. (2014). *Predicts 2014: Don't try to prevent the digital revolution, exploit IT now*. Gartner, Inc.

Gebauer, H., Fleisch, E., & Friedli, T. (2005). Overcoming the service paradox in manufacturing companies. *European Management Journal, 23*(1), 14–26.

Gephart, R. (2004). Sensemaking and the new media at work. *American Behavioral Scientist, 48*, 479–495.

Gibson, J. J. (1986). *The ecological approach to visual perception L.* Hillsdale, NJ: Lawrence Erlbaum.

Guzzo, R. A., & Shea, G. P. (1992). Group performance and intergroup relations in organizations. In M. D. Dunnette & L. M. Hough (Eds.), *Handbook of industrial and organizational psychology* (pp. 269–313). Palo ALto, CA: Consulting Psychologists Press.

Heisterber, R., & Verma, A. (2014). *Creating business agility*. Hoboken, NJ: Wiley.

Homburg, C., Fassnacht, M., & Guenther, C. (2003). The role of soft factors in implementing a service-oriented strategy in industrial marketing companies. *Journal of Business to Business Marketing, 10*(2), 23–51.

Jarzabkowski, P., & Kaplan, S. (2015). Strategy tools-in-use: A framework for understanding "technologies of rationality" in practice. *Strategic Management Journal, 36*(4), 537–558.

Kaptelinin, V., & Nardi, B. A. (2006). *Acting with technology: Activity theory and interaction design*. Cambridge, MA: MIT Press.

Kindström, D., Kowalkowski, C., & Nordin, F. (2012). Visualizing the value of service- based offerings: Empirical findings from the manufacturing industry. *Journal of Business & Industrial Marketing, 27*(7), 538–546.

Kowalkowski, C., & Brehmer, P. O. (2008). Technology as a driver for changing customer-provider interfaces. *Management Research News, 31*(10), 746–757.

Kowalkowski, C., Brehmer, P. O., & Kindström, D. (2009). Managing industrial service offerings: Requirements on content and processes. *International Journal of Services Technology and Management, 11*(1), 42.

Kowalkowski, C., Kindström, D., Alejandro, T. B., Brege, S., & Biggemann, S. (2012). Service infusion as agile incrementalism in action. *Journal of Business Research, 65*(6), 765–772.

Kowalkowski, C., Kindström, D., & Gebauer, H. (2013). ICT as a catalyst for service business orientation. *Journal of Business & Industrial Marketing, 28*(6), 506–513.

Leonardi, P. M. (2013). When does technology use enable network change in organizations? A comparative study of feature use and shared affordances. *MIS Quarterly, 37*(3), 749–776.

Markus, M. L., & Silver, M. S. (2008). A foundation for the study of IT effects: A new look at DeSanctis and Poole's concepts of structural features and spirit. *Journal of the Association for Information Systems, 9*(10), 609–632.

Matthyssens, P., & Vandenbempt, K. (2008). Moving from basic offerings to value-added solutions: Strategies, barriers and alignment. *Industrial Marketing Management, 37*(3), 316–328.

Oliva, R., & Kallenberg, R. (2003). Managing the transition from products to services. *International Journal of Service Industry Management, 14*(2), 160–172.

Orlikowski, W. J. (2000). Using technology and constituting structures: A practice lens for studying technology in organizations. *Organization Science, 11*(4), 404–428.

Orlikowski, W. J., & Gash, D. C. (1992). *Changing frames: Understanding technological change in organizations*. Center for Information Systems Research, Sloan School of Management, Massachusetts Institute of Technology, (236), 1–48.

Orlikowski, W. J., & Gash, D. C. (1994). Technological frames: Making sense of information technology in organizations. *ACM Transactions on Information Systems, 12*(2), 174–207.

Pinch, T., & Bijker, W. (1987). The social construction of facts and artifacts. In W. E. Bijker, T. P. Hughes, & T. J. Pinch (Eds.), *The social construction of technological systems* (pp. 17–50). Cambridge, MA: MIT Press.

Sawhney, M. (2006). Going beyond the product: Defining, designing and delivering customer solutions. In R. F. Lusch & S. L. Vargo (Eds.), *The service dominant logic of marketing dialogue debate and directions* (pp. 365–380). New York: M.E. Sharpe.

Schultze, U. (2000). A confessional account of an ethnography about knowledge work. *MIS Quarterly, 24*(3), 3–41.

Shollo, A., & Galliers, R. D. (2016). Towards an understanding of the role of business intelligence systems in organisational knowing. *Information Systems Journal, 26*(4), 339–367.

Thompson, J. D. (1967). *Organizations in action: Social science bases of administrative theory*. New York: McGraw-Hill.

Tichy, N. (1974). Agents of planned social change: Congruence of values, cognitions, and actions. *Administrative Science Quarterly, 19*, 164–182.

Vandermerwe, S., & Rada, J. (1988). Servitization of business: Adding value by adding services. *European Management Journal, 6*(4), 314–324.

14

Managing Risks for Product-Service Systems Provision: *Introducing a Practical Decision Tool for Risk Management*

Wiebke Reim, Vinit Parida, and David R. Sjödin

14.1 Introduction

Providing product-service systems (PSS), however, entails increased risks for manufacturing companies as they shift from pure transaction to relational engagements with customers, assume operational responsibilities for customers' processes, and engage in value co-creation (Meier, Roy, & Seliger, 2010; Reim, Parida, & Sjödin, 2016). In the context of PSS, providers are exposed to new types of risks at a significantly higher level, which are not fully understood. Prior studies have mentioned increased risk frequently and have noted that companies' inability to manage risks is the central issue prohibiting the PSS transition (Meier et al., 2010). However, detailed insights into different PSS-related risks continue to be a limited and largely neglected area of research (Erkoyuncu, Roy, Shehab, & Cheruvu, 2011). The unsolved view on risk has resulted in

W. Reim (✉) • V. Parida • D. R. Sjödin
Luleå University of Technology, Luleå, Sweden
e-mail: wiebke.reim@ltu.se; vinit.parida@ltu.se; david.ronnberg.sjodin@ltu.se

managers and executives becoming increasingly receptive to risk considerations; they lack a clear understanding of what constitutes risks and how they can be managed. The key to providing PSS successfully lies in systematically managing identified risks by implementing diverse risk management approaches.

Advancing the general understanding of PSS risk management requires matching different PSS operational risks to potential risk management responses. The ability to do so largely depends on identifying key decision-making criteria. In this chapter, we conceptualize and develop a PSS risk management decision support tool for PSS offers that can enable manufacturing companies to provide PSS successfully.

The practical purpose of the proposed tool is to effectively and proactively consider different contingencies related to PSS operation and match the potential risks with risk management responses (Erkoyuncu et al., 2011; Steven, 2012). The tool contributes to management practices by integrating insights of practical challenges for PSS provision with theoretical considerations from the risk management and decision-making literatures.

14.2 Theory

14.2.1 Risk for PSS Operation

Prior studies have highlighted that reducing risk for customers is the most common reason for adopting PSS (Meier et al., 2010; Sakao, Rönnbäck, & Sandström, 2013). The assumption that customers want more reliability and are willing to pay extra (i.e., a risk premium) for the reduced risk has driven providers to engage in PSS (Roy and Cheruvu, 2009). However, this implies that the risks for the providers will increase significantly (Ng, Ding, & Yip, 2013; Reim et al., 2016).

In PSS, several authors have identified various risks but without providing a holistic picture. Primarily, authors focus on unexpected breakdowns of the product (Erkoyuncu et al., 2011; Sakao et al., 2013; Steven, 2012), which leads to increased repair and maintenance costs (Meier et al., 2010) and other penalties. This view dominates because moving towards PSS usually implies that the provider is responsible for repairs and breakdowns, which is a new situation for most of them.

Other risk factors that are not yet well understood but are gaining increasing attention relate to unintended and adverse customer behaviour (Roy and Cheruvu, 2009). This can include less careful behaviour when using a product that the customer does not own. Examples include overloading or other extensive usage that has a negative impact on the condition of the product (Reim et al., 2016; Tukker, 2004). Opportunistic behaviour is another example of adverse behaviour, which occurs when the customer has no incentives to limit the providers' efforts and thus tries to maximize personal benefits (Ng et al., 2013). Adverse selection is another type of unintended customer behaviour that arises when a customer only buys PSS for the machinery that is prone to breakdown and the provider therefore ends up with a portfolio of unprofitable PSS agreements (Tukker, 2004).

Finally, risk can also be related to the company's competence and capability to provide the agreed-upon product service to customers. This is important for PSS because the company must acquire numerous new capabilities and resources to be able to offer PSS (Parida, Rönnberg-Sjödin, Wincet, & Ylinenpää, 2013). In many cases, the provider partly takes over the customer's operations, and the customer is therefore extremely dependent on the reliability of the PSS offered (Meier et al., 2010; Sakao et al., 2013). Thus, far more risks are relevant to PSS than only unexpected breakdowns. An increased understanding of such risks during the early development stages can enable improved risk analysis to reduce the complexity and ambiguity associated with both identifying and managing risk (Erkoyuncu et al., 2011).

14.2.2 Risk Management for PSS Operation

Although the field of risk management has matured over the last decades, the literature on risk management within PSS is still in a nascent stage (Meier et al., 2010). Risk management can be defined as a logical and continuous process consisting of three main steps: identifying risks, choosing the risk response strategy, and monitoring the outcomes (Dorfman, 1998). Prior literature has identified four main approaches or methods to respond to risks: risk avoidance, risk reduction, risk sharing or transfer, and risk retention (Dorfman, 1998; Rejda, 2005). Avoidance would mean evading all possibilities that the risk or loss can occur. For PSS, this could implicate to exclude certain customers or markets from the PSS offering when risks are deemed fatal. Risk reduction includes activities that reduce the frequency or severity of the loss (Dorfman, 1998). Reducing PSS risks can be reached by improved quality (Tukker, 2004), proactive risk mitigation activities (Romero Rojo, Roy, Shehab, & Wardle, 2009), and good data and information handling; for example, from sensors (Roy and Cheruvu, 2009; Steven, 2012). Risk reduction is usually connected to increased resource levels (e.g., more spare parts in stock or more technicians available).

Another approach related to risk sharing or transfer (e.g., insurance agreements) applies to cases in which the risks are completely or partly borne by someone else, including customers, retailers, or delivery partners (Parida, Sjödin, Wincent, & Kohtamäki, 2014; Rejda, 2005). In PSS, risk sharing is seen as a very important and effective method because with the right contract it can also create incentives for all parties to act as agreed upon (Caldwell and Settle, 2011). Finally, the fourth approach, risk retention, represents the situation where the provider bears all or certain risks and attempts to profit from retaining that risk by pricing the offering accordingly. This so-called risk premium is one of the reasons PSS has the potential to increase profits significantly (Tukker, 2004). This is the case because the provider is often better equipped to handle certain risks by pooling them together (Roy and Cheruvu, 2009).

In summary, several studies within the PSS literature have addressed issues of different risk responses, but the existing PSS risk management literature to date covers only limited aspects. As such, many researchers identify risk management for PSS as an important future research area, often discussed together with developing appropriate contracts and decision support (Meier et al., 2010). Hence, we argue that increased knowledge about the link between PSS risks and responses can help identify decision criteria to support risk management in PSS.

14.3 PSS Risk Management Decision Tool Development

14.3.1 Case Study Description

The present study is based on an exploratory single case study involving a global Swedish manufacturing company (hereafter Alpha) and eight of their global distributors that offer PSS. This research design was chosen because there is limited knowledge about PSS risk management and the decision-making criteria that affect the choice of risk response (Yin, 2013). This method allowed us to identify new aspects and phenomena derived from reality, in the context of a PSS risk management strategy. Alpha was chosen as the case company because of its long experience with PSS provision and operations in global markets. In particular, Alpha has directed significant attention to risk management due to its global operations and need to manage high diversity in customer requirements and value chain configurations. Furthermore, Alpha has undertaken significant steps to restructure the organization and processes to ensure successful PSS operations to global markets. Thus, Alpha represents an appropriate case for the present exploratory study.

Alpha is a global provider of construction equipment, and it conducts sales through internal and independent dealers globally. Currently, it offers several services in addition to its machines, including maintenance contracts, extended warranties, up-time services, and close attention to error codes and fuel consumption, as well as advanced services such as an agreed-upon availability level which is the main focus of this study. In total, we interviewed 32 respondents from different departments and distributors who have been actively involved in the current PSS development and operation at Alpha.

The present study's research approach was qualitative and based on semi-structured and open-ended interviews. The interview guide was designed to explore what risks the respondent perceived as most important in PSS operation as well as identifying possible risk management strategies to capture possible risk responses. The data analysis was based on open-coding content analysis where headings were written into the transcriptions based on different risks that were mentioned. The preliminary results of the present study were shared at the validation workshop, and the participants commented and added to the findings.

14.3.2 Empirical Findings on Operational PSS Risks

Our empirical findings clearly illustrate the importance of identifying and managing risks for Alpha and the term *risk* occurs everywhere in internal company conversations. But not all risks receive the same priority. These unexpected technical problems were identified as the first and major risks related to PSS. This risk also has an information-based aspect, because you need to know what is broken or might break when offering availability. Several respondents emphasized that getting accurate and reliable information at the right time is essential to offering a business model that promises a certain availability of the machine.

Although technical risks are most obvious and analysed, there are additional significant risks that the respondents highlighted. A global product manager noted that there is a risk that the customer always uses a machine very hard with the consequence that the machine will break quite soon. This described risk is a typical behavioural risk where customers behave less carefully if they do not own or are not responsible for the machine. Almost all respondents provided possible examples of behavioural risks such as overloading or careless behaviour.

Other respondents, for example, from the process planning for product services, saw major risk on the delivery competence side of the company. However, the financial loss is not the only aspect considered when looking at the risk of not delivering as agreed because you also lose the customer's trust in your competence when not performing as agreed upon. In summary, three risk categories are clearly visible at Alpha: *technical risks*, *behavioural risks*, and *delivery competence risks*.

Table 14.1 summarizes the characteristics of the identified risk categories and also shows some initial considerations about how the risks can be mitigated.

Table 14.1 Operational PSS risks

	Technical risk	Behavioural risk	Delivery competence risk
Characteristics	• Most acknowledged risk • Provider is in charge of unexpected breakdown • Dependent on reliable data	• Less careful product treatment from the customer • Opportunistic behaviour • Adverse selection	• Lack of capability and capacity to provide the offer • Decreased trust when agreement cannot be fulfilled
Mitigation alternatives	• High degree of monitoring • High resource levels	• Monitoring • Trust building • Customer segmentation	• High resource levels • Slow implementation • Training on provider side

14.3.3 Empirical Findings on PSS Risk Management

To manage the above-mentioned risks, many methods are in use or considered. Based on risk management theory, we categorize these methods into the four main risk response strategies: risk avoidance, risk reduction, risk sharing or transfer, and risk retention. These risk response strategies all present a way to mitigate risk but with different focus on limiting the risk or to back up for the results of the risk. In the following, all four are considered based on their appropriateness for PSS.

Avoiding all the risks related to PSS operation is almost impossible and would more or less lead to not providing PSS when the risks cannot be handled in a different way. With the help of customer segmentation, however, it is possible to filter customers that are not appropriate for PSS offerings. Technical or behavioural risks could possibly be avoided when the company does not have any responsibility for the current condition of the machine. For some PSS contracts, the risks can also be avoided when the dealer is selling the contract and has the responsibility. However, avoiding the risks is not possible when offering availability and is not one of Alpha's preferred strategies, because they, as the risk-bearing party, see the opportunity to make a profit off being good at handling the risk.

A lot of effort is devoted to *reducing* risks at Alpha, but the respondents also highlighted that it is important to consider that the costs for reduction should not be higher than the savings. We identified two general activities that help reduce operational PSS risk. First, reduction can be accomplished with the help of information and communication technology (ICT) (e.g., sensors or telematics systems) by collecting all the data necessary to monitor and organize the PSS. This, for example, would facilitate the reduction of technical risks by being proactive. To enable preventive maintenance, it is important to have the capability to collect and analyse the information from remote monitoring or analysis (e.g., oil analysis). One way to reduce behavioural risk is to have tracking tools such as a telematics system that identifies unintended customer use (e.g., overload or speeding). This should be done in combination with contracts that put obligations on the customers and exclude responsibility for failures that the customer causes. Well-working information systems reduce the delivery competence risk through better scheduling of service activities with access to technicians and spare parts in time. For these systems to work, it is crucial that all information is reliable in order to ensure that proactive maintenance and repairs are only performed where it is necessary.

Second, increased resource levels can significantly reduce PSS risks. Having additional spare parts or reserve machines reduces the impact of a breakdown because repairs can be performed quickly, and operations can continue with a reserve machine if necessary. Additional service personnel would increase the ability for good customer relations, because if they have more time for each customer, and close, trusting relationships can be developed that would reduce behavioural risks. Accordingly, delivery competence risks can be significantly reduced by increasing the resources are available to fulfil the PSS. It is critical, however, to compare the increased costs with the expected savings from such risk reduction.

The impact of the PSS risks can also be managed by either establishing risk and revenue-*sharing* agreements with the customer or *transferring* the risk to an insurance company. At Alpha, risk sharing, combined with profit sharing, is often discussed in relation to PSS operation. This creates incentives for both parties to perform as per agreement, and they both equally gain from successfully complying with the agreement. Risk sharing works well to manage technical risks, because the cost for machine breakdowns is shared, and the financial impact for the provider is much less. It works even better to cope with behavioural risks, as cost sharing creates incentives for the customer to behave properly; otherwise, there will be additional costs for the customer. Risk sharing to avoid delivery competence risks would work in a way such that additional availability percentages can be transferred to the next period and offset possible longer down times during that time.

Although risk sharing sounds great in theory, it brings a lot of complications that need to be handled carefully. The first complication relates to the percentages on which the sharing is based in order to make it an attractive option. A major problem, however, is that customers shy away from complicated contracts and may prefer to buy the machine without a service or availability agreement. The respondents also pointed out that it is hard to develop a sharing model for availability contracts because costs for fulfilling the agreement are much lower in the beginning and increase over time as the machine becomes older and the savings in the beginning would be needed to balance later losses.

The second strategy mentioned above is to transfer the risks to an insurance company. All the risks and the higher costs that are accrued when unexpected events occur can be transferred to special insurance companies. Even though this is possible, it cannot only be evaluated positively, a regional product manager pointed out that it sends negative signals to the dealers and customers if Alpha gives away the responsibility to someone else. Therefore, insurance companies are not the perfect solution but should be considered carefully in terms of whether they can manage the risks for a better price than the provider company can.

Our findings suggest that there are two types of activities that are related to risk *retention* in PSS. The first is risk pricing, and the second is customer segmentation. Risk retention may be the most convenient solution for the customers if they are willing to pay a certain risk premium to make it possible for the provider to take all the risks. The reason for doing this is that the provider company is much better equipped to pool the risks. To assume the risks, it is very important to have the capability to calculate an appropriate price that is neither too low, to cover the risks, nor too high that you will lose customers. Various aspects need to be considered while calculating the price, and this can become very difficult. Another problem is that the provider company has unlimited risks, and if those are too drastic, risk retention may not be the most favourable strategy.

Customer segmentation is a very important activity with regard to risk retention, because risk retention may only be feasible in certain cases. When the provider wants to retain the technical risk, it is suitable to only offer PSS for standardized machines with good historical data in order to calculate an accurate price. Similar arguments are valid for retaining behavioural risks. Similarly, our respondents suggested that PSS only be offered to loyal customers and not to new, unknown ones. This is accurate due to the established, trustful relationship that will prevent adverse behaviour, but also because of experience with the application among those customers for which they are using their machines. In terms of delivery competence risk, it is important to consider the geographical characteristics of the machine application (e.g., remote areas or constantly shifting locations) in order to ensure sufficient coverage of the services.

In Table 14.2, we summarize the findings of this section by presenting the characteristics of each risk management method in PSS as well as by stating the advantages and disadvantages of each method.

14.3.4 PSS Risk Management Decision Tool

The empirical results show that an important condition for risk management is the choice of the appropriate risk response (or set of risk responses) depending on the identified risks in each situation. Our analysis of the data discloses six key decision criteria that were found to influence the selection of the appropriate risk response in a given situation for PSS operation. These criteria are further connected to the three overarching risks associated with PSS operation found in the case study. Moreover, taking a more integrative approach, we are able to identify interconnections between the identified risks, criteria, and risk management response. This enables us to conceptualize and outline a decision tree (see Fig. 14.1), which can act as a PSS risk management decision tool.

Table 14.2 PSS risk management

	Risk avoidance	Risk reduction	Risk sharing/transfer	Risk retention
Characteristics	• Not providing PSS or not having responsibility for the condition of the machine	• Decreased probability of the risks through data collection and monitoring • Increased resource levels enable faster remedy of the risks	• Risks can be shared with the customers • Risks can be transferred to insurance companies	• Customer pays a risk premium that covers the risks • Provider balances good with bad agreements
Advantages	• No risks	• Better control of processes • Data can be used for future improvements	• Creates incentives for the customers • Costs for the risks are easier to calculate	• Provider captures all money from performing well • Based on a trust relationship
Disadvantages	• Not using the potential of PSS offers	• High costs • Resource intensive	• Bad signals to customers • No incentives for provider to perform well	• Provider bears all risks and costs • Only possible to establish with trusted customers

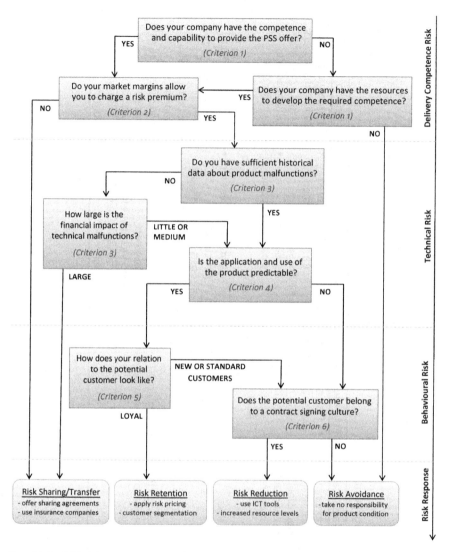

Fig. 14.1 PSS risk management decision tree

In an ideal situation for the provider, the appropriate risk response should be risk retention combined with risk reduction methods. However, such ideal situations are not always feasible. The *first criterion* in the decision tree relates to the resources and capabilities for providing the

PSS. This risk represents the inability of a company to offer the agreed-upon outcome, which can result in inhibiting manufacturing companies from successfully offering product services. Our results imply that to offer availability, it is crucial to have the competence to provide the necessary product services quickly and efficiently. This requires access to service delivery personnel with the appropriate skills and development of service routines. We argue that in situations in which such resources are absent or limited, PSS operation is not recommended.

The *second criterion* highlights the importance of considering market characteristics, especially based on the revenue margins that can be charged for certain offerings. Without sufficient possibilities to charge the customer for services, the company will not be able to deliver PSS profitably. In this sense, market margins affect the ability to offer PSS successfully. Therefore, risk retention works better in markets where providers can charge a high margin and the customer values the reduction of risks through the PSS offer. In low-margin markets, it will not be possible to charge a sufficient risk premium, and risks should be shared with the customer instead or transferred; for example, to an insurance company.

The product type is the *third criterion* that influences the risk response. This criterion is clearly connected to the technical risk, because it indicates how serious risks are for the breakdowns and other technical issues for the specific product. For a new or custom-made product with limited historical data, it is difficult to predict how well the product will perform. For products where limited historical knowledge exists about the quality of new products or the serviceability of specialized products, risks should be shared with the customers, especially when the financial impact of technical malfunction is serious. For standardized, high-volume products, it is much easier to calculate costs for product failures and their frequency; therefore, it is much more applicable to reduce or retain risks for such products.

Furthermore, the application of the product also affects risk management. This *fourth criterion* connects to technical risks as they affect the frequency of breakdowns and malfunctions. If the product is used for tough applications or longer durations, the risks are much higher and uncontrollable compared to easy or predictable work tasks. Hence, provided the impact of the application can be predicted sufficiently, it is possible to retain the risk. If that is not the case, a different response must be considered for those products.

The *fifth criterion* is the previous relationship to the customer. This criterion is related to behavioural risks, as it indicates the probability of unintended behaviour. Offering PSS to a new, unknown customer includes many more risks compared to a loyal, long-term customer, because the provider is aware of the application and use of the machines among familiar customers. Therefore, it is recommended that providers be more careful with new customers. For loyal customers, it is suitable to assume the risk, because the risk can be calculated reliably, and extensive contracts could damage the valuable customer relationship. For sporadic customers, it could be beneficial to bind them in agreements with lower risk such as service agreements and monitoring obligations (e.g., oil analysis) to reduce risks and obtain closer contact and thus provide the possibility of improving the relationship over time.

The *last criterion* is the culture of the customers with regard to contract-signing behaviour. Because contractual safeguards are so important for PSS provision, it is necessary to find customers who are willing to sign contracts. Without appropriate contracts, the potential for opportunistic behaviour is much greater. Consequently, when operating in regions or markets where signing contracts is not part of the normal exchange routine, the provider should be careful with PSS provision. It may be easiest in such situations to get paid upfront or not to take responsibility for the product's operating condition. With customers who belong to cultures that are accustomed to signing contracts, risk reduction mechanisms can be agreed upon to establish safeguards of unintended behaviour.

When using the proposed PSS risk management framework, it is important to remember that although the decision tree leads to a specific risk response (e.g., risk reduction, risk retention), it does not mean that the company should exclusively focus on that particular risk management strategy. Rather, the outcome of following the decision tree suggests a risk management strategy that should be given the most weight in a certain situation. Accordingly, a company may use all the risk management strategies in a given situation. Depending on the importance of different risks (e.g., behavioural, technical), certain risk management strategies may be used more widely. In particular, the combination of risk retention and risk reduction should be considered because the more the risks can be reduced, the fewer risks the company must assume. Furthermore, one fact that was until now ignored in the literature and which our decision support framework highlights is the importance of considering risk avoidance by not offering PSS, but offering it only with limited service components or by excluding certain customer segments from the offer.

14.4 Managerial Conclusions

For managers, responsible for developing and operating PSS offerings, it is especially important to realize that risk management is a vital activity that extends beyond technical risks that lead to breakdowns of the product to also include risks related to customer behaviour and insufficient competence at the providers' end (e.g., service delivery network). Our categorization of operational risks into technical, behavioural, and delivery competence risks structures the fragmented discussion of risks in PSS and represents a major step towards establishing a framework for assessing operational risks and risk management in the context of PSS. This is especially important because providers generally need to assume increased operational risks when providing PSS, which represents a key barrier towards their full-scale PSS transformation.

In addition, the present study establishes an overview of risk management strategies for PSS operation. Specifically, we have adapted four generic risk responses to the PSS context that are commonly discussed in the risk management literature (e.g., Dorfman, 1998; Rejda, 2005) and propose new insights into how different risk responses are used to manage each of the three PSS operational risk categories. In certain instances, the risks of offering PSS can be so significant that the only sensible action is to avoid the risks by not offering PSS at all. In most cases, however, it will be possible to handle the risks effectively by applying selected risk management strategies. The most convenient and potentially profitable way is to opt for risk retention by charging a risk premium. However, risk retention requires advanced skills in calculating offers as well as developing complex contractual agreements with customers. Moreover, risk retention also presumes significant attention towards risk reduction. However, a key point to highlight is that risk reduction needs to be balanced with its related costs, for it may, in certain cases, lead to more work without adequate benefits. Risk sharing can be efficient when making contracts with new customers or when new machines are involved. However, because risk sharing complicates the relationship with customers, it should only be used to establish a relationship or to develop sufficient skills to offer business models that include risk reduction or retention.

Finally, a major contribution of the present chapter is to identify and explain the key decision criteria that provide guidance to selecting an appropriate risk response. To guide the choice of the right risk response, the identified six criteria were combined in a decision tool. These criteria are resources for service provision, market characteristics, product type, product application, customer relations, and customer culture. The more a criterion leads to a predictable situation, in which the cost of the risks can be calculated by the provider, the more appropriate a strategy based on risk retention becomes. Identifying the criteria shows and motivates which factors affect PSS offering and also highlights the areas in which further consideration in relation to PSS operations is needed. This will help decision-makers critically evaluate their risk management strategies. Thus, the present chapter adds to the ongoing discussion on the contingency aspects of PSS (Kohtamäki, Partanen, Parida, & Wincent, 2013), underlining in which situations offering PSS is advantageous in order to advance financial performance.

References

Caldwell, N. D., & Settle, V. (2011). Incentives and contracting for availability: Procuring complex performance. In *Complex engineering service systems* (pp. 149–162). London: Springer.

Dorfman, M. S. (1998). *Introduction to risk management and insurance*. Pearson Higher Ed.

Erkoyuncu, J. A., Roy, R., Shehab, E., & Cheruvu, K. (2011). Understanding service uncertainties in industrial product–service system cost estimation. *The International Journal of Advanced Manufacturing Technology, 52*(9–12), 1223–1238.

Kohtamäki, M., Partanen, J., Parida, V., & Wincent, J. (2013). Non-linear relationship between industrial service offering and sales growth: The moderating role of network capabilities. *Industrial Marketing Management, 42*(8), 1374–1385.

Meier, H., Roy, R., & Seliger, G. (2010). Industrial product-service systems—IPS 2. *CIRP Annals-Manufacturing Technology, 59*(2), 607–627.

Ng, I. C., Ding, D. X., & Yip, N. (2013). Outcome-based contracts as new business model: The role of partnership and value-driven relational assets. *Industrial Marketing Management, 42*(5), 730–743.

Parida, V., Rönnberg-Sjödin, D., Wincet, J., & Ylinenpää, H. (2013). Win-Win collaboration, functional product challenges and value-chain delivery: A case study approach. *Procedia CIRP, 11*, 86–91.

Parida, V., Sjödin, D. R., Wincent, J., & Kohtamäki, M. (2014). Mastering the transition to product-service provision: Insights into business models, learning activities, and capabilities. *Research-Technology Management, 57*(3), 44–52.

Reim, W., Parida, V., & Örtqvist, D. (2015). Product–Service Systems (PSS) business models and tactics—A systematic literature review. *Journal of Cleaner Production, 97*, 61–75.

Reim, W., Parida, V., & Sjödin, D. R. (2016). Risk management for product-service system operation. *International Journal of Operations & Production Management, 36*(6), 665–686.

Rejda, G. E. (2005). *Risk management and insurance.* Person Education Inc.

Romero Rojo, F. J., Roy, R., Shehab, E., & Wardle, P. J. (2009). Obsolescence challenges for product-service systems in aerospace and defence industry. In *Proceedings of the 19th CIRP design conference–competitive design.* Cranfield University Press.

Roy, R., & Cheruvu, K. S. (2009). A competitive framework for industrial product–service systems. *International Journal of Internet Manufacturing and Services, 2*(1), 4–29.

Sakao, T., Rönnbäck, A. Ö., & Sandström, G. Ö. (2013). Uncovering benefits and risks of integrated product service offerings—Using a case of technology encapsulation. *Journal of Systems Science and Systems Engineering, 22*(4), 421–439.

Steven, M. (2012). Risk management of industrial product-service systems (IPS2)–How to consider risk and uncertainty over the IPS2 lifecycle? In *Leveraging technology for a sustainable world* (pp. 37–42). Springer Berlin Heidelberg.

Tukker, A. (2004). Eight types of product–service system: Eight ways to sustainability? Experiences from SusProNet. *Business Strategy and the Environment, 13*(4), 246–260.

Yin, R. K. (2013). *Case study research: Design and methods*. Sage publications.

Part IV

Solution Sales and Co-creation in Servitization

15

Selling Solutions by Selling Value

Pekka Töytäri

15.1 Introduction

Global competition, access to information, and industrial imitation even out competitive differences in increasingly short cycles, forcing selling firms to innovate differentiating products, services, and solutions to stay ahead of competition. A very visible outcome of the quest for differentiation and competitive advantage has been the service transformation of industrial companies. Service transformation brings about a rather fundamental change of business logic, offerings, relationships, structures, management, incentives, capabilities and resources, and most organizational functions, specifically sales. Not surprisingly, firms have found it difficult to implement such comprehensive change. Despite the challenge, the organizational ability to sell solutions by proactively demonstrating the life-cycle value of the solutions is one of the crucial goals to

P. Töytäri (✉)
Department of Industrial Engineering and Management, Aalto University School of Science, Espoo, Finland
e-mail: pekka.toytari@aalto.fi

achieve. Unfortunately, sales and sales management literature provide little support for the transformation.

In this chapter, I develop a solution selling framework of activities, goals, and tools, focusing on the distinctive features of the proactive value selling. I position selling as a concurrent and connected activity to organizational buying. Organizational buying is defined as a tool to implement changes that improve organizational performance toward business goals. I also illustrate the capability development activities preceding the actual customer engagement. To support the managers implementing the change, I illustrate the broader business cultural drivers of the change, including the barriers that impede the change, inside organizations and within the connected ecosystem of customers and suppliers.

15.2 The Change of Business Logic

Selling and buying are both strongly influenced and directed by the beliefs and norms of the actors engaged in the exchange (Thornton, Ocacio, & Lounsbury, 2012). Industrial buying has been strongly influenced by an approach that emphasizes transactional efficiency, product-based exchange, and independence for value capturing power. Value-based solution selling (Töytäri & Rajala, 2015), however, requires different supporting business logic to succeed. Selling and implementing a solution requires information exchange, evaluation of alternatives based on value created, and leads to a joint value creation engagement. The established industrial supply management practices often prioritize short-term transactional efficiency instead of long-term life-cycle value, sets purchasing criteria on optimizing price or capital expenditure over value-in-use or operational expenditure, seeks strong negotiation position by decomposing solutions to constituting elements for easy comparison, and prioritizes short-term value capture over long-term value creation. The solution vision is often developed based on internal knowledge rather than leveraging a broader knowledge base by involving the supply network. The value sharing (pricing) reference is quite exclusively "cost+" rather than the actual value created. However, despite the challenges, most firms and industries are investing in developing new capabilities and resources to support value-based strategies to escape the "commodity trap," improve value creation, and build stronger networks for competitive differentiation, to highlight some examples of the potential benefits. For an illustrative example, I label the competing approaches to industrial exchange and relationships as "product logic" and "solution logic," and I highlight the differences in Table 15.1.

The value-based solution selling builds on the solution logic, while much of industry operates under the product logic. This collision of logics clearly makes solution selling and value-based relationships difficult to achieve and manage. The change from the product logic to solution logic is equally difficult to achieve. Research has found a multitude of barriers to change at individual, firm, and industrial levels, including established beliefs and attitudes, experience and current skills, and the high cost and complexity of value-based approach. Similarly, product-oriented sales culture, prevailing managerial practices, incentives, IT systems, organizing principles, and other organization-level barriers impede change (Töytäri, Keränen, & Rajala, 2017). In the following, I illustrate some of the key solution selling related challenges, which directly influence the activities and goals of the solution selling process discussed later.

First, digitalization of industrial operations enables novel services that leverage the production data for diagnostics, operational control, predictive maintenance, performance benchmarking within a global fleet of

Table 15.1 Key differences between value capture and value creation-focused strategies

Key dimensions	Product logic	Solution logic
Exchange focus	Transaction	Relationship
Optimization focus	Exchange value (e.g. capex)	Use value (e.g. capex and opex)
Exchange scope	Product	Solution
Temporal focus	Short-term	Long-term
Relationship logic	Independence for value capturing power	Partnership for joint value creation
Initiator	Buyer	Seller
Market phase	Commoditized	Innovation
Solution vision	Buyer's	Jointly created
Value sharing reference	Supplier cost	Customer value

equipment, and similar. Those new services are, indeed, new to the customer. Hence, there is no active demand for the new services and no active understanding of the business benefits of the services. This "no active demand" situation puts all the responsibility on the sellers to motivate the buyers to proceed. Second, if the sellers get lucky and successfully convince the buyers about the value of the initiative, the next hurdle relates to the implementation of the value creating solution itself. Most often, the value creation by services and solutions involves a re-allocation of activities, business processes, or even complete operations from customers to suppliers. However, customers frequently find this service outsourcing of giving up on resources and activities risky in many ways, and hence it is a decision that is hard to take. Third, in contrast to the product-based exchange, the solution-based value creation engages the suppliers (and possibly other firms) in managing a joint business process, which requires new levels trust, common goals, information exchange, and sharing of risk and profit. Hence, suppliers need to offer credible and compelling evidence of the business benefits to overcome the barriers to change. Value-based solution selling must be and is designed to offer the evidence.

15.3 The Buying Perspective

Individuals and organizations buy to achieve their goals. All action is motivated by goals. Organizations and broader business ecosystems are built around goal achievement; organizations are social structures to support the collaborative pursuit of specified goals (Scott & Davis, 2016). Goals guide decision-making by providing criteria for selecting among alternatives. If set correctly, goals help recognizing and selecting those value creation opportunities that provide the highest potential value. Organizational goals are negotiated and set by powerful stakeholders (Cyert & March, 1992). Firms then devise business models, organizational structures, management systems, IT systems, and incentives to mobilize action toward the set goals. Organizational structures also reflect goals. Organizations can be portrayed as goal hierarchies.

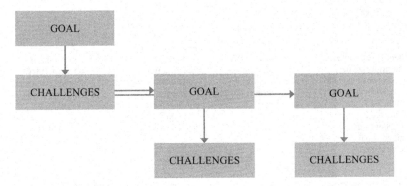

Fig. 15.1 An example of a goal hierarchy, where higher level challenges determine lower level goals

Goal analysis reveals challenges that impede achieving the goals. The identified challenges are then delegated as goals for the next organizational level. Continuing this process through all the organizational levels generates a goal hierarchy that spans the entire organization (see Gutman, 1982; Woodruff, 1997; Zeithaml, 1988). See Fig. 15.1 for an illustration.

The quest for achieving goals (by overcoming the identified challenges) initiates renewal of an organization, manifested as buying activities. The early buying activities include determining, evaluating, and prioritizing the gap between the current situation and the desired future situation. Once the gap is sufficiently large to motivate and justify action, the actor(s) involved engage in developing a vision of the solution that achieves the goal by overcoming the challenges within the given constraints. Once the solution vision is detailed enough for comparing and matching with available alternatives, a search for market alternatives is commenced. The solution vision is often adapted based on the new information on available alternatives. The rational part of the decision-making promotes a solution that maximizes value. Finally, the solution is chosen, and the roles, responsibilities, terms, and conditions that determine the value co-creation arrangement are agreed upon. Pricing, or more broadly, the value sharing among the contributing actors, is

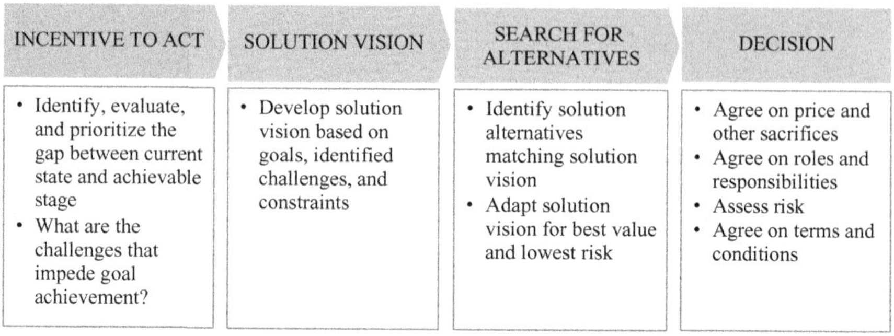

INCENTIVE TO ACT	SOLUTION VISION	SEARCH FOR ALTERNATIVES	DECISION
• Identify, evaluate, and prioritize the gap between current state and achievable stage • What are the challenges that impede goal achievement?	• Develop solution vision based on goals, identified challenges, and constraints	• Identify solution alternatives matching solution vision • Adapt solution vision for best value and lowest risk	• Agree on price and other sacrifices • Agree on roles and responsibilities • Assess risk • Agree on terms and conditions

Fig 15.2 The goal-driven buying process, adapted from Eades (2004), Rackham and DeVincentis (1999), Töytäri (2015)

agreed upon. Figure 15.2 illustrates the goal-driven buying process and the key activities within the process.

15.4 The Selling Perspective

The value-based solution selling is closely aligned with the organizational buying process, including activities that match the buying process activities. Key value selling activities explore customer goals, challenges, and constraints, and build a solution that addresses the goals and challenges within constraints, build on supplier strengths, quantify and communicate solution value, develop the value constellation to implement and operate the solution, and agree on terms of the arrangement, including pricing.

Value selling activities can be classified into three categories. (1) Relationship activities identify actors with influence, goals, and receptivity, and develop those relationships to enable information exchange and value communication. (2) Value activities develop, adapt, communicate, and quantify value to influence customer's incentive to proceed and solution vision. (3) Control activities gain commitments and devise shared plans to keep the buying and selling processes synchronized and aligned. Of these, I focus on the value process.

The above describes only the final implementation part of value selling. Proactive influencing must be planned for. Much of the value-based influencing builds on understanding and mapping customer segments' business processes and analyzing the processes for improvement opportunities. See, for instance, Bettencourt and Ulwick (2008) for an illustration of a customer value research method. Gaining customer insight is a crucial new capability of value-based solution selling, which creates a foundation for developing impactful value propositions. Specifically, customer insight is also a capability that highlights the differences between product logic and solution logic. Product-based exchange is quite possible without customer understanding, but solution-based exchange is not, simply because the solution-based value creation involves the supplier in the value creation process. Value proposition development is then grounded in the knowledge achieved during the insight process. The planning activities mobilize the value proposition for the sales organization by developing tools for value proposition communication, including success stories, value calculators, and benchmarking studies (Töytäri & Rajala, 2015). Figure 15.3 suggests a framework for value-based selling. The framework includes three stages from gaining customer insight to engaging in joint value creation. Each stage includes a selection of value-based solution selling specific activities. I discuss these steps next.

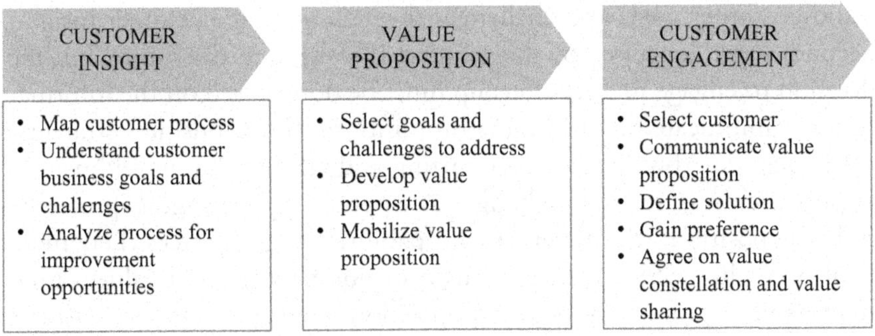

CUSTOMER INSIGHT	VALUE PROPOSITION	CUSTOMER ENGAGEMENT
• Map customer process • Understand customer business goals and challenges • Analyze process for improvement opportunities	• Select goals and challenges to address • Develop value proposition • Mobilize value proposition	• Select customer • Communicate value proposition • Define solution • Gain preference • Agree on value constellation and value sharing

Fig. 15.3 The framework for value-based solution selling

15.4.1 Customer Insight

Gaining customer insight seeks to understand and analyze customer activities to identify opportunities for improvement. In most areas of industrial activity, gaining customer insight focuses on (a) understanding and mapping a customer's business processes and (b) a customer's situation, goals, challenges, and associated key performance indicators. The goal of the business process mapping is to explore identifiable "pains" in the process as well as innovate improvement opportunities enabled by, for instance, new technology (such as the digital transformation), re-allocation of activities by service outsourcing, and (obviously) re-designing the process.

15.4.2 Value Proposition

Value propositions are the seller's primary tools to motivate a joint value creation opportunity (Anderson, Narus, & van Rossum, 2006; Vargo & Lusch, 2008). Value propositions are communicated, adapted, quantified, and ultimately verified (see Töytäri and Rajala (2015) for discussion on post-implementation value verification) to communicate value creation opportunities and to initiate business relationships. Many current change drivers amplify the importance of value propositions in the context of solution selling. First, value creation through solutions takes place increasingly as a result of collaboration in the customer's "value space" (Adegbesan & Higgins, 2011), putting pressure on suppliers to understand customer goals and challenges through gaining customer insight. Second, value generated by the solution is realized in the future, but the decision to engage in a relationship must be done based on the information communicated by the value proposition. Third, business strategies are increasingly building on recognizing and effectuating novel business opportunities as service exchange, as opposed to leveraging protected industry positions or differentiated capabilities and resources (Lengnick-Hall & Wolff, 1999). Hence, focus is on joint creation of value, rather than value capture only. Value propositions that quantify the business impact of novel opportunities likely determine the managerial attention those opportunities receive. Finally, the digitalization of economic activity disrupts established business models, shakes established power positions, promotes networked value creation, and greatly supports transparent value assessment (Kagerman, Helbig, Hellinger, & Wahlster, 2013). To gain management attention, value proposition needs to address timely and salient business drivers and (preferably) link to measurable key performance indicators. Salient criteria for evaluating the economic impact of the identified "pains" and "gains" include (a) revenue impact, (b) cost impact, (c) impact on asset efficiency (or return on capital employed), and (d) impact on risk and risk distribution.

15.4.2.1 Select Goals and Challenges

The business process analysis often identifies improvement opportunities. In an industrial setting those include such benefits as reduced energy consumption, higher production volume, improved resource efficiency, improved quality, reduced planned and unplanned production stops, and similar. Those value elements identified by the value research are not identical in importance. At least two value selection criteria are rather compelling: (1) impact on goal. Rather obviously, large financial rewards are more interesting than small ones. Suppliers and customers need to apply value quantification for each identified value dimension to determine the potential (financial) impact on key business performance indicators. Those value elements that have the biggest potential impact on business goals are then included in the value proposition. (2) Supplier differentiation: suppliers likely have differing capabilities and resources to create value. Suppliers should incorporate those value dimensions in their value propositions that differentiate themselves from competition (Anderson et al., 2006).

15.4.2.2 Develop Value Proposition

Investigation of the industrial value propositions reveals what value propositions are made of. Consider the following definition of a value proposition.

> *Value propositions are bundles of benefits that address business goals of specific target groups and offer significant value for the customer. Value propositions*

must help in differentiating from alternatives and resonate with the stakeholder's value views by addressing timely and salient business challenges.

Value propositions are expected to communicate value toward customer goals, explicate the business challenges that are addressed, and differentiate the supplier and the solution from the alternatives. These elements of the value proposition emerge from the need to connect to and influence the organizational buying process during the early stages of organizational buying. Figure 15.4 illustrates the connection.

Consider also the attached example of an industrial value proposition. The example is deduced from the actual value communication tools that the firm employs to mobilize its value proposition. The value proposition explicates three benefits (metal recovery, energy, and maintenance) and quantifies and aggregates the economic impact of the innovation.

A global supplier of mining and metals processing solutions has innovated an improved solution for their copper flotation process. Compared with their older technology, the new solution improves minerals recovery percentage, reduces energy consumption, and lowers maintenance cost. While the actual revenue improvement and cost saving are site specific, in an example case, an achievable two percentage unit recovery improvement equaled to two million euros in

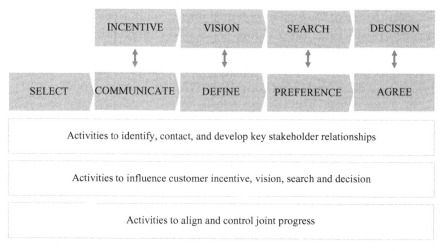

Fig. 15.4 Buying and selling process alignment

additional revenue. Correspondingly, a 50% reduction in energy cost equaled to EUR 100,000 savings, and a 50% decrease in maintenance costs equaled to EUR 50,000 yearly saving in maintenance expenditure.

15.4.2.3 Mobilize Value Proposition

Value propositions are embedded into and communicated by marketing messages, reference stories, and value calculators, in increasing order of customer specificity and impact. These value communication means greatly improve the influence and efficiency of value communication by leveraging wider organizational knowledge that is integrated and orchestrated by the sales force. In the past, the industrial marketing messages have been highly product-focused, reflecting their product logic (see Fig. 15.1). However, firms engaging in solution business are actively developing databases of success stories to influence customers at the different stages of their buying processes. Success stories seek to create urgency to act by demonstrating value creation opportunities and outcomes and to influence customer goals and challenges during the "pressure to act" phase. They also seek to build credibility during the "search" phase. Then, value calculators are tools for analyzing the value creation potential in a specific customer situation, using the customer's own data, goals, and identified challenges in adapting and quantifying the value proposition. Firms are increasingly building visually and technically sophisticated tools to help the sales force to conduct structured and fact-finding oriented conversations, for instance, by simulating the value impact of different solution alternatives and scenarios. In any case, impactful value proposition communication requires powerful IT tools, which hide the computational complications, connect to reference information databases, and present the results visually appealingly.

15.5 Customer Engagement

The customer engagement involves customer selection from the target segment of customers for which the value proposition is designed. After the customer selection, the customer buying process (Fig. 15.2) and the value-based solution selling process are tightly aligned (Fig. 15.4). The selling activities fall into three categories. The organizational buying is influenced through the coalition of powerful stakeholders (see discussion on buying center in Johnston and Bonoma 1981). Therefore, the first category of selling activities focuses on identifying, contacting, and developing key stakeholder relationships by supporting their goal achievement. The second, and perhaps the primary category of selling activities, seeks to understand and influence buying at every stage of the buying process. The third category of selling activities focuses on managing the joint progress by agreeing on joint activity plans and otherwise controlling process alignment and measuring mutual commitment to proceed.

From the value selling perspective, the second category of influencing activities includes the activities to (1) influence the customer's incentive to act by communicating the joint value creation potential, (2) influence the customer's solution vision by proposing a solution that addresses the identified challenges, and (3) influence solution selection by quantifying solution value.

15.5.1 Select Customer

Rather obviously, the customer and stakeholder selection made to initiate a sales process must comply with the criteria, which were applied when building customer insight, for value proposition relevance and receptivity. The better the match, the higher the likelihood of attracting interest. However, customer selection is complicated for three reasons. First, the actual selection criteria applied frequently violate the agreed principles. The opportunistic "we sell to anyone interested" attitude often overrules the more careful analysis and qualification of customer situation, customer relationship, and supplier brand credibility, often leading to costly mistakes and high cost of sales. Second, supplier category management allocates suppliers into categories based on criticality and differentiation (Kraljic, 1983). The innovative suppliers, which, however, may be perceived as non-critical and easy to replace, usually find it very hard to gain access and get their message heard, regardless of the potential value of their solution. Third, the value proposition may not be perceived attractive by the stakeholders. The practical and economically viable audience of value proposition development is the market segment or the stakeholder level. Hence, individual stakeholders, guided by their beliefs, past experiences, and incentives may fail to appreciate the value proposed. The final value proposition communication, adaptation, and quantification takes place during the sales process, and is only possible if the customer engagement is successful.

15.5.2 Communicate Value Proposition

Driven by their goals, organizational stakeholders initiate buying processes to engage in prioritized improvement opportunities and seeking strategic renewal of their organizations. Many key decisions during the buying processes, such as which goals are deemed important and which challenges are identified and prioritized, are all influenced by the actors' beliefs about what is relevant and critical in the current situation. Management history is rich of examples of managerial decision-making failures originating from repeating past recipes and being too strongly influenced by the prevailing organizational culture and industrial belief systems (Laamanen, Lamberg, & Vaara, 2016; Tripsas & Gavetti, 2000). Important value creation opportunities may be lost if they fall outside of stakeholders' radar screens. Value creation opportunities may also be lost if deemed irrelevant in the current decision-making situation. Hence, even with everything done right, the value-based solution selling process may still meet a stakeholder with severely outdated beliefs and goals.

15.5.2.1 Influencing Perceptions

The product-based buying culture is often unprepared and unskilled to evaluate the business impact of novel solutions. Instead, industrial buyers set minimum requirements for acceptable solutions, short-list qualifying vendors, and exercise their bargaining power for lowest price as a primary selection criterion. To influence buyers' value perceptions, value-based sellers need to gain access to their customers' buying processes at the early stages, while the customers are evaluating and prioritizing their situation, goals, and challenges, and skillfully employ success stories, value calculators, benchmarking studies, and other value communication tools to influence, align, and broaden perceptions. Specifically, guided by the product logic (see Table 15.1), industrial buyers often hold a narrow set of decision criteria, such as focusing on the capital expenditures of the investment decision. In contrast, progressive industrial sellers (guided by their solution logic) may promote a broader set of decision criteria, focusing on the life-cycle value of the solution (e.g. evaluating both the capital and operational expenditures). If the value creating and differentiating elements of the supplier's solution relate to improvements achieved by, for instance, higher operational efficiency, the supplier's solution fails to appeal to the buyer. The value creating elements of the seller's solution are not included in the buyer's value conception (see Rajala, Töytäri, and Hervonen (2015) for a definition of value conception); the product logic collides with the solution logic. Hence, the seller's pre-requisite for success is to influence the buyer's value conception by convincing value proposition communication.

15.5.2.2 Adapting Value Proposition

In addition to influencing buyer's decision criteria, seller potentially needs to adapt value proposition to a specific buyer situation and context. Designing a value proposition is an optimization exercise between impact and scope (Töytäri & Rajala, 2015). An impactful value proposition matches the individual stakeholder's views. However, the subjective nature of customer value renders this task impractical during the value proposition development stage; the pre-designed value propositions are crafted to address sufficiently large stakeholder segments, therefore potentially leaving a gap between the value proposition's generic scope and individual value perceptions. This gap can be filled in two ways; either the value proposition communication tools support adapting the value proposition to match individual views, and/or the value proposition communication is impactful enough to influence and align the stakeholder views with the pre-designed value proposition.

15.5.3 Define Solution

Ideally, developing a solution optimally integrates customer's and a supplier's resources (such as knowledge, skills, technology, and similar), and hence arrives at a solution that maximizes long-term value. I have already introduced the concept of solution vision as an elementary milestone of the customer's buying process. When implementing the buying process, the customer must develop a solution vision to proceed to matching the vision with real alternatives. Clearly, the supplier develops a solution proposal based on the information exchanged. Often, the customer's and the supplier's solution visions are different. For instance, the best value-maximizing solution could be the outsourcing of an entire business process to the supplier, while the customer wants to implement new technology and educate its own staff. Both alternatives get the job done, but differently. The parties likely have different experiences, knowledge, preferences, and perceptions leading to deviating solution visions and constraints. The buyer may be guided by the product logic, while the seller is guided by the solution logic.

The value proposition and the solution vision are connected. Consider the following extract from the value proposition example presented earlier: *the new solution improves minerals recovery percentage, reduces energy consumption, and lowers maintenance cost.* This part of the value proposition identified three sources of value (value elements or value dimensions), through which value is created. Revisiting the earlier discussion on organizational goals, we can now link the organizational (or stakeholder) goals, the challenges to overcome, and the solution to overcome the challenges to achieve the goal. See Fig. 15.5 for illustration. The challenges here are minerals recovery, energy, and maintenance cost.

Fig. 15.5 The connection between goals, challenges, and the solution

A stakeholder's solution vision can be influenced by quantifying the achievable value. Demonstrating a significant value creation opportunity involving specific challenges (or value elements) may well influence the stakeholder's value conception. For instance, showing significant savings potential by improving operational efficiency may persuade the stakeholder to expand the value conception from product logic to solutions logic. The value proposition quantification is implemented through the following steps:

1. For each involved value dimension (e.g. recovery, energy, and maintenance in the example), suppliers and customers need to determine the gap between the current level and the achievable level.
2. Then, each gap needs to be translated into a salient measure of value (such as revenue increase or cost reduction) by identifying an appropriate value function to calculate the monetary value of energy savings, production increase, and similar (Rajala et al., 2015).
3. Finally, the individual contributions of quantified value elements are aggregated into a commensurate measure of value created, as the measure of goal achievement.

The above quantification steps include a number of challenges for practical implementation. The current state performance is often difficult to determine. The growing volume of digital production information is helping to remedy the problem by creating volumes of component, equipment, process, and plan level production data, but currently the lack of information poses a challenge. Suppliers also need to determine what is possible to achieve and what level of risk in committing to the results is acceptable. Suppliers are actively building databases of success cases and verifying the results achieved together with their customers. However, goals involve risk, and risk sharing between the parties is a profound new business model-related topic on the agenda. Finally, the value function that translates the operational changes into (monetary) key performance indicators is often difficult to determine. In simple cases, the industrial process can simply be modified to reveal the impact of the changes, but often the value creating changes have delayed effects on the KPIs, or there may be other, uncontrollable variables also influencing the

KPIs. Hence, the equation between the value creating changes and the resulting KPIs may be difficult to determine and to demonstrate convincingly.

Proactive influencing of a stakeholder solution vision involves agreeing on common goal, salient challenges to address, and agreeing on other constraints to meet. Apart from the rather evident budgetary, resource, scheduling, legal, and other constraints, organizational identity and positional power also influence solution visions. Customers may be unwilling to give up specific business functions for identity and power-related reasons. In any case, the seller is more likely to succeed, if the seller succeeds in engaging with the stakeholder early enough, before the buying process has progressed past the solution vision development.

15.5.4 Gain Preference

During the search buying process stage, the buyer focus is on identifying a number of alternative solution suppliers with an ability to deliver the solution vision. The seller focus is on building a competitive preference based on a business impact (economic value), and a solution definition addressing the identified challenges. Clearly, such supplier-related decision criteria as the supplier's ability to deliver and participate in the value creation as agreed weigh heavily in gaining preferred supplier status. The remaining activities include building a shared plan of planning, evaluating, and decision-making activities and milestones extending over the remaining part of the joint process (Töytäri, 2015).

15.5.5 Agree on Value Constellation and Value Sharing

Once the value-based solution selling process by the buying process has arrived at a joint solution vision, the remaining value activities include agreeing on value constellation and value sharing. Value constellation denotes the coalition of actors with their associated capabilities and resources required to implement the solution. Solution implementation clearly requires commitment from both the supplier and the customer, but increasingly, value creation by solutions engages a multi-actor ecosystem to implement the joint value proposition (Adner, 2017).

Suppliers can improve their win rates and profitability by demonstrating value (Aberdeen Group, 2011). However, to fully benefit from the value-based approach requires tying pricing to value created (Töytäri et al., 2017). All the steps related to value-based selling require a significant upfront investment, are demanding and costly to implement, and require significant new capabilities and resources. To justify the investment, value-based selling should pay off in terms of improved profitability. Figure 15.6 illustrates the value-based and cost-based pricing logics. Both parties capture a share of the value created if the price is anywhere between the supplier cost and value created (Kortge & Okonkwo, 1993; Töytäri, Rajala, & Brashear Alejandro, 2015). In essence, price determines how the value created is split between the supplier and the customer. A price close to the supplier cost (cost-based pricing) favors the

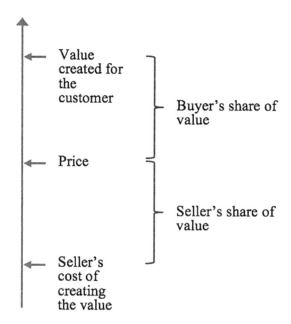

Fig. 15.6 Price in relation to value created and supplier cost (Adapted from Töytäri and Rajala (2015))

customer, and a price close to the value created favors the supplier, correspondingly.

Value-based pricing, however, is difficult to achieve. First, the product logic has a strong preference to the cost-based (or market-based) pricing, and considers value-based pricing greedy and going against the industrial norms of value sharing (Töytäri et al., 2015). Practically, value-based pricing requires (temporary) exclusivity to the solution and/or risk sharing arrangements.

15.6 Conclusions

This chapter ties value proposition and organizational goals as key elements of organizational buying and value-based solution selling. The value-based solution selling is embedded in to a broader, paradigmatic change from product-based exchange to solution-based exchange, where multi-actor constellations of firms, capabilities, and resources strive for improved value creation.

References

Aberdeen Group. (2011). *Value-based selling: Building a best-in-class capability for sales effectiveness.* Retrieved from https://www.zs.com/-/media/files/publications/private/whitepapers/valuebasedsellingaberdeen.pdf

Adegbesan, J. A., & Higgins, M. J. (2011). The intra-alliance division of value created through collaboration. *Strategic Management Journal, 32*, 187–211.

Adner, R. (2017). Ecosystem as Structure: An actionable construct for strategy. *Journal of Management, 43*(1), 39–58.

Anderson, J. C., Narus, J. A., & van Rossum, W. (2006). Customer value propositions in business markets. *Harvard Business Review, 84*(3), 1–10.

Bettencourt, L. A., & Ulwick, A. W. (2008). The customer-centered innovation map. *Harvard Business Review, 86*(5), 109–114, 130.

Cyert, R. M., & March, J. G. (1992). *A behavioral theory of the firm* (2nd ed.). Cambridge, MA: Blackwell Business.

Eades, K. M. (2004). *The new solution selling: The revolutionary sales process that is changing the way people sell.* McGraw-Hill.

Gutman, J. (1982). A means-end chain model based on consumer categorization processes. *Journal of Marketing, 46*(2), 60–72.

Johnston, W. J., & Bonoma, T. V. (1981). The buying center: Structure and interaction patterns. *Journal of Marketing, 45*(3), 143.

Kagerman, H., Helbig, J., Hellinger, A., & Wahlster, W. (2013). *Recommendations for implementing the strategic initiative INDUSTRIE 4.0: Securing the future of German manufacturing industry; Final report of the Industrie 4.0 Working Group.*

Kortge, G. D., & Okonkwo, P. A. (1993). Perceived value approach to pricing. *Industrial Marketing Management, 22*(2), 133–140.

Kraljic, P. (1983). Purchasing must become supply management. *Harvard Business Review, 61*(5), 109–117.

Laamanen, T., Lamberg, J.-A., & Vaara, E. (2016). Explanations of success and failure in management learning: What can we learn from Nokia's rise and fall? *Academy of Management Learning & Education, 15*(1), 2–25.

Lengnick-Hall, C. A., & Wolff, J. A. (1999). Similarities and contradictions in the core logic of three strategy research streams. *Strategic Management Journal, 20*(12), 1109–1132.

Rackham, N., & DeVincentis, J. R. (1999). *Rethinking the sales force: Redefining selling to create and capture customer value.* New York: McGraw-Hill.

Rajala, R., Töytäri, P., & Hervonen, T. (2015). Assessing customer-perceived value in industrial service systems. *Service Science, 7*(3), 210–226.

Scott, W. R., & Davis, G. F. (2016). *Organizations and organizing: Rational, natural, and open system perspectives.* New York: Routledge.

Thornton, P. H., Ocacio, W., & Lounsbury, M. (2012). *The institutional logics perspective: A new approach to culture, structure, and process.* Oxford, UK: Oxford University Press.

Töytäri, P. (2015). Assessing value co-creation and value capture potential in services: A management framework. *Benchmarking: In International Journal, 22*(2), 254–274.

Töytäri, P., Keränen, J., & Rajala, R. (2017). Barriers to implementing value-based pricing in industrial markets: A micro-foundations perspective. *Journal of Business Research, 76*, 237–246.

Töytäri, P., & Rajala, R. (2015). Value-based selling: An organizational capability perspective. *Industrial Marketing Management, 45*, 101–112.

Töytäri, P., Rajala, R., & Brashear Alejandro, T. (2015). Organizational and institutional barriers to value-based pricing in industrial relationships. *Industrial Marketing Management, 47*, 53–64.

Tripsas, M., & Gavetti, G. (2000). Capabilities, cognition, and inertia: Evidence from digital imaging. *Strategic Management Journal, 21*, 1147–1161.

Vargo, S. L., & Lusch, R. F. (2008). Service-dominant logic: Continuing the evolution. *Journal of the Academy of Marketing Science, 36*(1), 1–10.

Woodruff, R. B. (1997). Customer value: The next source for competitive advantage. *Journal of the Academy of Marketing Science, 25*(2), 139–153.

Zeithaml, V. (1988). Consumer perceptions of price, quality, and value: A means-end model and synthesis of evidence. *The Journal of Marketing, 52*(3), 2–22.

16

The Virtue of Customising Solutions: A Managerial Framework

Siri Jagstedt, Klas Hedvall, and Magnus Persson

16.1 Introduction

To gain competitive advantage, strengthen customer relationships and improve sustainability of revenues, manufacturers are increasingly integrating services with their physical products (Baines, Lightfoot, Benedettini, & Kay, 2009). A bundle of products and services that are integrated and customised can be referred to as a solution (Brax & Jonsson, 2009; Sawhney, 2006; Tuli, Kohli, & Bharadwaj, 2007).

S. Jagstedt (✉) • M. Persson
Department of Technology Management and Economics, Chalmers University of Technology, Gothenburg, Sweden
e-mail: siri.jagstedt@chalmers.se; magper@chalmers.se

K. Hedvall
Department of Technology Management and Economics, Chalmers University of Technology, Gothenburg, Sweden

Department of Aftermarket Technology, Volvo Group Trucks Technology, Gothenburg, Sweden
e-mail: klas.hedvall@chalmers.se

Accordingly, solutions not only require the integration of products and services, but also include a high degree of customisation to meet the demands of individual customers (Johansson, Krishnamurthy, & Schlissberg, 2003; Sawhney, 2006; Storbacka, 2011). The main motivation for customisation is to improve the effectiveness of the solution in relation to the operations of the customer. At the same time, however, manufacturers are guided by demands for internal efficiency. Manufacturers therefore often aim to increase their internal productivity and profit margins through standardisation efforts. Thus, researchers have noted that *the firm has to balance the trade-off between increasing customer satisfaction through customization and increasing firm's productivity through standardization* (Rust & Chung, 2006, p. 562). For many companies, this trade-off between internal efficiency and the effectiveness of the customised solutions becomes a challenging task. Ultimately, it is about being able to apply strategies enabling the achievement of both economies of scale and customisation of offerings (Labro, 2004; Meyer & Lehnerd, 1997; León & Farris, 2011; Aljorephani & ElMaraghy, 2016). Hence, to address the seemingly contradictory trade-off between standardisation and customisation in the provision of solutions, manufacturers require appropriate frameworks and tools (Baines et al., 2009). To address this need, this chapter will introduce a managerial framework for customisation of solutions. The framework, based on utilising commonalities among assets shared by solutions, is encompassing two phases. The framework is anchored in the extant literature and draws on the results from empirical studies in a transport industry context.

By exploiting commonalities among different solutions, a manufacturing company may improve efficiency and enable standardisation. At the same time, flexibility with respect to customisation, addressing individual customers' contexts and operations, can be achieved. To accomplish commonality, a wide range of assets might be shared among solutions. These assets can, for example, be components, processes, knowledge, or people and relationships (Robertson & Ulrich, 1998). By sharing these common assets among various solutions, a manufacturer will be able to address internal demands for efficiency, standardisation and economies of scale (Sköld & Karlsson, 2013) and still design offerings that are adapted to the requirements and needs of customers (Jha, Bose, & Ngai, 2016).

In the first section below, the drivers underpinning the need for a commonality strategy for provision of solutions are introduced. This is followed by a section discussing the first phase of the managerial framework, explaining how a solution may be subdivided into three elements: the products, the services and the manufacturer–customer interaction. Thereafter, as the second phase of the managerial framework, five steps guiding the process of customisation through utilising commonalities are described. In the final section, the main managerial implications of applying a commonality strategy when customising solutions are summarised.

16.2 The Virtue of Customisation

Customisation is about building or adapting something to fulfil the specific requirements of the individual customer. However, to improve internal efficiency, the manufacturer simultaneously strives for standardisation. Hence, firms often face a trade-off between the need for standardisation and the demands for customisation (Rust & Chung, 2006). The customisation can range from being completely unique, customer-specific customisation, to segment-specific or limited customisation (Johansson et al., 2003; Sawhney, 2006). By defining groups, or segments, of customers with similar—or near-to-similar—needs, a manufacturing firm may meet the demand for customisation while avoiding the need for development of unique and 'one-off' solutions. When utilising commonality strategies, manufacturers can simultaneously facilitate customisation and enable efficient development of the offerings (Robertson & Ulrich, 1998; Kim & Moon, 2016). A commonality strategy clarifies how customisation is achieved, while at the same time, the manufacturer leverages commonalities among solutions, hence, both enabling economies of scale and scope and meeting the demands of adaptation (Sköld & Karlsson, 2013). We argue that there are potential benefits for manufacturers in applying a commonality strategy for customisation of solutions. Moreover, these benefits may be arranged in groups addressing different drivers, or needs. In the extant literature, three main groups of drivers are identified: external drivers, internal

16.2.1 External Drivers

External drivers concern the needs and demands of the manufacturer's customers. Customisation is often highlighted as being essential for the customer, making the solution suitable for their specific, individual needs (Hakanen, Helander, & Valkokari, 2017). Hence, a main target for customisation is to improve the effectiveness of the solution offered. However, while customers demand a solution suitable for their context, they do not expect complete customisation per se (Brax & Jonsson, 2009). Rather, customers expect solutions to match their main needs and solve their key problems, while simultaneously attaining quality and limiting the lead time and cost of the solution. Such a match can be achieved, and even facilitated, if a manufacturer exploits the commonalities among offerings. Once the manufacturer understands the needs of its customer, and how to adapt the solution in accordance with these specific needs, the prospects of a match improve. With this approach, manufacturers can utilise knowledge from problem solving for previous customers to develop better solutions for new customers. Adding to the benefits, Sawhney (1998) proposes that the design quality of the offerings can be improved by exploiting commonalities. Testing and debugging of the common and shared assets can result in higher quality of the solutions being developed. Also, in the spirit of the arguments of Sawhney (1998), strategies leveraging commonalities among solutions may enable a reduction in development lead time for the customer who orders a solution. By reusing components, knowledge and competences, the time from identifying the customer's individual needs to the implementation of the solution can be shortened. For a truck manufacturer's fleet management offering, for instance, the on-board driver interface, the on-board communication unit and the off-board office system could be reused in several different solutions. Even if the complete fleet management system may involve some adaptation for the specific customer, the three units shared (the on-board driver interface, the on-board communication unit and the off-board office system) may be thoroughly tested and evaluated in advance, thus reducing the overall cost and the risk of quality-related issues.

16.2.2 Internal Drivers

The internal drivers regard the operations of the manufacturer. Standardisation is commonly highlighted as desirable from a manufacturer's point of view. Therefore, commonality strategies are often implemented in manufacturing companies to improve internal efficiency, enabling, for example, a reduction in costs. Through standardisation, the cost for production, procurement and development may be reduced by achieving economies of scale effects (Meyer & Lehnerd, 1997; Robertson & Ulrich, 1998; Sköld & Karlsson, 2013). A commonality strategy could also provide a means for firms to reduce development lead time. Moreover, through standardisation of assets and interfaces, internal communication and operational efficiency can be improved. While the development of completely unique solutions is associated with complexity, commonality strategies instead reduce this complexity in the organisation. For a manufacturer, the striving for commonalities is often reflected in the structure of the manufacturer's organisation. As a result, the organisation is often divided into separate organisational units with specific tasks and objectives (Scott & Davis, 2007). However, for the development and deployment of solutions, organisational units with different focuses, objectives and time horizons need to collaborate. Efficient and effective cooperation requires a common understanding of the overall objectives. In our studies, we have observed that a common 'language' based on commonalities among solutions may bridge these gaps between the organisational units concerned. Sales personnel, for instance, witness the benefit of a 'standardised offering' when they explain about the needs of customers to engineers in the development organisation. Moreover, for sales personnel, commonalities among offerings make it easier to initiate contact with new customers, showing the benefits of the solutions and the competence of the manufacturer. For a truck manufacturer, for instance, organising vehicle maintenance offerings as maintenance contracts addresses the needs for standardisation and a common language.

16.2.3 Interaction Drivers

In terms of solutions, interaction between the customer and the manufacturer is essential. A key objective for this interaction is to clarify and define the specific needs and demands of the customer buying a solution. Moreover, the manufacturer–customer interaction may facilitate the development and deployment of the solution and help to bridge possible gaps with respect to expectations and demands. Interaction, however, is also crucial with respect to the process of selling solutions, and in relation to this, referenceability is a key enabler. Our research shows that 'referenceability' (Sawhney, 1998) for customers is perceived as one of the major benefits of highlighting commonalities among solutions. A solution is often associated with large investments in terms of time and money for both the manufacturer and the customer. Referenceability to other solutions that have already been implemented in similar companies is therefore valuable for initiating a dialogue with customers. Through referenceability, a business case can be developed and presented, illustrating the benefits and potential savings of implementing the solution. For a truck manufacturer's solutions involving driver training, for instance, the value of the offering can be demonstrated to a new customer by referencing the fuel savings achieved by other hauliers who have implemented the solution in their operations. Commonalities among offerings can hence be used to reduce a part of the uncertainty experienced by new customers and strengthen the trustworthiness of the supplier.

16.3 Subdividing a Solution

Commonalities among different solutions can be identified and exploited in different stages of the development and deployment. While the architecture of the products is often used as the basis (Halman, Hofer, & Van Vuuren, 2003), it is important also to address the potential of other elements in an integrated solution. This is acknowledged by Brax, Bask, Hsuan, and Voss (2017), who argue that commonality strategies, which usually focus on the products only, need to be adapted to fit the conditions of solutions, which contain both products and services. By paying

The Virtue of Customising Solutions: A Managerial Framework

attention to various aspects of the offering, the potential for commonalities across the life cycle of the offering can be identified (Sawhney, 1998; Halman et al., 2003). As previously mentioned, solutions are commonly viewed as a bundle of products and services that are integrated and customised in order to better fit the needs of the customer (see e.g., Tuli et al., 2007; Brax & Jonsson, 2009). As a result of the bundling, the integrated solution often is characterised by high complexity. The perceived complexity of the integrated and customised bundle might, however, hinder the managers involved; it could become a challenge to identify the true and full potential for commonalities among solutions. By 'virtually' subdividing the integrated bundle forming the solution, the perceived complexity might be reduced. Commonalities could hence be investigated for the elements forming the solution as well as for the integrated bundle of the final solution. The ideas behind this virtual subdividing of a solution will be further developed below.

For many manufacturers, products establish the core of the solution. An example of such a product-centric offering is visualised in Fig. 16.1. Typical products are, for instance, a machine in a workshop, a refrigerator or a truck. The core, the product, is embedded in a service layer. This layer consists of services supporting the customers' use of the core products, services that support the customers' operational processes and services enabling product 'health' and uptime. In general, there are thus two main groups of services: those supporting the customer and those supporting the product (Mathieu, 2001). From the customers' perspective,

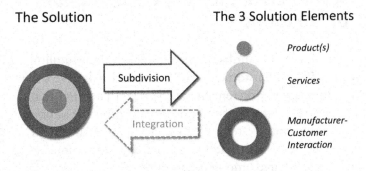

Fig. 16.1 Visualisation of the virtual subdivision of a solution

the services should enhance the value and the effectiveness of the manufacturer's offering. The service layer can thus include services as maintenance, operator/driver training and rental agreements. As such, the services might improve productivity throughout the life cycle of the product, or be associated with lowering the investment cost for the customer. We suggest, however, that the core products and the service layer are supplemented—and contained by—an additional layer: the layer of manufacturer–customer interaction. These interactions have been identified as a key enabler and integral part of the offering (Tuli et al., 2007). This third layer represents the manufacturer–customer communication and cooperation required for the definition, development and deployment of the solution itself. Moreover, this layer is essential for the improvement and further development of the solution in the long run.

Figure 16.1 visualises how the integrated solution is virtually subdivided into the three elements that together constitute a solution, namely, the products, the services and the manufacturer–customer interaction. Additionally, the act of integration is visualised as an arrow pointing in the opposite direction, that is, from the right to the left.

By a virtual subdivision of the solution into the three elements, the manufacturer will be better prepared to investigate the potential for commonalities among solutions. As a result, the manufacturer will also improve the opportunities to address all of the internal, external and interaction drivers.

16.4 A Framework for the Customisation of Solutions

Reflecting the desire of manufacturers to offer solutions fulfilling the specific needs of different customers, a manufacturer will have to manage a variety of solutions with different characteristics. That is, the manufacturer needs to manage a portfolio of solutions that exploit the same commonalities. These solutions are referred to as a 'solution family'. A solution family addresses the same underlying need of the customer group and commonalities are shared among the solutions. For hauliers, such a common need might be the desire to reduce fuel consumption. To address different customers with specific needs, aspects of the solution are then customised to fit the specific requirements of each customer. In the example regarding solutions targeting fuel consumption, this specific adaptation could concern adapting the solution to optimise the customer's usual journey routes or to fit the driving behaviour of specific drivers. Hence, although the final solution is adapted to the specific needs of the customer, each solution in the solution family is made up of elements from the same three groups of products, services and manufacturer–customer interaction. Customisation of the solution is thus achieved by varying the configuration and combination of elements from each group into different integration patterns. As a result, the solution family is concerned with both the commonality aspect and the requirements of the customers.

To efficiently manage the customisation of solutions, we suggest an approach involving two phases. The first phase involves the virtual subdivision of the solution (to be), while the second phase concerns customisation by utilising commonalities among solutions when combining and integrating the three layers comprising a solution. The second phase is managed in five iterative steps. The two phases will be further described and discussed below.

In the first phase, the solution is subdivided into the three groups of elements introduced earlier, namely, the (core) product(s), the services and the manufacturer–customer interaction (see Fig. 16.1). In fact, we propose a notional and imaginary unbundling of the integrated solution (to be) in Fig. 16.2, that is, a subdivision which enables us to study the solution as a whole as well as each of the three separate layers. For a product-centric offering built around a core product, the integrated offering being unbundled could thus be divided into (1) the product or

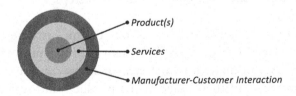

Fig. 16.2 A three-layer model representing a solution as three integrated elements: the product(s), the services and the manufacturer–customer interaction

products forming the core, (2) the services added to support the customer's use of the core product/products, and (3) the manufacturer–customer interaction required for the provision of the integrated and customised solution. For a haulier, an integrated and customised solution could encompass (1) a core vehicle involving a truck together with a trailer, (2) services for maintenance and driver training, and (3) a sales process resulting in the right vehicle and the interaction between the workshop and haulier for planning of service and repair. Although the final solution is adapted to the specific needs of the haulier, each of the three layers consists of elements shared also by other solutions, that is, in this case the solutions offered by the truck manufacturer to other hauliers. Hence, commonality is achieved as the solutions share elements—simultaneously as customisation is reached through the unique combination of elements and configuration thereof.

As previously discussed, a manufacturer aiming to become a solution provider must address different drivers when integrating and customising solutions: external drivers (associated with the customer needs), internal drivers (e.g., related to the company's efforts to achieve economies of scale) and drivers that concern interaction with the customer (enabling dialogue and cooperation). Thus, the process of integration and customisation partly becomes a challenge of how to address the various drivers simultaneously. As argued above, commonality is enabled by sharing elements of the three layers among different solutions, while customisation is achieved by varying the elements as well as how they are combined into the integrated solution. For customisation through integration, the second phase of this framework, we propose five specific steps, to be addressed jointly by managers at the manufacturer, see Fig. 16.3.

The customisation is carried out in an iterative process, in which various commonalities can be exploited in different steps. Each of these steps is described below.

The first step (1) concerns the customer's (or customer segment's) needs and demands to be addressed through the integrated and customised solution. Accordingly, this first step includes considering the customer's operations and their usage of the products and services. In this phase, managers should utilise knowledge about the customer as well as the products and their usage. That is, exploiting knowledge commonalities

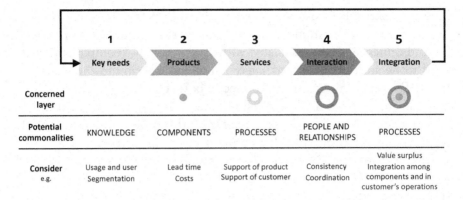

Fig. 16.3 Five steps guiding manufacturers when customising solutions

and thereby reusing the knowledge gained from solutions provided previously. For this first step, a customer segmentation that groups customers according to different types of operations could support the work of the solution provider. A truck manufacturer's customers operating in the mining industry might, for instance, have different needs than hauliers using trucks for long-haul transportation.

In this first step, key needs related to each of the three drivers are defined in relation to the segmentation. The external drivers concern the needs and demands of customers. For hauliers operating trucks for the mining industry, vehicle uptime and high load capacity may be such overarching objectives. Simultaneously, for a truck manufacturer, a demand for high and even utilisation of a network of maintenance workshops could be a key objective related to the internal drivers. Our research points to the importance of also involving the user when investigating the needs and demands as this could influence the segmentation. If a solution also influences the daily work of drivers, for instance, the solution is significantly different from a solution addressing only the owner of the fleet. Hence, this should be considered when identifying the key needs.

One way to establish knowledge about the customers' operations is by running 'learning projects'. That is, projects aimed for testing ideas and gaining new insights. In these projects, one customer is targeted and studied in depth. This knowledge is thereafter used as a basis for development of new solutions. Also, lessons learned from these projects can be used to identify key customer needs and core aspects of the customers' operations in specific industries. For instance, running vehicles in underground mines might be associated with several specific requirements that need to be addressed, such as safety issues very specific to the environment. By performing learning projects, both technology and business aspects can be tested in close collaboration with customers, constituting a basis for learning. Knowledge gained from this project can also be used for solutions targeting similar customer needs in the future.

In the second step (2), the focus is on the products, that is, the assets that establish the core of the solution. In this step, the manufacturer investigates which products are suitable and required for a solution addressing the needs identified in the first step. The products will display the basic characteristics of the group of shared assets—commonalities—but also the specific features that differ among the solutions of the group. As an outcome of this step, the manufacturer should have a clear view of which alternative products are needed for a specific solution, which characteristics these products possess and how they would influence the solution when combined with elements regarding services and manufacturer–customer interaction. In this step, component commonalities can be exploited, so that products are shared among a set of solutions. By exploiting such commonalities, it might be possible to reduce the development lead time of the solution (Sawhney, 1998), which might be important for both the customer and the manufacturer.

For a haulier performing transport of heavy goods to an assembly line, the specification of the truck establishing the core product should support an integrated solution enabling heavy loads, high uptime and reliable transport. That could imply that additional products to enable monitoring of the vehicle's 'health status' need to be included. For this step, manufacturers could consider internally developed products in the portfolio, but products could also be bought from a third party. To utilise already existing products could be beneficial in reducing time and costs. If there is a lack of sufficient products, however, new product development or adaptions of existing products might be needed. However, one should keep in mind that development of new products might be both costly and time consuming.

Step three (3) deals with the service elements of the solution. As in the prior step, the objective here is to achieve a clear view of which alternative service elements are suitable for the solution. For a haulier, for example, maintenance services are essential to reaching and maintaining the required level of vehicle uptime and reliability of transport. In the layered model, the service layer is also essential as it connects the product layer with the interaction layer. The service should therefore be fitted to both the products being used and the customer's specific needs. Manufacturers should hence consider both processes supporting the product and its condition, and processes supporting the customer (Mathieu, 2001).

The services are likely to establish processes being shared among several solutions either in relation to the products or needs similar to a group of customers. Such processes shared could be related to how to carry out the maintenance. The maintenance operations related to a specific engine, for instance, will be the same for all vehicles sharing the same type of engine. However, it might also be that customers in a specific segment share a set of key needs. For instance, a customer transporting food might require maintenance of both the vehicle and the fridge unit at the same time to minimise downtime. Processes supporting such coordination should therefore be considered.

In step four (4), the focus is on manufacturer–customer interaction, which is a key enabler of the solution (Tuli et al., 2007). Also for this task, the overall objective is to provide a clear view regarding which elements are available, what their specific characteristics are and how they would influence the features of the aggregated solution. The elements searched for should enable and support the manufacturer–customer interaction required for the definition, development and deployment of the solution. In this step, human interaction and human relations are essential to sealing the product and service layers. Manufacturers should consider the possibilities of giving the customer a perception of a unified and integrated offering, while leveraging on commonality benefits in terms of human assets—that is, aiming for consistency towards the customer. It is likely that personnel with specific customer knowledge will be in charge of the interaction with several different customers. This could also enable possibilities to gain leverage from referenceability as argued by Sawhney (1998), as communication between the manufacturer and the customer can be enhanced if it is possible to refer to solutions in use at similar customers.

Relationships are important in this step concerning manufacturer–customer interaction. Manufacturers should build on and take advantage of these relationships to provide a customised solution. In situations like these, key account managers could be important players, knowledgeable about both the customers' priorities and the solutions provided. It might also be that a specific group with consultancy competences is especially engaged in defining the solution together with the customers. Often, these employees will work as coordinators among various functions within the company to keep the solution together. For a truck manufacturer and a haulier, coordination with respect to planning of maintenance could form one of the elements in this layer of manufacturer–customer interaction.

In the fifth and final step (5), the solution will be formed by combining and configuring elements from the three groups: products, services and manufacturer–customer interaction. The overall objective of this step is to identify the configuration (or configurations) of elements (products, services and manufacturer–customer interaction) that best address the external, internal and interaction drivers. By varying the configuration, that is, the integration, of elements in the solution, various end results may be explored. If properly managed, the integration should enable a value surplus for the customer (Brax & Jonsson, 2009). Through integration, the solution will ultimately be customised and adapted to the specific customer. The integration concerns not only the integration among components, but also integration into the customer's operations. Hence, these integration processes are essential to achieving a customised solution when leveraging commonalities among assets. As customers' daily operations differ, all solutions will be customised to fit into their specific settings. Therefore, in this step, the customer needs and demands initially identified in Step 1 are revisited by the manufacturer; that is, the manufacturer should now evaluate whether the solution corresponds to the targeted need of the customer. If the results are deemed unsatisfactory, a new reconfiguration could be performed by exchanging elements belonging to one or more layers, resulting in a cyclic and iterative process that ultimately should result in the intended outcome.

It is important to note that the three layers of the solution—products, services and manufacturer–customer interaction—are interconnected and interdependent. Therefore, changes with respect to the elements in one layer may result in changes having to be made in one or both of the other two layers.

16.5 Managerial Implications

In the provision of solutions, manufacturers must simultaneously address the customers' demands for customisation and internal needs for efficiency. To guide companies facing this challenge, a managerial framework for customisation of solutions has been proposed in this chapter. By virtually subdividing a solution into three elements and thereafter developing a customised solution through integration, utilising commonalities, managers will be better equipped for the task of efficient customisation. The proposed framework involves the following two phases:

1. In the first phase, the solution is 'virtually' subdivided into three elements that together constitute a solution: product(s), services and manufacturer–customer interaction.
2. In the second phase, the process of 'customisation through integration' is performed according to five steps. The overall objective of this phase is to identify the combination and configurations of elements (products, services and manufacturer–customer interaction) that best address the needs of the customer.

In the process of customising solutions while exploiting commonalities, however, there are a few additional issues that require the attention of the managers involved:

- As the three layers of the solution (products, services and manufacturer–customer interaction) are interconnected and interdependent, changes in one layer may result in changes having to be made in one or both of the other two layers. Hence, an iterative approach to this process is required.

- Drivers (external, internal and interaction) often vary over time. These dynamics may result in the need for a reconfiguration of the elements of the integrated and customised solution. To identify the need for adaptation and reconfiguration, the manufacturer must strive for a close dialogue with its customers. Hence, the interaction layer of the solution model is critical to satisfy the long-term needs of customers. The involvement of the customer in the customisation process is also important to enable a better match between the needs of the customer and the features of the solution when integrated into its operations.
- A manufacturer involved in the provision of solutions may find that key elements or know-how is missing. If the manufacturer decides that the knowledge or element shall be acquired through suppliers or partners, this will require coordination and close cooperation among the stakeholders involved. To enable internal efficiency and customisation of the solution to be developed, the stakeholders should share a common view on the process as well as the final solution.
- A manufacturer concerned with the development and customisation of solutions may also need to review and adapt the organisational structure and the processes applied. For efficiency and effectiveness of the development and customisation of solutions, the manufacturer's organisation and processes should enable a common and holistic perspective on the combined solution. That is, creating an awareness of the function and purpose of each building block, a common strategy for manufacturer–customer interaction, as well as a common approach to the steps of subdivision and integration.

Our objective with this chapter has been to address the challenges facing managers in the industry when customising solutions. We hope that the managerial framework proposed will lighten the burdens of the managers involved, providing guidance for carrying out the tasks at hand.

References

Aljorephani, S. K., & ElMaraghy, H. A. (2016). Impact of product platform and market demand on manufacturing system performance and production cost. *Procedia CIRP, 52*, 74–79.

Baines, T. S., Lightfoot, H. W., Benedettini, O., & Kay, J. M. (2009). The servitization of manufacturing: A review of literature and reflection on future challenges. *Journal of Manufacturing Technology Management, 20*(5), 547–567.

Brax, S., Bask, A., Hsuan, J., & Voss, C. (2017). Service modularity and architecture—An overview and research agenda. *International Journal of Operations and Production Management, 37*(6), 1–15.

Brax, S., & Jonsson, K. (2009). Developing integrated solution offerings for remote diagnostics: A comparative case study of two manufacturers. *International Journal of Operations and Production Management, 29*(5), 539–560.

Hakanen, T., Helander, N., & Valkokari, K. (2017). Servitization in global business-to-business distribution: The central activities of manufacturers. *Industrial Marketing Management, 63*, 167–178.

Halman, J. I., Hofer, A. P., & Van Vuuren, W. (2003). Platform-driven development of product families: Linking theory with practice. *Journal of Product Innovation Management, 20*(2), 149–162.

Jha, A. K., Bose, I., & Ngai, E. W. T. (2016). Platform based innovation—The case of Bosch India. *International Journal of Production Economics, 171*, 250–265.

Johansson, J. E., Krishnamurthy, C., & Schlissberg, H. E. (2003). Solving the solutions problem. *McKinsey Quarterly, 3*, 116–125.

Kim, S., & Moon, S. K. (2016). Sustainable platform identification for product family design. *Journal of Cleaner Production, 143*, 567–581.

Labro, E. (2004). The cost effects of component commonality: A literature review through a management-accounting lens. *Manufacturing and Service Operations Management, 6*(4), 358–367.

León, H. C. M., & Farris, J. A. (2011). Lean product development research: Current state and future directions. *Engineering Management Journal, 23*(1), 29–52.

Mathieu, V. (2001). Product services: From a service supporting the product to a service supporting the client. *Journal of Business and Industrial Marketing, 16*(1), 39–61.

Meyer, M. H., & Lehnerd, A. P. (1997). *The power of product platforms: Building value and cost leadership*. New York: The Free Press.

Robertson, D., & Ulrich, K. (1998). Platform product development. *Sloan Management Review, 39*(4), 19–31.

Rust, R. T. T., & Chung, T. S. (2006). Marketing models of service and relationships. *Marketing Science, 25*(6), 560–580.

Sawhney, M. (1998). Leveraged high-variety strategies: From portfolio thinking to platform thinking. *Journal of the Academy of Marketing Science, 26*(1), 54–61.

Sawhney, M. (2006). Going beyond the product: Defining, designing and delivering customer solutions. In R. F. Lusch & S. L. Vargo (Eds.), *The service-dominant logic of marketing: Dialogue, debate, and directions* (pp. 365–380). New York: M.E. Sharpe, Inc.

Scott, W. R., & Davis, G. F. (2007). *Organizations and organizing: Rational, natural, and open system perspectives*. Upper Saddle River, NJ: Pearson Prentice Hall.

Sköld, M., & Karlsson, C. (2013). Stratifying the development of product platforms: Requirements for resources, organization, and management styles. *Journal of Product Innovation Management, 30*(S1), 62–76.

Storbacka, K. (2011). A solution business model: Capabilities and management practices for integrated solutions. *Industrial Marketing Management, 40*(5), 699–711.

Tuli, K. R., Kohli, A. K., & Bharadwaj, S. G. (2007). Rethinking customer solutions: From product bundles to relational processes. *Journal of Marketing, 71*(3), 1–17.

17

Servitization Practices: A Co-Creation Taxonomy

Per Carlborg, Daniel Kindström, and Christian Kowalkowski

17.1 Introduction

Servitization increasingly constitutes a strategic imperative for product firms, involving not just the introduction of value-added services and solutions to the core offering but also a reconsideration of the company's

---

P. Carlborg (✉)
Örebro Business School, Örebro University, Örebro, Sweden

Department of Management and Engineering, Linköping University, Linköping, Sweden
e-mail: per.carlborg@oru.se

D. Kindström
Department of Management and Engineering, Linköping University, Linköping, Sweden
e-mail: daniel.kindstrom@liu.se

C. Kowalkowski
Department of Management and Engineering, Linköping University, Linköping, Sweden

Department of Marketing, Hanken School of Economics, Helsinki, Finland

product-centric mindset, to actively involve customers in service processes (Kowalkowski & Ulaga, 2017). As companies climb the "value ladder," relationships typically become more long term in nature, and active customer participation in service deployment increases (Storbacka, 2011; Tuli, Kohli, & Bharadwaj, 2007). However, increased customer engagement also typically heightens uncertainty for the supplier (Larsson & Bowen, 1989), and it may be that customers lack the ambition or competence to play more active roles. Knowing how to harness the potential benefits of engaging customers in various service activities—as well as when not to involve them further—is therefore a vital question for any servitization initiative. In overseeing servitization, managers must consider different modes of customer engagement, ranging from passive to active (Chang & Taylor, 2016; Edvardsson, Tronvoll, & Gruber, 2011), and determine how to make the most of these relationships to ensure the firm's success.

Historically, research on servitization has tended to be one dimensional, addressing the managerial aspects of the firm's *own* (supplier-focused) servitization process (Luoto, Brax, & Kohtamäki, 2017), without considering the customer's transition to increased service reliance. But servitization entails increased awareness of co-creation (Kowalkowski & Ulaga, 2017), so both supplier and customer perspectives and practices are central to the process. This chapter accordingly explores both supplier and customer resource involvement and proposes a service co-creation framework that can support decision makers as they attempt to manage different forms of customer engagement behavior throughout the servitization process. The framework is grounded in the different roles a supplier may take and the various resource deployment issues that reflect the desired degree of customer and supplier involvement in the value-creation process.

17.2 Orientation of Servitization: SSP or SSC

Servitization processes differ in character, such that there are several ways a firm may approach servitization. A general distinction often has been drawn between two service types: those supporting the supplier's products (SSP) and those supporting customer processes (SSC). The former includes product support services such as basic maintenance and preventive services. This traditional approach to servitization is product centric and typically requires less in-depth knowledge of the customer's process because it relies on the supplier's knowledge of its own product. In contrast, SSC is geared toward supporting the customer's processes (Mathieu, 2001). From the supplier's perspective, it entails providing spare parts and routine maintenance, and managing the customer's evolving requirements (Tuli et al., 2007). For example, a component supplier might function as an expert about the customer's operating processes through process optimization and operations monitoring, thereby leveraging its knowledge of component use to improve the customer's own processes associated with using that component (Ulaga & Reinartz, 2011).

17.3 Servitization from Customers' Perspective

Because servitization is essentially a co-creation endeavor in collaboration with customers, it is not enough to consider only the supplier's internal processes or its inputs to the customer's processes. It also is necessary to address what happens on the customer's side, especially because servitization commonly induces changes in customer behavior. The potential for customer involvement in the development of *new* services has long been recognized (e.g., Alam, 2006), but the customer's role in service deployment is rarely discussed. For example, a fleet management service that controls and manages a fleet of equipment relies on the customer's ability to manage the system on a day-to-day basis. In many cases, the customer has a more visible role in this type of servitized context because the focus is inherently on customer usage. But when service deployment involves outsourcing, the customer actually becomes *less* involved. To realize the benefits of such outsourcing though, the actors involved must work more closely together, implying more interaction. As a good example of this, when they outsource the management of their networks to vendors such as Ericsson and Huawei, telecommunications operators no longer participate actively in network management operations. Yet these managed service contracts typically require closer relationships and increased trust between parties to address longer-term strategic issues, ensure incentive alignment, and, when needed, install an "open books" process (Kowalkowski & Ulaga, 2017).

17.3.1 Passive Customers

In many cases, service deployment entails some kind of *reciprocal* involvement of resources; managing joint resources is therefore a key issue (Grönroos & Voima, 2013). However, the customer may not be inclined to play a more active or proactive role; for example, more remote customers who rely on telematics-based solutions are likely more passive and rely on autonomous monitoring and data transmission and analysis, managed by the service provider.

Similarly, customers who lack time, money, or incentives may exhibit lower levels of engagement in service deployment (van Doorn et al., 2010). Without access to these resources, a customer may prefer to remain passive and rely solely on the service provider's capabilities. Such a preference implies a low level of human-to-human interaction, but relatively high levels of technology-mediated interaction still might take place across the systems. For example, remote control of machinery or equipment is commonly regarded as a provider-dominated service with a passive customer, but self-service requires the customer to be more active.

17.3.2 Active Customers

In some cases, strong drivers lead the customer to engage heavily in service deployment, integrating its internal skills, labor, and time to learn about and develop the offering and to achieve the best outcomes, in terms of the customer's own processes (Forkmann, Ramos, Henneberg, & Naudé, 2017). This motivation is especially relevant for advanced, integrated solutions that are interactively designed (Evanschitzky, Wangenheim, & Woisetschläger, 2011; Nordin & Kowalkowski, 2010). The customer's willingness to adapt its internal routines and processes to the service supplier is a central determinant of service effectiveness (Tuli et al., 2007), as are the customer's abilities to provide relevant operational information (Tuli et al., 2007), to offer feedback, and to use self-service options. Even in situations in which an active (i.e., highly engaged) customer is beneficial, increased engagement can have negative consequences if the customer's and supplier's goals are misaligned (van Doorn et al., 2010) and create runaway costs or unplanned customization efforts. It thus follows that service deployment requires varying levels of customer engagement, ranging from a passive installed base to active customer processes, according to the servitization strategy being used.

17.4 The 4C Framework (Constructor, Caretaker, Cicerone, Consultant): A Typology for Value Co-Creation in Servitization

This section elaborates and discusses the different roles a servitized firm can adopt, depending on its approach to servitization (product- or customer based) and the customer's service deployment role (passive/active). This 4C framework includes roles for Constructors, Caretakers, Cicerones, and Consultants; it provides a tool to facilitate managers' decision making. In Table 17.1, we provide examples and critical capabilities for success for each relational mode.

17.4.1 Caretaker

If a supplier's main business relates to capital-intensive products, and customer engagement in service deployment is low because of a lack of knowledge and experience, a *caretaker* role may be most appropriate. In such cases, the supplier is comfortable with the business and knows what to do because the services (e.g., maintenance, spare parts, and upgrades) are closely related to its own installed base. The customer is willing to allow a knowledgeable party take care of its problems or manage the equipment in question. For example, in the trucking industry, many

Table 17.1 The 4C framework: relational modes played by servitized firms

	Product-based servitization: Restoring or improving product functionality	Customer-based servitization: Focused on customer activities and processes
Passive customer (low degree of engagement in service deployment)	**Caretaker** Taking care of a specific activity for the customer to simplify the customer's life *Servitization in practice:* Remote monitoring of machinery and control over the performance of the installed base *Critical capabilities* • **Standardizing** to gain efficiency and an ability to scale up and "productify" services. Implies finding a generalizable service deployment approach in installations and interactions with customers. • **Modularizing** to enable internal standardization while maintaining external customization possibilities for the customer to choose among pre-defined modules.	**Constructor** Designing a function for the customer, using both products and services, to solve a real problem *Servitization in practice:* Preventive maintenance to support the customer's overall production process *Critical capabilities* • **Measuring** key indicators of performance to follow up on improvements to customer's process. • **Learning** from machine data to provide the right feedback and analytical support for the customer. Implies not only learning about data but making judgments about what data are relevant for each customer's problems.
Active customer (high degree of engagement in service deployment)	**Cicerone** Guiding the customer through an unknown landscape to acquire new knowledge through a high degree of engagement. *Servitization in practice:* Customer training and development of employee skills (e.g., new technical competence for machine operations) *Critical capabilities* • **Instructing** the customer through training, practical courses, and workshops to improve machine performance and worker skills. Instructing implies a pedagogic ability to find the customer's level of knowledge and adapt the training accordingly. • **Engaging** the customer to stimulate self-learning behavior. Includes emphasizing importance (improved safety, improved quality) and economic benefits.	**Consultant** Discuss and analyze a specific problem in collaboration with the customer to find customer-specific solutions *Servitization in practice:* Consultative guidance and long-term business development (e.g., providing research and development services to support customers) *Critical capabilities* • **Orchestrating** resources and skills from several actors find partial solutions among different actors in the network surrounding the firm. Includes communication skills and ways of sharing information. • **Collaborating** with customer to build a trusting environment in which ideas and solutions can be exchanged and discussed.

haulers prefer not to deal with repairs, maintenance, upgrades, or spare parts, so truck manufacturers can offer to take care of all these activities, leaving the customer to concentrate on its core business of transportation. The supplier's main task is to facilitate and support the customer's operational environment, rather than taking it over.

To ensure success in this relational setting, the supplier needs to standardize its service operations to a significant extent, so that it can offer generalizable, competitive services for many customers with different needs. This demand implies standardizing operating platforms, technology, and customer interactions. One way to maintain this level of customization is to modularize the service offering and allow the customer to choose pre-defined service modules. With standardized back-office modules and options for customers to choose among the modules, cost efficiency should increase, along with greater protection from low-cost competition by third-party suppliers. For example, in a highly competitive environment, an industrial robot producer decided to allow its customers to choose among pre-defined service modules (e.g., technical support, remote backup, and spare parts delivery) to balance its customization and operational efficiency.

17.4.2 Constructor

If a customer is less inclined to commit its own resources (labor, knowledge), the supplier can engage more actively with the customer's process by adopting the role of a *constructor*. This expert designs and plans some part (or several interrelated parts) of the customer's operational processes by deploying products and services. It is common among manufacturers of less expensive products (e.g., components as inputs for customer processes) that possess deep use knowledge. For example, the bearing manufacturer SKF works within customer processes, providing products (e.g., bearings, lubrication, and mechatronics) as inputs. For SKF, ball bearings are not just products; they are the "brains of the rotating machinery," transmitting real-life operating data to boost performance, reduce mission-critical downtime, and prevent accidents (Kowalkowski & Ulaga, 2017). With its advanced services and deep usage knowledge, SKF acts as an architect that sets up specific customer systems for different operational environments—for example, improved turbine efficiency in a wind energy park or more durable machinery for members of the shipping industry.

To comprehend the possibilities of such relational settings, the supplier must develop deep skills for systematically measuring and learning from information about the customer's situation and internal processes. Data are generated exponentially, so the provider must be prepared to learn how to collect, interpret, and analyze them effectively. Accordingly, it also must be able to follow up and imagine improvements to the customer's process, if it is to retain its credibility as an expert. For example, if a customer does not know how to manage data gathered from online machinery, the provider must motivate the customer to provide relevant data before it can make learning-based improvements for this customer.

The main risk in such relational settings is that the provider lacks the necessary competences to manage customer operations. For that reason, it is important to specify the limits of responsibility in advance, to minimize any risk of underestimating operational difficulties (and costs). There also is a risk of competition from other professional service organizations in the augmented product market (Salonen, 2011), such that success may depend on building strategic alliances with other actors in the network that can support the focal firm's service provision.

17.4.3 Cicerone

When services mainly are provided to an installed base and the customer actively contributes its own resources and labor to the deployment process, the supplier takes on a *cicerone* role. Acting more as a guide, this supplier instructs the customer, which then becomes increasingly able to manage the situations alone. Typical examples include customer training and product simulation, adapted to the customer's existing level of knowledge and specific needs.

To fully develop this role, the supplier must have the skills needed to instruct and engage with the customer. *Instructing* means having the right team to train customer representatives, possessing the required level of knowledge, and adapting the training accordingly. *Engaging* is equally important; servitization of this kind builds on the active participation of the customer. One successful example is Volvo Construction Equipment (VCE). In addition to its machines, VCE sells telematics-based services and hosts training to help customers increase their productivity through improved employee driving skills, which reduce both machinery breakdown rates and fuel consumption. It requires engaging the customer as an active participant in service deployment; without such engagement, the effect of such training may be very short term. Beyond the operational level, engagement must occur at the cognitive level to build more stable relationships (Brodie, Hollebeek, Juric, & Ilic, 2011). For example, the customer might log in to a system to gain a complete overview of its entire fleet (machinery status, spare parts library, planned maintenance) and interact with the service provider.

A potential risk in this scenario is that the *cicerone* might be replaced by machine-to-machine learning at the expense of human-to-human interactions. Online customer training (machine-to-human interaction) is already available in many industries, but machine-to-machine interactions also are a reality in a growing number of situations and application areas, such as business systems and online interactions. An important topic of discussion for managers will be how to leverage this situation to enhance customer value creation. Offering scalable solutions with lower labor costs potentially reduces customer training to a mere commodity. The challenge then is to build relationships with customers and engage them in service deployment, even in situations with minimal human-to-human interactions.

17.4.4 Consultant

This final element in the typology relates to services directed toward customer processes and customers that actively seek to contribute their labor and skills to service deployment. The *consultant* service provider seeks solutions to unique problems, in collaboration with the customer. This effort may involve resources provided by both parties, and there are usually no standard services on which to rely.

This type of relational setting, where both the supplier and the customer are active, may have the greatest value potential; existing research suggests that engaged, committed customers are more likely to remain loyal (Morgan & Hunt, 1994). Typical services include consultative programs and business development activities, which require deep knowledge of the customer's activities and deep trust between the customer and the supplier. The customer usually is motivated to deploy its own resources in long-term projects to develop the business over time. For the supplier, it therefore is pertinent to be able to integrate customer and firm resources and their uses, as well as to develop collaborative skills. Such efforts might include building teams of operatives that can work together and involving management at different levels. Linde Industrial Gas is one example of service deployment involving an active service provider and an active customer. To achieve improved customer processes, Linde staff work closely with the customer's own operating staff (welding, metallurgy) to find new ways to improve the process through better resource usage.

In the consultant mode, a major risk relates to the responsibility for the outcome. The service provider may stray beyond its usual operating area and thereby lose control of its costs and service deployment. This relational setting therefore can be seen as a development beyond initial servitization strategies, such that the customer and the service provider gradually develop different ways to collaborate by discussing their limitations and barriers.

17.5 Discussion and Managerial Takeaways

Servitization implies different strategies for product-based businesses that can leverage various product-based services as proactive weapons in their search for new opportunities for customer-centric growth. The framework presented herein accounts for the varying levels of customer engagement in service deployment and offers guidance for managers that are servitizing their business, in terms of the key activities to pursue and the risks associated with different roles. In doing so, this chapter complements existing servitization frameworks and road maps geared toward managers (e.g., Baines & Lightfoot, 2013; Kowalkowski & Ulaga, 2017). To conclude, we also note how current market trends are influencing customer interactions.

A major industrial trend in recent decades is digitalization. Real-time monitoring and connected machinery create a deluge of data, but these raw data need to be processed and analyzed. In this regard, a key issue is finding ways to develop sound relationships and systems that can systematically gather data from distributed business processes, then integrate each actor's resources to plan, and predict service outcomes. It requires a system for collecting and analyzing data and modeling capabilities for decision making. For suppliers, digitalization offers a means to initiate servitization by illuminating customer processes and thereby learning about the customer.

Another technology-related issue pertains to different interaction patterns, beyond human-to-human. As autonomous technology reaches new levels, machine-to-machine interactions likely will become elemental aspects of value co-creation, even though machines lack human intentions or awareness of agency. For managers developing servitization strategies, the many new interaction links offered by such machine-based interactions represent an opportunity to strengthen traditional interaction patterns.

Servitization also means that as markets become more intertwined, the co-creation of value may take multiple forms. Managers must prepare for an environment in which active customers make it difficult to control the situation, and they must function as part of a value-creating network with blurred boundaries between actors. This shift affects the customer's ability to be active but also requires a broader analysis of the behavior of ecosystem actors in their service deployment, through their roles as *caretakers, constructors, cicerones,* or *consultants*. In turn, managerial practices must address both interactions with members active in the ecosystem and collaborations with other actors.

References

Alam, I. (2006). Removing the fuzziness from the fuzzy front-end of service innovations through customer interactions. *Industrial Marketing Management, 35*(4), 468–480.

Baines, T., & Lightfoot, H. (2013). *Made to serve: How manufacturers can compete through servitization and product service systems*. Chichester, UK: John Wiley & Sons.

Brodie, R. J., Hollebeek, L. D., Juric, B., & Ilic, A. (2011). Customer engagement: Conceptual domain, fundamental propositions, and implications for research. *Journal of Service Research, 14*(3), 252–271.

Chang, W., & Taylor, S. A. (2016). The effectiveness of customer participation in new product development: A meta-analysis. *Journal of Marketing, 80*(1), 47–64.

Edvardsson, B., Tronvoll, B., & Gruber, T. (2011). Expanding understanding of service exchange and value co-creation: A social construction approach. *Journal of the Academy of Marketing Science, 39*(2), 327–339.

Evanschitzky, H., Wangenheim, F. V., & Woisetschläger, D. M. (2011). Service & solution innovation: Overview and research agenda. *Industrial Marketing Management, 40*(5), 657–660.

Forkmann, S., Ramos, C., Henneberg, S. C., & Naudé, P. (2017). Understanding the service infusion process as a business model reconfiguration. *Industrial Marketing Management, 60*, 151–166.

Grönroos, C., & Voima, P. (2013). Critical service logic: Making sense of value creation and co-creation. *Journal of the Academy of Marketing Science, 41*(2), 133–150.

Kowalkowski, C., & Ulaga, W. (2017). *Service strategy in action: A practical guide for growing your B2B service and solution business*. Scottsdale, AZ: Service Strategy Press.

Larsson, R., & Bowen, D. E. (1989). Organization and customer: Managing design and coordination of services. *Academy of Management Review, 14*(2), 213–233.

Luoto, S., Brax, S. A., & Kohtamäki, M. (2017). Critical meta-analysis of servitization research: Constructing a model-narrative to reveal paradigmatic assumptions. *Industrial Marketing Management, 60*, 89–100.

Mathieu, V. (2001). Product services: From a service supporting the product to a service supporting the client. *Journal of Business & Industrial Marketing, 16*(1), 39–61.

Morgan, R. M., & Hunt, S. D. (1994). The commitment-trust theory of relationship marketing. *Journal of Marketing, 58*(July), 20–38.

Nordin, F., & Kowalkowski, C. (2010). Solutions offerings: A critical review and reconceptualisation. *Journal of Service Management, 21*(4), 441–459.

Salonen, A. (2011). Service transition strategies of industrial manufacturers. *Industrial Marketing Management, 40*(5), 683–690.

Storbacka, K. (2011). A solution business model: Capabilities and management practices for integrated solutions. *Industrial Marketing Management, 40*(5), 699–711.

Tuli, K. R., Kohli, A. K., & Bharadwaj, S. G. (2007). Rethinking customer solutions: From product bundles to relational processes. *Journal of Marketing, 71*(3), 1–17.

Ulaga, W., & Reinartz, W. J. (2011). Hybrid offerings: How manufacturing firms combine goods and services successfully. *Journal of Marketing, 75*(6), 5–23.

Van Doorn, J., Lemon, K. N., Mittal, V., Nass, S., Pick, D., Pirner, P., & Verhoef, P. C. (2010). Customer engagement behavior: Theoretical foundations and research directions. *Journal of Service Research, 13*(3), 253–266.

Part V

Service Ecosystems and Service Supply Chain

18

To Servitize Is to (Re)position: Utilizing a Porterian View to Understand Servitization and Value Systems

Rodrigo Rabetino and Marko Kohtamäki

18.1 Introduction

Iconic cases illustrate how companies such as Rolls-Royce, ABB, Caterpillar, and GE (Huikkola, Kohtamäki, & Rabetino, 2016) have been increasingly implementing servitization while moving from offering standalone products to selling solutions. Selling solutions allow manufacturers to supply a combination of products, systems, knowledge, and lifecycle services (Rabetino, Kohtamäki, Lehtonen, & Kostama, 2015), but it requires a deep redefinition of manufacturers' business models (Reim, Parida, & Örtqvist, 2014); this redefinition involves implementation of different (re)positioning moves within the value system (Wise & Baumgartner, 1999) through different mechanisms to redefine the firm boundaries.

Previous studies typically downplay the discussion of strategic (re) positioning in servitization (Bustinza, Bigdeli, Baines, & Elliot, 2015)

R. Rabetino (✉) • M. Kohtamäki
University of Vaasa, Vaasa, Finland
e-mail: rodrigo.rabetino@uva.fi; marko.kohtamaki@uva.fi

and mainly recognize (re)positioning as a way of moving closer to customers, increasing the service portfolio and the serviceable installed-based, and obtaining new skills and competencies. However, the role of industry power and the study of particular strategic moves aimed at increasing companies' spheres of influence during strategic positioning within the value system are essential but often neglected concepts. Vertical (re)positioning is not straightforward and typically involves challenging the position of other players in the value systems when strategically moving not only to where the money is (Wise & Baumgartner, 1999) but also to where the money will be in the future (Christensen, Raynor, & Verlinden, 2001, p. 74). Consequently, distribution of power is central when explaining the dynamics of (re)positioning moves (Sturgeon, 2008). Throughout these moves, companies must "explore penetration points in multiple tiers that are not immediately adjacent" and look for "opportunities to influence customer demand" (Pil & Holweg, 2006, p. 73). Drawing on an in-depth single case study of a global company in the ship power sector that has been implementing servitization for more than 15 years, this chapter illustrates the implications of industry power and its consequences on firm vertical positioning within the value system.

18.2 Theory

Vertical positioning is built on boundary-related decisions that include considerations regarding the product range and decisions of investing/divesting in infrastructural activities and also decisions regarding moving downstream into servicing and upstream into component manufacturing (Chandraprakaikul, Baines, & Lim, 2010). Thus, positioning involves a firm's decision about which value-adding activities should be performed internally and which should be outsourced to suppliers, partners, distributors, and/or customers (Baines, Kay, Adesola, & Higson, 2005). Companies may either integrate or change their position in the value system to not only leverage the use of existing resources and core capabilities by following a diversification strategy but also acquire the necessary capabilities that firms do not currently possess. However, (re)positioning not only becomes a central notion for a focal firm but also involves moves that challenge other industry players' positions. Thus, distribution of power is central when explaining the dynamics of (re)positioning moves (Sturgeon, 2008). Companies must recognize the key actors in the industry, how the value system is governed, how the inter-firm division of labor is organized (Gereffi, Humphrey, & Sturgeon, 2005), and how value is created and distributed within the value stream (Ivarsson & Alvstam, 2010). Several concepts address these power-related issues. For instance, "platform leaders" (Cusumano & Gawer, 2002) and "keystones" (Iansiti & Levien, 2004) are used to describe situations where firms have the power of setting standards and rules in an industry. Governing "bottlenecks" within industries is a necessary condition to reach "architectural advantage" (Grant, 2010, p. 82), which can be achieved by enhancing mobility across the value chain, redefining roles and responsibilities by looking at other players' needs, and becoming a less replaceable bottleneck within the industry architecture (Jacobides, 2011).

Following the resource dependence (Pfeffer & Salancik, 1978) and industrial organization (Porter, 1980) traditions, firms may change their positioning within the industry value system to obtain capabilities, reduce the causes of external uncertainty, and control strategic relationships, knowledge, and resources. (Re)positioning becomes a tool to "determine the sphere of organizational influence, including its degree of industry control and its power over the external forces" (Santos & Eisenhardt, 2005, p. 491). Accordingly, firms may go downstream to offset (intermediate and end) customers' bargaining power or to improve product differentiation by providing a better service for customers and strengthening the firm's brand (Porter, 1980). Appropriating successive markups, dominating the linkages where purchasing decisions are made (Pil & Holweg, 2006), and establishing industry standards downstream while ensuring the consolidation of the main products on the original upstream market are also relevant reasons. Conversely, firms can move upstream to raise rivals' costs and establish entry and/or mobility barriers to gain power and reduce the dependence on a single supplier while guaranteeing a strategic supply under favorable conditions (Porter, 1980).

18.3 A Porterian Toolkit for Understanding (Re)positioning in Servitization

Many iconic manufacturers have been establishing competitive advantages from servitization based on different steps of vertical (re)positioning (Davies, 2004; Wise & Baumgartner, 1999). (Re)positioning has typically been studied as a way of reconfiguring the required resources and capabilities (Huikkola et al., 2016), which include system integration and project management, IT capabilities, consulting, financial competences, delivery, and post-sales service capabilities (Brady, Davies, & Gann, 2005). However, the successful development and deployment of new services is also related to the degree of control a firm exercises over a service value chain (Raynor & Christensen, 2002). Thus, the need for increasing industry power may also explain why servitizing firms move vertically to safeguard their domain (Cacciatori & Jacobides, 2004). Vertical control should guarantee access to end customers to enter a higher-return business. Furthermore, a vertically integrated structure can provide means to guarantee that product specifications and services can be adjusted to cater to diverse customer needs (Davies, 2004).

Baines, Lightfoot, and Smart (2011, p. 950) present two positioning practices between conventional manufacturers and service providers: (1) focusing on product-centric services while keeping a tail in production operations, or (2) combining original equipment manufacturer and product-centric services. Davies, Brady, and Hobday (2007) propose two ideal types of organizing the integrated selling and delivering of solutions: (1) the system integrator that coordinates the integration of components supplied by other firms, and (2) the vertically integrated system seller that produces all product and service components in a system. For instance, system integration is a deliberate "strategic business activity" that facilitates firms to shape "their position in an industry value stream" over time while "enabling them to decide who to compete with, who to collaborate with, what to make in-house, and what to outsource" (Hobday, 2005, p. 1136). Whereas vertical integration through mergers and acquisitions appears to be a common pattern of internalizing environmental sources of uncertainty for firms when moving downstream, the control of the value system can also be achieved successfully without full ownership by using quasi-integration, alliances, franchises, and joint ventures (Mahoney & Pandian, 1992).

18.3.1 Industry Structure and the Transition from Systems to Solutions

Let us consider a system supplier in the shipbuilding industry as an example. Shipping and shipbuilding industries started feeling the effects of deep globalization during the early 1980s. One of the most significant consequences was a deep change in the way the whole shipbuilding industry worked. By the late 1990s, looking for operational flexibility and technical integration efficiency while also being affected by their exposure to demand volatility, shipyards began to demand turnkey systems from their suppliers while becoming "system integrators". For example, shipyards demanded propulsion systems rather than their components in an individual way because the system procurement strategy enables the use of less providers. Today, many yards focus more on project management and cost efficiency and, in some segments, the value added in a new ship is increasingly coming from system suppliers. The installation of turnkey systems also simplified ship operators'/owners' daily processes while increasing operational reliability and cost efficiency. This strategy also enables the use of only a single life-cycle service provider (after the warranty period is over). Becoming a subsystem integrator was also convenient for component suppliers. Not only did they have the best knowledge of their components, but fulfilling such a role was an opportunity to add aftermarket services as part of the total offering.

Our illustrative case example seized the new opportunities by shifting the emphasis in its business from engine delivery to the integration of systems. Based on the combination of lowered total cost and enhanced performance for the customer, system integration was thought of as a differentiation strategy because of the competitive pressures from low-cost countries. However, the system integration strategy has turned into a highly spread industry recipe during the following years. In a highly globalized, volatile, and cyclical shipbuilding industry (Cho & Porter, 1986;

Stopford, 2009), the structural forces (Porter, 1980) of the marine propulsion industry pushed the hitherto system integrator to initiate an additional journey to become a solution provider (Fig. 18.1).

Regarding the rivalry, the market for propulsion systems is controlled by a few European and Asian manufacturers (and licensees), where the share of the latter group has been continuously increasing during recent years. The business is a mature and capital-intensive industry led by several global dominant players constantly struggling to improve their volumes and market share. Still, there is a need for constant investment in technology, and research and development (R&D), and the market leadership undoubtedly depends on the engine type and market segment. The major suppliers must invest in networking efforts to ensure a global presence (often through licensing) while combining the localization of production facilities in low-cost countries with constant innovation to maintain competitiveness. While some competitors have more

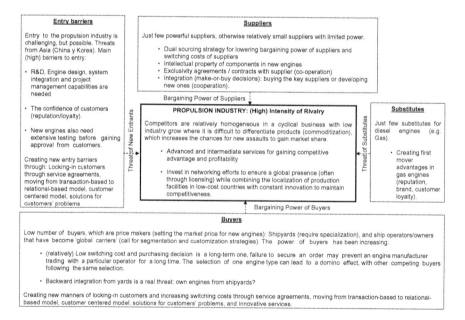

Fig. 18.1 Five forces in the propulsion industry. Source: own elaboration based on Porter (1980) and industry reports from 2000 to 2015

comprehensive portfolios and integrated offerings, other companies are only active in certain market segments.

Regarding the customers, the "propulsion business" consists of two connected markets: propulsion systems for shipyards (primary market) and after-sales services for ship operators (secondary market). Shipbuilding includes the assembly of new ships and its associated activities (repairing, maintenance, and conversion). Whereas backward integration from yards is a real threat (offering own engines), few large conglomerates dominate the industry today (mainly from South Korea, China, Japan, and Western European countries). The aim of shipyards is to meet the standard reliability and legal requirements at the lowest possible cost. Despite high barriers to entry (e.g., regulations, scale economies, capital, and expertise), new entrants have cyclically entered the shipbuilding industry, driven not only by demand peaks but also by local governments. Increasing arrivals lead to overcapacity once the demand peak is over, creating oversupply. Overcapacity has been promoting merger and acquisition waves for years. Due to the combination of high fixed costs, overcapacity, and high exit barriers, price is a key competitive factor. Thus, price-cutting practices and the search for cost efficiency based on economies of scale and low-cost locations for operations are common strategies.

In addition, the number of operators is relatively low compared with the number of shipyards once the market is properly segmented. Whereas many operators have become global carriers and have increased their bargaining power during recent years, the decision power regarding the ship design has been partially moved from shipyards to ship owners. Typically, ship operators demand uninterrupted operations at the lowest possible guaranteed lifetime costs (total cost of ownership). The relatively low switching cost and long-term purchasing decisions increase operators' bargaining power because a failure to secure an order may prevent a yard or a propulsion system provider from trading with an operator for a long time. Moreover, the selection of one engine type can lead to a domino effect within the industry, with other competing buyers following the same decision.

The provision of after-sales support to a large installed base during the system life cycle (30 years) is an important source of sales and profits.

Access to this secondary market depends largely on completing the original sale of new propulsion systems, which provides the opportunity for the provider to offer after-sales services. Ship owners in different market segments have dissimilar needs in terms of professional support and operational guarantees, ranging from those who want a low-cost service to those who need full-service contracts. In any case, neither the shipyards nor the engine manufacturers are able to control this secondary market entirely due to the existence of relatively low entry barriers. Attracted by the prospect of achieving significant benefits, a large but heterogeneous group of companies selling components and providing basic services (e.g., repair, maintenance, and overhaul) and spare parts has emerged near the most relevant system manufacturers over the past 20 years. Once again, system suppliers may increase the control of the secondary market by providing solutions provider and service agreements that include advance services (e.g., remote diagnostics, and operational services).

Finally, whereas the threats of substitute products and potential new entrants are weak (high entry barriers such as R&D investments, reputation and customer loyalty, and system integration and project management capabilities), only a few suppliers of engine components have some relative, but still limited, bargaining power (e.g., injection systems, cylinders liners, pistons sets, crankshafts, dampers, turbochargers, and coupling systems). Markets for other relevant components of the propulsion system are fragmented and highly competitive (e.g., propellers, thrusters, gears, seals, and bearings).

Facing such an industry structure, moving from a transaction-based to a relational-based model that is customer-centered and based on solutions and advanced services while locking in customers through service agreements and increasing the switching cost is a way to not only increase differentiation (reduce rivalry) and reduce the bargaining power of customers but also build stronger entry barriers. Finally, the bargaining power of suppliers may be reduced even further through dual-sourcing strategies, intellectual property of components in new portfolios, signing exclusivity agreements, and buying key suppliers or developing new ones though cooperation.

18.3.2 (Re)positioning for Solution Provision: A Value System Approach

Moving toward solutions involved a change in the organizational structure for the case company while reconsidering the scope of vertical positioning. For instance, the acquisition of a company specialized in propulsion systems (2002) and an agreement for manufacturing propellers (2004) were the initial steps toward becoming a system supplier. Then, our case company initiated a strategic step that has been broader than the change from an engine maker to a system integrator. The company acquired several service providers to develop new service products and speed up deliveries. Maintenance and operational services provisions for the systems sold became a necessary constitutive component of the new value proposition, providing means to maximize the customer value and create competitive advantages, revenues, and profits. Although the company already had services (field services, spare parts, and projects), they were still sold rather unbundled. Over subsequent years (2004–2011), the development and/or acquisition of new capabilities to offer solutions and service agreements composed of systems and services to support customer processes (Mathieu, 2001) became the company's strategic target. A detailed analysis of the last 16 annual reports of the case company allows us to translate this transformation into systematic and quantifiable strategic moves from 2000 to 2016. Pictorially, our service transition map illustrates that whereas upstream strategy was based mostly on joint ventures, alliances, and license agreements, investments and acquisitions were the chosen mechanisms for the downstream value migration from 2000 to 2015 (Fig. 18.2).

In project-based businesses with tailored outcomes, the need for cross-system coordination and knowledge sharing across complementary components and systems also reveals that modularization has limits. The transition from a system supplier toward a system integrator means that the firm becomes a knowledge integrator with a strategic role in designing and developing the system. Controlling key physical systems and the acquisition of service capabilities to guarantee the life-cycle performance of the system becomes a critical factor to assure system reliability and the profitability of the new business strategy. Controlling the interdependent

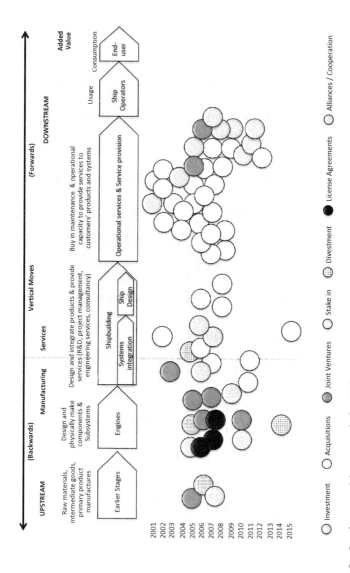

Fig. 18.2 Service transition map: (re)positioning within the value system. Source: own elaboration based on Davies (2004) and our case company's annual reports from 2000 to 2015. * Each sphere represents one strategic boundary-related move, including new companies, workshops, offices, service facilities, and training/education centers. ** The case company has approximately 20 license agreements worldwide. Only the new license agreements during the period are included in the figure, but not the extensions

links in a value system allows companies to capture the most profit, and thus, these component interdependencies will shape firm boundary decisions. Therefore, the case company needed a higher degree of vertical control to coordinate and guarantee system compatibility, as well as a threshold level of performance (Osegowitsch & Madhok, 2003), while ensuring that product specifications and services can be tailored and adjusted to the needs of different customers when supplying systems (Davies, 2004).

Technical aspects, such as lower engineering costs and faster construction time, as well as the dual need to minimize the "cost of response" and maximize the "speed and effectiveness of respond" to particular customer needs (Baines et al., 2011, p. 952), became relevant drivers for the case company when deciding how to provide solutions for the marine industry. In particular, customer preferences regarding performance features such as fuel consumption, emissions, and noise became a key to understanding the need to control how subsystems must be coupled and how the value system processes are organized (Baines et al., 2011; Fine, Vardan, Pethick, & El-Hout, 2002). In the presence of integral systems (Ulrich, 1995), these solutions can only be provided by controlling "knowledge in engineering and manufacturing domains" while allowing "significant dependence for supply in manufacturing capacity" (Fine et al., 2002, p. 73).

In addition, being close to the customer was an opportunity for the case company to not only access market information and a more profitable business but also acquire influence and new competencies upon which the company can build a non-contestable position in the propulsion industry (Porter, 1980). As suggested by Kaplinsky (2000), the ability to govern the value system often arises from intangible competencies, such as marketing, R&D, design, and branding. Additionally, by "understanding the anatomy of purchasing decisions", firms are able to make better choices "about ways to shift control over the demand and manage risk" (Pil & Holweg, 2006, p. 80).

The case company identified ship design as a permeable break/penetration point and thus bought design companies as a way of doing business and positioning itself in between yards and operators, and controlling ship design. This strategic move would favor the company's propulsion systems because the company could design the ship such that customers can derive the highest possible value from its systems. Furthermore, this move would enable the company to offer solutions and life-cycle service agreements to ship operators (including preventive maintenance). Therefore, entering the ship design market for the company became a strategy to achieve upstream market lock-in (Porter, 1980) and downstream knowledge by increasing the cost of switching the supplier of propulsion systems and the company's life-cycle bargaining power over both yards and ship operators. Another example is the acquisition of a UK-based producer of scrubbers in 2012. This acquisition was an important part of the case company's growth strategy in the marine gas, offshore, and environmental solutions markets. The acquisition was implemented for developing a first-mover advantage in a profitable business segment but also to control the competing environmental technology (different from the option developed in-house) before knowing which will become the industry standard. Since companies can make above-average profits when their technology turns out to be the industry standard (Funk, 2003), securing the adoption of the focal organization's industry standard is a way to increase industry power (Santos & Eisenhardt, 2005).

Finally, investing in the development of a global company-owned service network to acquire operational and maintenance capacity was also a major target. This move opens a direct channel to end customers (ship operators), which provides a source of information and knowledge that allows companies to offer improved services for the current systems while gaining knowledge from customers to improve future systems (Baines et al., 2011; Davies, 2004; Kohtamäki & Partanen, 2016; Osegowitsch & Madhok, 2003).

18.4 Managerial Implications

This chapter was set out to contribute to the literature on value system (re)positioning in the context of the servitization process of a manufacturer when migrating from a system integrator to a solution provider. To this end, we analyzed the patterns of (re)positioning moves made by the case company over the last 15 years. We discuss how structural conditions drive manufactures' servitization through different vertical moves to (re)positioning within the industry value system and shed light on both the role of market power during the implementation of servitization strategies and the use of different vertical practices as (re)positioning mechanisms. Moreover, this chapter illustrates how the power approach to firm boundaries complements the widespread capability view and contributes to value system analysis in servitization. Accordingly, (re)positioning within the value system was a double opportunity for acquiring new competencies and influence upon which the company can build a non-contestable position in the industry and lock in customers. In this situation, the power and competence notions are symbiotic.

Whereas the chosen (re)positioning mechanisms for downstream moves were investments and acquisitions that allowed for the control of core resources and key linkages in the value system, the upstream moves at the core of the company's traditional business were mostly based on collaborative practices, such as licensing, long-term contracts, strategic alliances, and joint ventures. The combination of the above mechanisms allowed the case company to access critical capabilities, decrease external dependencies, and increase its sphere of influence. Aligned with the findings of Pil and Holweg (2006), our case also demonstrated that (re)positioning goes beyond adjacent activities and involves detecting profitable points within the value system. The case company was able to recognize where money can be made (Wise & Baumgartner, 1999), as well as "…where, in an industry's shifting value chain, the money will be made in the future" and strategically move to where the money will be (Christensen et al., 2001, p. 74).

Using a forward-looking interpretation, our case seems to support existing evidence that shows how some industries may reintegrate when participant firms change strategies to cope with commoditization and changes in customer demands (Cacciatori & Jacobides, 2005). Once the firms within the value system and industry understood the new rules and opportunities, many of them intended to shift their position along the value system to find rents. Even component suppliers attempted to benefit from the new situation by offering spare parts directly to ship operators/owners or joining networks with other providers to offer a portfolio of after-sales services. Therefore, once the existing division of labor became inadequate to meet the changing needs of the customers, the new situation encouraged industry participants to reshape the value chain while searching for new forms of vertical structures with a new division of labor (Cacciatori & Jacobides, 2005). This discussion could be extended by adding further evidence on the nature of value creation and appropriation logics in different positions within the value system and on why value migrates from one value system point to another (Dietl, Royer, & Stratmann, 2009).

There are several strategic barriers associated with (re)positioning. Building strong joint ventures and alliances, and learning how to integrate knowledge and retain people from acquired companies are both critical and challenging. Furthermore, creating an extensive service network and finding competent people to offer field services are neither straightforward nor easy processes. In addition, industry conditions are key determinants of the smoothness of this value migration. While it can take some time to become familiar with the new practices, roles, and rules in the industry, rivalries in service markets will eventually intensify, and all services will turn into commodities (Matthyssens & Vandenbempt, 2008), which can alter the differentiating power of an advanced service strategy over time. Consequently, the real sources of differentiation and competitive advantage will be the implementation rather than the strategy itself (Rabetino, Kohtamäki, & Gebauer, 2017). An early understanding of the importance of key novel industry trends has given the case company the possibility to dominate, at least temporarily, the key sources of competitive advantages. Being the first mover allowed our case company to re-organize its value system functionally for the new customer-centric strategy and develop efficient and reliable systems, and an innovative portfolio of advanced services.

References

Baines, T. S., Kay, G., Adesola, S., & Higson, M. (2005). Strategic positioning: An integrated decision process for manufacturers. (H. Boer, Ed.) *International Journal of Operations & Production Management, 25*(2), 180–201.

Baines, T. S., Lightfoot, H., & Smart, P. (2011). Servitization within manufacturing: Exploring the provision of advanced services and their impact on vertical integration. *Journal of Manufacturing Technology Management, 22*(7), 947–954.

Brady, T., Davies, A., & Gann, D. M. (2005). Creating value by delivering integrated solutions. *International Journal of Project Management, 23*(5), 360–365. Retrieved May 12, 2015, from http://www.scopus.com/inward/record.url?eid=2-s2.0-21444441370&partnerID=tZOtx3y1

Bustinza, O., Bigdeli, A., Baines, T. S., & Elliot, C. (2015). Servitization and competitive advantage: The importance of organizational structure and value chain position. *Research-Technology Management, 58*(5), 53–60.

Cacciatori, E., & Jacobides, M. G. (2005). The dynamic limits of specialization: Vertical integration reconsidered. *Organization Studies, 26*(12), 1851–1883.

Chandraprakaikul, W., Baines, T. S., & Lim, R. Y. (2010). Strategic positioning of manufacturing operations within global supply chains. *Proceedings of the Institution of Mechanical Engineers, Part B: Journal of Engineering Manufacture, 224*(5), 831–844.

Cho, D. S., & Porter, M. E. (1986). Changing global industry leadership: The case of shipbuilding. In M. E. Porter (Ed.), *Competition in global industries* (pp. 1–585). Boston: Harvard Business School Press.

Christensen, C. M., Raynor, M., & Verlinden, M. (2001). Skate to where the money will be. *Harvard Business Review, 79*(10), 72–81.

Cusumano, M. A., & Gawer, A. (2002). The elements of platform leadership. *MIT Sloan Management Review, 43*(3), 51–58.

Davies, A. (2004). Moving base into high-value integrated solutions: A value stream approach. *Industrial and Corporate Change, 13*(5), 727–756.

Davies, A., Brady, T., & Hobday, M. (2007). Organizing for solutions: Systems seller vs. systems integrator. *Industrial Marketing Management, 36*(2), 183–193.

Dietl, H., Royer, S., & Stratmann, U. (2009). Architectures and competitive advantage: Lessons from the European automobile industry. *California Management Review, 51*(3), 24–49.

Fine, C. H., Vardan, R., Pethick, R., & El-Hout, J. (2002). Rapid-response capability in value-chain design. *MIT Sloan Management Review, 43*(2), 69–76.

Funk, J. L. (2003). Standards, dominant designs and preferential acquisition of complementary assets through slight information advantages. *Research Policy, 32*(8), 1325–1341.

Gereffi, G., Humphrey, J., & Sturgeon, T. (2005). The governance of global value chains. *Review of International Political Economy, 12*(1), 78–104.

Grant, R. M. (2010). *Contemporary strategy analysis* (7th ed.). Wiley.
Hobday, M. (2005). Systems integration: A core capability of the modern corporation. *Industrial and Corporate Change, 14*(6), 1109–1143.
Huikkola, T., Kohtamäki, M., & Rabetino, R. (2016). Resource realignment in servitization. *Research-Technology Management, 59*(4), 30–39.
Iansiti, M., & Levien, R. (2004). Strategy as ecology. *Harvard Business Review, 82*(3), 68–78.
Ivarsson, I., & Alvstam, C. G. (2010). Upstream control and downstream liberty of action? Interdependence patterns in global value chains, with examples from producer-driven and buyer-driven industries. *Review of Market Integration, 2*(1), 43–60.
Jacobides, M. G. (2011). Strategy bottlenecks: How TME player can shape and win control of their industry architecture.pdf. *Telecom & Media Insights*. Telecom & Media Insights, Issue 63, Capgemini.
Kaplinsky, R. (2000). Globalisation and unequalisation: What can be learned from value chain analysis? *Journal of Development Studies, 37*(2), 117–146.
Kohtamäki, M., & Partanen, J. (2016). Co-creating value from knowledge-intensive business services in manufacturing firms: The moderating role of relationship learning in supplier-customer interactions. *Journal of Business Research, 69*(7), 2498–2506.
Mahoney, J. T., & Pandian, J. R. (1992). The resource-based view within the conversation of strategic management. *Strategic Management Journal, 13*(5), 363–380.
Mathieu, V. (2001). Product services: From a service supporting the product to a service supporting the client. *Journal of Business and Industrial Marketing, 16*(1), 39–53.
Matthyssens, P., & Vandenbempt, K. (2008). Moving from basic offerings to value-added solutions: Strategies, barriers and alignment. *Industrial Marketing Management, 37*(3), 316–328.
Osegowitsch, T., & Madhok, A. (2003). Vertical integration is dead, or is it? *Business Horizons, 46*(2), 25–34.
Pfeffer, J., & Salancik, G. (1978). *The External control of organizations: A resource dependence perspective*. New York: Harper & Row Publishers.
Pil, F. K., & Holweg, M. (2006). Evolving from value chain to value grid. *MIT Sloan Management Review, 47*(4), 72–80.
Porter, M. E. (1980). *Competitive strategy. Techniques for analyzing industries and competitors*. The Free Press.
Rabetino, R., Kohtamäki, M., & Gebauer, H. (2017). Strategy map of servitization. *International Journal of Production Economics, 192*(October), 144–156.

Rabetino, R., Kohtamäki, M., Lehtonen, H., & Kostama, H. (2015). Developing the concept of life-cycle service offering. *Industrial Marketing Management, 49*, 53–66.

Raynor, M. E., & Christensen, C. M. (2002). *Integrate to innovate: The determinants of success in developing and deploying new services in the communications industry*. New York: Deloitte Research.

Reim, W., Parida, V., & Örtqvist, D. (2014). Product–service systems (PSS) business models and tactics—A systematic literature review. *Journal of Cleaner Production, 97*, 61–75.

Santos, F. M., & Eisenhardt, K. M. (2005). Organizational boundaries and theories of organization. *Organization Science, 16*(5), 491–508.

Stopford, M. (2009). *Maritime economics* (3rd ed.). Abingdon, Oxon: Routledge.

Ulrich, K. (1995). The role of product architecture in the manufacturing firm. *Research Policy, 24*(3), 419–440.

Wise, R., & Baumgartner, P. (1999). Go downstream the new profit imperative in manufacturing. *Harvard Business Review, 77*(5), 133–141.

19

Enterprise Imaging: Picturing the Service-Value System

Glenn Parry

19.1 Introduction

When faced with a complex service enterprise, there is a need to understand the basis of co-operation for the firms involved. Which organizations are involved, and how do they come together to create value? We were faced with this challenge when working with BAE Systems on the servitization of the Tornado fast jet. The aircraft was provided to the Royal Air Force (RAF) under a £1.3bn availability contract named Availability Transformation: Tornado Aircraft Contract (ATTAC). The contract initially ran from 2006 to 2016, and this was later extended to 2019 at an extra cost of £125m. The contract sought to save money on operations while guaranteeing the RAF Tornado aircraft's availability, capability, and effectiveness is maintained throughout its service life. Changing the Tornado aircraft from product to service provision meant that BAE Systems was to undergo a servitization journey. The change in business

---

G. Parry (✉)
Faculty of Business and Law, University of the West of England, Bristol, UK
e-mail: glenn.parry@uwe.ac.uk

model was not just going to impact BAE Systems; there were numerous organizations, including Rolls Royce, GE Aviation, and Serco that worked together to keep the aircraft flying and that, together with the RAF, would co-create the availability service of the aircraft. Successful delivery of the ATTAC contract required a co-operative discussion between stakeholders. A shared understanding of the organizations involved was needed. The tool described in this chapter was developed to provide a visual image that communicated how the organizations co-operated to deliver the complex service (Mills, Parry, & Purchase, 2011; Mills, Purchase, & Parry, 2013).

Enterprise Imaging has since been used extensively to map and understand complex services as well as simpler product delivery. Since undertaking the initial work on ATTAC, we have slowly developed the technique through application in over 100 firms, both large and small, as part of projects that include service design, new product introduction, supplier qualification, complex manufacture, client pitching, and event management.

19.2 Theory

Traditional product-based supply chain approaches mean that managers focus on optimization of their individual firm over any holistic measures of success (Spekman & Davis, 2004). Individual firms focus upon their own business model. A business model is the design of the value creation, delivery, and capture mechanisms used to engage customers to pay for the value offering of a firm and create profit (Teece, 2010). In its simplest form, the business model consists of three interacting elements: the value proposition, which is the product or service offered; the customer's use of the offer within their context to create value; and the firm's process to capture worth (Parry & Tasker, 2014). Manufacturers produce a unit by transforming materials and equipment as part of a production process, usually characterized as the "value creating" activity (Slack et al., 2013). Manufacturers perceive that value is realized when they sell their unit, at the point of exchange, where worth is captured by the firm. The customers' use of the produced unit is perceived as separate from the firm's value-creation activity, but it is an integral part of a business model. Value cannot be realized until some of the value proposition is integrated into a customer's enterprise. Enterprise is the complex system of interconnected and interdependent activities undertaken by a diverse network of stakeholders (Purchase, Parry, Valerdi, Nightingale, & Mills, 2011). In extended enterprises, many firms' offerings and resources are brought together to create a value proposition. It is the wider enterprise of customer and provider resource employed together that delivers the holistic service experience.

The value proposition is delivered through the combination of resources. Resources may be split into two distinct types: *operand resources* are resources on which an operation or act is performed to produce an effect, for example, physical objects such as equipment and materials. Operand resources can usually be applied to other operand resources, but not to operant resources. Operant resources are employed to act on operand and other operant resources, for example, knowledge, capabilities and competence, and so are often people-based resources; *operant resources* are applied to create transformations in other operant or operand resources.

When operating a complex extended enterprise, the need to have a holistic vision is well known (Dyer, 2000). How firms are aligned, interact, and how the required resources are co-ordinated determines the performance of an enterprise (Das & Bing-Sheng, 2000). However, co-ordinating resources that are managed by another firm toward goals that may not optimize returns for the resource owner is challenging. Not all parties have equal influence, but rather an enterprise forms around a small number of focal firms that are the key resource controllers, stakeholders, and beneficiaries to a contract (Mitchell, Agle, & Wood, 1997).

Understanding and managing the complexity of multi-organizational service enterprises is a challenge (Purchase, Parry, & Mills, 2011). In initial work on ATTAC, several different firm-level process-mapping techniques were used to try and capture a visual image of the enterprise-level offer. Techniques employed included simple upstream/downstream supply chain flow charts (Croom, Romano, & Giannakis, 2000); value stream mapping (Rother & Shook, 1999); and IDEF0 (NIST, 1993). The methods resulted either in images that were too complex to understand due to the numerous loops caused by non-linear flows within the enterprise or in processes that were aggregated to a level where they did not convey useful information.

Service blueprinting provided a useful approach to mapping an enterprise (Shostack, 1984). Service blueprints show a service process flow from a customer perspective. The process flows have a "line of visibility" that shows operations that the customer can see and may be part of, and operations that they cannot see that occur in a back office. For example, in a restaurant, the customer sees and interacts with the waiting staff and can see the other customers as these are all "front office". The customer does not usually see the food preparation activity of the kitchen, any staff rota, or purchase of supplies, as this is "back office" work. In service blueprinting, the process flows are placed in the appropriate place on the image each side of the line of visibility. The mapping approach works well for simpler customer-facing services where flows are linear. However, we found it was not quite appropriate for complex enterprises where contracts are between two organizations, but involve many other groups and process flows are often non-linear.

The service blueprinting concept was taken as the starting point for the Enterprise Imaging technique. Service blueprinting was adapted such that an image was created from the perspective of two contracting parties that have a shared front-office space where their activities and resources employed are visible to all, and both have a back-office support space where activities are not visible to others in the enterprise. Enterprise Imaging is a useful tool for managers or researchers working in complex service environments as it creates a picture that allows for shared understanding of the resources used in value creation.

19.3 Constructing an Enterprise Image

The method of construction of the EI draws stakeholders into evolving conversations that explore the multi-organizational service enterprises in which they work. EIs are described as "epistemic objects" as they capture knowledge that is often beyond the immediate grasp of an individual. The image is constructed with interviewees from firms involved in a contract, and as part of the creation process, their insight unfolds, revealing greater depth of information.

19.3.1 Who to Interview

EI creation is undertaken as part of an interview process. Creation of the image may be the central goal, or it can help in developing a deeper understanding of an operation. The approach is useful as it helps focus conversations on how a business works and uncovers details on which resources, both internal and external, are used to create the desired outcome for a client. Ideally, interviews would be undertaken with equivalent representatives from client, provider, and significant third-party organizations who have knowledge of the detailed current operation of the service, its problems, and its relationships with other organizations key to this service provision and its improvement.

We have constructed images using interviews from just a single-firm perspective. This was done as the firm did not wish to share information on its back-office functions with commercial partners. While this approach is valid for smaller firms where we can expect the interviewees to have detailed knowledge of their immediate network, it places a limitation on the validity of the images created. We believe a single perspective is less reliable for larger firms, and ideally multiple interviews from different perspectives would be required to ensure that the image accurately captures the enterprise resources employed. Interviews across many levels of a complex organization may be required from senior managers to shop floor employees to ensure the images are valid. Time is always an issue when undertaking interviews with key personnel from firms. Interviews typically take 1.5hrs to construct the first image and subsequent validation interviews take 30–45 minutes.

19.3.2 Drawing an EI

The EI begins with drawing a standard framework upon which the different resources/organizations that are used in the realization of the value proposition are placed. To define the areas, the EI uses the service blueprint concepts of "back office" and "front office". These terms define separate but co-ordinated areas within the enterprise that represent the space where provider and client interact (front office) and Client and

Provider organizations which support the service delivery but where the partners have no visibility of each other's operations (back office). The framework is shown in Fig. 19.1.

Over time, we have developed a standard that the provider's back office is placed at the bottom of the image. In the center is the shared front office and at the top is the client's back office. The front-office area represents the space in which the client and the provider interact and can "see" each other's resources. The front office may be in multiple geographic areas, including the provider and the client's own office/factory locations, if they permit client access. In practice, a judgment sometimes needs to be made as to if a resource is in the front/back office or is partially visible.

Selecting appropriate resource units is a skill developed with practice. Resource may be a business unit, an individual, organization, or piece of equipment. It is useful to consider the categories of operand and operant described above and decide what is appropriate and useful. We have found that resources described are usually sub-organizations, but in one case where a firm was selecting new suppliers and resources were to be shared,

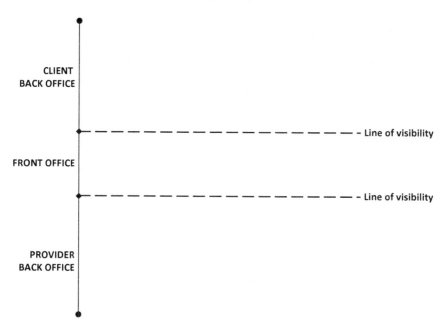

Fig. 19.1 The background framework for an enterprise image

the focus was extensively on the machines available for production. Specific shapes, and when possible colors, are used to describe the different resources employed. The shapes are standard in Microsoft PowerPoint, and the colors are also from the standard palette. The colors are selected as they can still be differentiated when printed in black and white.

Back-office resource	
 Governance	Governance resource • Triangle—dark orange where colored • Usually (not always) located in the back office • Representing the highest level(s) of the organization, so decisions made here affect the enterprise's ability to act • Operant resources/functional resources that determine what resources are available and dictate their co-ordination • Governance organizations may not be aware of the detail of the focal contract/operation Examples include groups such as board of directors; organizations such as a national TV channel, or the ministry of defense (MOD); or individuals such as a company founder, a CEO, an artist, or the prime minister
Internal Support	Internal support • Parallelogram—white where colored • Located in the back office • Owned and managed directly by the client or the provider • Often a shared resource providing services to numerous parts of the organization Examples include graphics teams, IT, estates management, HR, accounts, and shipping.
Third Party Internal Support	Third-party internal support • Rhombus—light blue where colored • Located in back office • Not a "visible" or directly accessible resource to the other parties in the focal contract • Contracted out/owned and managed by a third party Examples include legal advice, designers, HR, accounts, and logistics.

Front-office resource

Partnered Direct	Partnered direct • Rectangle—white where colored • Located in the front office • Jointly controlled/resourced by the provider and client • These represent the focal joint activity of a contract Examples include a client/provider jointly staffed office with a team of marketers and designers rebranding a major retail product; a children's playground developed by a design team with a council; a hangar where the client works with the provider to service aircraft
Third Party Direct	Third-party direct • Octagon—light gray where colored • Located either wholly in the front office or across the line of visibility as appropriate • Usually commercial contractors who provide significant resources to achieve an outcome • Often directly contracted to the client, but may contract to the provider or another party Examples include an event photographer; social workers within a health team; freelance animators working in a joint provider/client office
Third Party Indirect	Third-party indirect • Diamond—light gray where colored • Located either wholly in the front office or across the line of visibility as appropriate • Represents independently managed resources that are not directly engaged in the contract, and may not be aware of the contract, but can influence the outcome Examples include shops in an area where the council is seeking to reduce crime. Keeping shop units occupied, with no graffiti on their shutters, helps improve the residents' feelings of safety; a local government agency charged with road maintenance near a large factory reliant on road transport for supply. The agency knew when roads would be closed or restricted and informed the factory in advance to aid supply planning.

Contract-focused non-partnered
- Oval—light orange where colored
- Located either wholly in the front office or across the line of visibility as appropriate
- Resource solely owned or staffed by only one of the provider or the client.
- Focused (usually solely) on the contract

Examples include a sales and marketing team for a contract; a local HR function to support a client site service; a local project management team.

Customer voice
- Hexagon—white where colored
- Located either wholly in the front office or across the line of visibility as appropriate
- Customer representative resources that are routes of communication with groups such as customers, workers, or the public

Examples include neighborhood watch organizations and elected councilors in an area where the council is seeking to reduce crime; patient representative groups in a hospital; unions in a manufacturing plant during a process of redesign.

Each resource is described within the shape, for example, flight technician, machine press, and HR. Broadly, resources are placed on the image in order of them being used, from left to right, as in a process flow, except no linking lines are used. The resources are placed closer to the owner of the resources (client or provider). In placing the individual resource on the image, clarity of meaning and message is prioritized over strict chronology of use or ownership. Where placement may lead to ambiguity, a note may be written within the shape to provide clarity.

From experience, images are often best drawn on whiteboards or paper, and post-it notes are used to represent the various shapes and resource as they can easily be rearranged. A computer is not used in the first instance as a physical object means there are no barriers to interviewees changing the image. We photograph the image before moving it as post-it notes tend to fall off during transport. PowerPoint is then used to reconstruct the image and this is shared electronically with the interviewees to check representation of their enterprise is valid. In subsequent interviews,

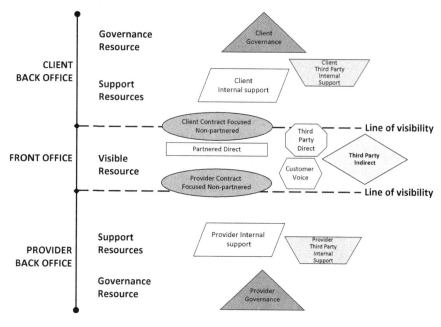

Fig. 19.2 The generic enterprise image

PowerPoint can be used, but images on a screen create an immediate barrier to interaction as the interviewees must learn to move the images or ask for them to be moved. It is better to print and let the client draw upon the image when suggesting modifications. When using EIs as part of presentations, the animation function within PowerPoint is useful to aid explanation. Revealing the shapes either one at a time or in small groups, starting in the front office and working outwards, helps people understand how the resources work together. Figure 19.2 shows the generic EI with resources placed on the framework.

19.4 Application Examples

To date, we have created over 100 images with firms from sole traders to global multinationals. Contracts examined have included nearly all types of business offerings including pitches, new product development, complex multi-agency service provision, simple product creation, design process, and summer festivals. Three examples are given here of services provided in different contexts: military aircraft servicing, the provision of intensive care units (ICUs) to local hospitals, and an organized tourist visit to a favela.

19.4.1 Case Study of Aircraft Servitization

The case example is between industry and government, specifically BAE Systems and the MOD. The contract of focus is ATTAC, a ten-year plus, whole-aircraft availability contract where BAE Systems take prime responsibility to provide support for fast jets with depth maintenance and upgrades, delivering defined levels of available aircraft, spares, and technical support at a target cost.

Researchers were able to create a preliminary image from secondary documents (Mills, Parry, et al., 2011; Mills, Purchase, et al., 2013). The initial image was presented to interviewees in turn, who changed it accordingly and assessed its validity until consensus was achieved. Over 22 organizational resource units were identified, and these were controlled by many different organizations. The EI was presented for critique at 17 different meetings involving personnel from many levels within the provider and the client. The image underwent many iterations. As the case study is drawn from the defense industry, for security reasons a modified version is been presented here. Though simplified, the public domain version still conveys the complexity of the enterprise, Fig. 19.3.

In the case example, four partnered direct resources are identified. The main activity of the contract was aircraft servicing. The operations resources were based within the main aircraft hangar, where the maintenance activities are undertaken named "Combined Maintenance and Upgrade". The hangar is located on an RAF airbase, but staffed with client and provider personnel. "Fleet Management" resource translates the client's aircraft requirements into the schedule of service maintenance. "Engineering Support and Airworthiness Management" resolve technical queries and safety issues and have resources at the airbase and additional offices in other client locations. "Materials Provision" resource provides spare part and repair requirements planning.

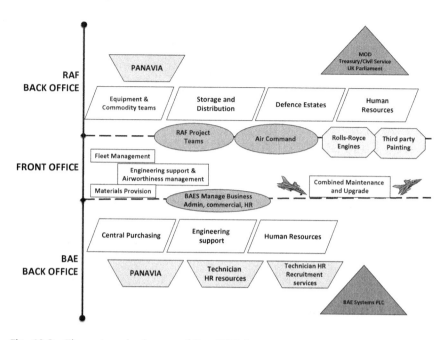

Fig. 19.3 The enterprise image of the ATTAC contract

Three non-partnered outcome focused resource groupings are identified. "BAES Manage Business" resource is a provider team that operates on the airbase, providing commercial, administrative, and human resource for local BAE personnel. The "Project Team" resource is responsible for delivery of the contracted output, though the staff are located some 50 miles away from the maintenance hangar. "Air Command" is a client team responsible for maintenance of the physical assets (hangars, electrical and hydraulic power supply, and information technology infrastructure).

Two main third-party direct resource providers are presented in the case example. Rolls Royce plc manages the repair and overhaul of aircraft engines via a separate contract with the client. A third-party company provides a painting service on a different site. Painting is a significant dependency as it is one of the last process steps in the aircraft maintenance process before the aircraft is returned to flying duty.

Internal-support back-office client resources provide services to several client operations. "Defence Estates" co-ordinate the client's real estate resources. "Storage and Distribution" is the provider of defense transport and storage for parts. "Equipment & Commodity teams" represent 20 different defense equipment and support (DE&S) client organizations, presented here as a single client resource, providing a range of equipment, for example, ejector seats, munitions, and compass. "Human Resources" controls the supply of engineering and supervisory staff into the partnered organizations.

Three provider internal-support resources have been depicted. "Central Purchasing" is located 200 miles away in the provider's main office. "Engineering Support" is also in the main office, providing in-depth technical back-up. "Human Resources" is again in the central offices and supply appropriate management resources and oversight of human resource development.

Client and provider third-party resources include a multinational alliance organization, PANAVIA, which formed the aircraft OEM, and two third-party HR suppliers of specialist aircraft technicians for the contract.

At the governance resource level, the provider has policies set at the corporate level within a functional structure. As a publicly traded company, its operations are driven by its ability to generate financial return on the money raised on capital markets. The MOD has civil service rules to work to, and beyond that, resources are determined and co-ordinated by the UK Treasury and ultimately the UK Parliament.

19.4.2 Case Study of a Nursing Agency

The image shown in Fig. 19.4 was produced as part of a project working with a manager to evaluate service provision for ICUs. In line with ethical approval guidelines, the groupings have been anonymized and simplified, and service performance will not be discussed.

Several front-office partnered direct resources were identified, which represent the ICU service provision located within three different hospitals. Provider contract focused non-partnered resource groupings include the provider's "Client Account Managers" assigned to manage healthcare purchaser (HcP) client accounts. "Food Services" provide dietary specific food for patients and a "Service Management Team" ensures the service

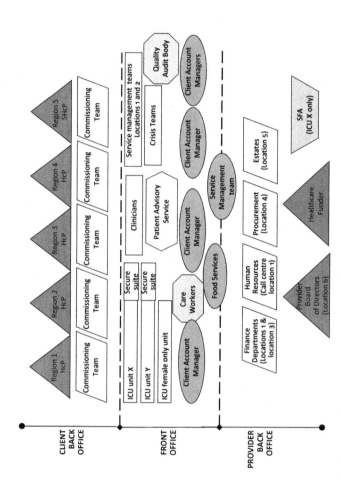

Fig. 19.4 Enterprise image of ICU provision

delivered to patients meets HcP requirements. "Patient Advisory Service" is a customer voice organization providing a channel for patient communication and complaint. Third-party direct resource providers included "Care Workers" who refer patients to the units and the "Quality Audit Body" that oversee standards. Each HcP client has a "Commissioning Team" managing its ICU provision and a separate governance structure. The provider has geographically dispersed service support resources. One of the ICUs was financed using special financial arrangement (SFA), identified as a back-office third-party internal-support resource. The provider had two governance structures: one relating directly to its organization with its board of directors and a healthcare funder who funded its operations. Each HcP client had its own governance. The image was used to communicate within the provider team how complex their service provision was. The work helped to simplify the operations and reduce cost.

19.4.3 Case Study of a Tourist Destination

Favelas are visited by ca. 40,000 tourists per year, though such visits retain an inherent potential danger. The value of tourism to the locals in these areas is not purely economic as tourism also provides status benefits for the population. A "safe" organized service experience requires an alliance between the parties engaged, ensuring that the areas visited are free from crime. The complexity of understanding the organization and the challenge of measuring benefits led to an EI being constructed as a way of identifying the resources utilized. The resultant image is shown in Fig. 19.5.

In the case example, two partnered direct resources are identified: local tour guides who take tourists through the favelas and the "designated tour zones". A client-contract-focused non-partnered resource involves representatives of the tour operator who sell tickets to the tourists and arrange their tours. There is a single customer voice resource, the "Community Office". This is the main point of liaison for the operators and the local community and the site that recruits and helps co-ordinate tour guides. Third-party direct resource providers are presented in the case example: a "Bus Company" that provides local transportation;

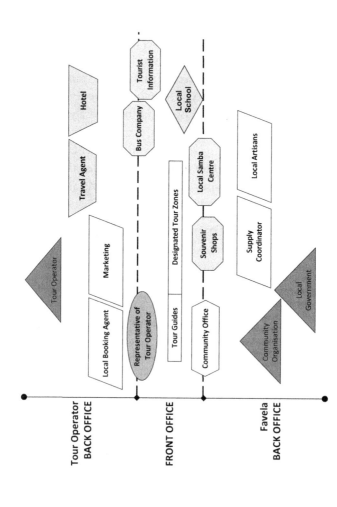

Fig. 19.5 Tourism enterprise image

"Tourist Information" that provides details and contacts to tourists so that they may join tours; and a "Samba Centre" based in the tourist area that makes significant revenues by providing dance lessons and displays to tourists. A single third-party indirect resource is a "Local School" in the tourist area that allowed partial access as part of the "tourist trail" and benefits from the perceived prestige from the tourists' awareness of their work, and subsequent financial donations. Back-office client internal-support resource includes a "Marketing" office to promote the tours and produce materials for hotels and tourist information offices, and a "Local Booking Agent" who creates the tickets and co-ordinates tour bookings information for the representatives. The provider internal-support resources depicted include "Local Artisans", a collective of local people who produce memorabilia and art for sale to tourists; and a "Supply Coordinator" who acts as a supply chain manager linking artisan producers with the local retailers. Client third-party resources include "Travel Agents" who promote the favela tourism experience to their customers and a "Hotel" that works with the tour operator and promotes the tours, among other excursions, as part of its accommodation package. At the governance resource level, the provider has two structures. A "Community Organization" works to ensure the success of the operation and the relationship remains equitable. In addition, "Local Government" agencies, tasked with the alleviation of poverty, support and monitor this venture. On the provider side, the "Tour Operator" seeks to co-ordinate resources and ensure the flow of tourists to develop location revenue.

19.5 Conclusion

Firms work in an increasingly intertwined fashion, often to such an extent that it becomes impossible to account for each partner's contribution. Managers need to have knowledge of the nature and structure of the resources and this knowledge in itself is a core competence for successful complex service management. Such knowledge is captured by the EI approach.

Organizations that engaged in the process have found Enterprise Imaging to be a useful tool for establishing a shared understanding of a complex enterprise where resources are co-ordinated to co-create value, but individual goals are not easily aligned. The EI provides an easy-to-learn and simple tool that captures and communicates the complexity of business-to-business relationships quickly and simply in a single picture.

Acknowledgment The author would like to acknowledge all colleagues whose work contributed toward the development of the EI approach and who provided source material for case examples: particularly, Trevor Mapondera (Nurseline Healthcare Ltd.), who helped with the healthcare case example; Ellen Hughes (UWE), who supported the development of this chapter, and extensively employed and tested EI as part of the Bristol and Bath by Design project, AHRC [AH/M005771/1]; and Dr Valerie Purchase (Ulster) and John Mills (IFM, Cambridge), who co-created the original approach as part of the S4T project funded by Engineering and Physical Sciences Research Council (EPSRC) and BAE Systems [EP/F038526/1].

References

Croom, S., Romano, P., & Giannakis, M. (2000). Supply chain management: An analytical framework for critical literature review. *European Journal of Purchasing & Supply Management, 6*(1), 67–83.

Das, T., & Bing-Sheng, T. (2000). A resource-based theory of strategic alliances. *Journal of Management, 26*(1), 31–62.

Dyer, J. H. (2000). *Collaborative advantage: Winning through extended enterprise supplier networks*. Oxford: Oxford University Press.

Mills, J., Parry, G., & Purchase, V. (2011). Enterprise imaging. In I. Ng, G. Parry, P. Wilde, D. McFarlane, & P. Tasker (Eds.), *Complex engineering service systems: Concepts and research* (pp. 49–65). Springer: London.

Mills, J., Purchase, V., & Parry, G. (2013). Enterprise imaging: Raising the necessity of value co-creation in multi-organizational service enterprises. *International Journal of Operations and Production Management, 33*(2), 159–180.

Mitchell, R. K., Agle, B., & Wood, D. (1997). Toward a theory of stakeholder identification and salience: Defining the principle of who and what really counts. *The Academy of Management Review, 22*(4), 853–886.

Ng, I., Parry, G., Wilde, P., McFarlane, D., & Tasker, P. (2011). *Complex engineering service systems: Concepts and research*. London: Springer.

NIST. (1993). Integration definition for function modeling (IDEF0). *Draft Federal Information Processing Standards Publication 183*. National Institute of Standards and Technology.

Parry, G., & Tasker, P. (2014). Value and servitizationE: Creating complex deployed responsive services? *Strategic Change, 23*(5–6), 303–315.

Purchase, V., Parry, G., & Mills, J. (2011). Service enterprise transformation. In I. Ng, G. Parry, P. Wilde, D. McFarlane, & P. Tasker (Eds.), *Complex engineering service systems: Concepts and research* (pp. 25–48). London: Springer.

Purchase, V., Parry, G. C., Valerdi, R., Nightingale, D., & Mills, J. (2011). Enterprise transformation: What is it, what are the challenges and why are we interested? *Journal of Enterprise Transformation, 1*(1), 14–40.

Rother, M., & Shook, J. (1999). *Learning to see*. Cambridge: Productivity Press.

Shostack, G. L. (1984). Designing services that deliver. *Harvard Business Review, 62*(1), 133–139.

Spekman, R. E., & Davis, E. W. (2004). Risky business: Expanding the discussion on risk and the extended enterprise. *International Journal of Physical Distribution & Logistics Management, 34*(5), 414–433.

20

Ecosystems Innovation for Service Development

Shaun West, Petra Müller-Csernetzky, and Michael Huonder

This chapter gives the reader a structured 'how-to' guide on creating new services within a business. Our approach is based on a six-step framework and will help you to understand your business ecosystem and innovate to deliver new services quickly and effectively. Often this can help you to leap-frog existing actors within the ecosystem, or identify ways to integrate digital services into existing systems to improve customer experience. The framework also helps to identify the gaps in value creation, pointing towards potential new disruptive innovations.

In our approach, we integrate elements of service design thinking, visualisation, and aspects of supply chain management to create the framework. The framework focuses on the value creation process for the fee-paying customers; it helps to understand the actors, and maps the complex web of transactions that support the overall value creation process. Transactions typically are in the form of goods, services, informa-

---

S. West (✉) • P. Müller-Csernetzky • M. Huonder
Lucerne University of Applied Sciences and Arts, Lucerne, Switzerland
e-mail: shaun.west@hslu.ch; shaun.west@mailhec.com; petra.mueller-csernetzky@hslu.ch; michael.huonder@hslu.ch

© The Editor(s) (if applicable) and The Author(s), under exclusive license to Springer International Publishing AG, part of Springer Nature 2018
M. Kohtamäki et al. (eds.), *Practices and Tools for Servitization*,
https://doi.org/10.1007/978-3-319-76517-4_20

tion, data, risk, or money. For each actor within the ecosystem, you will learn to answer the question 'what's in it for me?' Answering this will help you to build new relationships between actors, some of which may be new to the system.

We have tested the framework at different operational levels, from individuals to businesses and it has proved easy to apply and support when unfolding complex networks and creating innovative product-service systems. The framework has been tested in different product-service systems and every time it has provided new insights and created new business opportunities. It has been used in workshops with many participants, as well as in smaller working groups, and individually.

The value of this approach is that your participants will have a common shared understanding of the ecosystem and be able to point out the weaknesses within it. You will also be able to build new services more quickly and learn to grow existing services faster by building partnerships to share capability and capacity across multiple companies.

20.1 Ecosystems in a Product-Service System Environment

Product-service systems require ecosystem thinking to understand who and what is needed to keep the equipment within the overall system working so that it supports the customer's or end-user's business (Kowalkowski, 2011). Often a product is designed and manufactured by one firm, packaged by another, shipped by a third. A facility is built by a project team, handed over to the asset owner's project team, operations and maintenance are then undertaken by another company, and facility management is outsourced—the actors are diverse, as are their individual drivers and their know-how. Using an ecosystem approach, the actors and roles become more clearly visible, and from this it is then easier to manage and redesign, rather than is the case with the conventional value chain. A simplified supply chain is shown in Fig. 20.1 with direct actors and some indirect actors who are involved with the construction of a new

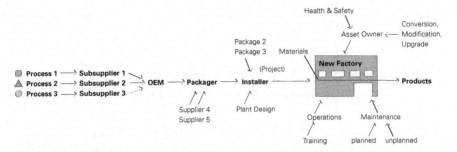

Fig. 20.1 Simplified supply chain around a typical product-service system (based on Anderson, Narus, & Narayandas, 2008; illustration by Müller-Csernetzky, 2017)

factory for a company owner who processes other raw materials in products.

Often different sub-suppliers in the ecosystem must interact or cooperate with the dominant equipment supplier, core company, and final end-user via different layers that constitute distributors, agents, service partners, installers, and system integrators. Between each actor, there may be different types of transactions taking place. The currency for these exchanges can be money, goods, services, information, or risk. Transactions may be single transactions, legally governed, customs-based, or relationship-driven, and they may be separated in time.

In the context of the Internet of Things (IoT), understanding customer value (co-)creation, risk allocation, actor dominance within the ecosystem, and who provides what are complex and important aspects that need to be characterised (Adner & Kapoor, 2010). With the IoT, and digitalisation in general, data is becoming the new enabler, allowing more effective decision-making to take place (Porter & Heppelmann, 2014; Iansity & Lakhani, 2014). However, often the data is spread out between different actors in the ecosystem, and it is important to close information loops in order to analyse data and make effective use of it. The data has often been poorly analysed with limited or wrong conclusions drawn from it. In the past, flow was considered to be in one direction, but it is clear that this is an oversimplification. This makes it more necessary for business leaders to understand and navigate their way through the ecosystem so that customer value is delivered and

20.1.1 Basis of Ecosystems—From Value Chains to Value Networks to Ecosystems

In the 1980s, Porter's value chain model (Porter, 1998) was the main tool used to describe relationships. It was product-centric and considered services more as an afterthought; on a supply chain basis, it was 'buying' or 'procurement' orientated. A more modern model (Anderson et al., 2008) expands to include the 'value network', extending from purchasing the raw materials to delivery of the product to the customer (Fig. 20.2). This model still lacks the operational phase of the equipment and it remains product focused. With digital integration, this becomes ever more complex (Libert, Wind, & Beck, 2014). This is now closer to the complex value networks that exist in product-service systems, particularly those based on equipment with a long operational life.

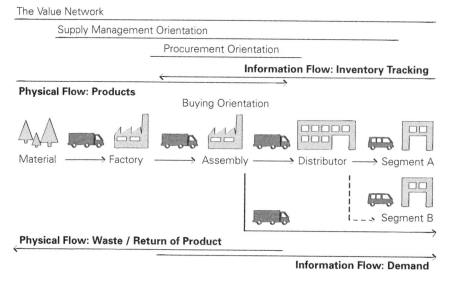

Fig. 20.2 Transformation of the value chain to a value network (based on Anderson et al., 2008; illustration by Müller-Csernetzky, 2017)

These models do not fit with complex product-service systems where value is based on goods, services, information, and risk. It also misses the timing aspects of the transactions, and the dominance and synergies that build up, based on co-creation. Clearly defined ecosystems allow these additional exchanges to be effectively described (often visually) allowing better analysis to be undertaken and conclusions drawn.

20.1.2 Learning from Ecosystems

Ecosystem thinking is the basis of many of today's business models. Uber and Airbnb are used constantly as examples of disruptive IoT-based ecosystems in B2C environments, yet there are many more (Ben Letaifa & Reynoso, 2015). Figure 20.2 shows that product-service system ecosystems are significantly more complex to understand than value chains (Chandler & Lusch, 2015).

Manufacturers do not often consider their ecosystem in their approach to their customers, suppliers, and partners. Consequently, they are missing the inherent value of the ecosystem and do not exploit its attributes fully since they do not understand it (Hui, 2014). Analysing business ecosystems, it is possible to:

- identify who consumes what and why;
- understand the different jobs-to-be-done for every actor;
- understand the timing and intensity/frequency of the interactions;
- improve adaption to different scenarios and situations;
- visualise and present the different flows of transactions;
- create empathy and understanding between and for the different actors.

In effect using the ecosystem approach it becomes possible to understand 'what's in it for me?' for every actor. This question is a very powerful tool as it provides new insights into individual motivations.

20.1.3 Co-Creation and Co-Delivery of Value in Ecosystems

Co-creation and co-delivery of value are inherent within services and ecosystems (Bennett, Peterson, & Gordon, 2009; Ng, Nudurupati, & Tasker, 2010). To complete a task that supports either the product or the customer in a product-service system, it is necessary to collaborate with others. The collaboration can be at a low level or at a more advanced level, depending on the situation. With conventional product thinking, there is often the assumption that the manufacturer creates the value for the customer. This is an oversimplification and is based on the top-down managerial approach. More applicable to services and their co-creation/co-delivery is the team-of-teams approach. Here value is measured by the actor receiving the service, and delivery of the service requires actions by many parties including the receiving actor (Kowalkowski, Kindström, & Carlborg, 2016). This represents the transition to co-creation and co-delivery of value in ecosystems from traditional command-like structures (McChrystal, Collins, Silverman, & Fussell, 2015) and is shown in Fig. 20.3.

20.2 An Approach to Ecosystem Innovation for Service Development

This approach to ecosystem innovation is an inclusive team-based approach; it is not a technology- or an expert-based approach and is best completed within a workshop environment. This is because interdisciplinary teams bring different views on the ecosystem, and where and how to innovate. The workshop is best run with a mix of people with different roles, including some real outsiders. Students can make excellent outsiders, and can bring with them a digital outlook that is unusual for more experienced participants.

A workshop to describe the current state of a firm's ecosystem requires around two to three hours of time, a large whiteboard, and printed empathy cards (see Fig. 20.8) for each of the actor. Assume that you will need

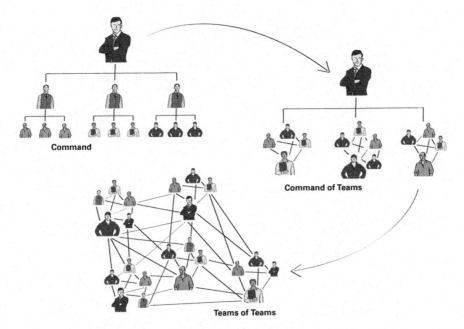

Fig. 20.3 Transformation of command and control structures to more adaptable team-of-teams (based on McChrystal et al., 2015; illustration by Müller-Csernetzky, 2017)

twice as many empathy cards as you expect. Make sure that sufficient time is allowed to get to a common agreement of the current state. Just completing the process as a group provides a forum to share information and build new knowledge and understanding. The framework is shown graphically in Fig. 20.4.

This method has the advantage that it is an inclusive, adaptable process that creates a clear visual of the current state. Its main limitation is that the output is dependent on the inputs, the content and the participants. To help overcome these limits, it may be necessary to undertake the process more than once, as new information is discovered. From the process, it is possible to create a shared understanding of the current ecosystem as well as to 'improve' the current ecosystem. This can help to bring a team together and, as in a lean workshop, to quickly identify improvements. Improvements can take place in many different areas, yet should always focus on delivering an improved outcome to the 'end-user'. Disruptive

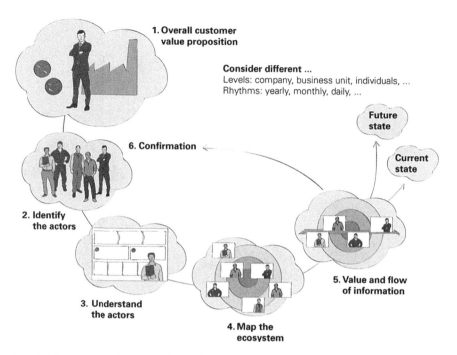

Fig. 20.4 Six-step framework for looking at ecosystem innovation for service business development (based on West, Granata, Künzli, Ouertani, & Ganz, 2017; illustration by Müller-Csernetzky, 2017)

ecosystems can be designed; these may be able to replace existing ecosystems or work side-by-side with them. In all cases, unanticipated reactions can be identified, and through role-play they can be further developed and more fully described, as this framework takes into account the emotional as well as the more rational aspects.

Context is important for ecosystem innovation. Research may be required before the workshop so that the context can be clearly described. All of the participants need to have access to the research and analysis. It is helpful if the background is simply described with graphics where possible. It may be possible to have the individual participants to provide the context, or it may be necessary for the facilitator to provide this.

It may be useful to hold a warm up session before running an ecosystem workshop on a business problem. This allows the team members to learn and understand the process in a risk-free environment as well as learning to work together. Two examples that can make insightful, warm up sessions are:

1. the introduction of electric vehicles—this example has many actors; with the status quo being challenged in many unexpected ways, it is also a good example of a complex product-service system;
2. the introduction of Uber into the existing taxi ecosystem—here, the overall value proposition is very simple to describe, and the process allows the value exchanges for all actors to be described and the weaknesses in the traditional business framework to be clearly stated.

20.3 The Six-Step Framework for Ecosystem Innovation

Some preparation should be done before embarking on the ecosystem workshop. A facilitator pack of pens and sticky notes are required, along with a room with a wall large enough for the team to work together around the ecosystem template. It is worth pre-printing 20 empathy cards (one for each actor plus spares), and to have an A1-sized ecosystem template. The templates are given in Fig. 20.5.

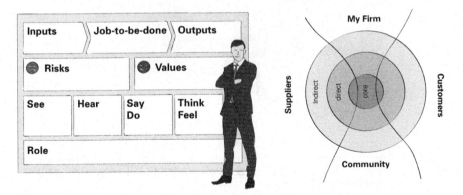

Fig. 20.5 The two most used templates (A5 empathy card and A1 ecosystem map) (based on West et al., 2017, adapted from Stickdorn & Schneider, 2012; illustration by Müller-Csernetzky, 2017)

20.3.1 Step 1—Overall Customer Value Proposition

The visual in Fig. 20.6 shows the actor who is considered to be the 'end-user' of the product-service system; in this case with a description of the overall customer value proposition (Osterwalder & Pigneur, 2014) and the outcomes that are critical to this actor. To ensure that all participants in the workshop are at the same level, it may be necessary to provide insights into the markets, the technologies, and the behaviours. The contextual aspects are needed, and having a common understanding within the team will speed up and improve the quality of the subsequent steps.

Hints:

- describe the actor(s) who could best be called the 'end-user(s)';
- describe the customer value proposition as a sketch and in words (maximum of three lines);
- list the critical outcomes for the 'end-user' in this case.

Fig. 20.6 Learning about the overall customer value proposition and critical outcomes (Adapted from Osterwalder & Pigneur, 2014; illustration by Müller-Csernetzky, 2017)

(Note: this is an excellent opportunity to conduct detailed market research with your end-users or invite representative actors to participate in the workshop.)

20.3.2 Step 2—Identify the Actors

All of the individual actors involved in the ecosystem need to be identified. It is important here to get to individual actors, rather than nondescript tasks that cannot be allocated to people, as this provides the key to the human aspects of ecosystem exchanges. Without the individual actors, the risk is that the system that is created remains a simple value exchange network or a process map, where rational approaches dominate. The objective here is to 'see and understand as others see and understand'. This means that the approach has to focus on individual actors as humans. It may be necessary to create 'actors' that are actually businesses. When this is done, it is worth returning to the individual actors that form the business or the firm.

Figure 20.7 shows sketches of four different actors in the ecosystem. Using sketches helps to capture the essence of the roles that they each perform. The job titles provide clarity and support the sketches. Here is it also possible to provide additional context, such as the equipment they work on or the environments in which they work. For example, in the case of electric vehicles, consider adding to the background of the sketch a petrol station if the person works in a petrol station; or in the case of a service technician, add the equipment that they are servicing.

Hints:

- work individually and then in groups to identify all of the individual actors;
- create a sketch for each actor and provide them with a 'job title' that describes their role(s);
- expect to add more actors later as it is unlikely that all will have been initially identified.

Fig. 20.7 Identifying the individual actors (based on Künzli, West, Granata, Ouertani, & Ganz, 2016; illustration by Müller-Csernetzky, 2017)

20.3.3 Step 3—Understand the Actors

A better understanding of the different actors (individual people or firms) in the business ecosystem can be achieved by analysing the environment, behaviour, concerns, and aspirations within the system. This approach, which was originally used in service design thinking to better describe the customer, and the question 'what's in for me?' help to understand the situation of every actor involved. This highlights the 'soft facts' such as beliefs, opinions, and feelings. Understanding these factors is an essential aspect of the ecosystem mapping, because behind every organisation there is a person making emotional decisions. The 'Inputs', 'Job-to-be-done', and 'Outputs' are a simplified way of documenting the process of every actor from beginning to end. These tools combined on one piece of paper help

Ecosystems Innovation for Service Development

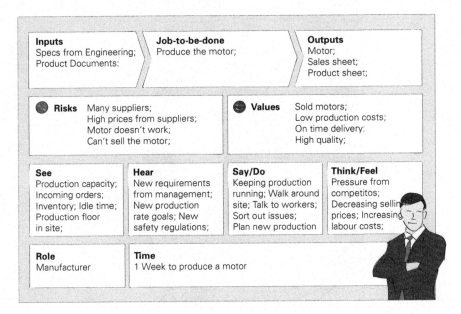

Fig. 20.8 Example of a detailed empathy card for the manufacturer (based on West et al., 2017; illustration by Müller-Csernetzky, 2017)

create a better understanding of every actor in the ecosystem including the goals and motivations; all of this helps us to build the picture for every actor of 'what's in for me?' One such example is shown in Fig. 20.8.

Hints:

- go beyond customer's demographic characteristics and segmentation;
- develop better understanding of environment, behaviour, concerns, and aspirations;
- fill out the empathy card for every actor (A5-size cards).

20.3.4 Step 4—Map the Ecosystem

The different empathy cards can now be placed on the ecosystem map as is shown in Fig. 20.9, to put individual actors in the most appropriate position for them. The layout with the four different segments (my firm, customers, community and suppliers) helps to place the different actors

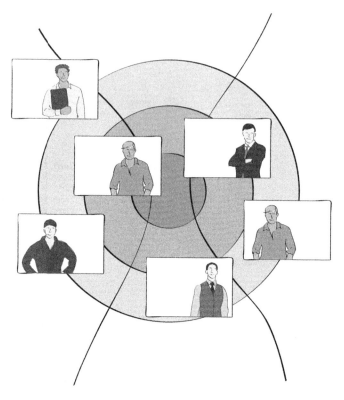

Fig. 20.9 Place the actors on the ecosystem map and cluster them when it makes sense to do so (based on Künzli et al., 2016; illustration by Müller-Csernetzky, 2017)

on the map and the circles visualise the distance to the focal point of your firm, which is in the middle. The product or service flows from the suppliers on the left to the customers on the right side of the ecosystem map. This can be done on an A2 or A1 canvas or drawn on a whiteboard and will create discussion within the team. Group actors together where it makes sense to do so; the groups may be representative of firms or of teams. New actors may be identified during this process and they should be added to the map (along with their empathy card).

Hints:

- place actor cards on the map in the four segments;
- add new actors and cluster actors where this helps to provide additional clarity;
- include the customers-of-customers to show all actors and the roles that they perform.

20.3.5 Step 5—Link the Value and Information Exchanges

This step links the value and information exchanges between different actors. This describes visually how the system works in reality, rather than how it 'should work'. The exchanges between actors are considered as transactions, each with individual inputs and outputs. As the transactions between actors are drawn, it may be necessary to review the inputs and output of the individual actors that were identified in step 3. A simple ecosystem map with transactions is shown in Fig. 20.10.

In complex product-service systems, it is likely that there will be five different types of transactions linking actors. These can be colour-coded to indicate whether they represent information (and data), goods, services, money, or risk. The thickness of the line connecting the actors can be used to provide insight into the relative value, size, or importance of the exchange. The timing of the transaction can also be added, as closure of a transaction may be delayed. Transactions, in reality, may not show a closed loop. Look for open loops where one actor is always taking from others—in the longer-term, this is not likely to be a sustainable relationship.

Hints:

- connect actors and groups of actors;
- colour-code the types of transactions (e.g., goods, services, information, money, and risk);
- highlight the relative intensity and timing of the transactions.

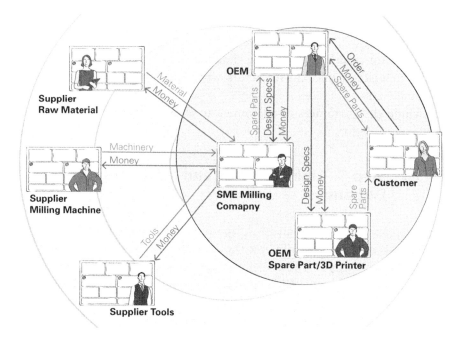

Fig. 20.10 An ecosystem map showing the transactions between individual actors (based on West et al., 2017; illustration by Müller-Csernetzky, 2017)

20.3.6 Step 6—Confirmation of the Current State and Future State

This step ensures that the ecosystem diagram is a good description of the current state and imagines the future(s). Step 6 is in part iteration, so that missing actors and their roles can be described; it is also partly sharing the findings; and partly developing new possible future scenarios.

20.3.6.1 Confirmation of the Current State

The aim of the current state ecosystem is to understand how the customer value proposition is delivered, and to confirm the effectiveness and efficiency of the delivery. This is shown graphically in Fig. 20.11. The analysis of the current state of the ecosystem provides detailed insights into many different aspects of product-service system delivery. The ecosystem facilitates

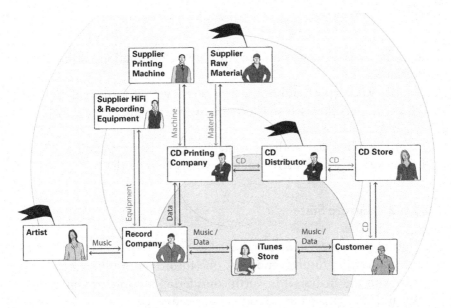

Fig. 20.11 Critical points red-flagged on a current state ecosystem map (based on West et al., 2017; illustration by Müller-Csernetzky, 2017)

good discussion within the team and creates an opportunity to red-flag areas of concern. When doing this, it is normally necessary to return to some of the previous steps, as some aspects may have been initially overlooked.

To open the discussion, start the questioning about the customer value proposition, as this helps ensure that everyone has a common understanding. Without a common understanding of the ecosystem, it is unlikely that all of the lessons can be successfully shared and new innovative solutions designed. A useful check is to confirm the fit with the customer's problem (i.e., is there a 'problem/solution fit'?) and if there are gaps, then these should be highlighted. Next, it is worth confirming the degree of alignment between actors, as many actors' roles may have poor alignment with the overall customer value proposition, or poor alignment between individual actors. During the discussions focusing on the actor transactions (e.g., information, money, goods, services, and risks) consider what is missing or unnecessary as well as the timing of the transitions and their route (e.g., direct, or via intermediaries).

Hints:

- identify key actors who control the information flows (e.g., bottlenecks);
- identify who is powerful in the ecosystem, who is actually dominant, who considers themselves as dominant, who is subordinate, and any synergetic relationships;
- assess the robustness of the ecosystem (e.g., what happens if one actor is removed, where is it stressed, and why is it stressed?).

20.3.6.2 Future State

The future state ecosystem exercise takes the lessons from the current state and imagines futures—not just one future but multiple scenarios. To help with the analysis it is worth considering both incremental innovation and disruptive innovation to the ecosystem. An example of a future state ecosystem is in Fig. 20.12. When designing new ecosystems,

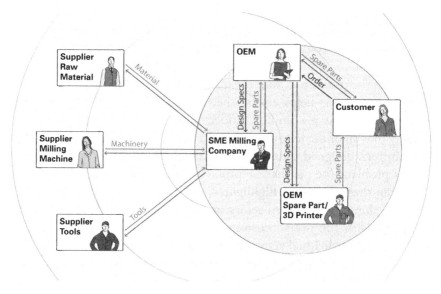

Fig. 20.12 An ecosystem redesigned to provide improve alignment of outcomes (based on Künzli et al., 2016; illustration by Müller-Csernetzky, 2017)

it may be necessary to introduce new actors or technologies. The need for new actors and their roles provides a basis to identify partners or new businesses that are needed to fill the gaps. Similarly, recognising that new technological advances could be beneficial allows technology scouts to find new technologies that could fulfil the role that has been identified.

The aim with incremental innovation is to improve the delivery of the existing customer value proposition. Many of these ideas will quickly fall out of analysis of the current state ecosystem. When looking to improve, it is worth having the team consider a series of issues: where can it be simplified and how can the information flows be improved? Could risks be better managed and where is improved alignment of outcomes needed? Could specific actors' dominance be increased or reduced? These questions are in no way exhaustive and could easily be extended. It is worth moving the actors on the ecosystem map and changing their connections so that the result is visible to the team. With each change, it is important to double check the value proposition that is delivered to see if it creates improvements.

Disruptive ecosystem innovation should be focused on delivering significantly more customer value and experience. It allows the design of new systems and the testing of digital technologies for their impact on the 'end-user' or other parts of the ecosystem. Uber, Airbnb, and iTunes are examples of platforms where the ecosystem innovation delivers improved 'end-user' outcomes (note: it is worth using this framework to analyse one of these examples yourself). They also all consider how to connect suppliers better with the 'end-user' so that the customer experience is improved. This partially explains why ecosystem innovation can be complicated in product-service systems. Nevertheless, the focus should remain on the 'end-user' in question and how to improve the value delivered, while improving engagement with and between actors in the new ecosystem.

Hints:

- do not limit the ecosystem actors;
- consider new technologies that would support the information flows;
- remove dominant actors and re-build the ecosystem to deliver improved customer value.

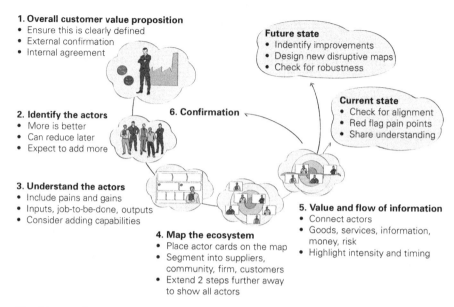

Fig. 20.13 The process overview with hints and tips (based on West et al., 2017; illustration by Müller-Csernetzky, 2017)

20.4 Managerial Conclusions

For product-service systems, it is clear that the linear supply chain, or even value networks, is no longer valid. Applying ecosystem thinking allows a broader view of the product-service systems, providing a richer analysis that remains a simplification of the real world. By working together as a team, it is possible to understand the ecosystem transactions and how they support (or otherwise) the outcomes for the 'end-users'.

The ecosystem has been shown to have many uses when it comes to innovation and supports business improvements, incremental developments, and disruptive innovation. The approach shown in Fig. 20.13 provides a methodology based on visuals that allow a team to work together to develop a current state ecosystem map based on an inclusive process. The expectation is that within a three-hour workshop, the current state ecosystem map will have been described, and all the participants will have had an opportunity to provide their own points of view and share their current understanding of the value proposition(s) of the 'end-users'. All participants should also clearly understand the complexities of supporting a product-service system and its users over its full operational life. The ecosystem map can provide a platform that can improve both collaboration and communication for a team, helping them to gain a joint understanding of what they are trying to achieve and where each person contributes.

The team should also understand the value creation process: the value creation (or destruction) that takes place at every transaction, and the outcome and value creation for the 'end-user'. The complexity of co-creation of value during the delivery of services and products will also have been described. This may come as a surprise to many within a conventional product-based firm, where it is often assumed that the value is *in* the product rather than from the *use* of the product.

The 'current state' ecosystem map will provide the team with many areas where improvements can be made. The initial focus should be on the customer, focusing on improving the customer outcomes via the customer value proposition. This may require internal realignment of resources and processes; often it may simply need improved communication. Other 'quick wins' can come from understanding who is dominant within the ecosystem, and what is actually important to them.

The 'future state' ecosystem enables potentially disruptive innovative improvements to be made. Often, this is based on incremental changes to reinforce the ecosystem, so that it is better able (more effective and more efficient) to deliver the desired customer outcomes. It may suggest in a product-service system that many tasks are better delivered by third parties rather than directly by the equipment supplier. This may be uncomfortable for a traditional product-based firm that prefers to have all of the resources to hand. However, for some mature manufacturers who are more used to 'make-or-buy decisions', it may be more acceptable. Interestingly, some firms may identify new actors in the ecosystem where they have no direct contractual relationship yet these actors are crucial to the success (or otherwise) of the overall customer value proposition. This approach can lead to new and disruptive models that are scalable and can support rapid growth.

This chapter describes a process of ecosystem innovation using a simple and clearly defined framework. The more you use it, the more effective you will become with the process and the more you will learn. It requires openness from all team members to get the best results. It can be coupled with other tools (e.g., customer journey maps) to help discover the actors or integrate with the business model canvas. It is a generic process—we have used it with individual teams, complex product-service systems and supply chains—and we have always learnt something new and useful.

References

Adner, R., & Kapoor, R. (2010). Value creation in innovation ecosystems: How the structure of technological interdependence affects firm performance in new technology generations. *Strategic Management Journal, 31*, 306–333.

Anderson, J. C., Narus, J. A., & Narayandas, D. (2008). *Business market management: Understanding, creating, and delivering value* (3rd ed.). Pearson Prentice Hall.

Ben Letaifa, S., & Reynoso, J. (2015). Toward a service ecosystem perspective at the base of the pyramid. *Journal of Service Management, 26*(5), 684–705.

Bennett, E. M., Peterson, G. D., & Gordon, L. J. (2009). Understanding relationships among multiple ecosystem services. *Ecology Letters, 12*(12), 1394–1404. https://doi.org/10.1111/j.1461-0248.2009.01387.x

Chandler, J. D., & Lusch, R. F. (2015). Service systems: A broadened framework and research agenda on value propositions, engagement, and service experience. *Journal of Service Research, 18*(1), 6–22.

Hui, G. (2014). How the internet of things changes business models. *Harvard Business Review, 92*(7/8), 1–5.

Iansity, M., & Lakhani, K. R. (2014). Digital ubiquity: How connections, sensors, and data are revolutionizing business. *Harvard Business Review, 92*(11), 19.

Kowalkowski, C. (2011). Dynamics of value propositions: Insights from service-dominant logic. *European Journal of Marketing, 45*(1/2), 277–294. https://doi.org/10.1108/03090561111095702

Kowalkowski, C., Kindström, D., & Carlborg, P. (2016). Triadic value propositions: When it takes more than two to tango. *Service Science, 8*(3), 282–299. Retrieved from http://pubsonline.informs.org/doi/abs/10.1287/serv.2016.0145

Künzli, M., West, S., Granata, T., Ouertani, Z., & Ganz, C. (2016). The use of ecosystem visualisation to identify value flows at ABB in the context of the internet of things, services and people. *Spring Servitization Conference*, Manchester.

Libert, B., Wind, J., & Beck, M. (2014, November). *What Airbnb, Uber, and Alibaba have in common*. HBR. Retrieved from https://hbr.org/2014/11/what-airbnb-uber-and-alibaba-have-in-common

McChrystal, S., Collins, T., Silverman, D., & Fussell, D. (2015). *Team of teams: New rules of engagement for a complex world*. New York: Penguin.

Ng, I. C. L., Nudurupati, S. S., & Tasker, P. (2010). Value co-creation in the delivery of outcome-based contracts for business-to-business services. *Business*, 1–48.

Osterwalder, A., & Pigneur, Y. (2014). *Value proposition design: How to create products and services customers want*. London: Wiley.

Porter, M. E. (1998). *Competitive strategy: Techniques for analyzing industries and competitors*. New York: Free Press, 1980. (Republished with a new introduction, 1998.)

Porter, M., & Heppelmann, J. (2014). *Managing the internet of things: How smart, connected products are changing the competitive landscape*. Harvard Business Review.

Stickdorn, M., & Schneider, J. (2012). *This is service design thinking: Basics, tools, cases*. London and New York: Wiley.

West, S., Granata, T., Künzli, M., Ouertani, Z., & Ganz, C. (2017). Identification of ecosystems actors and their behaviours in manufacturing and services. *Frontiers in service*, June 22–25. Gabelli School of Business, Fordham University, New York.

21

Service Supply Chain Design by Using Agent-Based Simulation

Petri Helo, Javad Rouzafzoon, and Angappa Gunasekaran

21.1 Introduction

Supply chain management plays a significant role in industrial product-service systems (PSS). Physical products are part of the entire delivery and intangible components of the delivery are becoming increasingly important, when companies are transforming to servitization. Operations, including tangible or intangible elements, are distributed in different locations and among different actors. Supply chain management encompasses activities aiming efficiently running, monitoring, and improving the performance of a supply chain. The traditional supply chain is concerned to all activities associated with conversions and flow of goods and services including funds and data flows from material sources to final

---

P. Helo (✉) • J. Rouzafzoon
Networked Value Systems, University of Vaasa, Vaasa, Finland
e-mail: phelo@uva.fi; javad.rouzafzoon@uwasa.fi

A. Gunasekaran
California State University Bakersfield, Bakersfield, CA, USA
e-mail: agunasekaran@csub.edu

users. Service supply chain includes planning and controlling activities from support functions to end-users, and development and modelling methods designed for operations management can be utilized in service supply chains. Service supply chains have been studied in various industries to create frameworks and modelling system-wide effects such as demand pattern changes.

Responding instantly to the demand variability is the most significant challenge for service organizations. There are several differences between service and manufacturing supply chain, but the most significant one is that fulfilling demands variability by creating inventory is not possible, but other approaches such as queueing, generating backlog, and creating reservation systems may take place in service organizations. Agent-based modelling (ABM) presents an efficient approach for the assessment of management decision options. This approach allows the use of geographical information systems, that is, maps, to provide the opportunity for analysing heterogeneity of spatial elements, which can be population densities, road networks, and landscape features.

Industrial companies moving towards product-service systems need to take account scenarios of delivery and plan how to maintain good asset utilization at the same time. Smart connected installed base is offering a possibility to see actual operations as well as raw data for analysing service demand and delivery. It is getting more common to have industrial companies where the business model is based on subscriptions and delivered service transactions only instead of one-time delivery of goods. This chapter presents possibilities of using agent-based simulation in service supply chain design by providing an illustrative example of service simulation modelling.

21.2 Theory

21.2.1 Service Supply Chain Characteristics

Traditional supply chains are managed by industrial companies by using material handling-oriented tools such as Enterprise Resource Planning

(ERP) or Advanced Scheduling and Planning (APS) systems. In the servitization context, new solutions are needed to consider the service delivery aspects. Service supply chains are defined as a network of service units that can fulfil one or more service tasks as required. Three major elements in service supply chain structure can be described as (1) service providers who present standardized, single service-type of companies and utilize collaboration and cooperation; (2) service integrators who are the primary enterprises in service supply chains and with access to efficient data processing and robust service design capability, facilitate collaboration and integration of tailored services presented by service providers to users; and (3) customers who can be an individual or a firm and service supply chain performance requirements are defined based on customers' needs (Sakhuja, Jain, Kumar, & Chandra, 2016).

Service supply chains have unique characteristics compared to supply chains focusing on material movements. In service supply chains, the service performance relies upon customers and subcontractor input into service production and delivery. These inputs can be managed or specified by contracting and inducement systems. Contracting can be considered as a method in service supply chain for coordinating the input through incentive systems across various parties. Contractual principles can be merged with functional features of service production and delivery to an integrated framework for realizing how operational and contractual aspects interact and develop each other (Lillrank & Särkkä, 2011). According to He, Ghobadian, Gallear, Beh, and O'Regan (2016), there are five major reasons for service supply chain diversification compared with manufacturing supply chain: (1) services comprises all business-related activities except for manufacturing, agriculture, and mining; (2) there is significant diversity between and within sectors in service supply chains; (3) compared with manufacturing supply chains, value chain procedures of service companies are less standardized; (4) service supplying is mainly decentralized due to decisions which are taken locally to fulfil various customers requirement; and (5) assessing and measuring service performance is complicated due to processes uncertainty, considerable human engagement, and service output variations due to diverse customers requirement.

21.2.2 Agent-Based Modelling

Simulation by using ABM is applicable when different participants exist in a system, and they act independently, interact with each other, respond to system alteration, and their total activity is nonlinear and not resulted from summation of each participant' behaviour. These requirements describe a typical service delivery operation.

Agent-based models are created with objects called agents that interact within an environment. Agents are distinct part of the programme and represent modelling actors which can be individuals, organizations, or bodies such as nation-states. From pragmatic modelling view, agents have following specific characteristics (Macal & North, 2009):

- Agents are social and communicate with other agents.
- Agents are independent and self-directed.
- Agents are traceable, discrete, or modular, each entity with set of features and principles controlling its behaviour and decision-making capability.
- Agents are located and living in an environment in which agents interact with other ones.
- Agents can have goals to accomplish considering its behaviour (not particularly maximization objectives).
- Agents are flexible and have capability to learn and adjust its behaviour based on experience.

Features of ABM can be described as follows:

1. Ontological correspondence: direct association exists between the model computational agents and real-world actors which facilitate model designing and outcome interpretation.
2. Diverse agents: each agent acts according to its own principles and preferences.
3. Environment representation: the environment in which agents are acting directly can be represented in an agent-based model. Furthermore, it can include physical aspects such as physical or geo-

graphical hurdles, other agents' impact on surrounding district, and effect of factors such as crowding and resource reduction.
4. Agent interactions: it is possible to simulate interactions between agents.
5. Bounded rationality: it can be defined as people are restricted in their cognitive capabilities and the level to which they can optimize their performance, and in an agent-based model, it is possible to create bounded rational agents.
6. Learning: agent-based models can simulate learning in both individual and population levels, and it can be modelled in three ways: individual, evolutionary, and social learning (Gilbert, 2008).

The challenges of service operations are related to structures and performance in a wide range. These include service quality, service performance, manufacturing principles, service dynamics, customer-related special requirements, coordination of information between supply chain actors, capacity management, demand management, outsourcing, and service provider selection (Sakhuja et al., 2016). Servitization generally shifts the focus from delivering the materials to synchronization of workforce, tools, and materials needed for the service delivery. ABM can help visualizing a combined view to demonstrate the expected performance in various conditions.

In designing a simulation framework, components are classified under three different clusters: (1) functional, (2) organizational, and (3) structural. Functional components encompass supply chain activities that are modelled as services—these elements are processing information by using resources, which are based on logical rules; organizational components are simulated as intelligent agents that represent business partners and structural components represent facilities in supply chain providing resources and constraints in the ambient environment. All components can be modified for assessing different scenarios. Furthermore, communications between members assimilated through interactions protocols, and they are conducted as set of services which can be initiated by members. These services set standard messages comprising business documents to be changed. This way, it is possible to have various executions of internal activities of each member and create an ordinary control on information visibility shared between members (Dorigatti, Guarnaschelli, Chiotti, & Salomone, 2016). Manufacturers transforming towards services and increasing the service part of the PSS need to have tools that are able to handle the delivery. ABM has been used to capture the service operation in the fields of transportation (Hilletofth & Lättilä, 2012), food assistance and locality services (Leung, Pun-Cheng, & Ho, 2015), health care services (Rouzafzoon & Helo, 2016), and evacuation planning (Esmaelian, Tavana, Santos Arteaga, & Mohammadi, 2015). These examples are typical for service delivery in a PSS context: coordination of transportation synchronized with other operations, operations that include people as both servers and customers in interaction, and managing time and space-related constraints are often presenting challenges. Traditional discrete event simulation has shown strong performance with material flow-related modelling, but the ABM can include the unique customer demand features of service and combine with the geographical aspects in service delivery.

21.3 Tool Presentation—Using ABM

ABM can be applied for testing various scenarios of service interaction and operational delivery by combining rules instructing the agent behaviour and the world described by using geographical information. This kind of approach allows analysing many questions such as:

- Where to locate service centres?
- How different customer areas are served?
- What is the performance of the service delivery at different times? (key performance indicators—KPIs)
- What is the resource utilization at different times?
- How system behaves under varying demand and supply conditions?

21.3.1 Geographical Information

Servitization broadens the focus of delivery towards the actual customer locations: where the customer asset takes place or where the service operation needs to be planned at each time. The availability of public geographical information, including maps, geotagged location data, population data, and open data provided by public administration, has enabled new possibilities for data scientists for modelling and visualizing data. Geographic information systems (GIS) technology can contribute in service organizations to comprehend their market scope, the location of their clients, and how to allocate resources in the district to fulfil service demands. GIS has also been applied for economic analyses in macro-level for enhancing accuracy in trip cost and benefit transfers. Open accessible public data can be used to discover patterns, resolving complicated problems, and make data-driven decisions. For instance, logistics-related service analyses can be performed by using OpenStreetMap (OSM) data source including diverse information such as routes types, speed limits, route directions, and length. Maps and spatial analysis enable servitizing manufacturers to model transportation network, estimate accurate service time frame, increase sale, gain market share, and decrease risk (Bateman, Jones, Lovett, Lake, & Day, 2002).

A suitable service area can be estimated by using maps, road information, and locating the service provider agent on the map. The reach for each possible location can be evaluated by time to access the service location. For example, based on OSM map and road information, three 10, 20, and 30 minutes' service areas are visualized in Fig. 21.1. The service location would be in the Helsinki city centre and with combination of driving speed and roads, the access map is generated (Fig. 21.1).

Service providing access and reach is very often combined with customer density information and, in business-to-business (B2B) commerce, it can be even merged with companies density information. Population data can play a significant role in service-oriented procedures. Population data is increasingly available in high details as open data and can be directly applied in B2C context. Data is available very often in postal code level at least. Many countries, including Finland, are sharing the population data in matrix of 1 km^2, which provides highly precise information on a very local level (Fig. 21.2). Population data, including age and gender, is a good source for generating the customer agents. Population density can be a driver for probability of having a service need for a customer on certain location. In the same way for B2B situations,

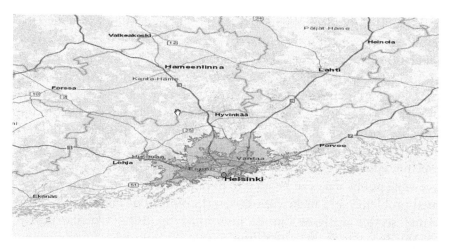

Fig. 21.1 Helsinki service areas from OpenStreetMap data source, © OpenStreetMap contributors (Data is available under the Open Database Licence and cartography is licensed as CC BY-SA: https://www.openstreetmap.org/copyright)

service providing access and service need for companies can be evaluated based on business density information. Many B2B operations have demand driven according to population density and, in order to generate probabilities, this data may be used as input. Linking population to demand of services can be used directly as an assumption in a model or by using an intermediate variable. For example, products related to construction, retail, wholesale, health care, and traffic are tightly linked to population. Road networks and other infrastructure are also provided by GIS systems. This information is highly useful for pure B2B cases as realistic information is available on transportation and access times for mobile fleets.

21.3.2 Agent-Based Simulation

To demonstrate how ABM can be used to support service supply chain design, we consider a vehicle service centre example, where the impact of centralized and decentralized service structure can be evaluated based on capacity utilization. In this case, a manufacturer of vehicles is expanding

Service Supply Chain Design by Using Agent-Based Simulation

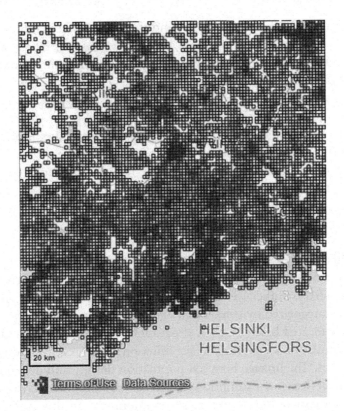

Fig. 21.2 Population grid data (1 km × 1 km) in Helsinki city (statistics Finland, 2015) (Licensed as CC BY 4.0: https://creativecommons.org/licenses/by/4.0/deed.en)

the business to cover life-cycle services and needs to maintain a certain service level of customer assets in order to get recurrent payments. In this example, vehicle service centres are authorized service shops which provide repair and service operations after the purchase of a professional heavy vehicle. The service network can consist of a number of different types of service providing units, having location and performance as object properties. Customers are attracted to closest service locations or ones with shortest processing times and lead-time to service can be used as a performance indicator combing the travel time, queue time, and the actual service delivery time. AnyLogic software was used to model the ABM simulation. Once the model has been constructed with agents and rules, the user can evaluate various conditions and extreme values regarding the number of service centres, their locations, operating working hours, and location impact on operational performance are evaluated (see also Rouzafzoon & Helo, 2016).

The simulation model focuses on following features:

- Service supply chain design by presenting network actors as simulation agents
- Key performance evaluation versus service location and geographical elements impact
- Demand pattern generation based on population density and geographical location

The first challenging issue is simulating population density in a way that it resembles to reality. Population data used to generate customers were provided by official Finland statistics data, which presents number of people categorized by gender and age in each square kilometre region. People are located based on their geographical coordinates with GIS feature of simulation software and Java function which retrieves population information. The linkage between population density and demand location for a service is an assumption, which can be adjusted to have a weaker or stronger correlation in addition to randomness. In this example, the assumption that customer demand follows the population density is taken as real-time tracking for customer asset is not available. Three potential service/repair shop locations suggested by managers, and in the next phase, customers are directed to the nearest repair centre. This process is implemented by Java functions which locate customers and repair centres based on their geographical coordinates. For instance, in (Fig. 21.3), some agents and a service centre are located in Helsinki centre area. Customers move to a service/repair shop based on routing information which is provided by the OSM server in the software. Furthermore, routing setting is defined based on road network and the fastest routing method.

Agents are the key building blocks of simulation, and in this automobile service centre example, the object classes Customers, Repair shops, and Mechanics are created as agents.

Service Supply Chain Design by Using Agent-Based Simulation

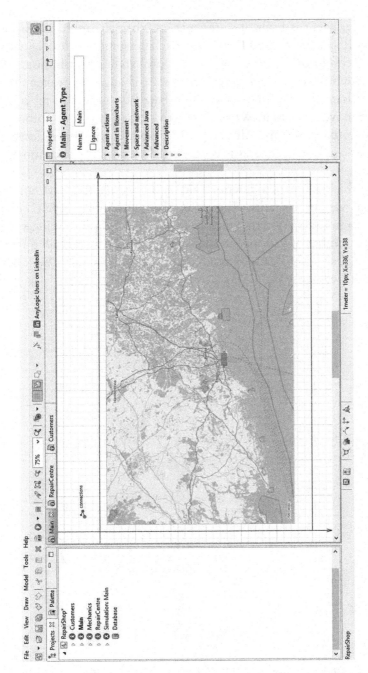

Fig. 21.3 GIS map with located agents and a service centre—AnyLogic simulation software screenshot

Customer agent is built of states such as NormalCondition, Broken, MovingToRepairShops, and Repairing. Each person's vehicle originally is in normal condition and then based on a probability distribution, vehicles become broken, and customer agent state changes to broken. Then, customers locate the nearest repair shop based on geographical coordinates and move towards it. When they arrive at repair centres, process of automobile fixing begins. After repairing process, customers leave the repair shop and the agent status is converted to normal condition again (Fig. 21.4).

Every vehicle requires different service and repair, and the system deals with large variety of tasks. Therefore, the automobile repair centres resemble to job shop system which is an order-based production system with large number of various products manufactured in a small quantity (Sharma & Garg, 2012). In this study, the repair shop agent is built based on simple three steps (Fig. 21.5).

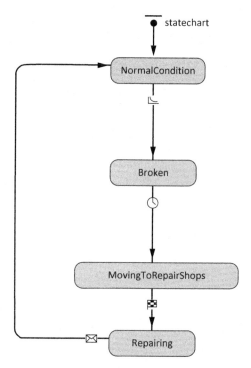

Fig. 21.4 Customer processing states and transition within agent

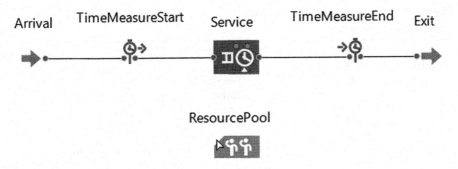

Fig. 21.5 Customer flow structure in service delivery

Customers receive service based on first-in-first-out (FIFO) rule. There is a resource pool for mechanics, and if there is no available mechanic, they wait in a queue. Furthermore, service time is defined based on a probability distribution.

To evaluate the simulation outcome, different KPIs should be defined. Length of stay and number of customers in queue can be introduced as service level indicators. Customers' length of stay can be defined as the time between customers' arrival and leaving the repair shop. In addition, a capacity utilization indicator is created to evaluate service level and operation cost, while resource managers can detect if resources are under or over utilized. Resources include mechanics in repair centres, and capacity utilization measures the ratio between actual working hours and total possible working hours. In addition, a ratio of the number of customers is created to compare the number of customers entering and leaving repair shops. KPIs are evaluated during the simulation and at the end of the simulation time (Table 21.1).

The described approach is too generic and can be applied to model various service interactions. Customers may interact with each other and spread demand (word of mouth effect) or have a varying need of service, as well as preferences for cost, lead-time or quality-related parameters. Probability of each customer parameter is randomized according to a statistical distribution and the simulation can show how KPIs behave under different conditions.

KPIs need to be built based on exact need of a company. Agents can provide information on actual resource consumption, event times, and

Table 21.1 Key performance indicators for evaluation, categorized according to agent type (example)

Perspective	Key performance indicators
Customer perspective – Customer agent	– Lead-time to complete the process – Time to access the service – Total cost of operation/customer
Service facility location – Automobile repair centre attracting customers and providing a service facility for service agents	– Capacity utilization – Cost of service operation – Operating cost/hour – Service supply chain flexibility time in demand increase
Service provider agent – Mechanic agent	– Capacity utilization for each resource type – Queue time for each resource type – Actual cost per service transaction

success rates of events. This is then translated into lead-time, costs, quality, on-time delivery, and other performance metrics, or towards more advanced indicators such as sustainability-related KPIs (Tseng, Lim, Wong, Chen, & Zhan, 2018).

Scenarios vary from one service operation to another. For instance, according to Pramod, Banwet, and Sarma (2016) the major issues in telecom service were stated as resistance to alteration, absence of trust in supply chain linkage, fear of information system or supply chain breakdown, low level of supply chain coordination, forecasting ambiguity, demographical aspects, and diversity between supply chain partners. Supply- and demand-related scenarios need to be built case by case as well as the KPIs, which are often company specific.

21.4 Managerial Conclusion

The process of designing and managing product-service systems is a demanding task. Systematic approach is needed to combine the data available for analysis and to test different scenarios. Aspects of structures, operational performance, perceived service level, business models, and role of technology need to be defined (Helo, Gunasekaran, & Rymaszewska, 2017). Large number of data needs to be analysed in complex situations, where system elements interact with each other dynamically. The behaviour may depend on previous actions. Updated and revised demand data may be needed to input for analysis and rapid decision support. For this kind of task, new tools beyond spreadsheet analytics are needed.

Contemporary agent-based simulation approach can solve the problem at least partially and be applied and developed in a service supply chain design. Modelling customers and service providers as intelligent agents with geographical location information is a generic approach for several service supply chains. Managers can evaluate the performance of service supply chain and there is possibility to conduct what-if analysis for assessing the decisions impact in a safe environment.

ABM requires knowledge of computer simulation and programming. Despite a learning curve, the advantages of ABM is concentrating on customer-level analysis. Additionally, the focus is not just on materials flow or resource utilization as in traditional discrete event simulation.

Agents can interact with each other and an agent has geographical location which can influence on its behaviour. The agents-based simulation approach can be used to analyse sophisticated customer-oriented systems, particularly for generating service network strategies. Service location analysis can be merged with service levels and operation performance associated KPIs in the same model. For analysing situations such as peak demand, time trigger events and demand patterns can be introduced.

Use of ABM can be incorporated in "DevOps" activities combining quality assurance, operational management of services, and continuous developments of services. Smart machinery and fleets of installed base will provide vast quantities of fresh data, which can be utilized for service business improvements. Agent-based simulation provides new opportunity to harmonize supply, demand, and KPI behaviour. ABM approach can capture the intangible aspects of the service process, and combine the "big data" from public sources (open data) and company-specific historical details of demand and service/operations.

The limitations of the approach are related to more complex modelling which requires programming skills in some extent. However, the ABM tools enable more comprehensive views and decision making which are based on data and documented assumptions.

References

Bateman, I. J., Jones, A. P., Lovett, A. A., Lake, I. R., & Day, B. (2002). Applying geographical information systems (GIS) to environmental and resource economics. *Environmental and Resource Economics, 22*(1), 219–269.

Dorigatti, M., Guarnaschelli, A., Chiotti, O., & Salomone, H. E. (2016). A service-oriented framework for agent-based simulations of collaborative supply chains. *Computers in Industry, 83*, 92–107.

Esmaelian, M., Tavana, M., Santos Arteaga, F. J., & Mohammadi, S. (2015). A multicriteria spatial decision support system for solving emergency service station location problems. *International Journal of Geographical Information Science, 29*(7), 1187–1213.

Gilbert, N. (2008). *Agent-based models*. Sage.

He, Q., Ghobadian, A., Gallear, D., Beh, L.-S., & O'Regan, N. (2016). Towards conceptualizing reverse service supply chains. *Supply Chain Management: An International Journal, 21*(2), 166–179. https://doi.org/10.1108/SCM-01-2015-0035

Helo, P., Gunasekaran, A., & Rymaszewska, A. (2017). *Designing and managing industrial product-service systems*. SpringerBriefs in Operations Management, Springer.

Hilletofth, P., & Lättilä, L. (2012). Agent based decision support in the supply chain context. *Industrial Management & Data Systems, 112*(8), 1217–1235.

Leung, Z. C., Pun-Cheng, L. S., & Ho, A. P. (2015). Locality service review and planning with GIS: A pilot study of spatial analysis of poverty data in Hong Kong. *Journal of Technology in Human Services, 33*(1), 38–52.

Lillrank, P., & Särkkä, M. (2011). The service machine as a service operation framework. *Strategic Outsourcing: An International Journal, 4*(3), 274–293.

Macal, C. M., & North, M. J. (2009). *Agent-based modeling and simulation*. Paper presented at the Winter Simulation Conference.

Pramod, V., Banwet, D., & Sarma, P. (2016). Understanding the barriers of service supply chain management: An exploratory case study from Indian telecom industry. *OPSEARCH, 53*(2), 358–374.

Rouzafzoon, J., & Helo, P. (2016). Developing service supply chains by using agent based simulation. *Industrial Management & Data Systems, 116*(2), 255–270. https://doi.org/10.1108/IMDS-05-2015-0220

Sakhuja, S., Jain, V., Kumar, S., & Chandra, C. (2016). A structured review of service supply chain discipline: Potentials, challenges, and integrated framework. *Journal of the Academy of Business Education, 17*, 270–295.

Sharma, R., & Garg, S. (2012). Capacity planning and performance measurement for automobile service centre using simulation. *International Journal of Modelling in Operations Management, 2*(3), 288–308.

Tseng, M.-L., Lim, M. K., Wong, W.-P., Chen, Y.-C., & Zhan, Y. (2018). A framework for evaluating the performance of sustainable service supply chain management under uncertainty. *International Journal of Production Economics, 195*, 359–372.

22

Servitization in the Public Sector: A Framework for Energy Service Companies

María Concepción Peñate-Valentín, Ángeles Pereira, and María del Carmen Sánchez-Carreira

22.1 Introduction

The public sector, as a large consumer, guarantees an initial demand and contributes to the promotion of new large markets through demand-pull. Public procurement of services has been increasing in the last decades, mainly due to the outsourcing of public services in many countries (Testa, Annunziata, Iraldo, & Frey, 2016). Energy Service Companies (ESCOs), which represent a servitization-based business model, have taken this chance to supply the public sector by offering innovative services and getting a competitive advantage (Bolton & Hannon, 2016; Pätäri, Annala, Jantunen, Viljainen, & Sinkkonen, 2016; Polzin, von Flotow, & Nolden, 2016; Stahel, 2010). Performance-oriented services, where the provider has to fulfill a function and the customer pays for having a specific work done, may contribute to dematerialization and to

---

M. C. Peñate-Valentín (✉) • Á. Pereira • M. d. C. Sánchez-Carreira
Department of Applied Economics, ICEDE Research Group, Universidade de Santiago de Compostela, Santiago de Compostela, Spain
e-mail: maria.penate@usc.es; angeles.pereira@usc.es; carmela.sanchez@usc.es

© The Editor(s) (if applicable) and The Author(s), under exclusive license to Springer International Publishing AG, part of Springer Nature 2018
M. Kohtamäki et al. (eds.), *Practices and Tools for Servitization*,
https://doi.org/10.1007/978-3-319-76517-4_22

achieve resource and energy savings (EPA, 2009; Rothenberg, 2007; Tukker, 2004). Thus, servitization may constitute a tool to achieve environmental goals by the public sector. However, public procurers face a major challenge when they have to choose among the multiple services offered by companies (Bertoldi & Boza-Kiss, 2017). In particular, ESCOs offer different types of services, such as energy-efficient solutions, specific services for buildings, and street lighting. Although the literature shows potential efficiency gains of lighting services provided by ESCOs, projects are scarce yet. Barriers faced by suppliers and procurers at different stages of the procurement process add complexities to the selection (Bertoldi & Boza-Kiss, 2017; Polzin et al., 2016; Roshchanka & Evans, 2016; Uyarra, Edler, Garcia-Estevez, Georghiou, & Yeow, 2014).

In this sense, enabling policies, such as public procurement law or procedures adjustments to enable ESCO project tendering, certification procedures, and benchmark projects are considered crucial to foster this innovative market (Bertoldi & Boza-Kiss, 2017). While some specific tools have been proposed that support manufacturing firms in the shift to offering customer solutions (e.g. Rabetino, Kohtamäki, & Gebauer, 2017), there is a dearth of models and tools that can be applied by the public sector to take advantage of ESCOs on a more standardized way.

This research attempts to fill this gap in the literature by proposing a framework for public procurers to take advantage of the potential of public procurement of innovation (PPI) to trigger servitization with environmental goals. To tackle this objective, a number of successful cases of ESCOs developed in the Canary Islands (Spain) are used.

This chapter shows several stages that the public sector should go through in order to take advantage of a servitized offer of lighting services. The proposed framework suggests a way to overcome barriers toward performance procurement. A set of scenarios faced by public procurers is presented regarding the different services provided by ESCOs. Each scenario corresponds with diverse solutions offered by these companies, being difficult for public procurers to make the appropriate choice. Public sector may demand different types of services depending on the specific need. In this sense, this study covers a gap in the literature, contributing to choose the most fitting set of ESCOs services, according to their specific needs.

The results provide a major understanding for public procurers on PPI as a tool to get benefits from servitization. The identification of needs and barriers as well as knowing and understanding the offer are crucial issues for a successful procurement process. In this regard, several successful practices for companies and public sector are set, which can be useful for the diffusion of these practices and their effective utilization.

Concerning the structure, the first section briefly identifies the main linkages between PPI and servitization. The second section presents several cases of ESCOs in the Canary Islands, reviewing successful practices and identifying key processes required to enable servitization through PPI. The third section shows a step-by-step guide for public procurers aimed at two main objectives: to overcome public sector barriers linked to performance procurement from ESCOs and to select the most appropriate set of services. Finally, some conclusions and managerial implications are derived.

22.2 Literature Review

22.2.1 Energy Efficiency Services Companies: Concept and Barriers

ESCOs represent one of the most promising models of servitization in the field of energy efficiency services. An ESCO is a company that develops and manages performance-based projects, focused on improving energy efficiency of facilities owned or operated by customers (Vine, 2005). As a type of servitization, ESCOs face some specific barriers, such as lack of government support, obstacles of SMEs and utilities to address costly changes, lack of proper legal frameworks and practices, lack of familiarity with performance-based services by the public sector, and financial obstacles (Bertoldi & Boza-Kiss, 2017; Hannon, Foxon, & Gale, 2015; Painuly, Park, Lee, & Noh, 2003; Polzin et al., 2016; Vine, 2005).

In addition, ESCOs usually deal with unfriendly response from incumbent energy companies and mismatch between the contract and the needs of the customers (e.g. lack of flexibility of long-term contracts, disruption to customer activities, need to access confidential data, perceptions about the actual level of energy efficiency, and existence of internal technical expertise) (Hannon et al., 2015).

A synergistic relationship between a business model, investor perceptions of risk, and a political framework is crucial to develop a successful energy project. In this sense, measures such as the modification of government procurement practices to facilitate energy performance contracts and governments backing up a portion of ESCOs guarantee to lending banks are recommended (Bolton & Hannon, 2016).

22.2.2 Public Procurement of Innovation: Potential to Promote Servitization and Barriers

The public sector plays a crucial role in any economy, due to the large amount of resources that it manages and the broad range of its actions. The role of the public sector as consumer triggers innovation in private companies in order to fulfill the bid requirements, in a process called public procurement of innovation (PPI). Thus, public procurement of innovative products and services can be a signal for private users. PPI opens opportunities for technological development in sectors that lack the minimum market, and contributes to develop new markets, offering a testing-ground for innovative products and services. Hence, the public sector provides a lead market for new technologies through demand-pull (Lember, Kalvet, & Kattel, 2011). In this sense, the development of certain technologies, mainly those related to the production of clean energy, is closely linked to the performance of the public sector.

PPI also contributes to generate an innovative environment, which supports learning and developing new organizational and technological capabilities (Rolfstam, 2013; Zelenbabic, 2015), the modernization of the public sector to meet current societal challenges (Caloghirou, Protogerou, & Panagiotopoulos, 2016), and less risk aversion in the public sector.

More specifically, Green Public Procurement of Innovation (GPPI) has been used by several countries in the last decade. The objective is to purchase any innovative product or service that results in fewer environmental impacts than other comparable products or services, and thus contributing to develop greener technologies.

The criteria used for the bids in any PPI project are critical to its effectiveness. When the public sector pursues environmental goals through PPI, sustainability criteria become crucial. In general, if the criterion is based on cost, GPPI projects are less likely to be chosen than non-innovative projects, due to the inherent costs of innovative activity. PPI sustainable projects could be benefited if requirements were formulated in functional terms. Setting performance objectives would leave room for innovation from the private sector (Edquist et al., 2015) and promote the creative interaction between demand and supply (Caloghirou et al., 2016).

Despite the important role that GPPI may play to promote the implementation of sustainable services, public procurers also face several barriers that prevent the effective use of this tool. Those barriers, which particularly affect the procurement of innovative services, can be summarized as follows: less experience in procuring innovative services in comparison with products, lack of experience of providers supplying the public sector, lack of flexibility in the procuring procedures, uncertainty about the adequate duration of the contracts, and so on (Testa et al., 2016). Moreover, there are a number of factors that hinder the public procurement of performance-based services and mainly affect the willingness of suppliers to compete (Uyarra et al., 2014).

Figure 22.1 summarizes the main barriers faced by stakeholders (private companies and the public sector) in servitization projects. The reviewed literature allows identifying the need for a specific tool that supports the implementation of performance-based contracting on behalf of the public sector and which, at the same time, acts as a driver for servitization in private companies.

22.3 The Case of the Canary Islands

To address the objective of this chapter, several cases developed in the Canary Islands (Spain) are used to identify scenarios faced by public procurers and the different services provided by ESCOs. This input serves as a basis for the framework that is proposed in the next section.

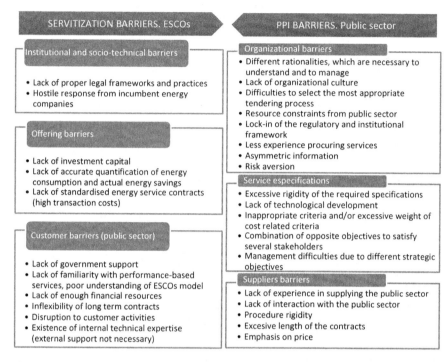

Fig. 22.1 Main barriers faced by private companies and public sector. Source: Own elaboration

22.3.1 Identification of Aims and Needs

Public procurers from the Government of the Canary Islands (Spain) started the process to procure energy services in official buildings in 2015. The call for tenders aimed at funding 158 projects to obtain energy savings and efficiency-related improvements in 54 municipalities of the region. The main goal of procurers was to reduce the energy consumption in official buildings and to adopt measures to preserve the environment. Before the call for tenders, procurers identified several problems that needed to be addressed (Gobierno de las Islas Canarias, 2015):

- high energy consumption,
- high energy costs,

- high level of emissions,
- high regional energy dependence, and
- necessity to improve on services provided by the public sector (mainly street lighting).

Procurers also identified potential gains from procuring energy-saving services, besides lowering energy consumption, such as cost reduction in the medium and long term, improvements on the services offered by the public sector, and decreasing emissions. The development of these projects amounted to a total of 5.9 million euros, of which 3.5 million were subsidized by the Ministry of Economy under the European Regional Development Fund (ERDF).

22.3.2 Preparation Phase and Call for Tenders

Once public procurers identified their needs and prioritized the most relevant and critical requirements, the regional government used the competitive dialogue procedure. This procedure allows public procurers and ESCOs to establish conversations, where procurers share their needs with the market and, at the same time, they receive inputs regarding the state-of-the-art current technology.

After this preparation phase, the call for tenders was initiated, specifying certain basic characteristics and criteria. Regarding the characteristics, the length of the contract was 15 years and was expected to run in a total of eight buildings. The awarded companies should carry out the following tasks:

- energy management,
- maintenance of energy facilities,
- improvement works and renovation of public facilities, introducing photovoltaic panels, interior lighting, and air conditioning system.

Procurers used performance-based and functional criteria to evaluate the different proposals. In this sense, the requirements attempted to specify just which problems needed to be solved, instead of establishing rigid conditions regarding the services. In addition, ESCOs capacity to perform the required tasks was assessed based on their previous experience in similar projects.

22.3.3 Awarded Companies and Results

After the evaluation phase of the procurement process, the public sector awarded three different ESCOs. One of them is the leader company in the provision of such services throughout the Spanish territory. Two of the awarded companies also sell energy and cleaning-related products, besides offering the maintenance service. In this case, the regional government decided to contract three different services from ESCOs: energy consultancy, energy consumption management, and new lighting materials provision. The projects developed by these ESCOs aimed to save 3.2 million kilowatts by year, implementing and integrating an overall performance that would improve energy efficiency. Table 22.1 shows the results of these projects in terms of energy savings and consumption reduction.

Table 22.1 Results of the implementation of ESCOs services

	Before ESCOs services	After ESCOs services	Savings
Interior lighting of buildings *Power (kW)*	462.74	201.24	261.51
Interior lighting of buildings *Energy consumption (kWh/year)*	1,516,181.02	659,490.3	856,690.7
Air conditioning equipment and management *Electric potency (kWe)*	332.94	73.99	258.95
Installation of solar control sheets on the windows *Thermal demand (kWht)*	1,201,950	1,165,892	36,059

Source: Government of the Canary Islands (2015)

22.3.4 Imitation Effect

The regional government pursued to become a model of energy efficiency to stimulate a similar behavior in other public buildings as well as in the private market. The procurement of ESCOs services for official buildings generated an imitation effect among local governments. Therefore, there are currently similar projects under development in the local areas of Arona and Granadilla de Abona (Tenerife), or Moya (Gran Canaria).

In the case of Moya municipality, only one company was awarded. This project implies the replacement of 277 lights to install LED lighting technology and auxiliary equipment in the central building, and 422 in the House of Culture. It is expected that the new high-efficiency lighting will save over 33,700 kilowatts/hours per year, and that it will reduce 75% of the current electricity consumption. In addition to the replacement of lighting in official buildings, this local government procurement process includes new services of maintenance and the operation of public lighting for a period of 18 years. The awarded company will also replace 2298 municipality luminaries for other more energy-efficient LED-based technology. The whole procurement process will involve an investment of 51,700 euro, co-funded by the Government of the Canary Islands and the ERDF.

22.3.5 Types of Services

The different services provided by ESCOs lead to the emergence of a set of scenarios faced by public procurers. Each scenario shows diverse solutions offered by these companies, being difficult for public procurers to make the appropriate choice. Public sector may demand different types of services depending on the specific need, as the case of the Canary Islands shows. Table 22.2 presents a framework aimed at helping procurers to identify the most fitting set of ESCOs services, depending on their specific needs.

ESCOs offer a variety of services that may be grouped in four categories: energy consultancy, provision of lighting material, energy consumption management, and consumer training. Some ESCOs may offer a combination of these categories of services or all of them.

Table 22.2 Type of service required from ESCOs depending on the barriers for public procurement

Diagnosis (public sector needs)	Types of services	Energy consultancy	Provision of lighting material	Energy consumption management	Consumer training
Lack of knowledge	At sectoral level	■ Necessary			■ Recommended
Lack of knowledge	Procedures	■ Necessary			
Lack of knowledge	Available technologies	■ Necessary			
Consumption	High energy consumption	■ Necessary		■ Necessary	
Consumption	High energy dependence			■ Necessary	
Service provided by public sector	Obsolete technology	■ Necessary	■ Necessary		
Service provided by public sector	Lack of quality in provision of public service/s	■ Necessary	■ Necessary		
Costs	High energy costs associated with consumption	■ Necessary	■ Necessary	■ Necessary	■ Recommended

Necessary   *Recommended*

Source: Own elaboration

Energy consultancy consists of providing strategical, technical, and environmental advice to other organizations. ESCOs offering this service usually have tailored skills related to renewable generation, the integration of low carbon technology, smart grid technologies, energy market analysis, noise assessment, and grid code compliance studies. In this phase, ESCOs measure the energy consumption and collect the data to find opportunities in order to save energy.

The provision of lighting material implies the delivery of energy-efficient and innovative products. It also involves the design and introduction of new structures and control systems in buildings or streets. Some ESCOs deliver these materials as a side-business or in collaboration with other companies selling these products, while others started in other sector, and moved to servitization later.

Energy consumption management involves controlling, monitoring, and saving energy. In this phase, ESCOs track the progress and analyze the data to assess the effects of the energy-saving strategies applied. Savings are monitored with regard to costs, emissions, and risks.

Consumer training refers to a type of service where procurers learn key facts about energy consumption and management, as well as environmental and economic costs. This process brings relevant advantages for procurers and ESCOs. Firstly, it helps procurers to distinguish their needs with precision and to select the most fitting set of services. Secondly, ESCOs receive a better and more accurate call from procurers, enabling and improving the connection between demand and supply.

22.3.6 Diagnosis

Four types of barriers and needs are mainly identified when public sector attempts to procure energy-related services, as it was observed in the case of the Canary Islands regional government.

The first kind of barriers refers to the lack of knowledge from procurers:

- If procurers are unaware of basic characteristics of the energy sector or the services provided by ESCOs, two main services should be contracted: energy consultancy and consumer training.

- If procurers ignore procedures (regarding the energy service and the procurement process of services) or/and the available technologies, the energy consultancy service is required to start the phase of identifying and establishing the needs from procurers.

The second group of barriers is related to energy consumption:

- If procurers identify high energy consumption, the awarded ESCOs should offer energy consultancy services, to determine the causes of such excessive consumption, and energy consumption management services, to maintain the equilibrium of consumption and costs over time.
- The existence of high energy dependence requires a similar set of services to the aforementioned barrier. Some regions are more prone to energy dependence than others; hence, it can be a key issue to be solved. The Canary Islands is a good example of this.

The third set of barriers is related to current services provided by the public sector:

- The existence of obsolete technology can have a great impact on the energy consumption and the emissions of public buildings. In this regard, three types of ESCOs services are necessary: energy consultancy, provision of lighting material, and energy consumption management. The second one is particularly crucial in this case, when the current technology is outdated and, therefore, more inefficient.
- Related to the previous one, obsolete technology can lead to a decrease in the quality of the service provided by the public sector. This issue is really important because the provision of quality service should be one of the main goals of any public administration. In this case, the same three types of services are required.

Finally, a fourth type of barriers is observed: high costs associated with energy consumption:

- In this case, the four types of services are required. However, only one of them, consumer training, is suggested and not always completely necessary. This aspect will depend on the previous knowledge of the sector and the processes that procurers might have. In some cases, it might be almost mandatory.

Table 22.2 shows the relationship between these barriers and the type of services offered by ESCOs, and the suggestion of contracting each service, depending on the barrier.

22.4 Framework for Public Procurers to Foster Servitization

Building upon the insights gained with the case of the Canary Islands regional government, this section proposes a framework with several stages that the public sector should follow in order to take advantage of a servitized offer of lighting services, while overcoming identified barriers.

Figure 22.2 shows the consecutive stages. Firstly, the public sector should identify its needs in order to start the procurement process. The project submission would be the next stage, where service suppliers

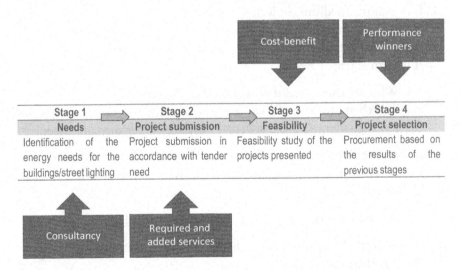

Fig. 22.2 Stages for the public sector to undertake performance procurement. Source: Own elaboration based on European Commission (2015)

present their offers. Next, the feasibility analysis is made in order to evaluate the offers presented. Finally, public procurers award one or several service companies, based on the previous stages. These four stages are described below.

22.4.1 Stage 1: Identification of Needs

The accurate identification of the procurers needs is one of the most important issues to address during the procurement process. Overestimating or underestimating the essential needs of the public sector is a major obstacle, which could hinder the whole procurement development. In the case of the Canary Islands, this stage was crucial for suppliers to understand the public sector aims and to develop the appropriate solutions.

Thus, procurers should ask themselves a set of questions to clarify the main objective they pursue with the procurement of services. The main questions are the following ones:

1. What are the main problems or needs identified?
2. Is it a short, medium, or long-term need?
3. What performance or set of objectives is the procurer pursuing?
4. Is the contract aiming at an extrinsic or intrinsic need?
5. If it is an extrinsic need,

    (a) Who are the agents that will receive the service?
    (b) Which are the specific views of those agents?
    (c) Do they identify any particular obstacle or performance need?

6. In the case of energy services, was any energy audit carried out?
7. If the energy audit was carried out, what were the key issues identified?

    (a) Do these issues happen at a given time or regularly?

8. If several needs are identified, will the procurer attempt to solve all of them at the same time?

    (a) If the answer is no, which is the main priority?

9. Can a procurement office collaborate with other offices that share the same needs?
10. Regarding the size of the tender process:

    (a) What is the size of competing companies?
    (b) Does it need to be separated in lots?
    (c) Is there any consortium among companies?

Once the needs have been properly identified and these questions answered, the procurer can proceed to the following stage. This stage is related to consultancy services. Companies trying to servitize their offering have an opportunity to support the public sector in the identification of needs, as the case of the Canary Islands shows. Thus, based on their expertise within a sector, they will be able to offer consultancy services to analyze the needs, identifying critical points and proposing the best adjusted offering.

22.4.2 Stage 2: Project Submission

The adequate transmission of information from public procurers to companies supplying services is crucial. At this stage, procurers should establish a well-defined set of parameters and criteria according to the observed needs in the previous stage. The tender should primarily include functional and performance-based criteria, instead of strict requirements. The case analyzed shows less rigid criteria make easier the path for innovative service companies and allow them to properly answer the call, adapting the offer to the procurer accurate needs. In addition, the criteria should be widely advertised among possible suppliers, facilitating the access to the process.

Suppliers can answer the call by offering the required services, as well as adding other services. A performance-based tender opens windows for innovation among the competing companies. Businesses may decide to implement different supplementary services that allow them to fulfill the public requirements, while at the same time improving their offering in comparison to competing companies. For instance, they may be able to go further in servitization by adding services that substitute products or that allow using them in a more efficient and effective way. The suppliers of the Canary Islands case were able to include additional services, such as maintenance or renovation works, and even sell and install innovative products, such as new types of lamps or photovoltaic panels. Supplementary services may be aimed at decreasing costs through a more efficient resource use, both at the production and consumption stages.

22.4.3 Stage 3: Feasibility

Two main subjects are addressed during this stage: abnormal proposals and suitability of the offered services. Firstly, some suppliers could be tempted to present offers with uncertain characteristics, such as an abnormal low price for the offered services. Procurers need to be cautious and, if there is not enough direct knowledge, a technical desk should be designated to avoid misunderstanding or undervaluing any offer. At the same time, service suppliers should be able to fulfill the terms of the tender. In this regard, public procurers will have to study the feasibility of each presented offer. This is a key issue that should not be ignored.

Secondly, public procurers have to check that each need identified during the first stage will be met. In this sense, and mostly when dealing with innovations and energy consumption services, the price should not be the main criteria to select offerings. It is suggested to use the most economically advantageous tender (MEAT) selection process, which involves that procurers have to take into account different parameters to evaluate the offers, being the price just one of them, but not the main one. The MEAT selection process was used in the case of the Canary Islands: several aspects were considered to select the most complete offer, such as needs fulfillment, company experience in similar projects, environmental criteria, or time to develop the innovations, apart from price. Cost-benefit analysis, which are frequently used to work out the efficiency and effectiveness of public expenditure, can offer a remarkable framework for this stage (see e.g. the tool proposed by Carbonara & Pellegrino, 2018). Therefore, setting a clear group of performance objectives at the beginning of the tender will pave the way for this analysis.

22.4.4 Stage 4: Project Selection

The final stage consists of choosing the most appropriate service offer to cover the needs identified during the first stage. It is the result of the work carried out in the previous stages. If properly done, it should lead to select the optimum service or set of services. In this regard, it is crucial that the awarded company or companies are able to answer the following questions:

1. Will they respond on time?
2. Have they surpassed procurers' expectations with their offer?
3. How does their offer fit with the requirements from procurers?
4. Is there any crucial aspect from the tender that suppliers will not be able to cover?
5. Do they offer continued services after the purchase?

All these questions were positively answered by suppliers in the Canary Islands. Procurers selected companies able to prove their expertise and on-time response fitting the needs, and to offer continued services. The assessment based on the above questionnaire will lead to identify the performance winners; that is, those service companies able to fulfill the requirements and achieve guaranteed results, as well as other added services.

22.5 Conclusions

Servitization constitutes a new approach that offers a wide range of opportunities for companies and procurers. However, this new business model can be hardly understood by procurers who are mainly used to purchasing goods. This aspect is particularly relevant in the energy sector, where the public sector attempts to push efficiency in energy consumption and increase the efforts toward environmentally technologies and services. In this regard, ESCOs and the public sector face several barriers that could hinder a successful procurement process.

The case of public procurers from the Canary Islands leads to identify several stages that should be taken into account before contracting servitized companies. Firstly, procurers need to know well the organization and its requirements, as well as the limitations they might face during the whole procurement process.

The first stage allows identifying certain obstacles, such as lack of knowledge regarding procedures or available technologies, high energy dependence and consumption, lack of quality of the public services offered, and high costs. A deep understanding of these issues is key to choose the most fitting service from the different options offered by ESCOs (consultancy, materials provision, management, or consumer training). The case of Canary Islands shows that the decisions adopted during this stage would greatly affect the following stages, favoring or hindering a successful procurement process of energy services. That is the reason why it is necessary to underline the importance of this stage.

Procurers should not underestimate the relevance of the following stages. In this regard, several key issues are underlined. Firstly, the use of performance criteria leaves room for companies to innovate and design the most appropriate solution, as it was observed in the analyzed case. During the first and second stage, procurers need to guarantee ESCOs participation, increasing the competition.

Secondly, the evaluation process should aim at choosing long-term solutions, instead of only evaluating the price. Cost reduction is crucial but not only in the short term. Procurers need to take into account all the benefits brought by the different offers from ESCOs as well as their feasibility.

The Canary Islands case has led to a sudden imitation effect from other public procurers in different regions. Nowadays, these regions are following these stages to achieve similar objectives. However, each region is adapting the scheme to its specific needs, being this aspect particularly relevant. A major task that public procurers should address from the beginning of the procurement process consists of clarifying and understanding the particular needs of each region. The adaptation of the stages to these singularities comes next, helping ESCOs to design appropriate solutions for each case.

The suggested framework has also managerial implications. If the public sector adopts standardized procedures, ESCOs can more accurately develop their servitization strategies and business models. ESCOs and other servitized companies may focus on the needs identified through each stage of the tool described in this chapter to better define their strategy to compete in a public tender and to set the most suitable bundle of products, services and outcomes.

References

Bertoldi, P., & Boza-Kiss, B. (2017). Analysis of barriers and drivers for the development of the ESCO markets in Europe. *Energy Policy, 107*(April), 345–355. https://doi.org/10.1016/j.enpol.2017.04.023

Bolton, R., & Hannon, M. (2016). Governing sustainability transitions through business model innovation: Towards a systems understanding. *Research Policy, 45*(9), 1731–1742. https://doi.org/10.1016/j.respol.2016.05.003

Caloghirou, Y., Protogerou, A., & Panagiotopoulos, P. (2016). Public procurement for innovation: A novel eGovernment services scheme in Greek local authorities. *Technological Forecasting and Social Change, 103*, 1–10. https://doi.org/10.1016/j.techfore.2015.10.016

Carbonara, N., & Pellegrino, R. (2018). Public-private partnerships for energy efficiency projects: A win-win model to choose the energy performance contracting structure. *Journal of Cleaner Production, 170*, 1064–1075. https://doi.org/10.1016/j.jclepro.2017.09.151

Edquist, C., Vonortas, N., Zabala-Iturriagagoitia, J. M., & Edler, J. (2015). *Public procurement for innovation*. Cheltenham: Edward Elgar.

EPA. (2009). *"Green Servicizing" for a more sustainable US Economy. Key concepts, tools and analyses to inform policy engagement*. Retrieved from http://www.epa.gov/wastes/conserve/tools/stewardship/docs/green-service.pdf

Gobierno de las Islas Canarias. (2015). *Proyecto de mejora de la eficiencia energética y prestación de servicios energéticos*. Gran Canaria: Gobierno de las Islas Canarias.

Hannon, M. J., Foxon, T. J., & Gale, W. F. (2015). "Demand pull" government policies to support product-service system activity: The case of Energy Service Companies (ESCos) in the UK. *Journal of Cleaner Production, 108*, 1–16. https://doi.org/10.1016/j.jclepro.2015.05.082

Lember, V., Kalvet, T., & Kattel, R. (2011). Urban competitiveness and public procurement for innovation. *Urban Studies, 48*(7), 1373–1395. https://doi.org/10.1177/0042098010374512

Painuly, J. P., Park, H., Lee, M. K., & Noh, J. (2003). Promoting energy efficiency financing and ESCOs in developing countries: Mechanisms and barriers. *Journal of Cleaner Production, 11*(6), 659–665. https://doi.org/10.1016/S0959-6526(02)00111-7

Pätäri, S., Annala, S., Jantunen, A., Viljainen, S., & Sinkkonen, A. (2016). Enabling and hindering factors of diffusion of energy service companies in Finland? Results of a Delphi study. *Energy Efficiency, 2010*, 1–14. https://doi.org/10.1007/s12053-016-9433-z

Polzin, F., von Flotow, P., & Nolden, C. (2016). What encourages local authorities to engage with energy performance contracting for retrofitting? Evidence from German municipalities. *Energy Policy, 94*, 317–330. https://doi.org/10.1016/j.enpol.2016.03.049

Rabetino, R., Kohtamäki, M., & Gebauer, H. (2017). Strategy map of servitization. *International Journal of Production Economics, 192*, 144–156.

Rolfstam, M. (2013). *Public procurement and innovation: The role of institutions.* Cheltenham: Edward Elgar.

Roshchanka, V., & Evans, M. (2016). Scaling up the energy service company business: Market status and company feedback in the Russian Federation. *Journal of Cleaner Production, 112*, 3905–3914. https://doi.org/10.1016/j.jclepro.2015.05.078

Rothenberg, S. (2007). Sustainability through servicizing. *MIT Sloan Management Review, 48*(2), 82–91.

Stahel, W. R. (2010). *The performance economy* (2nd ed.). London: Palgrave Macmillan.

Testa, F., Annunziata, E., Iraldo, F., & Frey, M. (2016). Drawbacks and opportunities of green public procurement: An effective tool for sustainable production. *Journal of Cleaner Production, 112*, 1893–1900. https://doi.org/10.1016/j.jclepro.2014.09.092

Tukker, A. (2004). Eight types of product–service system: Eight ways to sustainability? Experiences from SusProNet. *Business Strategy and the Environment, 13*(4), 246–260. https://doi.org/10.1002/bse.414

Uyarra, E., Edler, J., Garcia-Estevez, J., Georghiou, L., & Yeow, J. (2014). Barriers to innovation through public procurement: A supplier perspective. *Technovation, 34*(10), 631–645. https://doi.org/10.1016/j.technovation.2014.04.003

Vine, E. (2005). An international survey of the energy service company ESCO industry. *Energy Policy, 33*(5), 691–704. https://doi.org/10.1016/j.enpol.2003.09.014

Zelenbabic, D. (2015). Fostering innovation through innovation friendly procurement practices: A case study of Danish local government procurement. *Innovation: The European Journal of Social Science Research, 28*(3), 261–281.

Index

A

Advanced services, 8, 14, 45, 46, 51, 53, 86, 141–166, 173, 174, 176–179, 181, 185, 187, 189, 195, 201–211, 253, 315, 332, 338

Agent-based modelling (ABM), 15, 388, 390–392, 394, 395, 401

Agent-based simulation, 387–401

Agent processing states and transition, 398

B

Barriers, 7, 8, 27, 126, 227, 263, 270–272, 318, 327, 331, 332, 338, 351, 352, 406–409, 414–417, 421

Basic services (BAS), 28, 53, 89, 163, 202, 332

BI-in-practice, 233–244

Business intelligence (BI), 14, 233–244

Business model, 3, 4, 6, 8, 12, 13, 27, 28, 35–36, 61–77, 79, 80, 93, 97–99, 101–104, 106–118, 122–125, 132–134, 139, 175, 180, 186, 187, 193–195, 206, 209, 210, 213, 233, 254, 264, 272, 276, 284, 325, 343–344, 367, 384, 388, 400, 405, 408, 421, 422

Business problem, 154, 155, 157, 176, 370

C

Capabilities, 3, 4, 8, 13–15, 26, 28, 30, 34, 37, 44, 50, 62, 68–70, 72, 77, 90, 107, 109, 110, 123, 125–127, 175, 178–180, 191, 196, 201–211, 213, 215,

Capabilities (cont.)
    225, 227, 229, 238, 251, 255–257, 260, 269, 270, 275–277, 285–287, 312, 313, 319, 326–328, 332, 333, 337, 343, 345, 364, 389–391, 408
Case study, 15, 27, 86, 134–136, 224, 253–254, 258, 326, 353–359
Collective affordance, 238
Commonalities, 292–300, 302–305
Commonality strategies, 293, 295, 296
Competencies, 14, 45, 56, 69–72, 80, 192, 213–229, 251, 254, 256–258, 261, 263, 294, 295, 304, 310, 314, 316, 326, 328, 335, 337, 345, 359
Competency-based methodology, 214, 215, 218, 220, 222, 225
Competency definition, 214, 215, 218, 220, 222
Consumer goods manufacturing companies, 121–130, 132–138
Current service offering, 43–46, 48, 49, 51–53
Customer value proposition, 72, 149, 154–155, 157, 158, 163, 165, 277, 372–373, 378, 379, 381, 383
Customisation/customization, 13, 15, 36, 89, 121, 122, 126, 130, 132, 134, 135, 150, 186, 190, 193, 194, 196, 205, 237, 291–294, 298–306, 313–315, 330
Customising/customizing, 15, 190, 193, 291–306

D

Decision tool, 15, 249–264
Digitization, 8, 28, 30, 34, 36, 61, 225, 226

E

Ecosystem innovation, 15, 368–371, 381, 383
Efficiency, 29, 63, 66, 116, 145, 211, 237, 270, 277, 279, 282, 284, 292, 293, 295, 305, 306, 314–316, 329, 331, 378, 406–408, 410, 412, 413, 420, 421
Energy efficiency, 406–408, 412, 413, 415
Energy saving companies (ESCO), 16, 405–409, 411–417, 421, 422
Enterprise image (EI), 15, 343–360
Equifinality, 4, 62, 63

F

First-order change, 240
Framework, 2, 13–16, 48–50, 53, 57, 64–72, 74, 83–87, 93, 98, 99, 108–111, 116, 122–130, 132–139, 141–144, 149–151, 155, 163, 164, 188, 194, 202–204, 207–209, 216, 223, 262, 263, 270, 275, 291–306, 310, 313–318, 347, 348, 352, 363, 364, 369–371, 383, 388, 389, 391, 405–423
Framing contests, 233–244
Future service offering, 13, 46–48, 51

G

Geographic information systems (GIS) technology, 393, 394, 396, 397

H

Human capital, 214

I

Industrial service, 42, 43
Integrated solution, 5, 6, 9, 69, 73, 78, 84, 186, 187, 191–195, 203, 224, 296–300, 302, 312
Interaction, 9, 15, 47, 88, 122, 129–132, 154, 202, 203, 205, 234, 237–239, 244, 293, 294, 296, 298–300, 302–306, 311, 312, 314, 315, 317–319, 344, 352, 367, 391, 392, 399, 409

K

Key performance indicators (KPI) according to agent type, 41, 52, 53, 65, 68, 114, 152, 276, 277, 284, 392, 399–401
Knowledge skills attitudes (KSA) model, 215–218, 221, 223, 225

M

Maintenance, 45, 65–69, 71, 77, 84, 89, 91, 92, 114–116, 133, 145, 147, 148, 150, 160, 173, 179, 186, 203, 205, 206, 208, 211, 227, 242, 243, 250, 253, 256, 271, 278, 279, 283, 284, 295, 298, 300, 301, 303, 304, 311, 313–315, 317, 331–333, 336, 350, 353, 354, 364, 411–413, 420
Mass service customization, 4, 28–30, 35
Measures, 3, 13, 25–37, 41–55, 57, 68, 107, 116, 132, 138, 142, 157, 180, 208, 280, 284, 314, 316, 344, 357, 368, 389, 399, 408, 410, 415
Meta-model, 84–88
Modularization, 13, 121–130, 132–139, 314, 315, 333

N

Network, 6, 29, 80, 86, 90, 92, 93, 98, 129, 137, 138, 226, 270, 271, 277, 301, 311, 314, 316, 319, 330, 336, 338, 345, 347, 364, 366–367, 373, 382, 388, 389, 393–396, 401
Network management, 4, 28–30, 34, 36

O

Operand, 345, 348
Operant, 345, 348, 349
Organizational change, 9, 14, 53, 128, 186, 233, 240

P

Paradoxes, 8, 14, 185–196
Performance, 3, 5–7, 29, 37, 42, 43, 45, 47, 55, 61, 63, 64, 86, 98,

Performance (cont.)
115, 131, 132, 143, 145, 147, 148, 157, 162, 173, 175, 178, 181, 186, 188, 193, 201–210, 214, 219, 264, 271, 284, 314, 315, 329, 333, 335, 345, 355, 387, 389, 391, 392, 395, 396, 400, 401, 407–409, 411, 412, 418–422

Performance procurement, 406, 407, 417

Population grid data, 395

Positioning, 13, 107, 326–328, 333–336

Product-service system (PSS), 2–6, 8, 9, 12, 15, 26, 83, 85, 86, 88, 93, 100–105, 142–144, 146, 148, 194, 249–264, 364–368, 371, 372, 377, 378, 381–384, 387, 388, 392, 400

Profit formula, 63, 65, 67, 68, 70, 72, 74, 77, 79

Proposition, 282

Public procurement, 16, 405–411, 413, 414, 417–420, 422

R

Reconfiguring, 13, 28, 30, 34, 304, 306, 328

Resources, 7, 31, 41, 62, 88, 107, 123, 145, 175, 196, 218, 251, 269, 310, 326, 345, 383, 391, 406

Revenue model, 63, 68, 77, 79, 85, 88, 110, 142–149, 165

Risk, 7, 46, 51, 68, 99, 116, 130, 147, 148, 165, 174, 180, 181, 205, 221, 249–264, 272, 277, 284, 295, 316–318, 335, 364, 365, 367, 370, 373, 377, 393, 408

Risk management, 15, 75, 182, 249–264

Risk sharing, 252, 255–257, 264, 284, 287

S

Scale, 15, 26, 30, 36, 42, 43, 53, 66, 68, 79, 110, 122, 139, 202, 208, 210, 263, 292, 293, 295, 300, 314, 331

Scope, 3, 7, 44, 67, 85, 89, 106, 108, 122, 141–166, 282, 293, 333, 393

Seizing, 28, 30, 31, 34, 36, 329

Sensing, 11, 30, 31, 70, 132, 145, 194, 195, 234, 235, 242, 244, 261, 376, 406, 408, 411, 420

Service area analysis, 393

Service business development, 117, 370

Service delivery structure, 157, 242, 263, 390, 395, 399

Service deployment, 13, 26, 28–30, 34, 310–314, 317–319

Service design, 28, 141, 144, 160, 162, 163, 344, 363, 374, 389

Service development, 4, 13, 15, 26–28, 30, 31, 34, 36, 175, 192, 363–384

Service offering, 3–5, 7, 13, 14, 42–49, 51, 53, 62–63, 141–166, 173, 178–180, 182, 202, 204, 206, 207, 315, 344, 421

Service orientation, 13, 26, 29, 30, 36, 42–44, 47–49, 52, 63, 110, 244
Service revenue, 13, 42, 44, 48, 49, 52, 53
Service supply chain, 12, 15, 387–401
Servitization/servitisation
   capacity, 25–37
   strategies, 7, 8, 12, 15, 25, 27, 201–211, 318, 319, 422
   trajectory, 201–211
Shared affordance, 237, 238
Solution, 1, 26, 46, 61, 85, 97, 122, 142, 185, 206, 213, 233, 257, 269–287, 291–306, 309, 325, 379, 389, 406
Solution family, 298, 299
Strategic change, 10, 122, 123, 135
Subdividing, 293, 296–298, 305
Supply chain, 8, 12, 15, 98, 108, 207, 344, 345, 359, 363–366, 382, 384, 387–401
System, 6, 29, 53, 68, 111, 129, 148, 178, 195, 205, 225, 238, 256, 271, 294, 311, 325–338, 345, 363, 388, 411

T
Team-of-teams, 368, 369
Technological frames of reference (TFR), 235, 237, 244
Technologies-in-practice, 14, 234
Transition process, 4, 185, 194, 244

U
Unintended outcomes, 234, 239–244

V
Value
   appropriation, 5, 202–204, 338
   capture, 63, 123, 133–134, 136, 139, 162, 166, 270, 271, 276, 286, 335, 344, 366
   chain, 26, 84, 88, 93, 123, 253, 327, 328, 337, 338, 364, 366–367, 389
   co-creation, 8, 12, 124, 203, 204, 208, 249, 273, 313–319, 383
   constellation, 13, 83–94, 274, 285–287
   creation, 5, 15, 143, 144, 150, 152, 154, 163, 202, 203, 226, 270–272, 275–277, 279–281, 284–287, 310, 317, 338, 344, 346, 363, 383
   networks, 366–367, 382
   proposition, 5, 8, 63, 65, 67, 68, 72, 77, 78, 83, 85, 88, 98, 103, 104, 113, 114, 123–127, 129, 135, 139, 141, 143, 144, 146–149, 154–155, 157, 158, 163, 165, 206, 243, 275–284, 286, 287, 333, 344, 345, 347, 371–373, 378, 379, 381–383
Value-based pricing, 13, 74, 142, 147, 150, 151, 287

CPSIA information can be obtained
at www.ICGtesting.com
Printed in the USA
LVOW13*1604030618
579412LV00010B/414/P